PURDAH AND POLYGAMY
LIFE IN AN INDIAN MUSLIM HOUSEHOLD

PURDAH AND POLYGAMY

LIFE IN AN INDIAN MUSLIM HOUSEHOLD

Iqbalunnisa Hussain

Edited by

Jessica Berman

OXFORD

UNIVERSITY PRESS

OXFORD
UNIVERSITY PRESS

Oxford University Press is a department of the University of Oxford.
It furthers the University's objective of excellence in research, scholarship,
and education by publishing worldwide. Oxford is a registered trade mark of
Oxford University Press in the UK and in certain other countries

Published in Pakistan by
Ameena Saiyid, Oxford University Press
No.38, Sector 15, Korangi Industrial Area,
PO Box 8214, Karachi-74900, Pakistan

First Edition published in 1944 by Hosali Press, Bangalore

ISBN 978-0-19-940756-9

Typeset in Adobe Garamond Pro
Printed on 70gsm Offset Paper

Printed by Le Topical Pvt. Ltd, Lahore

Contents

Acknowledgements

This project was many years in the making. I was inspired to pursue this reprinting not only by Hussain's wonderful and important novel but also by the large community of scholars, colleagues, friends, and ultimately relatives of Hussain, who encouraged me to keep going. You put up with my constant queries and mad questions, even when all I had to go on was an old volume and an address 'somewhere in Bangalore'! I am pleased to be able to—finally—offer you this book.

First and foremost, I must thank Iqbalunnisa Hussain's grandson, Arif Zaman, and his family who joined me in the desire to make this wonderful author and thinker better known and who made this volume possible. Arif was indefatigable over the years it took to produce this volume, which I consider a joint project. I also thank Nick Brewster, archive assistant at the University of Leeds, who put two random queries about the same woman together and connected me to Arif. Iqbalunnisa Hussain's last surviving child, Dr Salima Ahmed, noted Pakistani feminist and founder and life President of the Pakistan Federation of Business & Professional Women's Organization, was instrumental in seeing both this volume and the earlier *Changing India* back into print. She passed away as this was going to press. We dedicate the volume to her memory.

I am very grateful to Arif, Suvir Kaul, and Muneeza Shamsie for their common cause and wonderful essays in this volume. It is much enriched by their contributions.

I am very grateful to the late Eunice de Souza, who died as this volume was in its final stages. Her inspiring work on Hussain first sent me looking for the later and she later encouraged this reprint project. I am sorry not to be able to present her with a copy. I thank Arvind Mehrotra whose enthusiasm for the project buoyed me and whose networking helped me on my way. I thank scholars Asiya Alam, Amy Bhatt, Feroza Jussawalla, Ayesha Kidwai, Ramachandra Guha, Jahan Ramazani, Sangeeta Ray, C.N.Srinath, Susie Tharu, and A.R. Venkatachalapathy for suggestions and support.

As an Anglophone scholar, I could not have completed the introduction and annotations for this volume without collaborators. I am very grateful to: Zain Abidin and Elham Fatma for sharing their knowledge of Urdu and Muslim practice; to Jean Fernandez for pointing me along the way and expanding my Indian background; and to Rahul K. Gairola for lending his network and support from India. Soha Tanwir Khan, our editor at Oxford University Press, saved me from lingering errors and added important insight and expertise. Aaron Berman Fernandez performed much appreciated copy editing at a crucial stage. Finally, many thanks go to Suvir Kaul for being an astute and insightful editor as well as contributor. I'm grateful for his willingness to be my sounding board through to the end.

Research for this project was made possible by funding from the University of Maryland, Baltimore County.

Contributors

Jessica Berman is Professor of English and Affiliate Professor of Gender + Women's Studies and Language, Literacy and Culture at the University of Maryland, Baltimore County (UMBC), USA, where she also directs the Dresher Center for the Humanities. Her scholarly interests include modernism from a transnational perspective, literature and politics, and feminist approaches to twentieth-century world literature. She is the author of *Modernist Fiction, Cosmopolitanism and the Politics of Community* (2001), *Modernist Commitments: Ethics, Politics and Transnational Modernism* (2011), and editor of *A Companion to Virginia Woolf* (2016), among other publications. Berman is a co-editor of *Futures,* the American Comparative Literature Association's decennial Report on the State of the Discipline (2017) and also co-edits, with Paul Saint-Amour, the Modernist Latitudes book series at Columbia University Press. In 2016–17, she served as president of the Modernist Studies Association.

Arif Zaman is Deputy Director, the Centre for Research and Enterprise (Enterprise and Internationalisation), London School of Business and Management, and on the visiting faculty at Henley Business School, University of Reading. He is Executive Director of the Commonwealth Businesswomen's Network, an accredited organisation to 52 Governments on women's leadership and economic empowerment. He is author of the bestselling book on Reputational Risk (*Financial Times,* 2004 and published in Russian, 2008). Arif was the first Associate Director of Mosaic, founded by HRH The Prince of Wales, which creates opportunities for young people of all backgrounds, and the Muslim community in particular, growing up in the UK's most deprived and disadvantaged communities. In 2011, he received an award from Malaysian Prime Minister Abdullah Badawi for his 'excellent contribution in the field of public relations serving world communities'. He is a Fellow of the RSA and the Royal Asiatic Society.

Suvir Kaul is A.M. Rosenthal Professor of English at the University of Pennsylvania. He has taught at the University of Delhi, Cornell University, Stanford University, the Jamia Milia Islamia, and the University of Illinois at Urbana-Campaign. He served as Director of the University of Pennsylvania's South Asia Center and Chair of its English Department. He was a Visiting Fellow at the Jawaharlal Nehru Institute of Advanced Study, Jawaharlal Nehru University (2016). He is the author of *Of Gardens and Graves: Kashmir, Poetry, Politics; Eighteenth-Century British Literature and Postcolonial Studies; Poems of Nation, Anthems of Empire: English Verse in the Long Eighteenth Century* and *Thomas*

Gray and Literary Authority: Ideology and Poetics in Eighteenth-Century England. He edited *The Partitions of Memory: The Afterlife of the Division of India* and co-edited *Postcolonial Studies and Beyond*. He teaches eighteenth-century British literature and culture, South Asian writing in English, and critical theory, including postcolonial studies.

Muneeza Shamsie is the author of a literary history, *Hybrid Tapestries: The Development of Pakistani Literature in English* (2017), Bibliographic Representative (Pakistan) of *The Journal of Commonwealth Literature,* guest editor of *The Journal of Postcolonial Writing*'s special issues: *Al Andalus* (2016) and *Pakistan* (2011). She was a jury member of the 2013 DSC Prize for South Asian Literature and Regional Chairperson (Europe and South Asia) of the Commonwealth Writers' Prize 2009–11. She serves on several advisory boards, has edited three anthologies, and contributes regularly to the Pakistani press.

Introduction

In this edition, the novel you now hold in your hands, *Purdah and Polygamy*, finds its way back into print after more than seventy years. It first appeared in 1944, published by the tiny Hosali Press in Bangalore, India, and has been largely hidden from view since then.[1] As of December 2016, only nine libraries worldwide list it in their collections.[2] At the time it was written, its author, Iqbalunnisa Hussain, had published articles in *The Deccan Times* of Madras and *The Daily Post* of Bangalore, as well as in other major English language newspapers across India. She was a writer and educator esteemed for her strong support for female education, especially of Muslim girls and women. Still, she was unknown enough that when asked to write the foreword to *Purdah and Polygamy*, Sir Ramalinga Reddy, a well-known educationalist and poet himself, felt the need to circulate the manuscript to several of his friends to assess its value. They confirmed for him the novel's realism, its freedom from a sense of inferiority to British or European models, and its sympathetic appeal. One reader commented that, 'the book gives an insight into a Muslim's life within walls, which is a sealed book to most of us'.[3] Despite earlier writing on domestic life by other Muslim women, such as Rokeya Hossain[4] and Ismat Chughtai,[5] and many texts by Indian men touching on the topic of purdah,[6] in 1944 that statement was largely true. Few non-Muslims knew much about the domestic life of Muslim women. There are still few literary guides to the complexity of Muslim women's lives within the zenana. Even fewer of these guides originate in English, as does this novel. Indeed, *Purdah and Polygamy* may well be the first full-length novel written in English by a Muslim woman. It is certainly one of the first in any language to take a full-length look at the domestic lives of secluded Muslim women. That it does so with elegance, empathy, and nuance, while also showcasing the difficulties posed by the twin practices of purdah and polygamy, is the marvel of this book and the reason why we reprint it here.

Iqbalunnisa Hussain was part of an expanding group of Indian women who were well travelled and well educated.[7] Even within this group, however, her accomplishments are remarkable.[8] Raised in strict purdah, her early home education was in Urdu, Persian, and Arabic.[9] She married at fifteen and her husband, Syed Ahmed Hussain, encouraged her efforts to master English and to continue her education. She had several children before becoming the first woman graduate of the Maharani College in Mysore in 1930.[10] With one of her sons, she travelled to study at the University of Leeds in England in 1933, and lectured both in the UK and upon her return, in India. She became deeply involved in the education of Muslim girls and women, founding an Urdu girls' middle school in Bangalore and a teachers' association for Muslim women. In the early thirties, she travelled as the delegate from Mysore to the All India Women's Conference, one of the most important national women's organizations of the late colonial period,[11] and in 1935, she spoke at the International Alliance for Women on Suffrage and Equal Citizenship (IAWSEC) conference in Turkey.[12] She was active as a supporter of the expanding Girl Guides movement, which in 1916 became open to girls of non-European descent.[13] She was well known and well respected as a representative for Muslim women in India and a speaker about their rights and needs.

Prior to writing *Purdah and Polygamy*, Hussain published a book of her collected essays called *Changing India: A Muslim Woman Speaks* (1940, reprinted in 2015 by Oxford University Press, Karachi). Along with such essays as, 'The Importance of the Mother Tongue' and 'The Educative Value of the Girl Guides Movement',[14] the book contains tightly argued and trenchant critiques of common practices among Muslims in late colonial India. It calls for Muslims in India to build a modern Islamic practice which would no longer condone either purdah or polygamy, and would endorse education for its girls and women. *Changing India* includes essays on the position of women in Islam, the differences between Muslims and Hindus, and on the distinction between true Islam and what Hussain calls 'Mohammedanism', which condones strict seclusion and polygamy (or more specifically, what we would today term 'polygyny'—a marital arrangement in which the man has more than one wife). Position pieces in *Changing India* argue that purdah interrupts social progress in India, that early marriage is a hazard, and that 'there is no polygamy in Islam'. Hussain reserves her harshest words for the overly ritualized practices of Mohammedanism, which differs from Islam in that it does not adhere to scriptural tenets and 'lays fixed religious dogmas and sets a rigid spiritual truth'.[15] These dogmas form the basis of the practice of both rigid purdah and polygamy, for which she finds no support in the spiritual texts. As the writer of the original foreword to *Changing India* puts it, 'her main objective has been to release the women of India and particularly the women of the Indian Muslim world from the state of ignorance and quiescent resignation which false tradition has imposed on them'.[16]

Hussain's novel, *Purdah and Polygamy*, is an attempt to illuminate in fiction the effects of this false Mohemmedanism on Muslim families and to chronicle the problems it poses for women's status, their bodies, and their lives. The novel takes place in a modernizing Muslim household, where a young man (Kabeer) marries four women in succession, looking to both satisfy his often-reactionary expectations of a perfect wife and satisfy his mother's desire for household stability. On its surface, *Purdah and Polygamy* presents a dispassionate description of the family's history, following its members through a series of life-events and challenges. But through the use of free indirect style to represent the characters' points of view, allusion to outmoded, extreme or ill-conceived habits of education and religious expression, or through occasional overt criticism by the narrator, the narrative constantly undermines the practices of Kabeer, his mother, and his household. The result is a trenchant critique of the practices of polygyny and the strict seclusion of women wrapped within the pages of a sophisticated and compelling domestic novel. The novel's excellence was not lost on its first readers.

In its original foreword, Sir Ramalinga Reddy noted *Purdah and Polygamy*'s 'deft touches' and the way that it 'deals with the ordinary and the familiar', and called Iqbalunnisa Hussain 'the Jane Austen of India'.[17]

And yet this brilliant novel, which raises so many compelling questions about Indian domestic life in the late-colonial period, and which dramatizes the issues facing Muslim Indians in the time period, was largely forgotten in the rush to support new writing in the independent states of India and Pakistan after 1947. The major histories of Indian literature from the mid– to late–twentieth century identify only a handful of women writers from this period and discount their influence. K.R. Srinivasa Iyangar's classic book on Indian writing in English remarks 'it is only after the second world war that women of quality have begun enriching Indian fiction in English'. Nonetheless, Iyangar praises *Purdah and Polygamy* as having 'tried with commendable success to present the currents and cross-currents in a typical Muslim family'.[18] In her 1974 study of Indian writing, *The Twice Born Fiction*, Meenakshi Mukherjee makes fleeting reference to the comparison between Hussain and Jane Austen.[19] Still, Iqbalunnisa Hussain's writings—both *Purdah and Polygamy* and *Changing India*—were allowed to slip out of print and become inaccessible to new generations of readers.

In the last fifteen years, however, scholars around the world have rediscovered Hussain's work and *Purdah and Polygamy* in particular. Despite the difficulty of scholarly recovery work, they have begun the process of bringing it the kind of readership and critical attention the novel deserves. In 2002, poet and scholar Eunice de Souza and Lindsay Pereira, published the anthology, *Women's Voices: Selections from Nineteenth and Early Twentieth Century Indian Writing in English* (Oxford), followed in 2004 by de Souza's *Purdah: An Anthology* (Oxford), both of which excerpted Hussain's novel. A review from the time commented 'de Souza and Pereira…want reputations reassessed, like that of Iqbalunnisa Hussain…[especially] her virtually forgotten, yet outstanding novel, *Purdah and Polygamy*'.[20] Reflecting back on the anthologies ten years later, de Souza commented, 'for me *Purdah and Polygamy* is one of the best Indian novels in English'.[21] At the same time, the novel began to be included in histories and critical studies of Indian writing in English, appearing, for example, in Teresa Hubel's essay, 'The Missing Muslim Woman in Indo-Anglian Literature: Iqbalunnisa Hussain's *Purdah and Polygamy*'[22] and in *Muslim Narratives and the Discourse of English* by Amin Malak.[23] Suvir Kaul, a contributor to this volume, writes importantly about *Purdah and Polygamy* in his essay, 'Women, Reform, and Nationalism in Three Novels of Muslim Life'.[24] In a discussion at the 2013 Lahore Literary Festival, Muneeza Shamsie, author of *Hybrid Tapestries: The Development of Pakistani Literature in English* and another contributor to this volume, cited *Purdah and Polygamy* as one of the crucial English language novels by women in the pre-Independence era.[25] Scholar Asiya Alam references the novel in her introduction to the 2015 edition of *Changing India*. The time has come for a new generation of readers to meet *Purdah and Polygamy*, enjoy its rich characters and nuanced portrayal of Indian domestic life in the late colonial period, and restore it to its rightful place in the literary history of the Indian subcontinent.

The Significance of *Purdah and Polygamy*

Hussain's *Purdah and Polygamy* takes its place alongside other late colonial writing by Indian women like Toru Dutt, Krupabai Satthianadhan, Shevantibai Nikambe, Rokeya Hossain, Ismat Chugtai, Cornelia Sorabji, and others,[26] who together develop an intersecting critique of genre and gender roles that helps resist women's social and political disenfranchisement. By focusing on the complexity of life in the zenana, their writings challenge the notion that the political contest for India is only a struggle for control of public space, or that the modern nation must turn away from the concerns of the domestic sphere, which is too easily connected to the traditional figure of 'Mother India', in order to progress. By placing domestic servants and secluded women at the center of their narratives, women writers in late colonial India not only raise questions about narrative voice and authority but also challenge the public/private, modern/traditional dichotomies that carry heavy political weight in the time. Their narratives shine a light on the ways that women in the zenana raise public as well as domestic concerns, and often exhibit their modernity by way of their very participation in traditional sites and practices. By troubling the distinctions between autobiography and fiction, and experimenting with narrative perspective and authority, many of the narratives by Indian women of the period—and Hussain's *Purdah and Polygamy* in particular—use irony and formal innovation as a means towards engagement in the political struggle over the role of women in India's impending modernity.

Much of the discourse surrounding the modernization of Indian domestic life in the first decades of the twentieth century assumed that modernity was being foisted on Indian households from outside and must either be resisted as a force for imperialism or embraced as a means around it. Modernization is double-edged, promising education, progress, and global connection, while often seen as Westernized, dangerously violent, and spiritually disruptive. The home is often seen as the space for resistance to modernity's discontents. At the same time, reform organizations, both male and female, voiced renewed interest in domestic efforts to make India modern, such as reducing the incidence of child marriage (through the 1927 Child Marriage Restraint Act), extending female education, and developing women's roles in social work. In many of these discussions, the household, and women's roles within it, become the proving ground for ideals about the public good and Indian modernity *writ large*—the example or limit case for public policies rather than the place where modernization itself might take place. However, in Hussain's *Purdah and Polygamy*, the domestic world takes center stage as the location not only of conflict over modernization, but also as a generating force of a particularly Indian modernity. The novel foregrounds the matter of domestic space as the crucial matrix not only of female coming of age but also of a potentially modern Islamic practice which, if realized, would help propel Indian modernity. The fact that throughout the novel, domestic arrangements remain tied to entrenched, outmoded practices shows the danger of ignoring social arrangements in the private sphere and the importance of changing women's lives to changing India.

At first glance, *Purdah and Polygamy* seems deeply tied to eighteenth and nineteenth century English literary traditions and to the work of Jane Austen in particular. The opening discussion of the household compound illuminates its inhabitants and their lives in much the same way that the description of Mansfield Park or Pemberley in Austen's novels introduces us to her characters and their relationships. The house itself, we read, was 'an imposing building, standing in the heart of a city' which 'commanded respect and awe'. It offers clues to the family within when it is described as 'peculiar...like its inhabitants' (6). But by the third sentence, we learn that 'its high blind walls made a stranger take it for an unguarded jail, and literally it was so for its women folk'. Thus by the third sentence of this novel, we already know that this household will not be benign and that the women within are in many ways prisoners. The awe-inspiring view from the outside belies the constrained and supervised view from within, and the novel fluctuates regularly between the two.

The comparison to Jane Austen is apt in another way too. Under what appears to be the realist surface of a novel of domestic life, Hussain, like Austen, presents her social commentary by way of deep narrative irony. The opening line of chapter V, 'It is a well-known fact that man is superior to woman in every respect' (35), it can be argued, makes explicit reference to the opening line of *Pride and Prejudice*: 'It is a truth universally acknowledged, that a single man in possession of a good fortune, must be in want of a wife.'[27] When Austen writes this of Bingley in *Pride and Prejudice*, we are immediately made aware that nearly every aspect of that sentence will be subject to revision and reinterpretation over the course of the novel. Is the man single? What makes for a good fortune and why does it matter to his desire for a wife? And most importantly, are the truths 'universally acknowledged' the ones we must abide by? For Hussain, that last question also underlies the pervasive narrative irony in *Purdah and Polygamy*. In what way is it 'a well-known fact that man is superior to woman in every respect' and is this kind of fact one we should accept as true?

Though we do not know what Iqbalunnisa Hussain might have read, her reference to Austen places *Purdah and Polygamy* into direct contact with the English literary tradition. Hussain invites us to hear potential echoes throughout the novel not only of Austen but also of other English-language writers, both those writing in the Indian subcontinent and those prominent in the English canon. She asks us to recognize the importance of themes about marriage and its relation to money or social standing, the complexity of family relationships within rigid social structures, and the limitations of prejudicial judgments about people that were common in English domestic fiction of the nineteenth century. In remarking on these references, we must be careful not to reduce Hussain's novel to an echo or imitation of Austen or any other author. Her achievement in *Purdah and Polygamy* must be understood primarily for its importance to the development of Anglophone literary traditions in India, and later Pakistan. Still, the novel's connection to the English literary canon helps us recognize the complexity of the domestic themes in *Purdah and Polygamy* and the novel's transnational sphere of meaning and influence. What might have seemed to early readers of the novel to be an idiosyncratic glimpse into the little known world of Muslim domestic life, appears from this perspective to be an innovative entry in the transnational tradition of domestic fiction. But Hussain's work revises, recasts, and revisions that important tradition by bringing it into the sphere of modernizing late colonial

India and connecting it to the religious and social issues of the enforced seclusion of women and the practice of polygyny.

The narrator of the story is bolder than Austen in her condemnation of the world of her characters and its expectations of them, immediately alluding to the 'plight' of the women in the compound (6). The plot of the novel, as it unfolds, makes clear that these characters will not redeem themselves in the end or become able to overcome their limiting situation. Though we may come to feel sympathy for its heroine, Nazni, Kabeer's first wife, there is little in her to admire throughout the novel. The 1944 foreword to this novel points out that Hussain 'deals with the ordinary, the familiar, not with the romantic and heroic', yet castigates her for the 'fervour of a moral and social purpose which sometimes leads her to didactic outpourings' (6). Yet we can see in this novel an extraordinary attempt to narrate what the author of the foreword calls 'social purpose' by way of an 'unsparingly ironic' tone. Under the unflinching gaze of the narrator in this novel, both men and women of the compound are seen as deeply limited. Their way of life, along with its distorted understanding of the rules of Islam, its insistence on strict purdah, and its unreflective espousal of polygyny, is placed under indictment, and the only possibility of an ethical or just situation must emerge through the ironic undermining of the unified narrative perspective and the multiplicity of points of view that develop by the end.

Social Commentary

In the world of *Purdah and Polygamy,* it is clear that a successful wife is defined by a body that will submit to supervision, domestic service, and strict enclosure, while retaining its strength and beauty. The matter of polygamy in this novel represents the family's quest for such a woman/body and stands as commentary about the futility of such a search, especially in the modern era, when matters of religion, commerce, and domestic economy are shifting. After the death of the father in the household, his widow, Zuhra, moves quickly to marry her son, Kabeer, to a suitable wealthy girl and Kabeer, who has not been consulted, becomes obsessed with her beauty: 'He was worried about her physical beauty. The question of temperament never struck him' (24). As it turns out, his new wife, Nazni, is a beauty, who at times is described as 'looking like Venus' (39), yet marriage has a clear bodily effect on her. As a new bride in her husband's home, she must restrain herself physically, making her presence in the home negligible. 'She was not expected to open her eyes in her husband's house for five weeks and not to talk for about two months…She was not expected to eat more than a morsel' (34). In fact, this physical self-abnegation becomes permanent as Nazni almost immediately becomes ill in pregnancy, retreats to her parents' house, gives birth, and is diagnosed with heart disease. The narrative makes clear that her illness is in part a physical response to her marriage and her enclosure in Kabeer's family compound: 'she felt better in her mother's house. As soon as she returned home, her illness reappeared' (45). On the other hand, from Nazni's first illness, her mother-in-law, who has counted on her new daughter to be present in the kitchen on a daily basis and to take on the cooking, is full of disdain. Once Nazni has removed herself from the kitchen and the compound, and shows her body to a male doctor, she considers Nazni an unsuitable wife, and immediately plans Kabeer's second marriage.[28] Because Nazni's body is unruly in so many ways, she is cast off as Kabeer's primary wife.

Within the space of four pages, Kabeer marries a second wife, Munira, a lower caste girl whose family has conspired to hide her ugliness from her prospective mother-in-law. If Nazni is described as 'small, thin, and delicate' (45), Munira is 'dark, with deep pock-marks, and her upper teeth projected prominently' (48). As Zuhra tells her 'you have neither beauty nor wealth…Your only weapons are your strength and spirit' (50). From the moment she arrives, she is constantly on the move, cleaning, cooking, and serving Kabeer and Zuhra, which ingratiates her to her mother-in-law, if not to her husband. Though she manages to seduce him once, enticing him with food and carefully closing her lips over her protruding teeth as she smiles, he disdains her, referring to her as an 'ape' and 'the negress' (67).

In placing such harsh and disdainful language in Kabeer's mouth, Hussain here makes reference to the long tradition of colorism in India that dates back to the ancient period of the Vedas. In the later period of the Delhi Sultanate and the Mughal era, distinctions also arose between the often lighter-skinned, foreign-descended Muslims and the wider populace—including those who converted to Islam. Yet the broad conception of the Mughal era as characterized by cultural rigidity, despotism, and a deep gap between foreign Muslim rulers and a Hindu populace 'were forged in a framework created by the British', which sought to create a pre-history for their own period of rule.[29] British colonial rule also served in many ways to reinforce racialized thinking by merging it with European notions of racial hierarchies and Darwinian concepts of evolution.[30] Colonial ethnographers described India as a place where racial distinctions remained intact (as opposed to in Europe), where they were almost synonymous with caste, and where differences between the foreign and native, Arya and the non-Arya,[31] non-Brahmin, or caste-less could be studied.[32] This body of knowledge constituted Sanskritic culture and Aryan people as European, cast Muslim rulers as invaders, and repudiated Dravidian cultures and lower caste or darker people as inferior. All of this colonial thinking contributed to divisions based upon color or perceived race among Indian people, some of which persist today.[33]

It is also important to note that the use of the word 'negress' here marks a connection to racial thinking both inside and outside India. The word 'negro' likely arrived in India via Portuguese traders who used it to refer to the peoples of Africa from the sixteenth century onwards. But 'negress' is a specifically English term and therefore carries with it the history of English-language usage. While in 1944, at the time of the novel's publication, the term was not always as derogatory as it is today, it must reference the evolutionary thinking that denigrated African-descended people as less advanced than Europeans, as well as the racial hierarchies that supported slavery and oppression. Kabeer's use of this language makes clear that he has imbibed this racist perspective and that it undergirds not only his attitude towards women but his entire worldview. His notion of the ideal wife includes expectations that she will be pale-skinned (as is Nazni) and untainted by all that darkness is thought to signify: lack of intelligence, culture, ability, and bodily integrity.

While Zuhra rejoices in having a daughter-in-law who obeys her meekly and works 'vigorously' (66), Kabeer responds to her color, her looks, and her energy as animalistic and unbefitting of his wife. While it is clear that Munira fits the servile role of wife better than Nazni and that her body is better able to sustain the rigors of becoming a mother, her darkness and lack of beauty nonetheless mark her as unfit. Ironically, neither woman embodies what a 'wife' is meant to be in this household. In fact, as the narrative makes clear, the expectations of women—to be both able housekeepers and frail, tremulous creatures, vigorous and yet contained, companionable and yet willingly servile—are contradictory and impossible to fulfill. The commentary on polygyny in this novel grows not only out of Zuhra's insistence on an outmoded model of patriarchal family life but also Kabeer's self-serving efforts to find the embodiment of a wife who doesn't and can't exist. Through their treatment of Munira, Hussain shows how the practice of atavistic and rigid Mohammedanism leads to shallow opportunism and mean-spirited treatment of women.

The inner rooms of the compound and the kitchen become contested territory as a third wife, Maghbool, is added to the household, and rooms are shifted. The architecture of private life thus comes to play a role in the possibilities for development among the compound's inhabitants and its confrontation with the modern idea of private spaces. The supervision of behavior within the communal enclosed spaces becomes paramount since, as a sign of his escape from his mother's control, Kabeer moves out of the house and into his offices. Zuhra, his mother, changes her quarters so she can observe and control the compound with almost panopticon-like discipline but, despite her constant watching and peeking through keyholes, she is unable to retain full control.

Maghbool is figured as the counterpoint to Munira since she is active and vigorous, but competent, learned, and worldly—like a man rather than a servant—and as such cannot fulfill the desired role of wife any more than can Munira, again making clear the coincidence of the reactionary practice of polygyny with antiquated notions of femininity.

> She was an institution in herself. Her mastery over the Urdu language had made her crazy after papers, magazines, romance and poetry…She was a good organizer and an economical manager of the house… Her father often said that she was a son to him, his secretary and his right hand. She was active and hated to while away her time…Everything she did was self-learnt (90).

Unlike the other women in the household, Maghbool benefits from the modern monetary economy and from Kabeer's willingness to sell off his patrimony for ready cash. The fact that she receives pocket money not only makes her able to purchase food rather than cook it in the kitchen (thus removing herself from identification with that space), but it also further defines her as modern, masculinized, and connected to the bourgeois economy which the household rejects for women. As Munira puts it, when hearing of Maghbool's bank account, 'How disgraceful! Then all the men know your name. It is only bad women's names that come to the notice of men' (125). Maghbool not only does not recoil at the idea of her name being known, she spends her money on the publication of a collection of her own poetry with her name attached, which she hopes will make the family fortune (153), thus underscoring both her usurpation of masculine roles and her connection to the modern economy and public sphere. In this way, she serves as a stand-in for writers like Hosain, Chughtai, or Hussain herself who transgressed into and transformed the masculine sphere of letters.

Further, although she does not fully conform to many contemporary Western models of transgender identity nor does she fit traditional Indian notions of hijra,[34] Maghbool might be understood here as a kind of trans figure, one who not only crosses over the gender binary, and inhabits a masculine position, but also challenges the assumptions that this household (and by extension, the institutions of purdah and polygyny) make about women, their bodies, and the roles they are expected to play. According to theorist Susan Stryker, transgender is a word that may be used to refer 'to people who move away from the gender they were assigned at birth, people who cross over (*trans–*) the boundaries constructed by their culture to define and contain that gender'. While some trans people feel strongly that they properly belong to another particular gender, 'others want to strike out on their own toward some new location [or] … get away from the conventional expectations bound up with the gender that was initially put upon them'.[35] For Stryker, as for many current thinkers, transgender thus becomes a capacious term that includes a wide range of 'gender-variant practices and identities' and the challenges they pose to socially constructed and historical categories of gender.[36]

In this way, much contemporary thinking about transgender identities pushes beyond a binary view of sex and gender, and considers 'anything that disrupts, denaturalizes, rearticulates and makes visible' the links we assume to exist between a sexual body and the social roles it is expected to play.[38] In other words, rather than understand the transgender position as a specific passage from one predetermined gender identity to another, contemporary thinkers like Stryker understand it as a position that destabilizes our assumption that embodied sex determines social or psychological gender. It broadly challenges the binary sex and gender system as a whole and at the same time often also questions intersecting assumptions about religion and social position, among other categories. When she takes on a public name, handles her own money, has a body marked as unfeminine, and over the course of the novel, increasingly rejects the behaviour expected of women within the confines of the female quarters, Maghbool sketches what we might call a 'trans' position within *Purdah and Polygamy*, one in which gender non-conformity also raises broad critiques of rigid religious, social, and cultural practices.

It is important to note that what we understand to be '[t]ransgender…is context-dependent' and multiple, taking on different forms and guises in different situations, locations, and historical moments.[39] The South Asian transgender practice of hijra, a way of living that goes beyond categories of gender and sexuality to encompass 'a variety of other axes of identity, including religion, gender, kinship, and class,' is a case in point.[40] Even as hijra cannot be subsumed into some kind of universalized category of transgender experience, neither can Maghbool's non-traditional role in *Purdah and Polygamy*. Yet while Maghbool never specifically embraces masculinity, her activity in the novel might be understood as part of what Roshanak Kheshti, writing about cross-dressing in Iranian film, calls a 'transgender move' that 'enables the manifestation of complex and contradictory openings in which gender and sexual transgression take place alongside other forms of social transgression.'[41] Viewing Maghbool in this light pushes us to recognize the diverse attitudes, behaviors, and lived experiences within a variety of global contexts that might coalesce and be mobilized under the rubric 'transgender' and their intersection with the critique of other categories of religious, social, and cultural identity.

Maghbool is further marked as an unsuitable woman/wife when her body is scarred in a kitchen accident. Afterwards, Zuhra sees Kabeer sneak in expensive medicines for her, recognizes Maghbool as a body she cannot control, and works to reassert her authority over her son, her surveillance of the inner compound, and the re-establishment of codes of gendered conduct. By the time Maghbool's wounds have healed, the potential of her modern attitudes and her 'trans' status to smash the complacency of the zenana and disrupt the gendered roles of the entire household has been both revealed and contained, and she is ostracized almost into non-existence.

The remaining chapters of the book succumb to a disorder of both plot and structure that mirrors the disorder of this household. The action of the plot speeds up, new events and characters are introduced with little preparation or context, and the final events are compressed into the novel's last pages. But the signs of this narrative 'disorder'—interruption of plot sequence, acceleration of temporal progress, shifts in point of view, gaps in knowledge—which grow in the final chapters of this novel are also visible earlier in the narrative and demonstrate the stylistic and formal challenges of this important text.

Stylistic Innovations

Indeed, although at the time of writing Iqbalunnisa Hussain was less experienced as a fiction writer than as an essayist, *Purdah and Polygamy* displays her sophisticated use of style, narrative voice, and structure. The novel thus participates in the late colonial movement among Indian writers to use formal innovation as a means towards engagement with social and political issues. As I have noted, *Purdah and Polygamy*'s characters are richly drawn and nuanced, its voice displays deep command of narrative irony, and its descriptive passages show Hussain's ability to evoke the significance of place. Hussain also periodically uses free indirect style to allow us to enter into the minds and voices of characters. For example, early on, Zuhra's voice and perspective on the value of marriage invades the narration: 'Why do people bring daughters-in-law if not to have real and well-earned comfort?' (35). Later, Maghbool's fear of refusing to marry is conveyed in similar fashion: 'no one would marry her if she was known as a rebel…Would not that life be a worse torture than merely being one of many wives?' (92).

Hussain also displays sophisticated use of temporal structure, not only accelerating the final chapters but also periodically leaping back in time and starting forward again from a different perspective. Between chapter VIII and IX, for example, when Nazni's family first learns of Kabeer's second marriage, the perspective shifts: 'Nazni's family thought about the remarriage very differently from Kabeer's people' (74). The narrative drops back in time, before the events that take place at the end of the previous chapter, and then moves forward again in Nazni's parents' household, as though the dyssynchronous perspectives demand a similarly dyssynchronous time frame. Nazni's brother embraces a modernized perspective on women's roles, defends Nazni's 'rights' (75) and considers it a 'blessing to make a woman independent and strong' (75). He argues that she should not be forced by his parents to return to the zenana. Hussain here uses structural innovation to highlight the conflict between false attachment to the practices of polygyny and an alternate, modern perspective on women's roles, complete with reference to the public matter of her rights. From the scene of dispute over Nazni's trip to the cinema, where the narration skips abruptly back and forth from Kabeer's conversation with his mother to his discussion of this conversation with Nazni (42), to the elision of several years before the final episodes, the novel often departs dramatically from the realism evoked by its connection to Austen and shows its commitment to a narrative technique we might call 'modernist'.[42]

One of the most obvious and significant formal features of *Purdah and Polygamy* is Hussain's syncretic use of language. That is, though we recognize the novel as written in 'English', its sentences are shot through with words from Hindi, Urdu, and Arabic, and the syntax and usage often depart from 'standard written English'. These vagaries of usage elicit an apology from the author of the original foreword, who attributes them to Hussain's lack of knowledge of the language.[43] Yet *Changing India*, written several years before *Purdah and Polygamy*, exhibits an extraordinary fluency of expression in English, making it unlikely that the novel's disruptions are the result of her inabilities in the language. Rather, I would argue, they show us the reverse—Hussain's competence in English allows her to use word choice, narrative structure, emplotment, and experimentation with narrative perspective as vehicles for her critique of zenana life. If modernity creeps into the novel through the byways—Nazni's mobility, Maghbool's authorship and financial independence, the changing architecture and use of the rooms in the compound, and the final disruption of the calm surface of zenana life—then it also invades the style and structure of the novel, making it vastly different, in the end, from a Muslim remake of *Pride and Prejudice*.

Purdah and Polygamy shares with the work of other Anglophone writers of the period, such as Raja Rao, Ahmed Ali, R.K. Narayan, and especially Mulk Raj Anand, interest in developing English as an idiom for Indian writing, distinct from its British and US traditions. Like Hussain, these writers bring elements of India's multiple languages into the English texture of their novels. Narayan's work has been described as an effort at representing Tamil speech patterns within an English language narrative.[44] Anand works to incorporate local languages and habits of speech into Anglophone writing. At times, he attempts to translate Hindi and Punjabi phrases into English; at other moments, like Hussain, he will mix the two languages, putting snippets of English within a Hindi phrase or vice versa. He incorporates new coinages without apology, arguing in his essay, 'Pigeon-Indian: Some Notes on Indian Writing in English', that the real everyday use of a combined language, no matter whether it is transparent in meaning or not, ought to be represented in the fiction that emerges out of India.[45] Hussain's practice in *Purdah and Polygamy* is similar. She weaves Urdu, the presumed native language of the family, Hindi, and Arabic into the fabric of this English-language novel, thereby creating a new Anglophone literary language reflective of and appropriate to the everyday life of Muslims living in late colonial India.

Purdah and Polygamy and Muslim Identity

Despite being written in a period of increased Muslim nationalism, Hussain also marks a certain cultural and religious syncretism in the habits and practices of daily life of her characters. While a notion of Muslim unity in India had been developing throughout the twentieth century, in the 1930s and 1940s, calls for Muslim cultural unity and nationalism grew significantly. As it became increasingly clear to Muslim leaders that Congress plans for a post-independence state would not include guaranteed representation and significant safeguards for Muslims, leaders began to advance serious arguments for considering Muslims in India as a separate nation and for forging a two-nation solution. In 1940, Muhammed Ali Jinnah, who served as the leader of the Indian Muslim League from 1913 until the creation of Pakistan in 1947 (when he became its first Governor-General), spoke to the League, proclaiming that Muslims 'are a nation according to any definition of a nation, and that they must have their homelands, their territory, and their state'.[46] In the years that followed, the idea of Muslim nationality became tied not only to the creation of Pakistan as a state but also to the broader ideal of Islamic unity.

At the same time, the everyday life of Muslims living in India reflected a complex mixture of influences and practices, both religious and secular, and *Purdah and Polygamy* often highlights that mixture. Many of the customs surrounding widowhood, death, and birth in the novel have little basis in Muslim scripture or Hindu teachings. Even when the characters are celebrating marriage or getting ready for a funeral, much of what takes place is not specifically Muslim practice or specified in the Qur'an. The novel thus shows us how, in the period, Muslim Indian life encompassed both a rising sense of religious unity and Muslim nationhood, which Hussain often endorses,[47] and the pragmatic syncretism of everyday life. Its complex treatment of the cultural practices of Muslims stands alongside its adoption of a dynamic and syncretic Indian English as a testament to its significant role in the development of the Anglophone literary tradition in the Indian subcontinent in the 1940s.

There has been an explosion of writing in both India and Pakistan in the more than seventy years since the original publication of *Purdah and Polygamy*. Women are among the foremost practitioners of Anglophone fiction and are prominent among social, cultural, and religious reformers. The case for Muslim national and cultural identity has been made; the practices of both polygyny and strict seclusion are on the wane. Many of the practices that Hussain illuminates and critiques in *Purdah and Polygamy* have disappeared. And yet, the novel's themes of female education and empowerment, of the importance of domestic life to notions of civic citizenship, of the multiplicity of gender roles and performances, of cultural, religious and linguistic syncretism, etc. remain surprisingly salient today. Its elaboration of a particularly Indian version of Anglophone domestic fiction and engagement with practices of modernism make it a crucial entry into the literary traditions of the Indian subcontinent. This novel, published quietly by a little-known press in 1944 Bangalore, has shown its importance and its staying power. We offer it to you again, in the hope that its reputation and readership will continue to expand.

Notes

1. The D.N. Hosali Press was named after D.N. Hosali and run by Philip Spratt, a noted intellectual of the time and former Communist Party activist. For more on Spratt and his life, see *Blowing up India* (Mumbai: Prachi Prakashan, 1955).

2. According to OCLC, these libraries are: The John Hopkins University, The US Library of Congress, Harvard University, Columbia University, University of Alberta, University of Manitoba, University of Toronto, McGill University, University of Regina. Last accessed 28 December 2016 <firstsearch.oclc.org>.

3. Foreword, *Purdah and Polygamy: Life in an Indian Muslim Household* (Karachi: Oxford University Press, 2017), 2.

4. See especially *The Secluded Ones*, published in serial form in Bengali in 1929, and selected in Hossain, *Sultana's Dream: A Feminist Utopia and Selections from the Secluded Ones* (N.Y.: Feminist Press, 1988). See Eunice de Souza, *Purdah: An Anthology* (New Delhi: Oxford University Press, 2004) for a capacious selection of writing about purdah in India.

5. Chughtai's controversial story 'Lihaaf' (The Quilt) was published in Urdu in 1942 though the majority of her literary work comes later in the century. See *Quilt and Other Stories* (New Delhi: Kali for Women, 1996).

6. See de Souza, *Purdah Writing*, for a selection.

7. See, for example, an early travel narrative, *Atiya's Journeys: A Muslim Woman from Colonial Bombay to Edwardian Britain*, ed. by Siobhan Lambert-Hurley and Sunil Sharma, (Oxford: Oxford University Press, 2010). For more on early twentieth–century movements for reform among Muslim women in India, see Siobhan Lambert-Hurley, 'Fostering Sisterhood: Muslim Women and the All-India Ladies' Association', *Journal of Women's History*, 16:2 (summer, 2004), 40–65. For more on the contexts for Indian writers in the UK, see Ruvani Ranasinha, *South Asian Writers in Twentieth-Century Britain: Culture in Translation* (Oxford: Oxford University Press, 2007) and Ruvani Ranasinha ed., *South Asians and the Shaping of Britain, 1870–1950: A Sourcebook* (Manchester: Manchester University Press, 2012) and the online database *Making Britain: South Asians in Britain from 1870 to 1950*, <http://www8.open.ac.uk/researchprojects/makingbritain>.

8. See the biographical sketch in this volume by her grandson, Arif Zaman, for more complete information on her life.

9. Asiya Alam, introduction to *Changing India: A Muslim Woman Speaks*, by Iqbalunnisa Hussain (Karachi: Oxford University Press, 2015), xiv.

10. The Maharani's College for Women was chartered in the early twentieth century to serve the women of Mysore by offering them classes and in 1920, began to offer degrees. In 1938, it partially merged with the existing Intermediate College for Women, Bangalore, which had access to science labs, to offer a full-fledged arts and sciences curriculum for women. This is now the Maharani's Science College for Women in Bangalore, <http://www.karnataka.gov.in/mscwb/Pages/History.aspx>. The Maharani's College for Women in Mysore became the Maharani's Arts College for Women; in the 1980's, the Maharani's Arts and Commerce College for Women. It is affiliated with the University of Mysore: <http://www.edubilla.com/maharani-s-arts-and-commerce-college-for-women-mysore/>. It is unclear which of these two institutions Iqbalunnisa Hussain attended.

11. She attended the 5th, 6th and 7th conferences, 1931–33. See Alam, *Changing* India, xv.

12. See her two talks at the Conference collected in *Changing India*. For a discussion of the content and importance of the Conference, see Asiya Alam's introduction to that volume. For more on Iqbalunnisa Hussain's biography, see the biographical sketch by Arif Zaman in this volume.

13. Alam, xxvii.

14. Hussain was active establishing the Girl Guides in India. See Asiya Alam's introduction to *Changing India* and Suvir Kaul's essay, '*Purdah and Polygamy* in a Changing India', in this volume for a discussion of the importance of that movement.

15. *Changing India*, 3.

16. Ibid., xi.

17. Foreword, *Purdah and Polygamy: Life in an Indian Muslim Household* (Karachi: Oxford University Press, 2017), 2.

18. Srinivasa Iyengar, *Indian Writing in English* (Vantage Press, 1973), 438.

19. Meenakshi Mukherjee, *The Twice Born Fiction* (Heinemann, 1974), II.

20. Chirosree Basu, 'Inner Persons: From the Kitchen to the Air Balloon', *The Telegraph*, Calcutta, 25 July 2003. Accessed 27 December 2016, <https://www.telegraphindia.com>.

21. Shabnam Minwalls, 'Rediscovery of Formidable Voices from the Past', 17 November 2002, 11.39, *Times of India*, Mumbai. Accessed 2 February 2015, <http://timesofindia.indiatimes.com>.

22. In V.A. Pai Panandiker and Navnita Chadha Behera, *Perspectives on South Asia* (Delhi: Konark, 2000), 141–51.

23. Amin Malak, *Muslim Narratives and the Discourse of English* (SUNY Press, 2004).

24. In Ulka Anjaria, ed. *A History of the Indian Novel in English* (Cambridge: Cambridge University Press, 2015), 133–46.

25. Zara Khadeeja Majoka, 'Lahore Literary Festival: Women's Writings about Women', *DAWN, Books and Authors*, published 3 March 2013. Last accessed 2 February 2015.

26. See Toru Dutt, *Bianca: The Young Spanish Maiden* (New Delhi: Prachi Prakashan, 2001); Krupabai Satthianadhan, *Saguna: A Story of Native Christian*, edited by Chandani Lokugé (New Delhi: Oxford University Press, 1998); and *Kamala: A Story of Hindu Life*, edited by Chandani Lokugé (New Delhi: Oxford, 1998); Rokeya Hossain, *Sultana's Dream and Selections from The Secluded Ones* (New York: Feminist Press, 1988); Ismat Chughtai, *Lifting the Veil: Selected Writings* (New York: Penguin, 2001); Cornelia Sorabji, *Love and Life Behind the Purdah*, edited by Chandani Lokugé (New Delhi: Oxford University Press, 2003). Suvir Kaul addresses Iqbalunnisa Hussain's connection to several of these writers in his essay, '*Purdah and Polygamy* in a Changing India', in this volume. For a broad perspective on Indian women writers, see Susie Tharu and K. Lalitha, *Women Writing in India: 600 B.C. to the Present*, 2 vols. (New Delhi: Oxford University Press, 1991).

27. Jane Austen, *Pride and Prejudice* (Oxford: Oxford University Press, 1986), 3.

28. Zuhra 'determined that Nazni should be punished for having…been treated by a surgeon' (45).

29. Barbara D. Metcalf and Thomas R. Metcalf, *A Concise History of Modern India*, third edition (Cambridge: Cambridge University Press, 2012), 2.

30. See Tony Ballantyne, 'Race and the Webs of Empire: Aryanism from India to the Pacific', *Journal of Colonialism and Colonial History*, 3, (2001); and Neha Mishra, 'India and Colorism: The Finer Nuances', *Washington University Global Studies Law Review*, 14. 4, (2015), 725–50. Last accessed 20 February 2017,

<openscholarship.wustl.edu/law_globalstudies/vol14/iss4/14>.

31. Aryanism is the notion that certain communities shared cultural features as a result of their sharing a common 'Aryan stock'. 'Although the Aryan concept is based upon the Vedic hymns, which record the incursion of nomadic pastoralists from Central Asia who called themselves "Arya" (noble) into north India, the birth of Aryanism as an ethnological framework was the direct result of what we might term "Company Orientalism", the body of knowledge about South Asian languages, cultures, and histories produced by the functionaries of the East India Company.' (Ballantyne, 'Race and the Webs', np).

32. See, for example, H.H. Risley, *The Tribes and Castes of Bengal* (Calcutta: Firma Mukhopadhyay, 1981; orig. pub. 1891) and his work on the early twentieth–century censuses in which the caste system, including distinctions between Aryans and Dravidians, was formalized for British India.

33. See Neha Mishra, 'India and Colorism: The Finer Nuances', *Washington University Global Studies Law Review*, 14.4 (2015), 725–50, <http://openscholarship.wustl.edu/law_globalstudies/vol14/iss4/14>.

34. Although there is variety in hijra practice, 'hijras are typically phenotypic men…who wear female clothing, grow their hair, and enact an exaggeratedly feminine performance. Hijra lifeworlds encompass a range of corporeal possibilities but tend to be characterized by hierarchies of authenticity, at the apex of which stand those who undergo complete excision of the penis and testicles'. (Rahul Rao, 'Hijra', in Rachel Dwyer, Gita Dharampal-Frick, Monika Kirloskar-Steinbach, Jahnavi Phalkey, *Key Concepts in Modern Indian Studies* [New York University Press, 2015]). While, as I have been arguing, Maghbool's gender identity in *Purdah and Polygamy* also raises questions surrounding religion, class, and nation, it overlaps very little with these aspects of hijra practice. It is therefore important to find other ways to characterize the challenge Maghbool

35. Susan Stryker, *Transgender History* (Berkeley: Seal Press, 2008), 1.

36. Ibid., 19.

37. Stryker, '(De)Subjugated Knowledges: An Introduction to Transgender Studies', *The Transgender Studies Reader*, ed. Susan Stryker and Stephen Whittle, (New York: Routledge, 2006), 3.

38. For further discussion of the issue of transgender in this novel, see my essay, 'Is the Trans in Transnational the Trans in Transgender?', *Modernism/Modernity*, 24.2 (April 2017), 217–44.

39. Susan Stryker, 'De/Colonizing Transgender Studies of China', in *Transgender China*, ed. Howard Chiang (New York: Palgrave, 2012), 287–92.

40. Gayatri Reddy, *With Respect to Sex* (Chicago: University of Chicago Press, 2010), 17.

41. Roshanak Kheshti, 'Cross-Dressing and Gender (Tres) Passing: The Transgender Move as a Site of Agential Potential in the New Iranian Cinema', *Hypatia*, 24, no. 3 (2009), 173.

42. For further discussion of the modernism of this novel, see my essay, 'Neither Mirror nor Mimic: Late Colonial Indian Narratives in English', *The Oxford Handbook of Global Modernisms*, ed. Mark Wollaeger (Oxford: Oxford University Press, 2012), 205–27.

43. Foreword (3, ref. page in this edition)

44. 'Through skillful use of the English language, he delineates people whose actions, behaviour, and responses are shaped by a language different from English', quoted in Feroza Jussawalla, *Family Quarrels: Towards a Criticism of Indian Writing in English* (New York: Peter Lang, 1985), 74.

45. Mulk Raj Anand, 'Pigeon-Indian: Some Notes on Indian-English Writing', *World Literature Written in English*, 21.2, (1982 Summer), 325–36.

46. Qtd. in Barbara D. and Thomas R. Metcalf, *A Concise History of Modern India*, third edition (Cambridge: Cambridge University Press, 2012), 208.

47. See *Changing India*.

Note on the Text

I have here reproduced Iqbalunnisa Hussain's *Purdah and Polygamy* essentially as it was published in 1944. In the text, she often uses translations or transliterations of words in Indian languages that are now considered non-standard. Where these are used consistently throughout I have retained them, often with a note indicating their meaning and the more standard spelling. On the many occasions where the transliteration is inconsistent, I have regularized it with today's more standard spelling (for example, 'hakeem' for Hussain's 'Hakim', and 'pir' for Hussain's 'Peer'). While Hussain often uses upper case for these terms, I have generally changed them to lower case, following contemporary practice. I have also corrected minor punctuation errors (such as when a comma appears in place of a period at the end of a sentence), some grammatical errors (for example, where subject and verb do not agree in number within a sentence), as well as a few spelling errors. While Hussain uses far fewer commas than contemporary usage would require, I have let her punctuation choices stand. I have not otherwise altered Hussain's grammar, diction, or word choice.

Purdah and Polygamy
Life in an Indian Muslim Household

Foreword

By

Sir RAMAALINGA REDDY, Kt., Hon. D. Litt., M.L.C.

Vice-Chancellor, Andhra University

Though by an author little known to fame, there is hardly a novel published in India and dealing with Indian life in any of its myriad phases and aspects which, in my opinion, has a better claim to become famous than Mrs Iqbalunnisa Hussain's *Purdah and Polygamy*. Without exaggeration I can hail her as the Jane Austen of India. She deals with the ordinary, the familiar, not with the romantic and heroic. It is by deft touches, each minute in itself, but together constituting life and reality, that she wins first the attention and finally the heart of the reader. Observation, analysis, a penetrating insight into the working of the minds of the men and women of the mercantile class of the Muslim community in India, the fervour of a moral and social purpose which sometimes leads her to didactic outpourings, and above all, the painter's gift of portraiture that brings out the very soul of the persons figured—these and other graces have given to us a novel in which all the characters, and more especially the women, live and move before our eyes true to life, simple, natural, unsophisticated, intimate. The women depicted are not types but flesh and blood individuals, particular, vivid, full of vitality and each an attraction in her own special way. I read the book at one stretch from cover to cover. For it was no task but an irresistible pleasure.

I sent it to some of my literary friends for their unbiased opinion without letting them know a word about the author or my interest in her who, I recently discovered, was one that I had helped in her education career. Mr Bezwada Gopala Reddi,[1] a Tagorean with an established standing in Telugu literature, writes thus: 'Her maiden effort at novel writing is quite a success. The book gives an insight into a Muslim's life within walls, which is a sealed book to most of us. She knows where the shoe pinches and has given expression to her agony through this book.' I would say that it is better than an agony. It is an analysis which is intellectually convincing as well as emotionally stirring.

The same thought has struck both Mr Gopala Reddi and myself regarding the psychological affinity between the Hindu and the Muslim women. As Mr Gopala Reddi says, 'The surface variety need not deceive us about the substratum unity.' Hindu readers of this book will realise, perhaps for the first time, how close to their women in heart, soul, thoughts, feelings and aspirations, earthly as well as heavenly, the Muslim women are. After all, they are the daughters of the same race. It is more easy to change one's religion than to change one's life. As I read of the joys and sorrows of the women portrayed in this novel, it was borne in upon me that not merely in their lives but in many of their customs, manners and superstitions, they were own sisters to Hindus. The trials and tribulations through which a Muslim daughter, wife or widow passes, her hopes and fears, the social inhibitions which suppress her personality, are hardly different from those that affect the Hindus of the same sex. In submissiveness, in the spirit of resignation, and many other traits of passivity and self-abnegation, differences in religion do not seem to have led to diversity in conduct and character.

I may be wrong but it strikes me that the Muslim men have diverged from the Hindu racial type to a far greater extent than Muslim women.

However, this story, so moving, so realistic like a French novel, yet free from whatever can offend the most delicate sensibility, mirroring characters, natural, unadorned, in all their lights and shadows, does not lend itself to moralising. It is life, throbbing, pathetic, tragic, and burdens the heart too heavily to permit of detached thought. It is after one has finished the volume that one awakens to deep indignation that such wrongs could be and a fervent hope of better conditions to be achieved.

Most Indian novels suffer from the reaction of the inferiority complex induced by centuries of subjection to foreign rule and an instinctive desire to stand well in the estimation of Europeans. There is in them a tendency to touch up, to gloss over, to interpret idealistically, to colour, to varnish and make of the ugliness marring our life a pale symbol of alleged spirituality. Mrs Iqbalunnisa Hussain is utterly free from this weakness. Either she is too proud to conceal and cover up, which I don't think is the case; or she has the French gift of sober objectivity and artistic realism. This is a very rare, refreshing and exceptional merit in an Indian novelist. But our authoress is no cynic, though one may detect a note of suppressed horror and disgust at the wretched levels of the lives lived by some of her co-religionists, the rich but uncultured mercantile community. Her heart is warm; her sympathy keen; her hopes of progress are not dead and cold. If she probes, it is to cure.

This same aspect appeals differently to a Tagorean like Mr Gopala Reddi: 'The ordinary and the obvious have come to us in the form of a story and have an effective appeal to our hearts. The familiar clothed in the garb of fancy has its own sweetness. Thus the novel is simple and sweet.' And now comes the Tagorean demurrer, 'There is nothing mighty about it. There are no whirls of depressed feelings not tempests of excited emotions. We do not find the solemnity of depths with loftiness of heights. It has not the romance of a hill brook. It is just a shallow-watered stream of the plains, useful and lucid.' This, in my opinion, is exactly what will give Mrs Iqbalunnisa Hussain's *Purdah and Polygamy* a very high and honoured place in Indo-Anglian literature.

Mr B. Muthuswami of the Department of English in the Andhra University[2] thus wrote after reading the book at my instance, 'In this book, almost for the first time, true Purdah life is depicted with utter realism.'

Mrs Iqbalunnisa Hussain has written this in English, a medium foreign to her. Yet her English, as far as another person like myself, to whom also the language is foreign, can judge, is simple, clear, correct and flows smooth and natural. She conveys her meaning both with power and with accuracy. But here and there the structure and the idiom may strike the English ear as strange, outlandish.

Occasionally, she translates the Urdu or Kannada idiom into literal English producing effects which are naive. But is this a defect? Does it not rather add to the faithfulness of the picture and make her narrative more natural and appealing? I have read some excellent novels in English by Japanese and Chinese writers. Their very deviations from standard English very often constitute an additional charm. The same may be said of the style of Mrs Iqbalunnisa Hussain.

C.R. Reddy
Andhra University
Guntur
12 August 1944

The author wishes to state that all the characters in this novel have no existence outside her own imagination and are not even distantly inspired by any individuals known or unknown to her. All the incidents also are invention.

Chapter I

Dilkusha was an imposing building, standing in the heart of a city. It commanded respect and awe, if premises have any such effect, among the neighbouring shops, restaurants, cafes and hotels. Its high blind walls made a stranger take it for an unguarded jail, and literally it was so for its women folk.[1] Dilkusha was divided by a high wall with a wicket gate into two houses and these faced opposite roads. The one opening on the high road was rented. The other was a peculiar one like its inhabitants. It consisted of a square courtyard surrounded by eight rooms, two on each side with a bath-room. All these rooms received light through a ventilator or a glass-tile in their ceiling. The only window that each room had opened on the courtyard, and so also the doors.

Umar, the owner, had let three of the sides and in the fourth he himself lived. In the absence of the male members the women of all the four families spent their time in the common courtyard. They ate, talked and worked together till the men began coming home in the evening. There was only one common door leading to the road, so all the males while going out or coming in had to give an alarm to the women of the other families. This was done by shouting three times the word 'gosha'.[2] One can imagine the plight of the women who had to run in and shut the doors and windows of their cottages before the word was said thrice. The presence of men at home meant the desertion of the yard which was their only source of light and fresh air.

Umar was a jageerdar (landlord). God had blessed him with a large family of nine children. The Creator proposes but man disposes where the principles of health are concerned. Lack of knowledge of child rearing had reduced the number to two. The poor man in spite of all his sincere efforts to serve his country was left with a daughter and a son, Kabeer.

Umar was very careful with his money. In fact the ancestral property had increased during his regime. He economised in all his expenses, abstained from polygamy, rented out every possible space. He knew well that women, being unreasonable creatures, could not be trusted in money matters.[3] He himself bought all that was necessary for the house. His wife's clothes were purchased once a year in Ramzan,[4] when he bought them in the way of zakath[5] for the poor. She needed no money because she never went out of the four walls of the house. No vendor was allowed near the house. He often said 'No virtuous woman will step out of the house and will see no third person.' Cinemas she had never seen. Arrangements for visiting religious places and picnics were made by the members of the other three families, but Umar neither participated nor allowed her to join them. When they left on such a journey he said to her 'There is none equal to you in virtue, modesty and obedience.'

He had made it a point not to eat anything cooked by a servant. No male servant was allowed into the house. There was never more than one woman servant, who did the washing and cleaning. The duty of a housewife is to see that the food is well cooked and her husband comforted. To feed the brute in him she cooked every meal herself. When he said, 'I had my food to my entire satisfaction,' Zuhra, with an expression of pride and joy, replied, 'I did my duty to the crown of my head for whose happiness nothing in this world will be spared.'

The property and the estate had been in the family for the last three generations. Their loss would mean a great disgrace to the great-grandfather, who had been a minister and nawab.[6] This feat kept all the successive heirs on tenterhooks. They had adopted a policy of all care and no expense. Umar was even more economical than his predecessors. The great trust had to be left to his only son, so no care in bringing him up to be a worthy heir was overlooked. He knew the old saying, 'spare the rod and spoil the child.' Corporal punishment was not an uncommon thing in the house. Whenever the blows were severe and needed plastering for days, Umar dropped a few parental tears. But the next time he transgressed Kabeer got his beating just the same. To justify himself Umar said 'I am not his enemy. I want to see him the best and the most worthy successor of mine.' He not only watched Kabeer's movements himself but engaged detectives.

Kabeer was given religious education at home by a mullah. After performing, very grandly, the school-going ceremony, he was sent to a madrasa (grammar school) to teach him reading and writing Urdu. Kabeer had a natural aversion for confining himself in the four walls of a classroom. Consequently he was often given a thrashing and on the plea of a headache or a stomach-ache he often stayed away. The parents' love for their only son was his protection. Alarmed at his supposed symptoms they permitted him stay in bed. After some time if Kabeer showed an inclination to play, his mother was very careful not to allow his father to see him. She did not believe in the child's going to school every day. She was of opinion that there was not much to learn. A boy who could consume four heavy loads of food a day could easily contain that of a book. Once or twice a week he went to school. The rest of the days, he left home with his books and after hiding them in the big gutter near the house he played marbles with the scamps of the locality till lunch time. If the afternoon was clear his companions planned an excursion to a neighbouring forest or orchard. But information of his movements reached home before his return. The evening brought him a flogging.

Umar fed and clothed Kabeer, but the boy needed money for his harmless enjoyments. How could he get it? The only way was to ask his father. One morning he went to his father's room and standing behind the door said 'I want some money.' This impertinent demand gave Umar the shock of his life. His needs, but for the modest eating and clothing, were few. He could not imagine how his son could be otherwise. For a minute he did not speak. Then controlling his emotion he said, 'You will never keep the property safe with your extravagant habits. Why do you want money? When I was of your age I did not know how to spend even a copper coin which stayed for months in my pocket.'

This gentle treatment was unexpected. Kabeer had gone to him to face a tyrant. For a time the boy gave up the idea of money. But only for a time. Soon, he was at it again. The fair means of asking for pocket money having failed he demanded it on the pretext of school subscriptions. The amount was given to one of the servants to be paid to the party concerned. This did not dishearten Kabeer. He invented an imaginary society and as usual he stood before his father dejected and pressed with the overwhelming idea of asking for money. The father knew his son's motive and made up his mind to put an end to such unnatural demands.

'Why are you standing like a criminal? What do you want?' he raved.

The sudden burst of anger froze Kabeer. He forgot all the bright ideas he wanted to express.

'The students have formed a junior league. All members have to pay ten rupees each,' he stammered.

'Nobody in the world has heard of such an exorbitant donation paid by a student.'

'They call me Nawab Sahib and say my donation should lead the rest.'

'They know you are the biggest fool. All idiots are flattered in that way. Resign your membership. It matters nothing if they call you a beggar.'

Saying these words Umar went out of the room. After a moment's thought he called his trustworthy servant and gave him a rupee to be given to the secretary of the junior league. No such organisation could be discovered. The father's anger knew no bounds. Kabeer was questioned and severely punished.

Need is the mother of schemes. Adolescence is the reservoir of designs—growing energy produces an abundant supply of them. Kabeer waited for hours for his father to leave his room. False keys were used to open the safe and his needs were satisfied. Sometimes the knitted bag of money looked small to Umar, but no one dared open it.

When Umar was bedridden with a cancer, the royal disease, there was no chance for such an enterprise. The mother found articles from the household missing. The woman servant was blamed and chastised. Who could suspect the heir to the family throne? Sometimes Kabeer himself solved the problem. He said that it was used by him and left in haste outside the house where there were swarms of beggars. At other times he said that he had lent it to a friend, but the article never made its appearance in the house.

Nature had dealt a heavy blow not only to Umar's offspring but also to his aspirations. His long-cherished hope of increasing the family wealth at any cost was shattered. For no fault of his he suffered from cancer and was in bed for years. Thanks to the efforts of the hakeem[7] his death was delayed. Umar hated doctors and their fantastic theory of operation, and always preferred physicians who charged no fees for their visits. When his condition was serious a friend suggested the name of a famous surgeon who was well known for the treatment of cancer. Unfortunately the man used to charge about five hundred rupees per patient. After hearing all about him Umar said, 'Pooh! Greed is personified in the wretched man. Selfishness in a physician is a curse. Sympathy is a great healer. If death is to come it will come anyway.'

The icy hand of death is gentle on the poor. It is torture on the rich. As a true Muslim Umar expressed his indifference to passing this sojourn happily, but in his heart of hearts a deadly struggle went on between two ideas: whether to get treated by the surgeon or be content with his destiny. The latter carried the day.

Expectation of his premature death made him hurry over the wedding of his daughter. One day in despair he said to his wife, 'It is the will of God that I should die leaving a big responsibility on your shoulders. It is my desire to get Jamila married in my presence and thus lessen the burden on you.'

The girl was only twelve years old. Although the mother had started to gather jewels and clothes in readiness she could not think it right that the marriage should take place in a hurry. There was no suitable man in view. It means a disgrace and giving room to scandal to send an offer from the girl's parents. But it had to be performed in the lifetime of the father or else there was no possibility of securing a husband in a good position for her. The son of Umar's brother was considered a worthless suitor when Umar was healthy. Zuhra, his wife, hated the young man for more than one reason. But the urgency of the matter made them send for Umar's brother and settle it. The marriage took place within a week. As a devoted husband and loving father Umar made his will. Zuhra was made the guardian of Kabeer who was only sixteen years old. To tell the truth he had no confidence in either—the wife because of her unreasonableness, or the son who had displayed such evident signs of extravagance. In view of his own relations, who would have squandered all his wealth but for the will, the lesser evil was given preference.

Umar's condition grew worse day by day. The famous doctor was sent for but he refused to take up the case. Kabeer stopped going to school as there was a reasonable excuse. He stayed at home and looked after his father. The illness had changed him and the helplessness made him kinder. His severe authoritativeness was replaced by gentleness of manner and sympathy for his wife and son. The father's changed attitude and behaviour drew out a response in Kabeer. A sense of responsibility took root. He heard the father's instructions and preaching with interest. They began to have one mind. Kabeer came to know of the exact amount of cash and other investments in various lucrative items. Umar on his death bed achieved the object of his life for which he had struggled so hard. Death separated them as good friends.

Chapter II

Messages were sent to the relatives living in the city and telegrams to those out of it. Early morning trains brought swarms of them. Deaths, births, and marriages are events of great excitement and bring hundreds of womenfolk together. People who do not know a certain family can make a voluntary acquaintance on such occasions on the plea of human sympathy.

Zuhra fainted when she knew that her husband was dead. Her mother and sister, who lived in the same city, had come a few minutes before Umar passed away. They looked after her and her belongings. A death affords a good chance to the poor to get away with portable articles which can be hidden under the full-size veil. All big and small things were locked up in a lumber room. They were wholeheartedly her sympathizers. The neighbours had to send food to the house of calamity. The days of such consideration vary but for three days at least, the bereaved family should be free from the worry of cooking.[1] Luckily the three families and the tenants agreed among themselves to feed the family a day each.

The dead body of Umar after washing and shrouding was kept in the common courtyard to enable hundreds of visitors to have their last look at him.[2] All those who visited them that day had to be invited to the funeral dinners on the 7th, 10th, 20th and 40th days.[3]

After the men finished their visits the doors were closed. The near and dear women relatives who did not observe purdah in front of him were asked to see the deceased. After all a man is a man even dead, and purdah before him is essential. The saddest ceremony in Zuhra's life had to take place before the dead body was taken for burial.[4] Neither the mother had the heart to do it nor the married sister. No woman with her husband living dared invite the calamity upon herself with open eyes. Umar's widowed sister came to Zuhra, an invalid who being aware of the dreadful ceremony began to sob which made all the women shed sympathetic tears. There was a loud cry by the nearest relations. Umar's sister did not care for the general wailing; she had to do her duty. Holding up Zuhra's arm she made her stand. She could not do it. The great strain of nursing for years and the shock of his death had made her lifeless. Another old widow rushed to help her. In between them she had to walk to the dead body. When Zuhra was nearing the dead man she felt her sorrow uncontrollable.

'Don't make me a dark spot on the radiant world of womanhood! Kill me here and bury me here with him!'

An avalanche of indigent shouts burst on her from numerous ladies: 'You get what you deserve.[5] You cannot go against God's will.'

'She will be a curse, a thing to be hated among women all her life,' said others.[6] 'If you were lucky you would have died before him. He would have made you the queen of the day,' said a kinder woman.

Naturally such bitter remarks touched her sympathizers to the quick. They retaliated.

'This day is seen by hundreds. You are not alone in the sinking ship.'

'Think of other widows who are in a more miserable condition. Be brave, face the wrath of God with the same spirit as you do his favour.'

But even the well-wishers spoke from a distance.

The two unsympathetic supporters of Zuhra had to do their duty quickly. They pushed her forward between them. Her sobs were converted into loud weeping.

'Don't for God's sake pull my arms. They are aching. I don't want to live. For whom have I to live?' said Zuhra, frantically struggling. The hold on her arms was tightened.

'Oh kill me! My life will be worse than death. What interest have I in the world? Who will be my supporter? Oh God, the world is dark to me.'

Umar's sister who was holding the arm lost her temper. 'Whatever one gets is in return for what one does. You must have made his life unhappy, and must have disobeyed him, so you are bearing the consequences of his curse. Behave yourself in acknowledgment of your evil doings.'

A desperate condition of mind breeds imagination and recollection. 'I had no sleep, no rest, no peace of mind, and converted my nights into days, yet I deserve this. Is there justice in the world?' she said still weeping.

Such desperate expressions by the helpless daughter put courage in the heart of the mother. She came near to console Zuhra, and holding her to her breast said, 'Don't lose heart. You are judged now. Your son will be your helper and protector. You have to live and do a double duty for him.'

On the approach of her mother Zuhra's grief knew no bounds. She entreated her not to make her a widow, but the mother could not help her. The ceremony had to be performed. So they brought her to the dead man. She screamed when she saw him in the shroud and said, 'Oh heaven! What a condition he is in! I cannot bear to see him dead. Leave me. I shall kill myself and be buried with him.'

Umar's sister, who believed that Zuhra had been the cause of her brother's death, indignantly said, 'Don't pretend by saying that you want to kill yourself. You killed him all right,' and with force she made her squat near the corpse and commanded the mother to leave her in her charge.

'Bring a stone,' shouted Umar's sister. It was given. She broke the bangles from both the hands of the weeping Zuhra, then she pulled and threw the latcha (black beads), the token of marriage, near the corpse, and removed the jewels and handed them over to a reliable widow relation.[7] 'Bring a sheet,' she shouted. Zuhra's sister had brought a white dress (sari and blouse) for the occasion and sent it with someone. Zuhra was clothed and her coloured dress was taken and thrown near the dead body.

One of the experienced women said 'Cover her face; let it not be seen by suhagans (married women).'

'Wash her face before you bring her inside the house,' cried another, 'Oh goodness, it ought to have been done before putting on the widow-clothes,' said someone else.

'One forgets what and how it is to be done because of the way she behaves. She is not ashamed of having caused the catastrophe; on the other hand she is howling and thinking of her own wretched self as if it is worth an atom. Shall I undress her, wash her face, and then put on the clothes?' asked Umar's sister.

'No, no, to put on the widow-dress twice means making her a widow twice,' said one of the onlookers.[8]

'Even if she is not made a widow twice, the curse will fall on someone else,' cried another.

It was decided that she should not be made a widow twice, nor to let the catastrophe fall on some innocent being, so she was taken back in the same way. She was not allowed to touch the corpse for fear of polluting it.[9] They brought the reluctant creature away by force and laid her on her bed.

The thousands of men waiting outside for the women to make room were agitated. It was Friday and the body had to be taken to the mosque before 1 o'clock.[10] Umar had been lucky even in his death. His death on Friday meant an easy salvation, which made others envy his fortune.[11] The news that the men were coming in made the members of the opposite sex hide themselves in rooms. But they could not help peeping through the windows and doors to see how the dead body was carried away. They were sure of their not being seen by the men. Even supposing they happened to see some women peeping no one could say who was who. The rooms were not enough to accommodate all. Some of the brave ladies sat down in the courtyard and shouted, 'Give us a sheet.'

It was searched for and given. Two old women beggars held the corners of the sheet. Thus it separated the women from the men in a corner of the open place. A second general wailing was started when the corpse was taken out. All women excepting the new widow came out to wash their faces and hands. The friends waited till the men returned from the burial ground and departed.

The relatives could not leave the place so soon. The near and dear ones coming from distant towns made up their minds to stay for forty days. They had to take part in various funeral ceremonies, and console the bereaved party.

The seventh day ceremony came on.[12] 'Do everything very grandly to keep up his name and fame,' said Umar's sister.

'I have invited for dinner about five hundred people,' said Umar's brother.

'Were there only five hundred visitors that day?' asked the sister.

'There were more than a thousand,' was the reply.

'It looks mean and insulting if all of them are not invited for all the functions. In what way are the survivors going to show their regard for the man who left untold wealth?' said the sister.

'Ask his wife if she has no objection to what you say. I shall do it with pleasure,' said the brother, who knew that without Zuhra's signature no money could be drawn from the bank. Kabeer went to his mother who was in bed and said, 'Uncle wants to know if all the visitors have to be invited for all the functions or a part of them for each.'

Zuhra could not yet think of her position. 'Let them do anything they like. As for the expenses he has left enough.'

The reply satisfied all the organisers. The amount for each function was calculated.

'We have to make the dishes he liked the best,' said his sister. 'What about the clothes to be given to beggars?' said someone.[13]

'They have to be clothed well or else the poor man will be seen naked in our dreams,' said sister.

This ingenious idea gave birth to a new problem: whether ordinary clothes were to be given to many beggars or a costly set to one.

'Whatever you give you will see him in it,' said the sister.

'Then let it be a costly dress. Who will not be pleased to see him in a grand dress? He will look as if he was alive,' said the cousin widow. After some discussion it was decided that at the other functions ordinary clothes were to be given and on the fortieth day costly ones.[14]

The fortieth day came. It had to be the grandest possible function. Many expensive dishes liked by Umar were prepared and the costly dress with gold embroidery was got made. It was arranged in a tray to keep ready for the night.

'No one will give such a grand dress to a beggar. No beggar will wear it. He will sell it and make money,' said the nephew of the deceased.

Kabeer was dissatisfied with all the extravagance, the daily expenses of maintaining five extra families and his mother's neutral policy.

'It was made for a fakir,' said Kabeer.[15] 'Let him have it. Why unnecessary discussion over a subject decided long ago?'

'The idea behind giving the clothes is just to part with them in the name of the dead man. It means the same even if it is given to a poor relation. Nazeer is getting married soon. It will suit him and will make a grand bridegroom's dress,' said the cousin.

The suggestion, as it was unselfish and useful, was unanimously supported. The prospective bridegroom was sent for and the dress was handed over to him after the fateha (prayer for the salvation of the soul).

The ladies who stayed for all these days did full justice to their sojourn. They helped, consoled and made them forget their sorrow. The motive of all of them was noble but the methods of carrying it out differed.

'What is the life of a woman after her husband? A woman lives for him and him alone. His death should mean the death of all her desires, comfort and happiness. Even the dogs are shown better consideration,' said one.

Once Kabeer was with his mother and heard someone saying, 'A widow has to be conscious of her sin in causing the death of her husband in thought, word and deed. She should avoid being present at happy events and not try to make others miserable.'

'My mother is different from other widows. I shall allow her to do anything she likes without caring for the ill talk,' said Kabeer.

Umar's sister, who was more tolerant to her nephew than to his mother, said 'You can allow her to do things after a long time, but now both of you should be very careful in what you do. So long as there is life in us we have to care for the opinion of others.'

The death of Umar had made Zuhra weak. Any mention of her husband or of her future wretched life made her shed tears for hours. Some of the guests were sincere and made a great fuss over her, attending to her needs in bed; some consoled her.

'God has chosen two extremes in writing your fate. One in giving you the best husband who sacrificed everything for you, and the other in making you the most unlucky in his loss. He has left money for you, but what is it? It does not give you happiness, respect and licence to take part in social activities.'

'He was very good to me. I was lucky in having him,' sobbed Zuhra.

'You didn't deserve the boon,' said one.

'If committing suicide was not a sin I would have done it long ago. The thought and the welfare of Kabeer prevent me. Oh, my son, who will take care of him? He will lose both father and mother,' cried Zuhra.

The over-crowded house, the seclusion, the constant counts, the direct and indirect condemnation of widowhood and the frugal food—she being afraid of looking healthy— had made Zuhra pale and haggard. She could not sit or stand by herself. One day Kabeer took her to the courtyard for fresh air. She felt better while sitting there. Her sister-in-law rushed to the place and said, 'What will people say if they see you here? They will say that you were just wanting his death to be free. No widow will leave seclusion before four months and ten days.[16] You are giving room to scandal. Even the servant will call you immoral.'

'Kabeer brought me here against my will. I am conscious of it,' said Zuhra.

'You should use your discretion. If you listen to children where is the difference between inexperienced boys and you? Unless you try to be careful in what you do and say I am afraid you will bring disgrace to the family,' said the sister-in-law rudely.

Days had passed since she had combed her hair. She had a constant headache. She asked someone for oil, and a comb. When it was taken Umar's sister said, 'You are not making her a bride?'[17]

The relations after performing the fortieth day funeral ceremony, and having exhausted all the cash in various banks, left one by one reluctantly. Thanks to the deceased the will was made and the property could not be sold before Kabeer reached his majority. This was well known to the male relatives.

Kabeer felt a great relief when the last family left. He did not ask anyone to stay behind and keep his mother company. He knew that he could do it better and make her forget her grief. The sense of responsibility had opened his eyes. Position in one's life works miraculously. He shunned his old friends and was the constant companion of his weeping mother.

'Don't make your life miserable in my company, Kabeer,' she said once.

'Your company gives me all that I need. You are to me both father and mother,' said he.

'You will be hopelessly disappointed in your expectations. No one will take his place. You lost in him everything in the world,' said she sympathetically.

Kabeer did not approve of her sentimentality. He felt that he was better able to look after himself. The sense of dependency had always been a cause of dissatisfaction to him. He was at liberty to spend and do what he liked, yet he did not exceed his privileges. His thoughts were turning towards the affairs of the estate. He had a sympathetic adviser in his mother.

'Both of us are equally afflicted. Let us feel the pang together. I would sacrifice my life to make you happy and comfortable,' he said with tears in his eyes.

'God bless you and give you long life, my supporter,' she said equally grieved.

Gradually he began to take an interest in outdoor affairs. All this time Umar's trusted servants and agents had managed the estate. He consulted his mother regarding the rent, interest and correspondence. He found her suggestions useful. This diverted her mind from the shock which seemed unbearable. They determined to keep aloof from their relatives. They felt that they were happier without their interference.

In a very short time he made the tenants, the staff and the people believe that he was sympathetic and lenient in his dealings. His generosity brought him more friends, and representatives of various associations for donations. His religious teaching had its effect. The pirs and the privileged demagogues whose high birth rules mankind were often invited.[18] They were fed for days and given gifts to enable them to carry out their noble professions. No other method of propaganda to make a name for himself was needed. People began to talk of him as a rich and great man. His numerous visitors made it necessary to vacate the other part of Dilkusha which had been let during his father's time.

The wealth seemed to have an outlet, but what is money for if not to live happily and comfortably? was the thought of both the mother and the son.

Chapter III

Kabeer's attempts to keep his mother engaged in estate affairs were not very successful. In spite of his interest in her, she stole a few hours a day for mourning. She kept awake very late in the night. She did not feel quite fit to take on domestic duties. Sitting near the fire cooking made her restless. She often said, 'I don't know what has happened to me. I am not the same person after his death.' The lifelong hard and selfless work had created a craving for well-earned rest. After the relations' departure, the maidservant, expecting higher wages as cook, took to it and forced her mistress to stay in bed.

Kabeer seemed to care more for quantity than quality. It is a blessing in a man which makes the work of a woman easy. The mental sufferings, which in the case of the mother amounted to physical pains, in his case had just the opposite effect. He looked round and overfed. The unnecessary flesh all over the body and especially on his cheeks, chin, and breast made him look older than his age.

Thanks to the costly dress they had given Nazeer, the second cousin of Kabeer, he became their ever-grateful supporter. He often visited them and cheered them up by his conversation. Indisposition on account of indigestion was the disease Kabeer often suffered with. Nazeer came one day when Kabeer was unwell and said, 'You need half rationing and exercise. Get yourself weighed.'

'Nothing of the kind. Weighing and measuring reduce one's span of life,' said Zuhra.

'He is too fat for his age and height. I think he is only five foot five, but his weight is not less than fourteen stone.'

'Don't cast eyes on him. He is just nice. Everything in him is equally balanced. He will look consumptive if he is reduced.'

'He is still in his teens but he looks like a man of middle age,' said Nazeer

'I am nineteen now,' interrupted Kabeer.

'His body is bulky but not strong,' said Zuhra.

'Exercise will make him strong.'

'He is busy from morning to night with visitors and estate affairs. Is that not enough exercise?'

Nazeer knew that Zuhra's point had only one side. No one could convince her against her conviction. Those who argued with her were called cranks. He could not break his friendship with her. As a safeguard, it was better to pocket the insult and be a hypocrite.

'When will you give us the pulao (a rich preparation with rice and meat) of your marriage?' said Nazeer.

'You can have it today for lunch. We have prepared it.'

'I want not the ordinary one but the marriage pulao.'

'What difference does it make? You can imagine that you ate it.'

'It makes a world of difference in taste,' said Zuhra.

'Because it is cooked in large quantity, the taste differs,' said Nazeer.

'Not only that; the name attached to it increases or decreases the taste. The pulao made at the funeral ceremonies tastes bitter,' said Zuhra.

'You mean the one made on the fortieth day. Naturally it tasted bitter because you were sad that day,' said Nazeer.

'That is not the only time. I have experienced it on several occasions.'

'You may be right, but it makes no difference to me,' said Nazeer humorously.

Whatever was the idea of talking about Kabeer's marriage, Zuhra's mind began to work in that direction. She felt that she had not done a mother's duty. She had neglected him and had left him to be satisfied with the cook's preparations. Why should he suffer on account of her? No, it was unjust. She must get him married and transfer her responsibility to younger shoulders.

'You have to help him to settle down in life. How can he get himself married without the help of his elders?'

'Your agent, Mustafa, is a good matchmaker. I shall speak to him about it.'

Kabeer felt uneasy when talk of his marriage was going on. He left the room.

'Have you any particular girl in view?' asked Nazeer.

'What do I know about the people and the girls here?'

'I shall come some other day to see Mustafa,' said Nazeer. He had his food and left.

Zuhra was a person who would never allow the grass to grow under her feet. She knew that the sister of her cook was a good matchmaker and the matter could be decided quicker through her. If she had to depend upon Mustafa she could not do it directly. She needed the help of a third person. Nazeer was not a daily visitor. The same evening while helping the cook peel vegetables, she said, 'What does your sister Zainab Bi do?'

'Her work is quite different from mine. She earns ten times more than I do, yet it is easy work. No grumbling.'

Zuhra felt the hint. The cook was hard-worked and low paid. She would steal things but they were not counted. She could not be rude to her. A lot was expected from her, and through her.

'Does she know many people here?'

'She knows almost everyone. She rarely stays at home during the day. During the time of weddings, even her nights are engaged. She is popular both among the rich and the poor.'

'What does she get from the poor except a plate of pulao?'

'She fixes up her fees before deciding the matter. If the girl is poor, she tries to get her married to a rich man and takes double from him.'

'No rich man will marry into a poor family.'

'Why not? What does a polygamist need but a girl? If the girl is beautiful, her fee jumps up to hundreds. She is in touch and keeps an eye on every young man and never lets an opportunity slip.'

'Has she been successful in her profession?'

'Sometimes, the marriages arranged by her come to an unhappy ending. Then she effects a reconciliation between the parties concerned. But such cases are rare.'

'Ask her to see me tomorrow,' said Zuhra.'

'Is it about Kabeer miyan's marriage? It is high time you thought of it. You will lose him and the money if you don't get him married soon.'

Zuhra's pride was wounded. The cook could not understand her sorrow. The death of a husband meant nothing to her. These low class people care nothing for social talk. Their world is shallow and they live in the present. Her son was not a squanderer of money. The cook was insulting and condemning her son. But it was not the time to break with her.

'There is time for everything. No one can perform a marriage unless and until the time comes for one's marriage flowers to blossom. Even now, we don't know which day they will come out. No human hand can force it,' said Zuhra.

'Yes, yes, you are quite right,' said the cook, and promised to bring her sister the next morning.

Zainab Bi, though illiterate, was not uneducated. Her general knowledge and experience were wide. She could act boldly and could make her opponent take to her point of view without humiliating herself. Her success in her occupation had made her over-confident. She acted hypocritically till the question of her fee was decided. Then she could arrange a match in any house with any person.

Zainab Bi was punctual and alert in spite of the superfluous flesh all over her body. She was annoyed because no conveyance was sent and she had to plod. She always wore decent clothes, presented by the benefitted parties. On that day, they were costlier than those of Zuhra.

As soon as Zainab Bi entered the house, Zuhra looked at her own clothes and felt self-conscious. 'Never mind, I am in mourning,' she said to console herself. The visitor addressed Zuhra as an equal.

'Did you want to see me?'

'I am glad you could come.'

'You were lucky I was available. People wait for months to catch me,' was the proud reply, which made Zuhra indignant. But she would undergo any insult to make her son happy.

'I hope what you do will be lucky' was the considerate reply.

'There is no doubt about it. I never take responsibility if I am not sure of its success.'

'Your sister knows my son well. He is a home bird.'

'I have been keeping an eye on him, and waiting for this opportunity. Tell me whether you want a rich or a beautiful girl. I shall fix it up.'

'He is my only son in whom all my desires are concentrated. I want a girl both beautiful and rich. She must come from a well-known and respectable family. I have to be very careful in my choice. The criticism will be bitter if I am wrong. The same thing, if it were done by the master, would have been called a virtue,' said Zuhra.

'You want high family, beauty, and wealth. These things rarely go together. You being a rich person must be contented with beauty. There is one place where you can get all these three things. The father is very proud of his daughter and refuses proposals on the slightest excuse.'

'Who are those people?'

'Doulath Khan, who lives in a mansion in the street named after him.'

'Is he not a Pathan?'[1]

'Yes, a better Muslim than all of us.'

'But people object…'

'Your demands can't be supplied in other houses. The girl is rich and beautiful and comes from a respectable family. Syeds and Pathans are all human beings.'[2]

'It is a matter of destiny. No one can prevent their union if they are fated to each other. You try in other places too,' said Zuhra.

Zuhra was known for her intuition. She could definitely say that a certain thing was possible.

'Doulath Khan might have refused other offers but he will surely give his daughter to my son. This is his first marriage, he is a jageerdar, and he has no dependents.[3] A girl's fate must have been written with golden letters to be destined his wife,' said Zuhra emphatically.

'It depends upon them to say. She has had many offers but none of them was accepted.'

'This case is quite different. They will give their consent unhesitatingly.'

'The offers I took were not of ordinary people. They were unmarried men, holding very high positions. They had promised me a hundred rupees each.'

'If it is your commission that makes you bargain, I shall give you more if I am satisfied. After explaining to them about Kabeer, you fix a date for me to see the girl.

'They will not allow a widow to see her.[4] You must send for your daughter.'

'I know, you need not teach me. It's more my concern than theirs. I shall be the greater loser in casting my shadow on my daughter-in-law,' said Zuhra dejectedly.

As was expected, the offer was welcomed in the houses of both the officials and non-officials. They were informed of the mother's desire to see the girl. The dates had to be fixed.

'Kabeer, write to Jamila's husband to send her for a week,' said Zuhra.

'Her husband gets annoyed if we call her often. He has to ask his parents. It is not even six months since she went back.'

'Tell him that I want her on some important affair.'

Kabeer was surprised by his mother's stern tone. He hesitated to ask her the cause. If it was about his marriage, she would not tell him nor would he be able to face it.

'We must give him the reason, otherwise he will take it amiss.'

'Whatever it is, you can't write. Just say that I want her.'

Kabeer's quick imagination guessed the truth. How could he ask her where it was and who was arranging it? Was it Nazeer? He hadn't turned up again after that visit. He left her so as not to create suspicion or to show his anxiety in the matter. After some time, he brought the short letter to read to her.

'Yes, it is all right.'

Jamila arrived and asked her brother, 'Why did Amma call me?'

'How do I know? I know as much as you.'

'It must be in connection with your marriage. Where has she fixed it up?'

'I tell you I know nothing. I don't think it is about that.'

'Didn't you try to overhear her talk with others as you used to do? After going home I shall let you know all about it.'

'Will you?' he said with a smile.

'What a shameless creature you are! Already in smiles.'

'Before you know what it is, you call me shameless as if you were not married,' said Kabeer, with a broad smile.

Brother and sister arrived home from the station.

'Was your husband angry with me?' said Zuhra.

'He was worried not knowing the reason. He thought someone must be ill so he sent me immediately.'

'Rubbish! When happy events are planned, no ill thoughts should be contemplated.'

Kabeer's guess was confirmed. He left them to talk to their hearts' content. The more time he gave them, the more information he would get through Jamila. He didn't go to them till bed time and then began his rounds to catch his sister alone, but in vain.

'What do you want, Kabeer? Go and sleep, it is very late,' said Zuhra.

'I just came to drink water. Drinking a glass of water before going to bed gives me a good sleep.'

'Don't drink too much or you will catch cold.'

Next day, Zainab Bi was sent for to send word to different houses about their going to see the girl. Dates were fixed. There were three houses in the city itself and three outside. They had to go by train. The mother, the daughter and her two little ones, with Zainab Bi and Mustafa left home every morning and returned in the evening, stuffed too much to eat any more.

They took sweets, fruits, and flowers in abundance to enable the bride's people to distribute them to all their relations and friends. Both the bride's and the bridegroom's parties had to create a good impression on the other. The bridegroom's people had to create the first impression and the others had to make the people believe that their girl was given to a rich man. No economy would help to achieve this object. They took a costly jewel to every house but it never made an appearance. Presenting it to the bride meant the decision of the matter.

After giving a grand tea or lunch to the bridegroom's party and showing the girl, the eyes of every well-wisher of the bride were on Jamila's hands to see if she was going to give any present. In the absence of such a consideration on the part of the bridegroom's people the opposite party had to do the job. In one or two houses, one hasty woman said, 'Is the girl accepted?'

'She is nice, there's nothing wrong with her,' said the austere Zuhra from a distance. The bent head of the prospective bride with her closed eyes was lifted by Jamila to show her face to the mother who was standing in a corner.

In another house, a more curious woman said, 'Is the girl liked? Then give her a present.' The poor woman did not understand the dissatisfied attitude of the mother, who had turned her face away after a glance at the carelessly created face of the girl. Zuhra said, 'The girl is pretty. I shall let you know of our decision in a day or two. If she is destined to my son, none will prevent their marriage.' But Zuhra was thinking of getting out of the place as soon as possible. The ladies were shabbily dressed, and many street woman with their filthy clothes had crowded into the place, pushing Zuhra out of the door. The hospitality also was inadequate; cheap stuff from hotels.

The day to go to Doulath Khan's house came. Everything was done lavishly. They needed two extra cars to take the things. Their arrival at the bride's house was a tumultuous scene. Everyone received them cordially and made a great fuss over them. The ladies were grand looking and sociable. A very expensive tea was served and many relations and friends did full justice to the generosity of Doulath Khan. What more could one want?

The girl was brought. Jamila did her duty of face showing to the anxious mother. Zuhra gave a sign to Jamila to present the necklace. The jewel which had escaped from all other houses at last had its day. The sign was welcomed by the expectant bridal party. They were all in smiles. Jamila put the necklace round the girl's neck and said, 'She is zulekha (unrivalled beauty) and needs no decoration. The jewel on the other hand feels its incapacity to do its work efficiently.'

This high appreciation of the bride thrilled the hearts of all those who were keen on her marriage. Doulath Khan's habit of finding faults in all the offers had greatly dissatisfied the ladies. They believed in the saying that the first offer should never be refused. They passed congratulatory glances to one another and all in smiles, applauded the appreciation.

Jamila asked her mother to fix the date for the betrothal ceremony. 'Ammajan, let it be celebrated before I leave.'[5]

'You are so much excited at seeing your sister-in-law that you would like to take her with you this minute if they would permit you.'

'God bless them both. Let there grow everlasting love and friendship between them,' said the grandmother of the bride in approval of the mother's statement.

'Let the engagement be the day after tomorrow,' said Jamila.

'How is that possible? It needs months for preparation,' said the bride's people.

'Let us have it next week at least. I can ask Jamila's husband to prolong her visit for a week more,' said Zuhra.

The ladies said that they had to ask their men. They would let them known about it the next day.

Kabeer was waiting as usual to catch his sister alone. The over-enthusiastic mother hardly left her alone till very late in the night. The question of her son's marriage was to be decided. No effort, no thought could be spared. Any indifference might mean his unhappiness. She had to consult the soothsayers and know if his life with her was going to be long.

Kabeer couldn't wait any longer. He thought of trying his luck by mixing with them. He sat near his sister and described the day's activities. Neither the mother nor the sister could understand his motive. Their minds were occupied with the ensuing engagement.

'Some people have been asking for the front building. They want it on a long lease,' said Kabeer.

'Write a letter to Jamila's husband asking him to allow her to stay for ten days more,' said Zuhra.

'Shall I let the building?'

'I want the services of Mustafa for some days more for our work.'

'I shall do both,' said Kabeer, disappointed by their distraught attitude.

Mustafa was asked through the cook to bring jewels and clothes to be bought for the betrothal ceremony. A big bundle of gold embroidery and gold-threaded saris and blouses was brought for selection. The cook brought it to Zuhra.

'Jamila, come and open the bundle,' shouted Zuhra. Jamila was busy with her infant who had been neglected during all the days of tumult.

'Come soon, give the baby to the cook,' she shouted again.

Jamila left the crying child and ran to her mother.

'Open it and show me the different saris. Yes, the one in your left hand is nice. Unfold it, let me see the design inside. That is right. Keep it apart. Tie up the bundle. Tell the cook to ask Mustafa to buy it.'

The same process went on with jewels and other presents. The day for the ceremony came. Mother and sister with an army of more distant relatives went to the bride's house.

After refreshments the bride was brought for the ceremony. She sat quiet with her head bent and fully covered. A lady relative sitting near tugged her dress, a sign to start crying. The droning began instantly. There was no need of music. The long process of clothing, jewelling and painting of sandal-scent continued with the bride's sing-song. People were given a grand dinner, and food for the bridegroom was sent to his house.

Next day a similar ceremony took place at Kabeer's house. The poor man sat patiently and underwent all the process performed by the bride's young brothers under the able instruction of an old woman from the bride's house.

Thank God Zuhra had overstrained herself, and satisfied at having performed the ceremony she left Jamila to look after the rest. She felt extremely tired and went to bed. Kabeer seeing his mother in bed ran to Jamila, 'You are a promise-breaker!'

'Why? What have I done? Is this the reward for my labour?'

'Remember your promise on our way home from the station.'

'What was it? I can't recall it.'

'You said you were going to tell me all about the activities going on at home.'

'Oh goodness! I forgot. Amma was with me from morning to night and my mind was busy with so many things. Your engagement took place with Doulath Khan's daughter.'

'As if I don't know that much.'

'How did you know?'

'I asked Mustafa indirectly and today I was with his people.'

'Didn't you feel shy to ask that old man, who is like your grandfather?'

'If you had told me I wouldn't have done it. Now tell me all about it.'

'What more is there to say?'

'How are those people?'

'Grand, rich, rolling in wealth. They are giving us lots of jewels, clothes, a car…'

'Then?'

'Then what? Nothing. The marriage is fixed for this month next year.'

'That I will come to know somehow. But…how is…'

'How is the bride? What a cunning fellow you are! How you brought me to that point!'

'Yet you don't say.'

'She is very beautiful. She is like a fairy.'

'Just like our cook?'

'No, no, there's no one in our family to give an example to you.'

'What a person to ask a description of! You are a savage. Can't you describe everything separately?'

'Don't be impatient. People will laugh at you. Someone is coming.'

Their talk was disturbed by one of the relatives. The house was crowded with them.

Jamila went back and the relatives also. Several thousands of rupees were spent. A share bond was sold at a very heavy discount. The grandeur of the function was the talk of the town. Every house described and exaggerated every minor item, and every man and child in the street gazed at Kabeer whenever he passed by. Even the women on being informed ran to the doors and windows to get a glimpse of the wonderful bridegroom.

Kabeer's mental condition now amounted to physical pain. He had not felt it when his father died. He gave up many of his activities on the pretext of being gazed at by the neighbours. He was impatient to know what kind of person his prospective bride was. But whom to ask? How to ask? He dared not ask his mother. His sister's description was funny. She did not know whom to call beautiful: often ugly women with fair complexions she called beautiful. His sister called him shameless. What would his mother say if he attempted to ask her?

He took the daughter of the cook, who was only four years old, to his room and asked her about the bride. She said the bride was good. He showed her a good-looking woman who passed on the road and said 'Is the bride like her?' The girl said yes. Then he showed an ugly woman and with painful expectancy asked the same question. The girl said yes.

He was worried about her physical beauty. The question of temperament never struck him. To him as to all other men there is no such thing as temperament in a woman. A woman is supposed to live under any circumstances. Her only needs are food, clothing and decoration. The larger they are in number the greater her happiness.

How could he see her? He dared not walk along the road she lived in. He might be seen by her people. Such a thing might lead them to break off the engagement. A man should be firm from the beginning to the end. Even after marriage he must keep his dignity.

Soon after the marriage is decided a girl confines herself in a corner, preferably a pantry or a store-room, where no male member of her own family can see her.[6] She keeps aloof. Her immediate needs are supplied by her mother or sisters who to save her from the social taunts do extra duty. She is not expected to laugh or to hear the talk going on in the house. She should assume an air of dejection, disappointment and despair at leaving the parents' house or else she will not be doing justice to all their sacrifices for her. She should cry during the marriage and show her unwillingness to meet a man.

He remembered what he knew and what he had seen at the time of his sister's marriage and gave up the idea.

Wait, wait, not one or two days, but a year! It was better to think that he was not engaged and be content.

Chapter IV

Human nature is not good everywhere. 'Birds of a feather flock together'—this is particularly true of business men and men with the mania of acquisition. When this instinct becomes a master sentiment it acts ruthlessly and knows no point of satiation.

When the capitalists and exploiters of the town came to know of the offer of a valuable house by a woman, all of them stuck together and offered a rock-bottom price. There was no time to wait for a better one. The building which had brought in nine hundred rupees a month was knocked down for fifty thousand. Zuhra's plans for the marriage were too grand to be carried out with that amount. She believed in being noticed.

'Kabeer, can you manage to raise a loan? We can easily economise in the future and repay it.'

'We shall have to sell or mortgage another property. There is no other alternative.'

'It will come to the notice of Doulath Khan. If he comes to know of our financial condition he will not respect you. I am told that he is spending double the amount yet he is not selling any property. He offered more money for the building, yet I refused his offer.'

'Then the only way is to buy things on credit. They charge more…'

'Let them take a few rupees more. We shall be able to pay soon after the marriage.'

'From where?'

'Out of the presents and the cash you get at the time of jalva.'[1]

Kabeer in spite of his anxiety to say more could not do so freely in front of his mother. She spoke to him about it only when it was necessary. He wanted to say that she could not sell the presents, but it was too much for him.

'We have fifty thousand.'

'It is not enough for the jewels. I want to buy different kinds of sets. What about clothes and other expenses?'

'They won't be much.'

'The celebration will last fifteen days and the guests will be here eight days before it begins. We need at least twenty five thousand for feeding and clothing the near relatives.'

'Why all that? They know father is dead and we have spent a lot already.'

'Knowing our condition and expecting gifts are two different things. If we don't give them at least half of what they expect we will be making enemies.'

'Tell me what to do.'

'Send for one of your uncles. He knows what to do.'

'Yes, swindle us. We know where we stand with our servants. Even if they steal it wouldn't come to hundreds.'

'If we do it ourselves there will be open hostility. If he were alive no one would have dared ask for the responsibility. Didn't you hear the sarcastic talk after the betrothal ceremony? Although I told them it was done in a hurry because of Jamila.'

'If father is dead you are alive. No one can blame you for it.'

'Have you ever heard of a purdah woman doing it? There are a thousand and one things to be bought, people to be consulted, houses to be hired, servants engaged, and what not?'

'If we ask one to be responsible the others will be annoyed. We have had enough experience of their work and their grumbling. Didn't they say if they had not rallied round father would have been left unburied? Their anger will not do us much harm. We shall try to face their taunts boldly and patiently.'

'There must be a male member to look to things. You can't do them. What will people say? You can't put Mustafa in charge. It will make them furious. They will never be bossed about by him.'

'He will not order them to do things.'

'He dare not. Even if he commands servants it will put them off. They will set up their servants against him, and even us.'

'We shall ask Jamila's husband.'

'While his father is alive he will not accept.'

'Then let Mustafa do all that he can before they come. Then you can ask Jamila's father-in-law to act for father.'

It was decided. No relation was asked to come in advance. All those who had played important parts formerly waited anxiously for months. Nearing the month of the wedding they realised that they had to play a secondary part. The decision divided the relatives into two groups. Some of them were pleased and called Kabeer and Zuhra wise. They even prayed for his long life. 'The world will be better for the existence of such a clever young man,' said a very sincere relation. These came exactly on the date fixed for their arrival. This prompt action displeased the others who held meetings to discuss whether to go to the wedding or not. Women are keener than men on participating in marriages. The aunt said: 'Our presence at the marriage as mere spectators will not look so hideous as our non-cooperation. People will openly say that we did not attend because we were not made responsible.'

'To be at a distance and hear such talk will not be so humiliating as to be there on the spot. You will have to obey the orders of that insufferable Mustafa. I am sure he is acting the father. I shall murder him if he acts master to me,' said Umar's brother, who had been in charge of all the funeral ceremonies.

'You are prejudiced. He will neither be made responsible nor will be command you,' said his sister. The women supported the aunt, so they decided to start as soon as possible not to create any suspicion about their willingness.

Intimation of their arrival was sent. Conveyances and escorts were sent to the station. Umar's brother suspiciously looked at the guides to discover Mustafa, but he was not there. He had many other important things to attend to. Jamila and her husband came with the first batch but her father-in-law arrived only with the malcontents. His excuse was that the house could not be left to itself for months, so he would try to engage a reliable watchman and join them.

The party reached home. Every one of them looked proud and serious as they had come with the policy of non-cooperation and non-violence.[2] It gives a reasonable excuse to an unwilling partner.

'We want a separate room for ourselves. We are not quite well, that is why we came so late,' said Umar's sister.

'I see,' said Zuhra. 'The separate rooms have been kept ready.'

Unfortunately the rooms meant for them were occupied by distant relations who had come earlier. So rooms in the other corner of the house were shown to them. The luggage was carried in and the party followed. Aunt and uncle exchanged glances.

'This is the first humiliation, and many will follow,' said the uncle.

'The corner rooms will be much safer. We can give full vent to our feelings,' said the aunt.

All of them went to their rooms. Zuhra asked Jamila to seek out her father-in-law and tell him that the whole management had been done by her, but now that the men were there she wanted him to take the responsibility and to allow her to attend to other domestic duties.

Jamila told him confidentially. He said 'I shall think it over and send word to her.' He went to the sister and brother who were busy in talking over the insults and informed them about it.

'Something is better than nothing. The servants all least will have respect for us if you act prominently,' said the sister.

All of them grouped together and expressed their grievances to their hearts' content. When the meals were announced they intentionally went late.

'What a dirty place and plates! Do they take us for dogs?' said Umar's brother.

'You have to make the best of your position. Try to be patient and pass the days,' said the sister.

'This looks like a doll's marriage to me. The arrangements and the food at the funeral ceremonies were a hundred times better.'

'This is not the time to pass remarks. Even the walls have ears. As it is we are unwelcome guests. Our criticism will do us no good,' said the sister.

'We are insulted and treated like strangers. We ought not to have come to a place where we are not respected,' said he.

'Hush, someone is coming,' said the aunt.

'Rasam has been brought. Mother wants you all,' said Jamila to the ladies.[3] The participation in the rasam would give them fresh ideas and cause for more gossip. All of them stood up quickly and departed.

Kabeer was made to sit on a stage in the middle of the famous courtyard which was brightly lit. It was packed with ladies, those who did not observe purdah in front of him, and children. Numberless trays with presents, eatables and flowers were set in front of him.

'Uncover the trays and show us the presents,' said the aunt.

One of the married women obeyed her faithfully.

'What a cheap sort of ring, and shawl! This gives an idea of what they think of the bridegroom. If the bride's people had any respect for him they would have presented him lavishly,' said the aunt.

Kabeer's mother overheard the remarks from a distance.

'Those are a few of many. Other costly ones make up for them. We shouldn't judge the people on the basis of less expensive things,' said Zuhra.

'If it were my only son's marriage I would have picked a quarrel on that matter. I would have thrown them in their faces and asked them to replace them by suitable ones immediately,' said the aunt.

The girls, boys and the maidservant who had come from the bride's house looked horrified and stood like statues. They did not know whether to commence the ceremony or return with all their paraphernalia. Zuhra without caring for the suggestion asked them to start the ceremony. This annoyed the aunt, but there was nothing she could do. She pocketed the insult and gazed earnestly at the performance. Her associates also found many more grievances for discussion in their den.

The next morning nikha was being performed.[4] The bridegroom's party went to the uncle for permission to start.

'In the absence of the bridegroom's father your permission is to be obtained,' they said.

'You did not need any at the time of fixing the marriage and till today it was not necessary. Carry on with your work,' said the uncle.

'Does it mean you disapprove?'

'My approval or disapproval has nothing to do with it. The marriage is almost finished. One should know the time for such permission,' said the uncle.

There was confusion and agitation among the male members of the bride's party.

'What does it mean? Are they against the marriage?' said Doulath Khan.

Jamila's father-in-law overheard it and going to the over-anxious group said 'Carry on the nikha with my permission.'

Many agreed and said 'He is one of Umar's brothers. His permission is equally valuable.' The nikha among men was over.

The bride was brought to the ladies for tying the latcha. The poor thing was crying pathetically. Now was the time when she really felt the separation from her near and dear ones. She knew nothing of the people among whom she was going. She had not even seen them. She had been frightened to death from her childhood by stories of cruel mothers-in-law. How she would be criticised and faults found in everything she did. She had been given examples of heartless husbands who inflicted corporal punishment on their wives. She was asked to forget herself and be ready to face a hell in her future home. All these precepts began to crowd into her mind. The pathetic cry of the bride made almost all the ladies shed tears, thinking of their daughters who would one day have to face the same situation. Zuhra also shed tears thinking of her son who would not be so loving and obedient after that day.

'Go and ask aunt who is an old suhagan to tie the latcha,' said Zuhra to Jamila.

If a married woman who has lived long with her husband ties the latcha the bride will have the same good fortune. So an old couple is particularly invited and the lady is requested to perform this act. As the demand for such a privileged woman is so great naturally she feels proud of her position.

Jamila went to her aunt. 'Ammajan wants you to tie the latcha.'

'Is your mother dumb? From when did she lose her power of talking? Perhaps she thought it was beneath her dignity to come to me for it.'

'She is sitting at the other end of the hall. The place is overcrowded. She can't stir from her seclusion,' said Jamila.

'When you could manage to reach me, why couldn't she?'

'I pushed them and squeezed myself through and jumped over the children. One can't expect all that from Amma.'

'Just because there's no alternative she had to ask me. Ask her to do it herself, just as she did everything else,' was the curt reply.

'Don't be absurd and ask a widow to do it,' said the bride's grandmother who happened to be seated close by.

Jamila went back to the mother who gave her permission to do it herself. As Jamila approached the bride the aunt's better sense prevailed. She got up and tied the latcha without more ado. One of the ladies said, 'If she had done it without making a fuss, she wouldn't have brought ridicule on herself.'

'Don't talk through your nose without knowing the circumstances,' said one of the aunt's companions. The aunt finished her most sacred job and returned to her place. The widow sister of Umar, who had played a prominent part at the time of the funeral, said, 'Our talks and actions are watched and criticised. We must not show indifference or we shall leave the place with their enmity. It is better to preserve a nominal friendship.'

Experience is a good teacher, and bitter taunts are better. The aunt's friends in appreciation of her wisdom nodded their heads as a token of approval and jingled the heavy jewels in their ears and necks.

Jalva, when the bride is first shown to the bridegroom, now took place. Relations and friends from both side had to give presents to the new couple. Kabeer's relatives who were annoyed, were discussing in a corner whether to give presents or not. The majority were against the proposal for more than one reason, but the opposing party though small carried the day. Some of them had brought with them superfluous articles from their homes and so felt an inner urge to deliver the goods. They stealthily handed them over to Zuhra with a request not to betray them. The rest followed suit.

The bride was brought home after the jalva. A ceremony to make her coming an auspicious event took place, when her feet and hands were washed with milk.[5] Similar observances were going on, to the utmost disgust of Kabeer, till he said that he was exhausted and needed rest.

The next morning the bride was sent for by her parents. Kabeer was left alone and had to wait for an invitation.[6] The hours of separation were taxing. He was not allowed to go out of the house as on these days men literally observe purdah. He sat about impatiently or played with the children, keeping his eye on the front door not to miss the messenger bringing the invitation. The hours dragged on. He felt furious at the clock, which seemed cruelly antagonistic to his feelings. He thought of turning the hands of the clock to seven, but who would do the same in the bride's house? He went from one room to another, and to his surprise he found everyone asleep. He felt jealous, could not believe his eyes to see them so thoughtless; he went to his room and lay in bed till it struck seven. Each stroke put life back in his nerves. Each sound of a footstep thrilled him. But in vain. At eight o'clock, disappointed, he came to a decision not to go when the invitation arrived.

'It is past eight, and no sign of those people. Are they sending for you or not?' said the aunt, who came to him to put oil on the burning fire.

'I am not going there even if they send for me,' said the enraged Kabeer.

'Don't pretend. You will jump up and forget your determination,' said Jamila who had entered the room.

'Have your dinner with us if you are feeling hungry,' said Zuhra who followed Jamila.

'I shall go to sleep right away. I don't want any food.'

This satisfied the opponents who felt sourly triumphant. Their spirit of revenge was making its way naturally.

'What inconsiderate people they are! Do they want to separate their daughter from him? The poor boy is pining from ten o'clock in the morning. One can imagine their treatment in the future if it is such the very first day,' said the aunt very lovingly.

'Coming events cast their shadows before. You have to be ready for worse things. After all they are rich people. Pride and wealth go together. It suits them even if they do it,' said one of his cousins.

His mother's pride was touched to the quick. It was an open insult to her. The fear of hearing such a remark had made her spend thousands of rupees. She wanted people to say that both parties were equally rich. If they had said that her son was richer than his father-in-law she would have had nothing to complain of, as man being the superior animal everything that belongs to him ought to be so.

'If they are proud of their wealth we are prouder. A man after all is not the loser in such circumstances. If he is dissatisfied with one woman he can marry many. If they don't behave better I shall put down my foot and see that they come to their senses,' said Zuhra.

While the talk between the ladies was going on in his room Kabeer was becoming more and more exasperated. Patience has a limit. Once it is passed no one can control himself.

'Why this discussion on a subject that does not need any? I tell you I am not going there. If they send a car return it saying that I am not well,' said Kabeer.

'There will be many such hitches in life. If you begin to make a fuss over petty matters life will be impossible,' said Jamila, who by now had experience of a mother-in-law.

'That's your valuation of life,' said Kabeer.

'Don't be silly, Bhai.[7] What will they think of you? After all what did they do to you? This is just the time for dinner. When there are guests dinner takes place at ten,' said she.

'What did they do to him? They treated him like a servant. They will send for him to feed him, as if he has no food in his house. You call him silly. You are a silly goose not to understand the situation,' said the aunt.

It was past nine. The car was announced. They young brothers and sisters of the bride came running into Kabeer's room, and seeing him in bed they began to pull his shawl and arms and made him sit up. A girl brought his shervani (long coat) and turban from the hanger and forced him to put them on.

'Abba and guests are waiting for you. He asked us to bring you soon,' said they.

Kabeer forget all about his decision. He said to the little ones, 'All of you go to the car. I shan't be long.'

But one of the girls with more perseverance said, 'I am not going. You will sleep again.' She held his finger tight and pulled him out of the room. He did not resent it. The little girl had charmed him. The idea of asking his mother's permission went clear out of his head. He followed the girl from the room.

The spectators exchanged sarcastic glances. The aunt was overjoyed. Revenge had laid the foundation and the construction of the edifice was in her power.

'To expect respect from sons especially after they are married is to build a house on sand. Soon after seeing his brothers-in-law he forgets all, even his own mother who is sacrificing her life and happiness and is working like a servant for him. If children only thought how difficult it is to bring them up they would have more respect for their parents' feelings. I can't get over the sight of how he acted and treated all of us,' said the aunt very affectionately to Zuhra.

Zuhra was astounded at her son's behaviour and began to feel that her sister-in-law was her real friend. She controlled her emotion but in the absence of the aggressor wrath must find a satisfactory outlet.

'I shall serve him out if he does not mend his manners,' said the defeated mother.

'Unless you take this matter seriously and nip his impertinence in the bud he will treat you like a slave. It is up to you now to keep up your dignity. You have to deal with a person who has no blood relationship and respect for you. If he is indifferent to you she will be worse.'

'You have confidence in me. I won't allow anybody to have the upper hand with me. From the very first day I shall make her understand her position here.'

This was a matter of no small elation to the aunt. She had put the poisonous seed in the cultivated ground. Circumstances would see to its proper watering. Zuhra's spirit towards her daughter-in-law was bitter; but would she not yield to the whims of her son?

'You have to be strict to both. There's every possibility of his losing his head. I can't imagine how he marched out of the room without looking at you when you were all the time supporting him.'

'Yes, I know.'

'I don't think the bride is chaste. I have my own reasons for saying so,' said Kabeer's cousin, who had been waiting all those years to give her daughter in marriage to him. His wedding was an irreparable shock to her.

Jamila had not heard the conspiracy going on among the ladies. She had left the room after Kabeer went to put her babies to bed. She entered the room when the last remark about the bride was passed. Her blood boiled with fury. From the first sight she had liked her sister-in-law.

'Don't start talking ill of the poor thing. She is an innocent child. Such suggestions will result in the destruction of both. You will make Bhai's life miserable. They are respectable and very orthodox people. One should think twice before condemning anyone.'

'I didn't mean anything ill. I just mentioned what struck me. Hereafter we will act like puppets,' said the cousin.

'It is better to be silent than to harm someone,' said Jamila.

Zuhra and the aunt looked at each other meaningly. The former detected a contemptuous look in the eyes of the latter which was rather disagreeable to her. She thought it was wise to support her daughter, or the mischief might take a hideous turn.

'The world will be better without presumption and hasty remarks. Sensible people avoid such expressions even if they are certain of it,' said Zuhra.

'Our own relations are our enemies. How would you feel if someone said such a thing about your daughter?' said Jamila to the cousin.

'They would be mad to say it. Nothing is said without cause,' said the cousin and left the room.

The matter was dropped. The mischief-monger was not very proficient. The design was erased before it could make its appearance. All of them had a quiet dinner and went to their rooms. The aunt thought that she had done her duty for the day. Her plan would have been more efficacious if the cousin had not unwittingly poked her nose into it.

Zuhra and Jamila were together for some time. 'It is mere jealousy that made her talk so nastily. If she is angry with us she ought try to take revenge upon us and not on that poor creature,' said Jamila.

'Let us not think about it anymore,' said Zuhra.

The next day the bridegroom and the bride came to spend the day. Everybody contrived to seem busy, except Jamila and the numerous children who came to welcome the pair. Jamila led the bride to her room while Kabeer paused to please the little ones. A servant came: 'Begum Sahib wants you.'

'Is anything the matter?'

'I don't know. She looks serious.'

'Why, what has happened?'

The servant went away.

He hesitated to go to his mother, but he had to. He went and greeted her very politely. Zuhra without blessing her son said, 'What happened to you last night? Had you gone off your head? You could see no one except your new friends.'

Kabeer stared at her and tried to recollect what he had done. 'What did I do?'

'What did you do? Are you still dreaming? Is it hypocrisy?'

'But what happened?'

'The very first day of your marriage you forgot your mother and your obedience to her.'

'All of you were waiting for the car to send me. The children worried me so much that I forgot to ask your permission.'

'That's what I say. You forget that your mother is alive. I wouldn't have prevented you from going. Isn't your interest my concern?'

'Ammajan, it was done unwittingly, and it shall never take place again.'

'Well, so long as I am alive you and your wife are expected to obey me implicitly. If you learn to obey, you will be able to rule. For whom am I labouring if not to make your life happy?'

Kabeer left her room and made to go out.

'Why are you so serious?' asked his aunt. 'A new bridegroom should be all happiness. When we are happy we don't know what we do.'

'Oh, nothing,' said Kabeer.

'Did you see your mother? She was rather upset last night. I tried my best to console her.'

'Thank you.'

'Zuhra is rather hasty in her actions. She should remember that a boy after losing his father is sad beyond words. Your sorrow will make that poor girl unhappy.'

'Please leave me. I have to go to the office. The business has been neglected for a long time.'

Kabeer knew his aunt's character well and couldn't be easily led astray. He entered the front building of Dilkusha. All the workers were having an easy time. No one would expect a bridegroom to go there.

'Something is wrong somewhere,' said one of the old clerks.

'The poor man seems used up,' said Mustafa.

Kabeer sat there checking and rechecking the accounts mechanically. A servant came and called him for lunch.

'I am not well. I don't want it.'

He sent servants for food and sat alone in his room.

'What made her so changed? She has never been so cold to me. Her attitude was quite different from what it has been all my life.'

The servant came back after an hour.

'Begum Sahib is waiting for you and wants you to have some light food.'[8]

He stood up. If he did not obey the second call there would be a break in the family. Her anger had a cause. She must have felt awkward when he went away without her permission. Four hours had passed since he was separated from his wife. He decided to go to his mother first and on the pretext of not feeling well go to his room.

He found her kinder and she smiled as he entered the room. She made him sit near her.

'Kabeer, I live for you and you alone. I wanted to kill myself after his death and save myself from lifelong misery. Only the thought of your loneliness made me surmount unbearable sufferings. What do I want from you but a little regard? You will have many wives but not your mother. How long will she live? Her days are nearing their end.'

'I am extremely sorry for what has happened. It has upset me. I shall have tea and no lunch.'

'Do as you please. Go and have a rest. I shall send for you.'

After bowing respectfully he left her and went to his room. He found Jamila and all the little ones there entertaining his bride who looked to him like the Sleeping Beauty. All of them were talking and laughing but she had closed her eyes and lips tight. Nothing made her smile or look about her. If there had been a competition to behave like a statue in the presence of mischievous spectators she would have won the first prize. She was not expected to open her eyes in her husband's house for five weeks and not to talk for about two months. The woman servant from her mother's house supplied all her needs. She closed the door when she fed her. She was not expected to eat more than a morsel. When Jamila found her brother in the room she sent all the little ones away and taking the bride's servant with her closed the door after her.

Chapter V

It is a well-known fact that man is superior to woman in every respect.[1] He is a representative of God on earth and being born with His light in him deserves the respect and obedience that he demands. He is not expected to show his gratitude or even a kind word of appreciation to a woman: it is his birthright to get everything from her. 'Might is right' is the policy of the world. To express thankfulness to such a creature as she is humiliating. She should be proud, happy and thankful to him for having accepted her services. If he is depressed she must make herself so. It should matter nothing to him if she is indisposed. On the other hand he has every right to be aggrieved if the meals are not punctual or well cooked. A woman as a wife should be subservient in everything to man's comfort and exist for him and him alone. She should have no particular liking for anything. Her world should as a matter of course begin and end with him.

His polygamous nature has an excuse: a man doing brave deeds needs every sacrifice by others. A woman who does not show the proper spirit of gulping down ready-made beliefs is condemned by the rest as douzakhi (hellish).[2] The great fuss made over him gives him no time for introspection. He has accepted and assimilated the dogmas without analyzing them. Unequal distribution of labour and regard is the social code made by man in his own interest. There are some who relinquish their birthright, but their number is not legion.

There is a miraculous change between wifehood and motherhood. A wife aspires long to achieve the position. When she does it even her husband recognizes some merit in her. Motherhood is sanctified. A mother holds the highest position in the estimation of her children. Even highly educated sons obey her implicitly. They owe everything to her, their birth and their upbringing. Heaven is under her feet. The greater the obedience to her the easier is admittance to it. She is the queen of the house and rules over all her subjects with an iron hand. Her administration needs more attention when strangers unfortunately take shelter in it. Her government is not constitutional, so the laws are flexible and specially formulated in the interest of the earning member. There is no court of appeal. Everybody recognizes her court of justice. The elasticity of judgment depends upon the greater application by the convict. Those with supernatural powers of cunning and flexibility of mind can get on splendidly with the legislator and executive.

Nazni, Kabeer's new wife, a girl with little tact and no knowledge of the world, fell an easy victim to the tactics of the experienced ruler of the house. Nothing but her beauty pleased her mother-in-law. But what could she do with her prettiness? She wanted a young woman to look after the house, to cook and take away her responsibility. Why do people bring daughters-in-law if not to have real and well-earned comfort? One can't keep a person for her beauty and worship her as an idol.

Three months after the marriage, when Zuhra was anxiously waiting to transfer her responsibility, Nazni fell ill on account of pregnancy. Now how could the poor mother-in-law get her rest? Her hopes of dominance which soared so high at the time of marriage came down to earth. With a person in bed her work was increased. Although nothing special was prepared for the sick daughter-in-law yet the meals had to be sent to her room. Whenever she vomited someone had to be near her and attend to her. Nazni's mother engaged a woman for it.

The presence of an extra servant was a cause of annoyance to Zuhra. A servant from Doulath Khan's house was a spy in hers.

'What a clumsy woman your wife is!' said Zuhra. 'Mothers think of getting a girl married before training her to be a good and useful wife. They just think of transferring the burden from their shoulders to another's. If they thought of us they would come half way to mitigate our sufferings. She's such a shabby creature. Any china she touches exists no more.'

Kabeer did not know whose side to take. Second thoughts made him flatter his mother. 'She's frightened in a new place. Under your training she'll be all right. You have trained worse people.'

'Why is she frightened? Girls of her age undergo tortures day and night in the hands of drunken and cruel mothers-in-law. It is not fear but fearlessness and indifference. She's a spoilt child. Don't you see her munching the whole day? What does she eat and from where does she get it?'

The food sent to Nazni was returned untouched. Pregnancy is a peculiar disease which makes the very sight of food repugnant. Kabeer knowing that she starved the whole day brought fruits and sweets and put them on Nazni's window sill from outside. The servant was given instructions to wait and remove the packet quietly. Kabeer was alarmed to think his mother had come to know of the secret supply of nourishment.

'Her brothers and father keep on bringing things for her.'

'They come empty-handed. I watch them when they pass through the corridor. Perhaps they carry it in their pockets,' said Zuhra.

Kabeer felt satisfied that no suspicion about him had arisen.

'It seems childish the way she behaves. She knows nothing of responsibility and the care of her husband. She spends the day either in sleep or talking and laughing when her people come. I have never heard a woman laugh so loudly. In my absence she'll never manage the house even for a day.'

'She's so quiet and grave in my presence. I can never make her cheerful. She is serious by nature.'

'She does not laugh in my presence either, but I hear her shrill voice from my room. It's not good for girls to laugh so loudly. What will people say?'

'You tell her that. Even my gentle words make her cry,' said Kabeer.

'You should never feel pity or trust a crying woman. They shed crocodile tears.'

'I've often heard that but I can't understand it,' said Kabeer.

'The point is that a woman's nature is not constant. Her weeping or laughter has no value. You shouldn't take her tears seriously. Your love must be in your heart. Your eyes and lips should express gravity and command. Once you become familiar and expose your weakness she'll be your ruler. You'll lose control over her forever.'

Kabeer thought over his mother's precepts for some time and came to the conclusion that she being an experienced hand and his well-wisher her instructions should be his guide. After some time he went to his room, but seeing his wife's pale and thin but smiling face he forgot his mother's teaching. He said nothing about their talk but enquired of her health. Nevertheless he felt that something prevented him from being free with her. 'Once you become familiar she'll be your ruler and you'll lose control over her.' He couldn't say it to his wife. Already unwittingly he had been too familiar with her.

He never allowed her to discuss his mother. Her name was sacred. Any mention of her had to be in her praise. Nazni on the other hand had a hundred and one grievances to get redressed. But how? During the six months of her married life conveyances and escorts from her parents had been sent back at least thirty times. When permission was asked from Kabeer he told her to go to his mother. Once in every third call she permitted Nazni to go home and return the same night.

'Mother wants to send the car tomorrow for Eid,' said Nazni's brother.

'Why does she want to humiliate herself? They will return it,' said Nazni.

'Have they not humiliated us many times? What do we care? We just want to have you with us. You can come back the same night.'

'For my wretched self my parents have to be insulted. Tell them to leave me to my fate,' said Nazni with tears in her eyes.

'I can't dictate to father and mother. You just listen to what they ask you.'

'I'm not master of myself or my time and wishes. Tell mother plainly it is no use to send the car.'

'I see it is you who does not want to come.'

'I wish to heaven that they would send me there. I'd really enjoy my feast with mother.'

'I shall ask Kabeer to send you.'

'He never permits it without his mother's consent.'

'Let him take it.'

'He wouldn't do it himself, knowing her attitude.'

'Can't he do even that to please you?'

'Whenever he has asked it he has been snubbed.'

'Then you ask her.'

'I can't. Last night she was telling him to stay at home on the Eid day. There's only one way to do it. Bring the car and say Granny is ill,' said Nazni.

Zuhra had already drawn up the menu for Eid.[3] The preparations had begun two days in advance.

'Wear your red sari and green blouse on the Eid day,' said Zuhra.

'Can't I wear the red blouse with the red sari?' asked Nazni.

'Do as I tell you.'

Nazni was annoyed, but knew that she was going to her mother's so she could wear anything she liked.

The car was brought on the morning of Eid. The old woman who accompanied Nazni's brother entered Zuhra's room.

'Big Begum Sahib suddenly got ill this morning. I am asked to fetch Nazni Begum as she wants to see her.'

'Your Nazni is not a hakeem to cure her. Old peoples' diseases are common and they are rarely serious. Your mistress should have more sense than to send for the girl so often. That girl has no interest in this house. This is her house. In her mother's house she's only a stranger. Why does a man get married? Is it to destroy his home and live in his wife's house?'

'She's still young. Young brides before they are encumbered with the responsibility of children do have an attachment to the house where they were born and brought up. Moreover she'll be alone here. Let her enjoy her Eid with her brothers and sisters.'

'You came here with the excuse of someone's illness and saying she has to do the work of a maseeha.[4] Now the truth has come out. Our arrangements for Eid will be upset. She can't go.'

Nazni's younger sister, who had been listening to the argument, ran to her: 'You are not coming with us!' Nazni seeing her dear ones could not make up her mind to stay away. She thought of the lonely room. None to speak to her cheerfully, but commands and fault-finding. In spite of herself tears began to flow. Her young brother ran to Kabeer's office in the opposite building and said, 'Apa is crying. I wouldn't leave her here.'

Kabeer thought that his interference was necessary.

'What's all this?' he asked Zuhra.

'As soon as your wife sees her relations she begins to cry.'

'God forbid!' retorted the escort. 'Why should she cry to see her brothers and sisters? They are not starving or suffering. She's crying because her grandmother is ill. She loves her dearly.'

'I have often seen her crying after their visits. She loves them more than her husband,' said Zuhra.

'Send her, otherwise she will make us unhappy by her wailing.'

'She knows well she can bring you down on your knees by her tears. I told her not to go and you ask me to send her. What respect will she have for me?' said Zuhra.

Kabeer did not like Doulath Khan's people in the room when his mother was angry. He gave his mother a sign to send them all away.

'Why are you wrangling here? All of you go to her room.'

'Shall I take her?' asked the old woman.

'She wants to have her own way in everything. We are puppets in her hands. Take her and bring her back tonight. We are not beggars to be elated at the invitation to celebrate the feast in somebody's house. We have to think of our own visitors and the dead.'

Though the permission was not polite the children were pleased and ran to Nazni. Mother and son were left alone, but neither felt like speaking to the other. Kabeer was coming round to her view. Nazni loved her parents more than himself.

Nazni wiped her eyes to be ready to go to her mother-in-law to pay her respects before leaving the house.'

'She sent her permission. You needn't go to her. Your eyes are red like flames. She'll pick up a fresh quarrel and abuse you,' said Nazni's brother.

'She won't leave me alive if I go away without her blessing. Even he wouldn't forgive me for it,' said Nazni.

'Crying makes you prettier. Do cry every day to make your cheeks and nose pink' said her mischievous younger sister.

Nazni smiled and looked at herself in the mirror of the dressing table and rubbed her swollen eyelids.

'Go soon and be done with it,' said her brother, who was going to the car with all the little ones. He turned to the old woman and said, 'Accompany Nazni to her mother-in-law's room and bring her to the car.'

Nazni entered Zuhra's room. She dared not look either Kabeer or his mother in the face. Bending down she touched her mother-in-law's feet, who put her hand on Nazni's head. When Zuhra was in a good mood she would say a few words by way of blessing, but now she said nothing. Nazni stood there like a penitent looking at her own feet.

'Your obstinacy has had its way after all. Try to be sensible and think of your home and husband, who cares for you more than your parents. Once you are married your parents have nothing to do with you. Their unnecessary interference in your life will only destroy it. We love you and you love others.'

Nazni standing there looked like Venus. She expected no support from her husband who was sitting there with head bent. The little ones in the car blew the horn.

'It is time for lunch. We came hours ago. Come, let us go,' said the old woman from behind the door.

'These rogues spoil her. Go,' said Zuhra.

'Did the convict take such a long time to be released even after the judgment was passed?' said her brother as he made room for her in the car.

'She wouldn't have come even now if the children had not blown the horn,' said the old woman.

Nazni was all smiles as if nothing had happened.

'The situation is out of your control. She's proud of her people and their wealth. They'll destroy her home and life,' said Zuhra. No reply came from Kabeer.

She went on: 'Did you notice her clothes? She went with those she wore at home.'

'Perhaps she forgot to change.'

'She went in them with a purpose. You don't know her. She did it to defy my orders to wear a certain sari on the Eid day, and to show her parents how badly we keep her. Sincere and loving girls borrow costly clothes from others while going to their parents' just to keep up their husband's dignity.'

'She must have taken them with her to change there.'

'I hope so,' said Zuhra.

In the evening the car was sent by Doulath Khan for Kabeer.

'Father wants you for dinner,' said Nazni's brother.

'I'm sorry I can't come. Mother will be furious if I don't stay for dinner. I shall come there after it.'

'Shall I bring the car after some time?'

'No, I shall come in ours.'

Zuhra knew nothing of the invitation, so after dinner Kabeer said, 'They sent for me for dinner, but I said that I would go there later.'

'If you don't go there she'll feel the pinch and avoid deserting you on feast days in future.'

'I'll go there to bring her.'

'She must come herself as she went.'

Kabeer had promised his brother-in-law and was in a fix. He couldn't go there without her knowledge. That would create more trouble. It was better to touch her weak point and extract permission from her.

'If we leave her to herself she might not come for khutba.[5] Moreover we'll be making her more independent.'

Zuhra felt that she was loosening her iron hold which would result in Nazni's separation.

'Yes, perhaps it is better to go and bring her for tomorrow.'

Although Kabeer had definitely said that he was not going for dinner Doulath Khan and the guests were waiting for him and forced him to have it a second time. Kabeer never missed a good opportunity. He did full justice to the delicious, rich dishes.

The children wanted to go to the pictures and compelled Kabeer to accompany them. He agreed after some hesitation.

'Let us take Apa,' said one of the young brothers who did not know that it was objectionable for ladies to go to the cinema.

All of them welcomed the idea and shouted 'Yes, let us take her with us.'

Kabeer wondered what to do. He imagined his mother's anger.

'What's going on here?' said Nazni's brother, who was also going to celebrate Eid.

'We want to take Apa with us,' said the children.

'Are you afraid of your mother? There's nothing wrong in taking Nazni to a picture. Hundreds of Muslim women go these days. We shall reserve box seats and there is a purdah arrangement.'

'I...I didn't ask mother's permission. She has never been to a picture and does not have a good opinion of those who do,' said Kabeer.

'These old women's world is quite different from ours. They have neither desires nor strength to take part in life's enjoyments. You shouldn't try to mould your wife's life according to your mother's,' said the brother, who was annoyed by Kabeer's servile behavior.

'We'll have to take her permission. She's both father and mother to me.'

'She won't know. Even if she does, you tell her that father took you both.'

'He's not going,' said Kabeer.

Kabeer respected his father-in-law. Being fatherless he took him for his guardian and well-wisher.

'He does not often go to late pictures, but I can make him take Nazni and you. This is her first picture. Don't stop her going. Be a sport,' said the brother.

'If he takes us I shall have a good excuse.'

All the little ones danced with excitement. They often described pictures they had seen to Nazni, as she liked them. Now the trouble of description was saved.

Zuhra waited for her son's return till past ten. Then she began to worry and imagine things. She asked the cook to wake up the watchman and sent him to Doulath Khan's house.

The watchman made enquiries of the servants.

'Kabeer Miyan and Doulhan Begum have gone to the pictures with the children,' said the watchman, vexed at being disturbed from his sleep and having to walk the long distance. He said nothing of Doulath Khan.

Zuhra and sleep were poles apart. Kabeer had taken his wife to a cinema, and without her permission! All her teachings had no value for him. She did not know that the ladies of Doulath Khan's house were so shameless. She should never have consented to bring a girl from that house. Her blood boiled. Yet she made up her mind to postpone punishment. The morning would bring numerous visitors and they would come to know about it. To pretend innocence was the best policy.

At about two o'clock Zuhra heard the car stop. She did not stir from her bed. The young couple went to their room silently and slept. In the morning Nazni said, 'If Ammajan asks me about coming home late what shall I tell her?'

'She's bound to come to know of it. We must tell her now.'

'I've no courage to face her,' said Nazni.

'I shall try to get her into a good mood, then I'll break it, putting the blame on Bavajan,' said Kabeer.

'If she asks me?'

'You try to avoid her for some time.'

Khutba is a grand function in every Muslim family. Even a poor Muslim spends one or two months' income on that day and does not mind suffering on account of it for several months after. Clothes for everybody have to be made and grand dishes to be prepared and sent to relations. The more numerous the dishes the greater is the valuation of one's wealth. Presents have to be given and visitors to be fed. Because of the new relationship Zuhra's plans were elaborate.

Early morning at five Zuhra got up for prayers. Soon after cooking was started she herself went to the kitchen. She believed in direct action to persuade others to follow suit.

Nazni before going for her bath forgot to ask her mother-in-law for the clothes to wear that day. She could not go after it without being properly dressed. She called the cook and told her to ask the mother-in-law for them.

'Doulhan Begum wants to know which sari she should wear,' said the cook.

'Who asked you to go there? You mind your work,' said Zuhra.

'She's standing in her kimono.'

'If she really wants to know let her come herself.'

The cook felt sorry for Nazni but couldn't please two mistresses.

Nazni waited for the cook but didn't dare call her for a reply. She wore a sari she liked.

Kabeer returned home from Eidgah and paid his respects to his mother.[6] He looked for Nazni this side and that. She hadn't come out of her room. As he was trying to be on the good side of the mother it was better to neglect her. He sat down. Nazni knowing of Kabeer's presence went to her mother-in-law to pay the Eid respects. After touching her feet she stood up.

'Was it humiliating to ask me about the clothes yourself? You sent the servant, treating me as her equal.'

Nazni's eyes were full of tears.

'Why do you cry? What have I done to you? You threaten us by your tears. You knew that I was cooking alone. You not only failed to come to help me, but also called the servant to help you. Do you think I am your servant?'

Kabeer had asked Nazni to avoid his mother so that she should not be asked about the previous evening, but she had misunderstood him.

Nazni sobbed loudly. There was a knock on the door. Relations had already started their visits. Zuhra did not like the scene to be noticed by others.

'Go and change your clothes. Who asked you to wear them now?' Zuhra commanded the culprit.

Nazni felt a relief as the ordeal was over. She could cry to her heart's content in her room. Kabeer felt like going after his wife to console her but the barrier between him and his mother was still greater. Any regard shown for her meant that the gulf between him and his mother widened still further. The matter of going to the pictures had not yet come out. He had to be careful and gather courage.

Nazeer entered and paid his respects.

'I saw you last night at the pictures. As there were ladies I didn't like to go to you.'

Kabeer's face turned blue. He had not seen Nazeer at the pictures or he would have been prepared for the ordeal.

'I was sitting with the children and Doulath Khan. You could easily have seen me,' stammered Kabeer.

'Do the ladies of his house go to the pictures? It is a surprise to me. I didn't know of that before,' interrupted Zuhra.

'They followed us in a separate car. There was a strict purdah arrangement.'

'So your wife also went there?'

'Yes, her father took her.'

'Nazeer saw us last night at the pictures and he mentioned it to mother,' said Kabeer, who was so confused that he did not think of consoling her first.

'What did she say?' cried Nazni.

'Not much. Don't worry. She'll be all right. I told her Bavajan took us and I being his guest could not refuse him.'

'So it is over. The very thought of it was killing me.'

'Yes. If she asks you can repeat what I said.'

'Change your clothes before you go to her. She did not notice your latcha. Otherwise that would have given her enough cause for anger.'

'I removed it to have my bath and forgot it.'

'Don't you keep it on when you bathe?'

'I feel sticky when it gets wet.'

Nazni was thankful to her husband because of his warning.

'Her father had no right to take a married daughter. Seeing you a coward he made a fool of you. She's your property. No one can have any interest in her without your permission. If you had any regard for your mother you would have flatly refused his suggestion.'

'It was not a suggestion. It was compulsion, and I thought of him as my father and yielded to it.'

'Since when have you given him that sacred position? You should rather die a hundred times than own it! Remember a woman going to the pictures can neither be virtuous nor an obedient wife!'

'It was her first picture and it may be her last. It was all arranged within a few minutes after dinner.'

Zuhra thought it was not an appropriate time to discuss the matter. Nazeer would let others know of their differences. She asked him to have lunch with Kabeer.

'Shall I go and change my clothes? These are so heavy and I am perspiring,' said Kabeer.

'Yes, be ready for lunch.'

He found Nazni in bed lying on her face.

He really did not like his mother's ill-treatment of her.

'If you try to be a little more careful there will be no trouble at home. She will have no cause to grumble. She's our well-wisher. She's old and how long will she live? Soon you'll be the mistress of the house. She has reached that position after passing through similar days. You must strive and achieve it.'

'She sees nothing good in me. The more I am afraid of her and try to be careful the more causes she finds for grievance,' said Nazni.

'Old people are always like that. If you try to be patient and obey her even if she is wrong she'll come to love you.'

Although Kabeer's talk was not very encouraging Nazni felt relieved because it was expressed gently and in her own interest. She thought that she would undergo any suffering for his sake. One must not expect a bed of roses in this life.

Chapter VI

Nazni was small, thin, and delicate. When she was ten years old, she had fallen victim to a severe attack of rheumatic fever and was under treatment in a ladies' hospital for months. Her mother and grandmother spared no efforts to get her treated by hakeems, pirs, and even witches. At length Doulath Khan took up the matter and consulted good doctors. A special nurse was appointed for her care. The fever stopped and the swelling disappeared. She was given tonics and cod liver oil for years. At last came a day when she looked healthy and blooming, but still the least exertion caused her fatigue and palpitation. Nature had taught her to rest to get relief. Sometimes she would have pain in her left shoulder. Her mother and grandmother massaged it. They said that all these small ailments would heal of themselves if she were married.

From the month of conception her health gradually declined. She had constant headache and giddiness. In her seventh month symptoms caused by her weak heart began to appear. She felt better in her mother's house. As soon as she returned home her illness reappeared.

According to custom the first child must be born in the mother's house. The pregnant daughter is usually sent for in the seventh month. Doulath Khan had her examined by a heart specialist. Unfortunately it was a man.[1] Zuhra who had lived a healthy life could not believe her ears when she heard of the heart disease. She had refused to consult a male doctor when she was ill after her husband's death, and by good luck she recovered without it. She formed a strong belief that all those who go to doctors are either fussy or immoral.

'A man can't own a woman as his wife after she has been touched by a man. There were men in former days who used to cut off that part of the body which was touched by a stranger,' said Zuhra.

'I felt a sort of repulsion when the doctor was examining her heart, lungs and back. I felt that I could not be proud of her any more,' said Kabeer.

Zuhra was pleased to hear him endorse her opinion. She determined that Nazni should be punished for having gone to the pictures and having been treated by a surgeon.

Under the careful nursing of a trained nurse from the seventh month Nazni withstood the strain of delivery. A baby boy was born to the rejoicing of all. Nazni's parents spent thousands of rupees on various ceremonies. On the fortieth day hundreds of people were invited to dinner. Many expensive gold presents were made for all including Zuhra.

Nazni now had to go back home, but the very idea of going there made her cry. There was a relapse. She was put to bed and was not allowed to stir from it for three months.

Zuhra often went to see her grandson. She and Nazni's grandmother became close friends. The old lady exaggerated Nazni's sufferings to gain Zuhra's sympathy and make her leave Nazni for some months more in her mother's house.

'The doctor says it is a serious disease. She should not be allowed to get up from her bed for six months. Her heart is weak and will stop working if she exerts herself.'

Zuhra thought of her son. Another six months was terrible. 'What's that heart trouble she's suffering from?' said she to Kabeer one day.

'Her heart has been affected from the time she was a girl.'

'So they got rid of her by putting the burden on you. No one said anything about it before the marriage. They deceived you.'

'Who will say anything about one's health except doctors? They also didn't know of it till the specialists examined her. One who has heart disease has to be cared for all her life.'

'What do you mean by cared for?'

'She shouldn't be allowed to lift heavy things and exert herself too much. She must have peace of mind and complete rest, and be kept under proper medical treatment. Then she'll live for some years.'

'If not?'

'She'll soon get worse and die. At least for six months we can't expect anything from her,' said Kabeer.

'So what do you want to do?'

'What can I do? It is fate. One has to be content with it.'

'Become a fakir and give up the world. Go to a cave and live there. Young men like you can't pass their days single. If she's suffering from an incurable disease why should you be punished for it?'

'I don't know what to do. I had a talk with the doctor about her. He is of the opinion that she'll never be normal. She must be kept at home as an idol.'

'And you will worship her, I suppose.'

'That's what many people do.'

'They do it if they are not men,' was the nasty reply.

'What else can be done?'

'Get yourself remarried and leave that whore in her mother's house.'

The idea did not vex Kabeer. On the contrary it roused him.

'How can I do that?'

'As if it is an impossible thing! Hundreds of men have done it. They do it on lame excuses, or none. Your need is great and is quite reasonable. It can be arranged easily. If you just open your mouth there'll be hundreds of offers.'

The optimistic expression encouraged him and he began to think seriously about it.

'Before the thing is settled the whole town will know.'

'We have to be very careful till the wedding is over. It must be done through Mustafa,' said Zuhra.

'Zainab Bi could do it quicker.'

'A secret matter can never be entrusted to a woman. She's popular in Doulath Khan's house. It is not the hurry we have to think of but the secrecy.'

When Kabeer mentioned the idea Mustafa welcomed it.

'I can do it in no time. I'll see that a healthy, obedient and faithful girl is brought to you. She'll make you and your mother happy and comfortable. You can't expect to live with a sickly woman,' said Mustafa.

In a week's time Mustafa brought numerous proposals from rich and poor families. Kabeer repeated them all to his mother for approval. When he mentioned a rich family's name she said, 'We have had enough of them. No rich girl can be obedient and loyal to you. You'll have to adjust yourself to their whims and fancies instead of being humoured by them.'

When the name of a poor fatherless girl came up she agreed.

'What does Mustafa say about the girl?' said she.

'He's a man of experience.'

'What shall I ask him to do?'

'The difficulty is that I can't go to see the girl. The whole town would talk of it. Your father-in-law will come to know of it before the matter is settled, and he'll get it broken off. Our going to a poor widow's house in a dirty locality will rouse suspicion. They will humiliate us. If we bring a girl from a decent family we risk our happiness and comfort. We should care for our interest, not for the opinion of others. As we did at the first marriage.'

'They'll call us heartless if you do it when she's ill. If she comes to know of it she'll have another relapse.'

'If you can't do it when she's ill you'll not dream of doing it when she's well. You have a good cause in her long illness.'

'We can't go to see the girl and we can ask no one else to do it. We have to depend upon Mustafa's version. We are defying her and her people by the second marriage. They will have a good cause to condemn us if something goes wrong,' said he thoughtfully.

'You are a coward. We are not defying them. On the other hand we want to help her by lessening her work and responsibility. They ought to be grateful instead of condemning us. An extra healthy woman at home is no more than an extra servant.'

'If she's treated like that...'

'You can't argue. Ask Mustafa to send his sister to see the girl and settle the matter soon. You are not a saint to live with a bedridden woman. Your comfort is more important than her happiness.'

Mustafa's sister went to see the girl. They showed her a decent-looking girl from the locality. There was no need for the matter to leak out. Both parties had their secrets to keep. Kabeer was hiding it from his wife and the new girl's people had to hide the name of the man who had come to their house.

The girl's mother acted dramatically and promised an expensive garment and cash to Mustafa's sister on the success of the marriage. The sister in turn praised the girl to heaven in front of Mustafa. She was very optimistic regarding her health, sense of duty, and ability to adjust herself to any circumstances. She added that Zuhra would not see a day of discomfort. She would make her sit like a queen and would be a source of joy to Kabeer. She was a girl who would eat crumbs and work like a horse.

Mustafa in his turn exaggerated these womanly virtues in Kabeer's presence. When Kabeer repeated them to his mother she thought that this was just the type of daughter-in-law she had always sighed for. The girl's mother was asked to keep the matter strictly secret in her own interest, and the marriage was to be a very quiet affair. The conditions were welcomed and arrangements in a modest way were made on both sides.

On the day of the nikha Zuhra went with Kabeer and Mustafa's sister. It was over very soon. As everybody was in a hurry to leave the place unseen by others, Zuhra asked the girl to be brought for tying the latcha. The bride's relations said that the girl was not yet ready to be shown. She was to be given a bath. It would take an hour more. Zuhra over-ruled the long-established custom of the latcha ceremony done by the husband's people. She asked them to do it themselves and left the place with Kabeer.

The jalva was to take place in the night at about three o'clock. The mother and son reached the bride's house safely. When the bride was brought to Kabeer her face was covered. The face of the bride is shown in a mirror which is placed between the bride and the bridegroom. When he saw her face in it he could not believe his eyes. He rubbed them and looked again. He was not wrong, the face was ugly and dark.[2] He looked at his mother furiously. She was at a distance and had not seen the bride. She smiled her congratulations. His blood boiled. He called up before his mind's eye the fair and beautiful features of Nazni. What a contrast! Even his mother was laughing at his discomfiture. He got up from the stage without a word and went out. He stood there for some time thinking of what he should do. After some time Zuhra sent for him. He would not go in. He left the house alone.

Zuhra was in an awkward position. She did not know the cause of her son's anger. She looked for Mustafa's sister, who however had disappeared.

'Why did he go away like that?' said she to one of the ladies.

'Go and see the girl. All her younger sisters were married years ago but she... You have been deceived. We knew of it so we came to see the fun,' said the kind spectator.

Zuhra went to the stage and asked a girl to lift the bride's head. 'I won't,' said she, and ran away. Zuhra called her informative friend and asked of her the same service. Zuhra screamed.

'What wicked people! This is sheer deception. Where's Mustafa's sister? She has ruined my son's life!'

Who would help her? She was alone, and all of them were united. Zuhra went and saw the bride a second time. She was dark, with deep pock-marks, and her upper teeth projected prominently.

A woman of Zuhra's caliber even if she loses her temper can be serene and practical after some time. Nothing could be done as the marriage was over. If she left the girl and went home as her son had done the bride's people had every right to file a suit against him. It was she who had forced him to remarry, so she was responsible for the consequences. There would be no chance of getting him remarried soon. When people came to know of this no one would give him a girl. And why waste all that money? She decided to take the bride with her and coax Kabeer to accept her. If he refused she could take her for herself. She would be an unpaid servant entirely at her disposal.

Leaving the bride in her room Zuhra went to Kabeer. He was in bed and pretended to be asleep. But she would not leave him. Yet the pill had to be sugar-coated.

'Your first wife will be pleased to see her rival. Her sense of importance will by no means be lessened and your love for her will be increased. All your desires in your first marriage are fulfilled. This one will only be a head-servant,' said she to her sleeping son.

Kabeer turned and looked aghast. 'One should feel inclined to be in the company of a woman whom one calls wife. The very sight of her is repulsive. You can't think of her as both servant and wife.'

'After your first wife you can't expect such beauty in the second. She's not very ugly. There are uglier women living happily with their husbands. When you find her more useful and obedient you'll love her. It is usefulness that matters.'

'You always have your own way. What do you want me to do after making me an object of laughter?'

'Have I to tell you that after the marriage is over?'

'I hate to touch her. I can't live with her.'

Kabeer had never been so rude and obstinate. Zuhra thought she had said enough.

'I did not mean any harm to you. If you don't want her I shall have her for my service. You do as you like.' No reply coming she began again. 'In spite of all our precautions she has come to us. It's a matter of destiny. You can't change it. No human hand can do it.' Zuhra left his room.

Kabeer began to think about his mother's words, his wife's health, his inconveniences for the last nine months with no hopes of having a healthy wife in the future. Reading always bored him and thinking gave him a headache. So he released himself from his worries by sleeping soundly.

Zuhra asked the cook to make a bed for the bride in her room.

'Whose bride is she? Where's the bridegroom?' asked the cook.

'You mind your own business. You have nothing to do with our family affairs.'

'I have seen you buying clothes and jewels. I thought they were for Doulhan Begum. You gave her no present when she gave birth to a child. Other mothers-in-law overload their daughter-in-law with gifts, especially if she gets a boy.'

'I tell you not to interfere in our home affairs. If you open your mouth again I'll sack you on the spot. Your position in the house is like that of this slipper. It must know its place and lie down there.'

However the bed was made and the bride was laid on it. Munira, the bride, listened to all that took place. She had aspired all her life for marriage with no hope of getting it. Her last desire was to call herself a married woman. She would have been happy with the title even in a poor man's house, but luck is blind. The wheel of fortune brings down the most deserving to earth and raises the vilest to the top. The one satisfaction was that she was married. Let the quarrels go on. Why should she care?

If her features were the cause of her misfortune she could change it by her tact and spirit. She would not mind the work of a menial. She would work for her husband like a Russian soldier and win him. Let him love her or not so long as they lived like husband and wife.

While these thoughts were passing in the mind of Munira, Zuhra who was sleeping on a cot opposite to hers said, 'You know what has happened to you? I did my best to plead for you but my obedient son has disobeyed me—the first time in his life. I am helpless. You have to make your way to win him. Even if he treats you like a khawas, you must be thankful to him.[3] You have neither beauty nor wealth, which are the two considerations that make a man love a woman. Your only weapons are your strength and spirit, and though they are secondary ones you can make the best use of them. Your rival is seriously ill. He has been undergoing great suffering on account of her. It is up to you to exert and acquire the wealth a woman aspires for in the world. Many women in spite of their ugliness have been loved by their husbands.'

Munira had been thinking just the same thing. She made up her mind to put her ideas into practice forthwith.

'Go to the kitchen from tomorrow and see to the cooking. If you feed the brute he will want nothing else. Serve all his meals yourself. Don't leave it to the cook. After all he is a hungry man. If you try to please him sincerely without thinking of your own interest your deficiencies will be overlooked.'

Early in the morning when Zuhra returned from her prayers she found the bride's bed empty. She went to the kitchen and saw her busy preparing chapaties. As soon as she saw Zuhra she bent down her head. Zuhra was please to see her obeying implicitly and went to her room to keep an eye on her movements. She saw the bride carrying in the tray with numerous dishes for breakfast. The strong and tempting smell of kichdi and fried kabab made Zuhra feel hungry.[4]

Kabeer came to the dining room and seeing the ugly face of his wife turned his head. He pretended not to look at her and began eating. Munira not caring for his indifference went to the kitchen and brought some more dishes. She arranged and rearranged them on the duster-kuhan.[5] Kabeer was forced to look at the person who was interfering in the quarrel of his mouth and fingers. He looked at her as a grave master to punish her for her audacity. She gave a broad smile with closed lips, as all those with projecting teeth do. Her smile was pleasing, her eyes shone. As a bride she was sweet with flowers, amber and sandal. She was wearing new and gorgeous clothes. Even an inhuman being would respond to such a smile. Kabeer was firm and did not smile, but he felt he was acting like a hypocrite. He had made her his wife, and for no fault of hers he was ill-treating her. He had been unjust to her. As for her features she was not responsible.

After his breakfast he went to his mother, who seemed serious. She asked him when he had last seen the baby.

'For the last three days I haven't been there.'

'I sent the servant and got information of both the mother and the baby,' said she.

'I might go there this evening.'

Zuhra did not like the idea of his going there so soon. She wanted him to go there when things at home were more developed and his hatred for his new wife had lessened.

'You are a bridegroom and are not expected to go out,' said she. She had confidence in the new girl's tactics. She would make him yield to her in two or three days. Her own absence from home would enable them to be free.

'I shall go there now. It makes no difference,' said she.

Kabeer was repenting for what he had done. He thought that his treatment of her had been horrid, and nothing but yielding to her would make things up. So he said 'As you please.'

Zuhra left the house after breakfast. Kabeer went to his room to sleep.

Munira on the pretext of giving him fruit juice, which he had never taken in his life, went to his room with a glass in her hand.

'Please taste if the sugar is all right,' said she, holding it out to him with a smile.

Kabeer sat up on his bed and took the glass from her hand looking into her eyes. As his mother had said, she was not so very ugly. Youth and its charm were on her side. The rich blood running in her veins made even the dark complexion attractive.

Zuhra returned home in the afternoon and found them in his room. Her plans which had fallen to earth only the night before had been fulfilled and quicker than she had expected.

Munira running from his room helped her to carry her shawl and the pandan and asked if she wanted a hot drink as the journey might have made her tired. Zuhra was pleased with the voluntary offer of service. Before the order was given Munira ran to the kitchen and asked the cook to boil water for tea. She arranged the tray herself, carried it to her mother-in-law, put it on a chair and made two cups of tea.

'For whom is the other? Has Kabeer finished his tea?'

'Yes, but I shall give him one more hot cup. The evening is so cold, he'll feel better with it,' said the new loving wife.

'Call him here. He can have it with me.'

Munira disappeared for a long time. The tea was getting cold, but it did not displease the mother. It all added to the success of her own efforts. Finishing her cup of tea she asked the cook to remove the tray.

'How is Akram?' said Kabeer paying his respects to his mother.

'He is lovely, smiles, tries to talk and goes to everyone. He is not timid or frightened of anybody. She is still the same. They say she is getting better and they will send her home next month. But I don't think she'll be well so soon. She breathes so fast one can hear the loud beating of her heart sitting near her. She's pale and anaemic. She is a sight to make a healthy person sick. I told them not to hurry and follow the doctor's advice strictly. I even said they could keep her as many months as they liked.'

'So they don't know of this?' said Kabeer.

'I don't think it has reached them; none of them behaved differently. We must congratulate ourselves on the clever way we've managed things. They are bound to know in a day or two. Our cook is enough to inform them. What a fright she gave me last night!'

'Why? What does it matter to her? Tell her not to mention it.'

'I am not a coward like you to ask her. Let her talk. Who cares now? Are you funky to face her? I have heard of people called henpecked husbands but now I can see one with my own eyes.'

'Oh, no… no, I shall tell her it was done in her own interest, and to make her comfortable and to live long.'

'Better put it another way. You did it because you couldn't suffer any more. Ask her to come to her home when she is well.'

'That depends upon her parents,' said Kabeer.

'If they don't like to send her let them keep her for life. No woman will take the drastic step of separating herself from her husband,' said Zuhra.

'Many have done it.'

'If you go into the details of their history you will always find something immoral. Modern girls do it but they are exceptions. What'll you lose even if she refuses to come? If she really loves you she must be pleased with all that pleases and comforts you. The presence of an extra woman at home should not displease her. She was happy with the cook and she is hand and glove with her. Your fears are baseless. You will see that both of them will be happy.'

Kabeer's point had only one side where his mother was concerned. Whatever she said was an authorized fact. None could contradict it. He himself could not see beyond it. Her arguments to him were sincere and right. After all man is man and woman is woman. Why should he not do anything he liked for his own comfort and happiness? He was not living for his wife's happiness but his own. He was not going to discard her for life. What more could she want than food and shelter? His needs would be satisfied and her children brought up. If she was faithful to him she must be contented with her life.

The cook on the pretext of stomach-ache left the house after Zuhra's return. Munira was busy with the dinner. Her experience in cooking was coming in handy. She believed not only in quantity but in quality and variation. She asked the cook indirectly how many dishes were prepared and what were the things Kabeer liked. Both Zuhra and Kabeer were pleased with her cooking, as the one liked quality and the other quantity. After her work was over Munira spent her time with her mother-in-law. Unlike her rival she either stitched her clothes or massaged her body. Old age was showing itself and she needed special attention. Till very late in the night she worked for her mother-in-law.

Chapter VII

The cook was more fond of Nazni than of Zuhra, partly because of her beauty, and partly for the tips she got now and then from her. The presence of a new woman at home and her connection with the master had given her brain rich food for digestion. She went straight to Nazni and sat down panting near her bed.

'Why are you panting? What has happened to you?' asked Nazni's mother.

'I came running from Doulhan Begum's house to give her a terrible piece of news,' said the cook.

'Ammajan was here the whole day. She did not say anything. How is he? What has happened to him?' interrupted Nazni anxiously.

'Has he come to see you?' said the cook proudly.

'For the last four days he hasn't been here,' said Nazni.

'Why would he come here? He has been enjoying his life with his new wife,' said the cook.

'What! Who is she? When? How is she?' said Nazni puzzled, excited and breathing heavily.

The mother was shocked not only by the news but also because it was broken so sharply to Nazni. She got up and giving a sign to the cook to follow moved towards the door. She wanted to know the details, but they would upset Nazni.

'Amma, don't take her away. You'll kill me! I want to hear more about it,' said Nazni, breathing heavily.

'You shouldn't hear anything saddening in your present condition. He will not forgive me if your health is upset,' said the mother.

'There's nothing more saddening than what I have heard already. Nothing more will happen to me if I hear the details. I get the palpitation only when I talk. I promise you not to open my mouth, or put her questions,' said Nazni.

The mother sat down reluctantly. After all Nazni knew the worst, and it would be better if she heard direct the treacherous ways of her husband. It would lesson her sorrow.

'When was he married?' said the mother, while Nazni stared eagerly at the cook and prayed to God to make her say it was a lie and said for a joke.

'He was married yesterday morning. Both the mother and the son left home at about eleven o'clock. I thought they had gone to Nazni Begum,' said the cook.

'Didn't you suspect it before? You were there day and night,' said the mother.

'If I had I would have informed you beforehand.'

'Didn't they buy jewels and clothes?'

'Yes, they did. I thought they were for Nazni Begum because she had given birth to a boy. I was hoping to get her old saris after she got them.'

'They came here like beggars empty-handed on the day of chilla,' said the mother.[1]

'Yes, I was here that day. I thought they wanted to give her presents after her return home,' said the cook.

'When did the bride come home? Was he very pleased?' interrupted Nazni.

'You promised not to speak. I shall send the woman away if you don't keep quiet,' said her mother. 'Didn't you hear them talking about it at home?' She went on. She wanted to hit upon those facts that would reveal Kabeer's treachery.

'They did everything so cunningly that even when they went for the jalva I didn't know. I was sleeping in the kitchen,' said the cook.

'You must have known of it when the bride came home,' said the mother.

'No, not even then. Master came alone and asked me for water to drink. I asked him about Begum Sahib but he went to his room without answering,' said the cook.

'How funny! When did she come?' asked the mother.

'I slept again. I was awakened to make a bed for the bride in Begum Sahib's room,' said the cook.

'Why? Why there?' cried both the mother and the daughter.

The mother looked a warning at Nazni. Nazni was pleased that the bride and Kabeer were not friendly. She guessed that he had not liked to take a second wife and it was his mother who had forced her on him. So she must leave her mother's house at once to help him in his determination. She must tell him that she would give her life at his feet. She would never go back to her parents. She admired his self-control and was anxiously waiting to get the proof of her guesses.

'I was equally surprised, so I asked Begum Sahib whose bride she was and where was the bridegroom. She was furious and said if I said one word more she would sack me.'

'Then what happened?'

Nazni's hopes were still high. She was waiting for a favourable reply.

'I made the bed and laying the bride on it I went to sleep,' said the cook.

'So the bride and bridegroom are at sixes and sevens,' said the mother.

'I knew he would never remarry. Even when a woman is forced upon him he rejects her. He often said that the charm of my eyes had a magical effect on him and that he would never be able to look at another woman. Amma, please let me go home with the cook. It doesn't matter even if I die there.'

Her mother looked at her sternly.

'Nazni, why don't you have patience and leave the thing to me? I have more experience in such matters. Whatever I do is in your interest. Every second minute you break your promise.'

'It is not exactly that,' said the cook. 'In the morning when I was lighting the fire in the kitchen the bride came. I got a shock to see her. I hadn't seen her face in the night.'

'Don't tell us what happened to you. What took place there?' said the mother.

Nazni's hopes were not yet shattered. Her only consolation was that her husband was faithful to her. The sin of getting him remarried was his mother's.

'She's dark like Amavas. She has four long teeth. They don't fall below as some have them but go up like this.'

'Oh woman, come to the point!' cried the mother.

'When I describe a person I do it fully.'

'Don't describe her but tell us what she did.'

'She has deep holes on her face.'

'What, holes! Are they due to leprosy?'

'I don't know what they are due to. Don't you know, like those the night nurse has?' said the cook, who was bent upon exaggeration and irritation.

'They are marks of smallpox. What happened then?' said the mother.

'She's fat like an elephant, and looks like this when she walks.'

The mother could not help laughing. Nazni was overjoyed. She looked at her slim body and arms, touched her thin cheeks, and noticed her fair complexion by half closing her right eye and looking at her nose. A sense of superiority over her rival took root in her mind.

'Again you have started your rubbish,' said the mother.

'Amma, dear, please let her say all she wants to. I feel happier,' said Nazni with the most pathetic appealing eyes. Her mother decided not to check the cook and let Nazni have a few happy minutes.

'Come on with your narration. How does she walk?' said the mother. This revived the cook's spirits who was bent upon derision. She had tied over her bag a string with tiny bells. She removed it and tied it to her leg to imitate the silver jewels on the bride's legs. She began to walk up and down the room with exaggerated gait and gestures, jingling the bells. Each movement made Nazni burst out laughing.

'She has lots of leg-rings then?' said the mother.

'Oh yes, three different kinds on each.'

'Did she bring them from her mother?'

'Tut! She's a beggar like me, even poorer. She brought only a bundle of clothes. Whereas I gave my daughter boxes, trunks, a chair and a cot. I went and examined her clothes. They are very ordinary ones like this.'

'What more did your new bride bring?'

'Peesh! My new bride! Why she's just fit to bring water for me to the lavatory. I was very fair and beautiful at her age. Even now I beat her any day. My Doulhan Begum is my dear mistress. I shall live and ide for her. Why, I should have left the house long ago if she was not there,' said the cook, kissing Nazni's feet.

Nazni's eyes were full of tears. At least there was one person in that house to feel sympathy for her.

'What happened after she came to the kitchen?'

'She asked me about the meals and the dishes cooked for each, especially what things master liked.

I was furious and felt like pulling her hair and kicking her out of the house, but I only asked why the devil she wanted to know all that. I had more right to keep them sacred to my heart, having served there for so long. I said that she was a newcomer so she should obey me.'

'Then what did she say?'

'She said that she was not a servant but master's wife. I asked her then why didn't she come with him and why did she sleep in his mother's room?'

'What did she say? Now give us the exact words.'

'She said that master after looking at her face on the takhat left the place without a word,' said the cook.[2]

'Just because she was ugly he left her. Otherwise he would have brought her quite happily,' said the mother.

'Then the mother-in-law brought her and pleaded for her to the master but he refused to accept her.'

'Didn't I tell you, Amma? He's not a man like that,' interrupted Nazni.

'Wait a minute. What happened then?' said the mother.

'What a treacherous woman your mother-in-law is! She persuaded the bride to do her best to win him. She asked her to cook and serve all his meals and see to his needs.'

'Did she do all that? Did he speak to her?' said the mother.

'She served the breakfast but came back to me with tears and said that he did not even look at her. She ran in with another tray and did not say a word after that.'

'So he still does not talk to her?' said Nazni.

'Soon after Begum Sahib left home she made orange juice and took it to him. I told her that he did not like it but she wouldn't listen to me. She disappeared till two o'clock. Then she came back all smiles. The lunch was ready. She took it for him. She gave him tea. When the mother-in-law came she ran to her and helped her and gave her tea without being asked.'

The mother and daughter looked at each other meaningly. Nazni felt a pain at her heart. She began to cry. She needed an outlet for her pain.

The cook was suddenly frightened. 'Bibi,' she said, 'if you give them my name for telling you about it they will sack me.'

'Not only will you lose your job but there'll be no one to look after Nazni in that house. You are safe with us. We shall protect you,' said the mother, and hurried out of the room to fetch medicine. She went to Doulath Khan to consult him about the medicine. She was not allowed to do anything by herself. Meanwhile one by one the whole family entered the room. The father came himself with a dose of medicine and administered it immediately.

'Why did she get it so suddenly? What did you tell her?' said the father, seeing the still trembling cook.

'That wouldn't do her any harm. It is her disease,' said the cook.

Doulath Khan's presence revived Nazni. She thought that her father had come to punish the culprit and revenge her. Tears were still falling from her eyes.

'I don't want this latcha and the bangles anymore,' said she and pulled it from her neck.

'The bangles are ours. You have worn them from the time you were born. What's the matter?' No one answered.

'Why don't you say what you did to her?' he said to the cook.

'I told her that master has remarried.'

'So she's killing herself for that. It's a wonder he did not do it earlier,' was the calm reply.

'What! He has remarried!' screamed the grandmother.

'Leave her to me. I shall look after her. All of you go out,' said he.

Some obeyed the command immediately and some hesitated to leave the place of excitement. When the cook left the room all followed her to get first-hand information from her. They took her to the dining room. She was an important personage. All of them either sat or stood round her and put similar questions. The cook repeated every item with more exaggeration. Every second or third sentence was followed by an assurance that she did not know of earlier or she would have informed them all about it in time. The event gave them a matter to discuss for months, and to gather information from the place through other sources.

Nazni's elder brother came home. The little ones ran to him and shouted.

'Doula Bhai (Kabeer) has got another bride![3] Apa is crying.[4] She was dying. Bavajan is still in her room.[5] He sent us all out.'

He went straight to Nazni's room and knocking on the door entered it. His father was sitting on Nazni's bed. Nazni looked like a corpse. He sat on the chair.

'How do you feel now?' said he.

'I'm all right. Nothing'll happen to me even if you kill me. There are many more sufferings reserved for me,' said Nazni with tears in her eyes.

'Why do you cry as if all of us were dead? I would sacrifice my life to make you happy and to serve you. Your wailing won't help you or help us. He has acted treacherously. We must punish him for it,' said the brother.

'I am asking her to get herself cured first. When she is well we can decide whether to send her there or not. If she still wants to go to him let her. We are ready to help her and support her either way,' said the father.

'Never think of going to that brute, a coward, a cad, a puppet in his mother's hands. He thinks of his cleverness too much but I have never met such a dunce. It's a disgrace to go to him when he stabbed you in the back. Live with us happily. We will file a suit against him and get your mahar and maintenance for both,' ejaculated the brother.[6]

Nazni liked her brother's sympathy, but she was sad because of the vulgar words he used about her husband. But on second thoughts her brother was right. She had lost him and in that loss she had found a loving and supporting brother. What more did she want than her own people?

'Going or not going there we shall leave for a later date. Let her decide when she feels stronger. Our house welcomes her under any circumstances. Nothing serious has happened to her. It's her imagination. On the other hand she will be more free from the home responsibilities,' said Doulath Khan. He knew the human heart.

'She can't decide anything in her present state of health,' said he again.

The brother's anger had cooled down. He listened to his father. He always admired his forethought and sound judgment, yet the sight of the weeping sister made him say, 'He is a rogue and a cad. He did it without her permission, when she's in bed.'

'Often second marriages take place without the first wife's knowledge,' said Doulath Khan. 'It is neither uncommon nor a sin according to social injunctions. He has every liberty to do it. Her precarious health gave him a good excuse. Men with the polygamous instinct fish for an excuse. The minute they find one even if it is not a reasonable one they interpret it in such a way that any stranger hearing it puts the whole blame in the opposite party. They know the first wife would not permit it so they do it on the sly. Some first wives go themselves and get it done.'

'He was forced by his mother to do it. Even when the woman was brought home without his permission he refused to look at her. So she asked her to make her way,' said Nazni despairingly.

Doulath Khan expected his daughter to side with her husband in spite of his action. He was pleased with her careful expressions. Nazni's love for her husband was blind. A separation from him or hatred for him should be by her own decision.

'What gives me more pain is that he did it on the sly. He came here almost every day and never said even a word about it,' said she again.

'You wouldn't have permitted him. He knew the futility of approaching you for it. Don't bother about it. He will tell us now when everything is over and there's no fear that we'll prevent it. It's a mistake to think that he did it without your permission. Your dignity is wounded as he didn't give you as much importance as you give to yourself. The thing has taken place without your permission and it would have taken place with it. It matters nothing.'

'Why didn't you do it with all your money, and why are many others contented with one wife?' asked the brother.

'My dear son, the number of such men is not great. Those who develop a power of thinking impartially, and see the harmful consequences of a plurality of wives, remain contented. Some remain single all their lives because they know the responsibility and their inability to fulfill it.'

'Knowing that he has more money than he needs, that his life is idle and that he is not a thinker, why did you give her in marriage to him?'

'Your mother and grandmother are more responsible for this catastrophe. They had no peace of mind and rest till they got it done. Every rejection of an offer by me brought on a new quarrel at home. Knowing that I find fault with new men they decided almost everything between themselves this time. I gave my consent to satisfy them. It was a mistake.'

Nazni was feeling extremely tired and the philosophical discussion between them made her feel sleepy.

The cook had gone, and the ladies, finding their excitement diminishing thought of going to Nazni to get fresh matter for discussion. The grandmother gently opened the door and entered the room. The mother followed suit.

'Don't say anything to her,' said Doulath Khan. 'You people can't understand when to talk and what to say. He is married. You can't make him divorce his wife by unnecessary discussion.'

'We know it. We have not grown our grey hair in the hot sun,' said grandmother emphatically.

'That's why she was bad,' said the father.

'Your wife was with her all the time. I came just one minute before you,' said grandmother.

Doulath Khan looked at his wife. 'All of you sail in the same boat. Let her be left with the nurse for some days.'

'As if the nurse is more loving than we,' said grandmother.

'You don't understand what I say but take it amiss,' said he, and left the room. The son also followed him.

The grandmother sat comfortably on Nazni's bed and put her hand over her forehead. Nazni began crying noiselessly.

'Don't cry. God ought not to have shown you these days so soon, especially when you are bedridden. What kind of a man is he? He is a beast. Other husbands don't think of their lives when their wife is ill,' said grandmother.

'Don't mention his name any more in this house. Let us think of him no more. After what he has done she can't forget us for him,' said mother.

'I don't want to go there. There'll be none to ask me whether I ate or not,' cried Nazni, who knew nothing more of love than that.

'The cook said both of them are very happy, so your presence there will annoy them,' said grandmother.

'Don't talk of those things. Let her forget she was married,' said mother.

'I am not saying anything to her. She herself says that she'll not go there' said granny.

'How can I forget, Amma? When I think of Akram my heart breaks,' said Nazni.

'He can live with us as one of our children. His father has no right to take him till he is seven years old,' said mother.[7]

'After bringing him up for seven years I have to give him to be tortured by his stepmother.'

'How badly stepmothers treat their stepchildren! We have seen with our own eyes a woman scarring her stepdaughter's feet with burning wood,' said granny.

Nazni with tears in her eyes was thinking of Akram being beaten by his father and scarred by his stepmother. The nurse entered with food and asked them all to clear away. Doulath Khan had given her strict orders.

In the night the whole family was as quiet as if someone was dead. Nazni had a restless night in spite of a sleeping dose. The report of her health was given to Doulath Khan in the morning. The day nurse was reengaged.

Kabeer did not know that the cook had already created mischief. In the morning he went to see her and his son. He intended to reveal the secret tactfully after preparing the ground for it.

'No one's allowed in the room' said the nurse to Kabeer.

'Why? What has happened? How is she?'

'She's having temperature. The condition of her heart has caused anxiety.'

'I have every right to see my wife if she's not well. No one can prevent me,' said he.

'Wait a minute please. I'll ask her father's permission. I shall be held responsible if anything goes wrong.'

'Damn you and her father.'

She closed the door and disappeared.

Kabeer stood thinking. Has she come to know of it? How could she? The cook was not well; she would not have come here. She resumed her duty this morning. It might be the usual relapse. He felt like going back without seeing her, but sin makes a man a coward. He decided to stay.

The nurse went to Doulath Khan and informed him of Kabeer's arrival. He was puzzled. He could not treat him ill. It might mean lifelong suffering for his daughter.

'Don't let the patient cry,' he said at length.

'She's getting crazy and cries for nothing. You keep an eye on her when he is there.'

The master's warning increased the nurse's curiosity. She opened the door and putting a chair for Kabeer, planted herself in the next room.

'How are you? The nurse said you are worse and no one's allowed in your room,' said he.

'What do you care for my health?'

Kabeer had never known her to be sarcastic. She was annoyed because he had not seen her for the last four days.

'Who wants to know of you if not I? Have I not cared for you without caring for myself? Have I not suffered alone all these months while you have been enjoying yourself in your parents' house? Am I not living the life of a sanyasi, thinking of you, praying for you and crying for your sufferings? I am not lucky enough even to have my own son with me, for whom I am ready to give my life.'[8]

'Now you have someone else to care for.'

This was unexpected. It was of no use to ask her about the informant. There was no way out. He was caught. The only thing he could do was to condemn the newcomer down right.

'Phoo! What a silly person you are to think that I care for that wretched negress.[9] I hate to see her face. I didn't know that you were so foolish.'

'But Ammajan asked her to exert her influence on you and to win you. You were with her for hours in your room,' interrupted Nazni.

'That's rubbish. Who told you all that? You come to know of things about me before I know them myself. I'm the master of my mind. No one can make me change unless I want to. Why don't you allow me to tell you? Then you can ask anything you want to know,' said Kabeer.

Nazni began to feel despondent. It was foolish to put questions in between. Her hesitation gave Kabeer his chance.

'Do you know I locked myself in my room? I had a quarrel with Ammajan for having brought her home. When you see her you will understand why. She's not suitable even to wash your bathroom. I am surprised that you compare yourself with her. There's no one in the whole world to take your place in my heart. How can it be? None possesses even a hundredth part of your beauty. God has specially made you with his own hand and chosen me to enjoy that boon. I don't know how I deserve it. I am at a loss to know why it pleased God to grant you to me.'

Kabeer was the only man she had seen in her life. The poor girl fell an easy prey to his open flattery. She thought that she would be unjust and cruel to him if she tried to make him sad. The woman who makes her husband sorry goes to the Seventh Hell where the fire burns eternally.[10] She is burnt alive and is recreated and burnt again. This process goes on forever even after the Day of Judgment. Tears were generously falling from her charming eyes. She did not know whether they were in sympathy for her suffering husband or in her own interest.

'Is life with you possible for me now? I am afraid of going there,' said she sadly.

'If you ask how your life is possible without me, there's some sense in it. I have answered already. I can live with no one but you. She's only a head cook and your servant as well as mine.'

'You got married without telling me. I was thinking that you hide nothing from me.'

'It was again because of your health. I came to tell you how it all happened but someone has already misrepresented it.'

'You did not care to see me after it. It is five days since you came.'

'It was due to you and in your interest. I had tried to persuade mother not to bring an extra woman into the house. She said you were coming home next month and she wanted you to have complete rest. You don't know how she adores you. One servant was not enough for you and Akram. By the by, did you tell her that you were coming soon?'

'Yes, mother told Ammajan.'

'That's why she was bent upon getting her soon. She wanted to train her in advance. When you come home you'll have nothing to do.'

'If you wanted to remarry why didn't you get a decent woman?'

'Because she will demand equal rights and status with you.'

Nazni felt that all she had heard was true. His regard for her was constant.

'Did the cook come to see you? She is very fond of you. Who wouldn't be? She was wanting to come here yesterday evening.'

Nazni was in a fix. She had promised not to mention her name. Kabeer realized that she was the culprit. No answer coming he said, 'Do your people know of it?'

'Yes, every one.'

'What did your father say?'

'He said my health is more important and he leaves it to me to decide whether to go back or not.'

'He's a sensible man and your well wisher. Obey him implicitly. You will never repent it.'

'But Bhai is against my going back to you. He was very angry. I felt so sad to hear him.'

'He's a fool. What does he know of the world and my love of you? If he had loved you as I do he would have felt for my feelings. These young men after learning a few words of English think too much of themselves. Our sense of justice and our ways of love are more reliable than those of the imitators of the West. They have illegal connections with many and yet believe in their fidelity.'

Nazni was admiring the philosophy of her husband. She thought that God had created him with unique talents and had bestowed this personage on her.

'Yes, he was angry at first. After hearing father his anger cooled down and he didn't open his mouth till he left the room,' said she.

'What do the ladies say?'

'Granny was crying and asked why God had to show me these bad days so soon.'

'Tell her that there's nothing bad in it. You'll have one extra servant to serve you. What did you say?'

'I also cried, thinking of Akram and how he'll be ill-treated by his stepmother.'

'So you are the only person who is responsible for his birth? I have nothing to do with him? He is my first-born and is a source of pride and pleasure to me. You'll have to cry for him when I die. I'm ready to give my life for him as Babar did for Humayun.'[11]

That was the only instance in the whole history of India he remembered. He thanked his memory.

'You'll have other children.'

'Don't you know that a throne is given only to the first son? Others work under him like servants. When are you coming back? I live a lonely and sad life. Ammajan couldn't see me unhappy. She wouldn't have brought that ugly woman if you had been at home.'

'I used to come here only for the day. This time I came because I was not well,' said Nazni.

'If you were ill my mother was there to look after you. Is your mother the only person who loves you?'

'When I was ill your mother never came to see me, whereas my mother hardly leaves me.'

'My mother's love is reasonable. She supplies all your needs and keeps information of your health. What more does your mother do?'

'When you are ill her treatment is quite different.'

'So you grudge the little pleasure she gives me. You ought to be pleased with it. What does your mother do to me when I am ill?'

'She can't do it because she is gosha in front of you.'

'Even if she were not she wouldn't do so much as she does for you.'

'That's what I say and that's why I came here.'

Kabeer thought that the matter needed some more time and flattery, though it meant a great strain.

'You are not bad by nature. Your people spoil you and will break your home. They sent for you almost every day but you refused to go there and stayed with me. Don't listen to anybody and as soon as you can come home. This is your mother's house. Your home is longing to have you.'

'I am having fever and there are two nurses to look after me.'

'Bring them with you. We shall send them here once a month for their salary.'

He got up and was trying to go but sat down quickly. 'I can't go without seeing my son,' said he. He rang the bell. The nurse came. 'Bring Akram soon.'

'Baby's nurse won't let me bring him to a sick person's room. She's having fever.'

'You are an owl. The fever is in her body not in the room.'

The nurse smiled at the ignorance of the man. 'What makes you laugh? Go bring him soon.'

The nurse left the room and returned after five minutes.

'The baby is sleeping,' said she.

'He sleeps at this time. He wakes at five when they get up for prayer,' said Nazni.

Kabeer got up with a sigh. 'If he were in my house I would have kissed him in his bed. I go leaving my heart here.'

'Come tomorrow to see me,' said the poor wretch in bed.

All the doubts that Nazni had entertained were solved. He had been married, without her permission because of her health. She found that her husband loved Akram more than she did. Her fear of losing his love and care was baseless. He loved her more than ever and she would now have more comfort. She felt sorry that because of her love for her parents a new person had to be brought into her home.

Kabeer on his way home was very thoughtful. He was lightly gratified by his success in dealing with an awkward position. He thought over the discussion and his flat denial of having had any connection with the new wife. He made up his mind to keep his word, not to live with her and to try and get a decent woman in the future to wipe away the disgrace caused by this pariah woman.

Nazni's words 'Why didn't you get a decent woman?' rang in his ears.

Chapter VIII

Zuhra's prohibition was not of much avail. Kabeer determined to see Nazni and particularly Akram, in whose praise she was very liberal. On the pretext of going to office he left home and drove to his father-in-law's house. Zuhra made enquiries in the office and found her son absent.

'Where did you disappear from the office?'

'I had an intuition of her illness and to my surprise she is seriously ill,' said Kabeer.

'I see, you are a prophet. You can do wonders by your prophecy. Her sickness is not an unusual thing. She gets many attacks without your intuition,' said she.

'She was getting better but this is a sudden one.'

'All her attacks are sudden.'

'This one is due to the recent incident. She knows more about it than myself.'

'You are a wonderful man who keeps less information than a woman.'

Kabeer was annoyed but could not retaliate. Her words were sarcastic. He thanked his stars that he never spoke to her in the presence of his wife.

'She knows more about yourself and that negress's conspiracy to entice me.'

'What do you mean by conspiracy? You talk without meaning. I am a conspirator against whom?'

Kabeer thought it wise to change the subject.

'She has had a serious attack with fever. They have again engaged two nurses. I asked her to come home,' said Kabeer.

The coming home of the sickly Nazni taxed Zuhra's brain more than the former stimuli. Moreover she could not forget the contemptuous title 'negress' for her favourite daughter-in-law

'How can she come here if she is seriously ill?'

'I asked her to bring the nurses with her.'

Zuhra's fury knew no limit.

'Are you mad? What has happened to you? You behave like a lunatic! Those nurses don't eat our food. You'll have to cook their meals.'

'If they care for their job they'll eat anything they get. I told her to send them to her father for their remuneration,' said Kabeer.

Zuhra was pleased with her son's wisdom in sending the nurses for their pay to Doulath Khan.

'We had the bitter experience of keeping a servant from their house. To have two English women here will involve unsurmountable difficulties.[1] Let her come here when she is quite well. You are not in need of her. That wretched cook must have informed her of the details of the wedding. We'll have to treat her as a spy in this house.'

To Zuhra there was nothing like love between Kabeer and Nazni. When he had a wife at home there was absolutely no need for him to think of Nazni.

'Yes, she is the person who created the mischief there. I had to rack my poor brain to bring her round.'

'I'll warn her strictly not to step in that house any more.'

Jamila was anxious to go to her mother for her third confinement. Her parents-in-law were against it. They said it was beneath them to send her there for all her deliveries. Zuhra was of the opinion that the third confinement is dangerous. Apart from that a baby boy in the third delivery undoubtedly meant the loss of one of the parents of the newcomer. She sent letters and even escorts to Jamila's place, to no avail.

Jamila's home was in a village. There was a hospital for men with two nurses who went round from home to home to attend to the women. A rumour was rife that only the lucky few survived the catastrophe. The nurse, being informed by Jamila of the tragical consequences of the third delivery, told the parents-in-law the seriousness of the case and its alarming symptoms. The news melted the heart of Jamila's monogamous husband. He pleaded for her and the old couple agreed to the proposal, against their will and to the great loss of their prestige.

'Are you not going to receive Jamila today at the station?' said Zuhra

'I can't. I shall send Mustafa,' said Kabeer.

'You don't mind going to your wife many times unnecessarily, but to go to your only sister once in a way you can't. Your valuation of a sister is nothing in comparison to your wife.'

Kabeer took the car near the compartment to save the trouble of screening Jamila all along the long platform.

'A penny for your thoughts, Bhai. You seem quite changed,' said Jamila.

'Do I? said Kabeer.

'Is anything the matter?'

'Oh, nothing.'

'Perhaps Bhabi's health has upset you.'

'Maybe.'

Kabeer instead of following his sister into the house got down near the office to avoid her meeting with the new wife. He knew that she loved Nazni, and that she would revolt and condemn his action.

'Hai, hai, who's that? The children will be frightened to see her. I'm not allowed to see ugly faces. Ask her to go away from there!' ejaculated Jamila to Zuhra who was standing behind the door to receive her daughter. Munira was also anxious to see her sister-in-law and was standing at a distance behind her mother-in-law.

'Keep quiet! Don't exaggerate your condemnation,' whispered Zuhra as her daughter bent down to pay her respects.

'But who is she? She can't be a servant with all those jewels and grand clothes. What has happened to the old cook?'

'Don't call her a servant. She's your sister-in-law.'

'My sister-in-law! My sister-in-law! Don't pull my leg. She's the most beautiful creature in the world,' said Jamila with open mouth and eyes.

'She's your second sister-in-law. You shouldn't condemn God's creation.'

Since her daughter's marriage Zuhra could tolerate her remarks and humour her fancies, just the opposite of her attitude to Kabeer.

'What madness to have a woman of that type and call her a sister-in-law. Where was the need of such a creature when you had the most superb woman at home? How did Bhai approve of her? He's blind.'

'He refused downright to accept her. Even my pleading had no effect on him. He just tolerates her. Don't try to prejudice his mind again.'

Turning round to see if Munira was still there Zuhra saw her frightened look. She had overheard them.

'It is getting late. Go and see to the lunch,' said Zuhra to Munira.

The poor creature obeyed her mother-in-law meekly. She went to the kitchen and started work vigorously. But her thoughts returned to Jamila's contemptuous words and she shed a few bitter tears. For a moment she felt she must show her indignation, but said to herself that Jamila being rich and beautiful had every right to call her names.

Zuhra took Jamila to her room.

'You seem more angry with the poor woman than your brother.'

'Couldn't you have got a better woman? People will say you picked up a woman from the gutter because no one was willing to give him a girl. Suppose my people did the same. How would you feel?'

'Why should they do it to you? You are not sick and bedridden. We did our best in our first choice and everyone was pleased. This we did only for our comfort, not for others' opinion. We are quite happy and you'll feel the same in course of time,' said Zuhra.

'I can't help laughing when I see her face.'

'Don't look at her face. I never do. I just command and get work done.'

'You could have engaged an extra servant.'

'No servant would be so cheap or useful. She's here day and night. She feels this is her house and the work is hers. That makes all the difference.'

Kabeer came from the office thinking that he had given them enough time, but found his mother and sister still discussing the unpleasant topic. His mother left the room as she saw him.

'Bhai, now I know the cause of your moods. I was surprised to see how you'd changed,' said Jamila in sincere sympathy for him.

'You aren't changed after your marriage.'

'You weren't changed after your first wedding.'

'This one has brought me nothing but disgrace and sorrow. I must fight it out. But then I don't know what to do.'

'It is no good saying you'll fight it out now. You ought to have done that before it took place.'

'I'm fed up. I have to say something to mother, something else to her, quite a different thing to the negress. Oh I'm disgusted.'

'You've given her an appropriate title. I've been wondering these two hours what to call her.'

'Negresses don't have long teeth, so ape is better.[2] She's mother's favourite and she's benefited by my name. My ideas of a wife are quite different.'

'Why don't you make mother understand your ideas?'

'She's changed from the day I was married. We never talk freely now. She misunderstands me in everything. I obey her implicitly without caring for the consequences.'

'Mother's old fashioned. She can't differentiate between a daughter-in-law and a servant. My parents-in-law aren't rich yet I don't cook at home. Cleaning of the house and children's work's enough for me.'

'Ammajan has been a cook all her life. How could she tolerate others not being so? One reason why I yielded to her proposal of remarriage was her health. She can never be handled roughly. She will have to be treated like an aged woman all her life.'

'It seems barbarous to have more than one wife.'

'When one is fed up with life one can have any number of them. I shall do what I think fit for myself hereafter.'

'Your best way is not to act independently but to co-operate with mother. Change her instead of suiting yourself to her temperament.'

'Does Bhabi know of it? What did she do, poor thing?'[3]

'What'll she do but cry? I made her believe that I hate the negress and still love her.'

'She's an innocent girl and good hearted too. She's very sweet. Even her people are polite and well behaved in spite of their wealth. Ask Bhabi to come home. We shall sack this one. Her mahar won't be much.'[4]

'Mother wouldn't allow you to do that. She needs a servant.'

'Do you think that Munira will live like a servant all her life? Once she gets children she'll fight and demand equal rights with Bhabi.'

'That is another consideration which never struck me. Let Ammajan bear the consequences.'

'You can't escape so easily. You'll bear the brunt of it more than anybody else.'

'Oh goodness, you make it all the more difficult for me,' said Kabeer desperately.

'Come for lunch, Jamila,' said Zuhra, who did not feel it beneath her dignity to call them for food. If there were her son and daughter-in-law talking she would have asked the servant.

'How many delicious dishes she has prepared! The very sight of the dastarkhuan is tempting. Even a person without an appetite would yield,' said Zuhra, forgetting the help she had given in the preparation.

'I can't do these things any more. There must be someone to look to the food and to entertain guests,' said she again.

Both brother and sister were extremely pleased at the sight of the grand and appetizing food and realized the truth of Zuhra's statement.

'Taste this one, how delicious it is. Even I couldn't have made it so well,' said Zuhra, who knew how to bring round an opponent.

'She can cook. There's no doubt about it,' said Jamila condescendingly.

'She's a hundred times better than the cook, and much less expensive,' said Zuhra.

'Cooking is not the only thing that we have to think of. The whole house is dirty. Look at the cobwebs in the corners. Why, all the things in the rooms are covered by them. Dust is an inch deep everywhere. The cook must be made to clean these things. If both of them are left in the kitchen after some time the food will not be up to the mark,' said Jamila, who had been trained in her husband's house. He was a high official and she often met ladies of different communities including the missionaries.

Kabeer wanted to say that from the time Nazni left home it was neglected, but dared not in the presence of his mother.

'That woman knew nothing and did nothing but stand near a cupboard or a chest of drawers for hours with a piece of cloth to show people that she worked. What's there to do every day? In a kitchen the fruit of one's labour is shown. All idle mongers take to nominal duties. One can judge a person by the kind of work he assumes,' said Zuhra sarcastically.

'I do nothing but cleaning of the house and children. There's a lot to be done in that way. Who comes to know of cooking? It is the house that's seen by all. Let one of them cook and the other see to these things,' said Jamila.

In Zuhra's view nothing in the world was so difficult and important as cooking.

'Feed, clothe and on top of that pay the cook and give her the easiest work! You seem to have a very strong sense of justice. The animosity of a sister-in-law is a proverb but now I see it with my own eyes. How is it that you treat her so differently from the other? Is it because she's dark?'

Jamila realized the truth of Kabeer's complaint. Her mother was changed. She hated her first daughter-in-law, who had won Kabeer's love and was responsible for the less regard he had shown to his mother. Jamila thought it was useless to persuade her mother of her new ideas but determined to get the work done through the cook.

'Give a bath to the children and wash their clothes,' said Jamila to the cook.

'I have to cook. Who'll give you food?' was the haughty reply.

'Munira does the cooking. You needn't keep her company. Do the washing and grinding masala. That's the only difficult thing in the kitchen,' said Jamila. The cook retired grumbling.

'I'll bathe the children, you do the cooking,' said Munira.

Jamila was a problem to her. She had been against her from the day of her arrival, but she resolved to win her. She gave Jamila's two daughters their bath, dressed them, combed their hair and washed their clothes.

Jamila was listening to their appreciation of Munira's work.

'When the cook bathes me my head and body burn. I won't have a bath if she gives it. Munira must bathe me,' said her daughter. She had long and curly hair and it was the most difficult thing for Jamila to comb it. The girl had neither patience to sit still nor to bear the pain. She would often cry and her mother would slap her.

'Look at my nice hair. I don't get it combed by you. I didn't cry. She told me a shaitan's story,' said the girl again.[5]

Jamila was pleased. She was waiting to comb her hair. Munira entered the room.

'The water is ready for your bath. I thought you would like it. You don't look quite well. It'll do you good.'

Jamila felt pity for her and understood why her mother liked her. Zuhra was not an easy person to please. Except for her own children she was horrid to everybody. She pictured the lovely presents Nazni had sent for herself and the children. She knew that Kabeer never gave his wife any money yet she managed to send many things. While she was having her bath these ideas were crowding her mind and her pity for Munira dwindled.

'Shall I wash your hair and back?' said Munira, entering the bathroom.

'I'll do it. I'm used to it.'

'You'll feel tired. When my sisters were expecting they often said they were exhausted after a bath. I used to wash their hair. It makes no difference if I do it to you.'

'You've been busy with the children the whole morning. The cook'll spoil the meal. Ammajan'll be furious. Don't bother about me. I'm all right,' said Jamila.

'I gave her instructions and I've been supervising the curries.'

Munira began washing her hair. She gave Jamila her bath, helped her in dressing, combed her hair and dried it with incense.

'There'll be a lot of extra work when the baby comes. Ammajan is too old to do it all,' said Jamila feeling fresh after her bath.

'I used to do the work at the time of my sister's confinements. You needn't be worried. I'll look after the children as well.'

'I'll engage a woman to help you.'

'I'll manage everything without anybody's help.'

'The children are very fond of you. I'm not at all worried about them.'

Munira gave a big smile. She felt proud of her contrivance in winning her sister-in-law.

Jamila averted her face to avoid any unpleasant feeling re-entering her heart.

'Munira says that she'll look after me and the children during the days of confinement,' said Jamila to her mother.

'You'll see more of her goodness in course of time. I didn't know comfort in this house all my life. Now I understand what a blessing it is. Why don't you call her Bhabiman?[6] Even your children call her by her name. She'll love you more if you respect her,' said Zuhra.

'When I go home I'll make a nice jora (dress) for her.'[7]

'Why do you want to make a new one? Give her your old clothes.'

'I want to give them to the cook.'

'Don't give them to that wretch. She gets lots of them from Nazni. She does not even wear them. She makes money out of them.'

Zuhra with all her fondness for her favourite daughter-in-law could not bear the idea of her getting a new expensive dress. Jamila made up her mind to give Munira both the old and the new clothes, the old ones to be given soon and the other after her delivery.

The children liked Munira more than their mother and grandmother. She told them stories and sang to them while feeding and putting them to bed in her leisure time. The stories were often of ghosts, devils and of women who were possessed.

'Give these saris to Mumani,' said Jamila to her daughter.[8]

'Who's Mumani?' said the little one in surprise.

'Munira,' said Jamila with a smile.

'I don't call her Mumani. She's dark. My Mumani is nice. She's like a moon. She gives me lots of dolls. Munira's the cook's sister. She works for us.'

'You shouldn't talk like that. Granny'll spank you if you call her by her name.'

'I feel shy to call her Mumani. Ask Looloo to do it first. I don't call her Munira in front of Granny,' said the girl. Though she refused to call Munira aunty she was pleased to give her some gifts. She ran to the kitchen with the silk saris.

'Bibi gave these to you. See how nice they are. Touch them with your fingers. See, your sari pricks my fingers. Look at the nice flowers on them. They are roses. Bibi asks me to call you Mumani.'

Munira's joy knew no bound. No one had hitherto called her anything but her name. 'Did she? Won't you call me Mumanijan?' said Munira with a big smile.

The girl looked at her face and ran away. Munira was hesitating whether to accept the clothes or refuse them. If she accepted them she would always be treated like a servant. There would be no hope of getting new ones. If she rejected them she would be sowing a bad seed in the ground which she had tilled with such labour. If her husband had shown any regard to her she would have done anything she liked. The response from that side was nil. She would leave his room every morning at five and never spoke to him the whole day. After her day's work and massaging of her mother-in-law's body she would go to him at about eleven o'clock in the night. One or two sentences about Zuhra, the cook, and cooking were exchanged. Often he would warn her to be very careful and please everybody at home.

Reluctantly Munira got up as she could not bear the angry look of the cook and went to her room.

The cook's anger had no limit. She had had an eye on those saris from the day Jamila arrived. She was doing her best to get on the good side of Jamila to get them. Now here was a rival to share her rights. She was not allowed to go to Nazni. She could not lose her job. In spite of all the drawbacks it was the only way to keep her home going. She gave a bang with a burning log on the big earthen pot. It gave a loud noise and burst. The water flowed all over the kitchen and the small mat on which Munira used to sit was floating with the saris. She kicked them into the water and trampled them under her feet till they looked like the kitchen rags. Jamila's daughter seeing the water rushing out of the kitchen ran to see the fun. 'Granny, the kitchen is swimming in water,' said the little girl to Zuhra.

'What nonsense you talk, child.'

'The water jar is broken. Bibi's saris are swimming.'

'How did her saris get there?'

'Bibi gave them Muni ... Mumani.'

'Say Mumani again.'

The girl ran away. If Zuhra had not been agitated with the news she would have given her a slap.

'You bitch! What have you done?' cried Zuhra seeing the muddle in the kitchen.

'The jar was very old. It broke.'

'It was not possessed to break itself. Don't tell lies. I heard a big noise. I thought you were chopping wood.'

'It cracked with a loud noise when I was sitting here,' said the cook showing a place very far from the pot.

Zuhra waddled over and found the piece of wood lying near the broken jar.

'You are twenty cats!' said Zuhra, but controlled herself when she thought of Jamila's confinement. She could not sack her before getting another cook.

Munira hearing her mother-in-law's voice in the kitchen ran to see what was wrong. She took the saris from the ground and began squeezing them.

'The cook was jealous. She was grumbling and looking daggers at me when the saris were sent. I left her to herself for some time to let her anger cool down,' whispered Munira to Zuhra, who thought the fault was not the cook's so much as Jamila's. She said nothing to either of them.

Kabeer wanted to engage a doctor for Jamila's confinement.

'It is better to engage the doctor who came for Akram. They say she's clever.'

'How much did they pay her?' asked Zuhra.

'For the case and for ten days visit they paid her three hundred.'

'It's lunacy to send for a doctor. What is there to do? God sends the baby into the world. What wonderful things does the doctor do there but sit about and look on? Send for your old Dai.⁹ She did all of mine and Jamila's confinements. They are fashionable people. They must have called her for show.'

Accordingly the midwife was sent for in advance and engaged, and was asked to be ready whenever the call came.

The day came and the pain started in the night, to Zuhra's regret. She could not send for all her relations in the middle of the night. However she sent word to the midwife. Early morning a messenger was sent to inform them all. Carts, cars and rikshaw loads arrived before noon. All assembled in Jamila's small room. They planted themselves there the whole day and gossiped and now and then said a few sentences to encourage the crying patient.

The day passed, and again and again the midwife gave hope for half an hour more. But the time never came. In the evening the patient had become too weak to bear any more pain. Zuhra was not allowed into the room as the very sight of her would prolong the labour.

'I'm dying. Send for a doctor,' said Jamila faintly.

The doctor came and chased everybody from the room, opened the windows and prepared for an abnormal delivery. The unwanted baby boy made its appearance in the world, to the displeasure of many, who began to associate sayings to facts. The tedious and prolonged labour and the coming of the doctor were in favour of their doubts. But all was well in spite of the time wasted in getting a maternity expert.

Munira was now indispensable. She was needed everywhere, in the kitchen, in Jamila's and Zuhra's rooms, and for the children. Even her husband was not neglected in spite of her indifferent health. Munira's pregnancy, unlike Nazni's, was a matter of course. She could eat well and digest any food. She had her meals only when she found time for them. After all of them finished theirs she had hers with the cook.

Nazni's grandmother had made up her mind to go to Zuhra and have a good fight with her for having remarried her son, but Doulath Khan was in her way. Even when Nazni's mother went to see Jamila's new baby, she was not permitted to accompany her.

Nazni's mother, tall, fair, perfectly made, with a very good countenance, came to see Jamila's baby with lots of presents for both the mother and the child. When she was entering Jamila's room Munira peeped through the half-shut window of the kitchen.

'What a lovely person she is! Is the daughter like her?' said Munira to the cook.

'Her daughter's like an angel. She's fairer, with big eyes, parrot nose, well shaped face, long hair, high forehead, fine mouth, teeth like pearls, as tall as her mother, and straight limbs. The more you see her the more you want to. For hours I used to stare at her but never was I satisfied,' said the cook with pride in her expression to humiliate her colleague.

Munira's spirits fell. She had to attend to many things in Jamila's room, but she felt that her whole body was paralysed. She now made Jamila's daughter take and bring things from there. She expected more humiliation and more degradation when Nazni came to live in the house. Then she thought she should be proud to be called the rival of that beauty. She should take it for luck to be near her and serve her.

'Nazni also wanted to come but the doctor wouldn't allow her. She sent her love to you and asked me to tell you that you too have forgotten her,' said Nazni's mother to Jamila.

'She's unforgettable. I had no face to go to her after I came here. I was shocked to see the change of events at home,' said Jamila.

'She's very sad and says the world's cruel to her,' said Nazni's mother.

'I was annoyed with mother and Bhai. It took me a long time to reconcile myself to it. Tell her to come to her home.'

'She shudders at the very idea and cries whenever she thinks of it.'

'She need not be afraid of anything as far as the new woman is concerned. She's treated here like a servant by every one of us. There can't be any cause for jealousy between them.'

'We never expected that from your brother, especially when she was ill,' said Nazni's mother.

'I assure you of his love towards Bhabi. He hates that woman. We have never seen him speaking to her. Bhabi's ill health made Ammajan bring her against his will. I believe he left the wedding house and came home alone.'

Nazni's mother was anxious to see her daughter's rival. She expected her in Kabeer's room, where she could not go. She went to the kitchen to see the cook and found Munira sitting with her legs stretched out and Jamila's daughters sitting on them. As soon as she entered Munira jumped up and stood like a penitent with her head bent. The cook pointed towards Zuhra's room and made signs to indicate that she was prohibited from going to Nazni and it was her fate that she should not see Nazni for so many months. Nazni's mother stood there for a few minutes and without a word left the house.

Chapter IX

Nazni's family thought about the remarriage very differently from Kabeer's people. Nazni's brother was wild with anger. His father's philosophical discussions restrained him for a time. His silence in her presence was because his anger was so great. If he had been allowed he would have murdered Kabeer. He had disliked him from the day they met and now he hated him. He was planning to give him a thrashing and compel him to divorce his second wife.

Thoughtfully he followed his father to his room to discuss the matter. Neither the father nor the son liked to talk in Nazni's presence.[1]

'What shall we do to him? He has not only stabbed her in the back but has brought disgrace on us. We have been tolerating many meannesses but we can't do it any more. We bore them, thinking at least he wished well to Nazni,' said the brother very thoughtfully.

'In such circumstances we must act with patience and understanding. We have to behave like hypocrites, keeping her interests in view. She loves him immensely, so wisdom lies in encouraging her to go back to him when she is well,' said the father, who was really more pained than the rest.

'It is in her interest we have to create hatred for him.'

'No one can create anything in anybody's mind. Hatred for him will develop only when she studies him well and sees his ill-treatment of her. She is not in a position to draw her own inferences from the events. Husband and wife are like two blades of a scissor. A third person going in between them is cut. Their quarrels are temporary and soon are made up by themselves.'

'They are no more husband and wife.'

'Who said that? He will come to her soon and beg of her to treat him leniently for having fallen an easy prey to circumstance.'

'She is no more his wife. A man remarries to prove the disloyalty, incapacity, ill-temper and barrenness of the first wife. Once he takes that attitude he no more respects her. He openly disgraces her in home and society. He lives with her as he would live with a prostitute. No respectable woman would humiliate herself by calling him her husband. He has kicked her out of his home. She should not re-enter it if she possesses self-respect.'

Doulath Khan listened to his son with surprised admiration. He was pleased to hear the young man expound his ideals. His education had not been wasted. He was older than Nazni by four years, but what a difference there was between that dumb, passive and easily deluded creature and the young man in front of him. He debated whether to support his son and effect a separation. He would have done it if the matter had been between his son and his wife, but not with a girl with no power of decision, no judgment or practical knowledge of the world.

'That is all right in theory, my boy, but practice differs immensely. Your brother-in-law has not kicked your sister out of his home. He married her when the romance in him was just springing up, when he wholeheartedly concentrated all his feelings on the object of his first love and gave her all. The first marriage is the only one worthy of its name. Subsequent marriages are nominal and are caused by necessity. He has brought in a woman by the back door and is more conscious of it than anybody else. Men of complex nature are not satisfied with fair dealings either at home or in society. He will regard your sister more if she tolerates his mistake as he realizes it himself and appreciates her superiority.'

'I gave him an honourable place. Now I know he has not kicked her out but stabbed her in the back. He's a knave, a murderer and a coward in guise of a gentleman.'

Doulath Khan smiled and said:

'A man depending upon one wife feels himself equal to her. Plurality of wives maintains his self-importance. His mean action is a source of satisfaction and pride to him: we must recognize his weakness and should not condemn him for it.'

'So his faithlessness should be interpreted as virtue! A woman in spite of her loyalty should be submissive and servile. Why this double standard of morality? Is it not the creation of society and man? Has she not the same feelings as he? Would he be submissive to her?'

The father scratched his head, took a deep breath of smoke from the huqua and leaned back in the easy chair to prepare himself for another deliverance. Dealing with his son was not easy.

'She would not dare to do it. There are more harmful consequences in the case of a woman. A man faces his opponent with hatred and may even kill him. A woman's attitude towards a powerful antagonist is fear and submission.'

'That's all humbug. Man being both the legislator and executor has brought in laws to suit his interests. He has monopolized freedom and luxury. A woman has no right to question even when she is wronged. She must retaliate now. No one will blame her. Her cause is right and just.'

'It is not practical for a woman, especially a Muslim girl. She is weak both bodily and mentally and should be kept under restrictions. A woman discards a man only when she has someone else to take his place.'

'Whose fault is it? If she were given the same education and training she would have been quite a different person today. The flaw lies not in her but in man who keeps her a slave all her life in his own interest. His selfishness is responsible for her helplessness.'

'It was nature's design to make one strong and the other weak. Or else co-operation between two members of opposite sexes coming from strange families would have been impossible. If both try to have their own way happiness in life and peace at home will be a dream.'

'It is again the interest of the aggressor kept foremost. It is a blessing to make a woman independent and strong irrespective of man's interest. It is a crime to leave her in a dejected, hopeless and helpless condition. Her helplessness makes a man more selfish, inconsiderate and cruel. A fear of her getting on without his support checks his whims and fancies.'

'It has been the way of the world. The man earns, and supports and looks after the weaker ones, so he deserves comfort and satisfaction. She is ill. Why should he suffer on account of her?'

'Love is unselfish. A woman undergoes more sacrifices. Should she deserve treachery and heartlessness for her devotion? Shouldn't he at least show some consideration when she is in need of it?'

'There was no need. He had shown enough already. If he had not remarried it would have been an obligation to her. You would have called him a generous man. But that virtue can't be a part of everyone's life. Man is selfish. The whole world is based on selfishness.'

'The words love and respect should be erased from the dictionary. One should gain and benefit avariciously; the other should yield. Is that the policy of marriage? Why do we read books giving the life of an ideal man and woman both devoting their lives to save and make happy the life of one another?'

The father again was thoughtful and looked about for fresh ideas.

'Ideal books are written to eradicate the ills of the world. They, no doubt, set us examples, but man takes his own time to realize the truth and to follow them. Men with a spirit of self-sacrifice don't need any injunctions. Their very nature is a great teacher.'

'The question is what will be Nazni's position in that house with a rival creating hell for her day and night?'

'Many women have done it. Man's nature can adapt itself to any circumstances. A woman being ill trained, ignorant and ill used to her environment is more so. Living away from him is also wrong. It makes her feel guilty and incur blame. The lesser evil is to yield to him.'

'Yes, live in a hell,' said the son sarcastically.

'Hell or heaven is in one's mind. If she takes life as a sojourn, luck and misfortune as mere chances without attaching much importance to either of them, she can be happy in the worst surroundings.'

'Has she no rights? Should she be a product of circumstances, a puppet without feeling and life? Should she be a mere machine, an unpaid servant doing certain duties for the food and clothing she gets? Do you think the children of parents of unbalanced mind with different motives in life can develop strong characters? We are her well-wishers and must not leave her in a ditch,' said the son emphatically.

'As far as our support is concerned we will not grudge her anything, yet her life will be empty and devoid of womanly ambitions. A woman's ideal life is to have her home and children. Anything less than that seems vacant. Once a girl is married our responsibility towards her decreases. We maintain her not as a bounden duty but out of charity. Similarly she feels a stranger here. With all our efforts she will be as unhappy here as there. By the description of the woman he has brought I feel there will not be much trouble for Nazni.'

'Should we force her to go back to him?'

'We should force nothing upon her. We must leave it to her to decide. Her decision in the long run will be lasting. There are two antagonistic powers working before her. If one compels her to do something the other makes her do the opposite. Naturally she will yield to her husband. If she still loves him let her make a fair trail. Our concern now is for her health,' said Doulath Khan and asked the young man to go to bed and sleep over the idea. The next day would make him a better judge.

Nazni's brother still could not see eye to eye with his father. He held the strong opinion that his sister should have no connection with her husband. Should he force her to do it? His father's words that the decision should be her own rang in his ears. He lay in bed tossing restlessly. He thought of going to Nazni's room and converting her to his ideals, but the nurse was there and it was past twelve in the night. He dared not enter it. He had a disturbed night and in the morning he overslept. The disturbance at home due to Kabeer's arrival awoke him.

'Who's that running about?' he asked the servant who brought coffee for him.

'Nazni Begum's husband has come. The nurse is running about to get master's permission to allow him in.'

He could not believe his ears. The man after doing this atrocity—to come to see his wife! How was it possible for him to show his face to her? He jumped from his bed and stood in his pyjamas wondering whether to go straight to Kabeer and strangle him or kick him out. But second thoughts prevailed. He drank his coffee and lay down in bed.

'Tell me when he goes,' said he to the servant who returned to remove the tray.

'Who?'

'The visitor.'

'Kabir Miyan?'

'Yes, the dog.'

The news of the second marriage had spread among the servants. They had made inquiries as to the parentage, social status and character of Munira. The servant had intended to annoy him, and was elated at the burst of his anger. He turned with the tray and grinned.

Nazni's brother got up, had his bath, and dressed. He made a few rounds to the closed door of Nazni's room and heard a gentle sobbing. The nurse spied him and asked him what he wanted.

'I came to see Nazni,' said he and went to the portico to see if Kabeer's car was still there.

When he was having his breakfast, the nurse came to take Akram to his father.

'What are you doing?' he asked.

'Baby is wanted by his father.'

'Have you no sense, to take him to a sick room? Tell him he's asleep,' said he to the nurse who was pleased at this easy solution to the problem.

After breakfast, he went straight to Nazni's room.

'You seem better this morning,' said he.

'He has really remarried,' was the irrelevant answer.

'So you are free, like a bird. You are no more a slave. We had cruelly and heartlessly put you in chains, but you escaped. Luckily, you can live with us.'

'No, I can't. He asked me to go home soon, and said because of my stay here his mother remarried him.'

'In your present condition, to be taken in an ambulance accompanied by the nurses, I suppose,' said he sarcastically.

'Yes, he asked me to bring them there.'

'Will he pay ten rupees a day for them? His mother will die a hundred deaths before she pays them for a day.'

'He asked me to send them to Bavajan for it,' said Nazni shyly.

If Kabeer had been present he would have killed him then and there. But the fragile figure on the bed with tears flowing profusely moved him. He bent his head and stared at his clean shoe.

'Well, that's all right. The doctors won't allow you to go so soon.'

'Bhai, don't tell Bavajan. What'll he think of his meanness? I hope the doctor will not permit me to stir from my bed. I don't want to go there.'

'I am glad you are trying to be sensible. Your going there will mean our humiliation. I shall never see your face again,' said he hastily. 'We'll always be the same to you but not to your husband. We hate him and his very existence. You'll lose us all in caring for him.'

'Bhaijan, the world is cruel to me. I am tortured. I can't bear any more pain. Poison me,' said she, weeping.

He was agitated. Why should she be ill-treated for no fault of her own? He took her in his arms and wiped her tears.

'Don't think I am angry with you. You know I'd do anything for you. My anger towards your husband and your blind love for him made me cruel to you. In the sacrifice of his love you have won that of all of us. You don't know how sad we are,' said he stroking her head like a father.

Nazni felt as if she was in heaven, a world that had no ills. She felt comfortable on that brave breast. The gentle stroking seemed to take away all the worries from her head.

'Don't cry, you break my heart,' said he.

'I can't decide anything for myself. The world looks hideous to me. I don't know what to do.'

'There's time for everything. Forget him completely. When you are healthy we shall see what's to be done,' said he and laid her down gently as he heard the loud beating of her heart. He stretched her straight on the bed and covered her with the gold embroidered blue shawl.

'Bhai, keep your hand on my head. I feel happier,' said she.

He did so, and she was quiet for a time.

'Why can't I die and end all my worries? I feel as if I have lost everything in the world,' said she still crying.

'Hullo, you are here? Didn't you go to office?' said Doulath Khan who just entered.

'I forgot all about it. I don't feel quite well either. I shall send a leave note,' said the son.

'Nazni is improving. She'll be all right soon. If the doctor allows it we shall take her to the hills. It will do her a lot of good,' said the father.

'I should love to go to a place where I could hear nothing but birds' songs and see nothing but trees and flowers and rivers. I'll walk and run like a mad woman in the hills. Leave me there forever,' said she boldly.

Normally she would hardly speak in front of her father, even after her marriage. She was desperate and cared for no one and nothing.

'So that's that. You don't want us and even your sweet baby to be with you. Unless you make up your mind to be healthy and strong to travel you can't go anywhere.'

'I don't want to be healthy nor to go to him. If I get well I'll have to go there.'

Doulath Khan was surprised to hear her talk so boldly. Has she really made up her mind not to go there, or was it just a passing show?

'You are blind with anger, my dear child, and don't know what you are saying. Keep your head cool. You can judge better,' said the father. The hint was useful to both son and daughter.

'I tried my best to keep my head cool and temper humble. I tolerated every possible insult not to let this take place, but what's the use?' cried she.

'If you don't want to go you need not. We don't force you to do it,' said her father, who was disheartened to see her so dismayed.

'We shall go to Kashmir for a long stay. I shall take leave to keep company with you,' said her brother.

'Is it very far from here? Let it be very very far so that he may not know where I am and what has happened to me. Are there rivers? I shall drown and make my whole body cold. Oh it burns! I feel the heat unbearable. See how it is.'

'Yes, it is fever. Even we feel hot when we have it,' said the father despairingly.

'No it is not fever. This is something new. I never used to feel like this. The heat comes from my heart. I'll go mad, Bavajan, if you don't save me,' she began to cry.

'Send telegrams to house agents there and arrange everything immediately. We can take her in an ambulance to the train and can reserve a first class compartment,' said Doulath Khan.

The son was upset but controlled himself. 'Kick him and don't take anything to heart,' said he.

'Bhai, you don't know what it is and how I feel. Oh it is terrible! No one can understand my sufferings,' cried she.

'Let us go. She'll come to her senses when she's alone,' said the father. Nazni dreaded to be left alone. She could not bear the torture of her thoughts.

'I must go somewhere immediately. I don't want to see him again.'

'Well, we are arranging it. You need a change badly and it is decided,' said her brother.

Strict orders were given to the ladies not to enter Nazni's room, and for some days they obeyed implicitly. They had created a new whirl of excitement through the servants who generously kept them informed of the daily events in Kabeer's house. Their curiosity was satisfied to the point of satiation and sometimes they felt an inner urge to run to Nazni and reveal it. But the nurse held an iron rod over the entrance of her room. At length as her health ceased to cause anxiety the restriction was relaxed.

'Amma, we are going to Kashmir. It's very far from here. No one will come to know of me and compel me to go to that wretched house,' said Nazni to her mother.

'Yes, he told me all about it. We are making arrangements to go there soon.'

'I shall never come back once I go there.'

'You can do anything you like,' said the mother, knowing full well that Nazni after a few months would want to go back to her husband.

'How can she live there? Will her husband leave her?' said Granny.

'I am going there because I don't want to go to him.'

'People will throw stones at our house if we keep you here. You'll bring a bad name to your father. Who'll marry your sisters? You went to his house in a douli[2] and must leave it only in a doola,'[3] said the grandmother. Mother made a sign to her not to mention such things.

'It's her will and pleasure. She's free to do anything she likes. When he does what he likes why shouldn't she?' said mother.

Kabeer's visits to Nazni became less frequent and more formal. He no longer urged her to go home. On the other hand when he came to know of the whole family going to Kashmir he was pleased to be free of the bother of visiting her.

It was the season in Kashmir and Nazni got on well. She could walk long distances and ate normal food, but the painful feelings did not leave her. She kept an eager watch on the post peon to know if Kabeer wrote to her father or brother. Letter writing was Kabeer's weakness. He was afraid of spelling and grammar mistakes. He could not ask his clerks to do it. A letter to his father-in-law meant a good deal of deliberation and pain in recasting and rewriting. Moreover after his second marriage he had not met Doulath Khan, who also kept aloof.

The family stayed there for three months and it was getting cold. They returned and Nazni forgot all about her former plans. After her return she came to know that Jamila's new baby had come. As Kabeer had not been there to see her she did not like to accompany her mother when she went to see the baby.

'Jamila is still your friend. She said that she was sad to see the new woman at home and she told me to ask you to go back to your home,' said mother to Nazni.

'Did you see the new woman?' was the reply.

'Yes, she's nothing but a servant. Even a servant is paid and works for certain hours. Jamila said that no one has seen Kabeer speaking to her.'

'He never spoke to me in the presence of his mother and relations.'

'But you did not live in the kitchen and work as she does.'

'He is a man and can do anything he likes,' interrupted grandmother. 'Your only duty is to obey him. He can marry many wives or keep many outside. You are not supposed to pry into his private life. If he gives you food and clothing and looks after you there is nothing more you can ask for. Thank your stars he has brought an ugly woman and wants her to serve you. Other men marry young, rich and beautiful girls and make the first wife work for them.'

Before she went to Kashmir Kabeer had visited Nazni once in three or four days. After her return he did not turn up for about ten days. Nazni was miserable. She had not felt the waiting for him on the hills, but even where he lived she had to wait. On the third day after the visit of her mother to Jamila he came

'I didn't know of your return. Jamila told me your mother had come to see her and said that you were not well enough to accompany her. Aren't you well? You look quite well.'

'I have been waiting for you every day from the day I came here. Even on the hills I was anxious to hear from you.'

'Those miserable days of waiting for us are over. Come home soon. I have vacated my rooms for you and Akram.'

'Where do you live? What will the house be without you?'

'I have shifted to the front building. The clerks and the managers were having a good time at our cost. The income was falling and the expenses were increasing. Now I sit on their heads day and night. I have my food there also. Jamila's children keep up a sing-song the whole night. I used to get hardly any sleep.'

'Why should I come and for whom?'

'After you come home I shall see you more. I am disgusted with her ugly face, so I keep aloof.

'Akram's nurse is not willing to come with us.'

'Engage an ayah.⁴ These Anglo-Indian nurses are no good. They are the most discontented creatures on the face of the earth. I have private money now and no longer depend upon Ammajan. I shall pay all your expenses. How long will your parents help you?'

Nazni began to think that her fears were false. She now felt like laughing at them. Her husband had not only thought of her comfort by vacating his rooms but also had provided money for her expenses without his mother's knowledge. He was considerate even to her parents.

'Shall I come after Akram's birthday?'

'That's next month. Yes, it will be better. Jamila will soon go back and there won't be much disturbance at home.'

'Won't you come to see me again?'

'Of course. All my time, after my duty to earn our bread, is yours and Akram's,' said Kabeer and tried to kiss Akram, who was brought there on Nazni's instruction. The poor child did not know he was his father and gave a push to his cheek and screamed.

'He has forgotten me so soon. He will be all right when he comes home,' said he.

Chapter X

Marriage among Muslims is a lottery. Only those on whom luck smiles get a square deal as far as temperament, interest and beauty are concerned. Love does not begin before the marriage. It arises only from observation and use of the object. It is nourished not by intellect but by the service the woman renders the man. The greater the need the greater is the valuation of the idol.

Kabeer's disappointment with his second marriage gave him an urge and a firm determination to select a girl of his choice. But how? The choice had to be made by the ladies, the settlement by the elders, and performance by both the ladies and the gentlemen. What was his part during all those days of anxiety? A dumb spectator of the deeds and deliberation of others. His part started after the girl was brought home. Even then it could not be bold and straight-forward. The slightest expression of sympathy and support towards the object of his love might cause him to be dubbed a hen-pecked husband.

He could not give vent to his anger in the presence of his mother. He felt murderous towards Mustafa and many times thought of sacking him. But his sincerity and regards for his beloved master's son were unimpeachable. He was grieved to see Kabeer moody and made up his mind, if Kabeer permitted him, to get a decent girl for him and to get the stigma wiped out. He had indeed already made enquires through women he knew. He was satisfied with one girl coming from a respectable family, but had no courage to face Kabeer and put the proposal before him. He was waiting for an opportunity, when Kabeer himself provided it by calling him.

'Do you know the harm you did to me? For how long were you waiting to destroy my life and happiness? My confidence in you is lost by your one lunatic action,' said Kabeer one day in the office when everybody else had left.

'I am more conscious of it than you. I have been wretched all these months and ready to sacrifice my life for your happiness. From the day of the catastrophe I have spared no effort in looking for a suitable girl for you. Your second marriage was not the end but the beginning of your future happiness.'

'Yes, as you did it last time.'

'It was a blunder done through a woman. I was not wholly responsible for it. I gave you a list of girls with every possible description and acted according to your orders. You definitely gave me to understand that you cared for nothing but a healthy girl. A good-looking girl was shown to my sister. She was under that impression till the day of jalva. When she was dressed for it my sister happened to see her. She felt the shock of her life and left the place like a thief before you arrived there.'

'The same thing will take place even this time.'

'All that I have done this time is above reproach. I not only sent ladies to see the girl but I disguised a man as a woman-vendor and sent him. He became so familiar with the ladies of the house that they gave the history of the family and told him all about the marriageable girls and boys and the offers received. He saw your girl very closely and by the description he gave me I concluded that she is a beauty.'

'Who are they?'

'Faiz Mohammad Tahseeldar.'

'I have seen the father and the sons. They are quite fair.'

'I believe the girls are fairer and prettier. The girl I chose is the eldest among the girls. She manages the house, keeps an account of the father's income and expenditure, sings beautifully, plays the harmonium, and is good at needlework. This time you will have a wife to your entire satisfaction.'

'If my mother knows her she will die of heart failure.'

'She chose the first and second wives for you. Let this one be entirely of your choice.'

'Without consulting her I can do nothing. She is the financier and the ruler of the home,' said Kabeer.

'If you make up your mind there is nothing impossible. We can arrange for money. I shall ask them to keep the bride for a time you think suitable before bringing her home.'

'Will they agree?'

'I shall try. There is nothing like it.'

Kabeer had a difficult problem to face. To obtain permission from his autocratic mother and his sophisticated sister, who in her own interest supported monogamy, was an impossibility. He could play with Nazni in any way he liked as she was the most easily pleased person. Even more than permission the idea of finance distressed him. He had never cared to have private money. But now he needed a monstrous amount of money. As there was no hope of realising it by fair means he planned to get it by foul. He determined to sell some land, and get married. The days of guardianship had passed and it was not difficult to do it.

The second problem that faced him was Nazni's homecoming. The best plan was to shift to the front building before she returned and visit the zenana whenever necessary.[1] Shifting to the front building involved a complication. Except the front two rooms the rest were occupied by the office staff. He had to get them vacated and the pay of the occupants increased to meet the extra demand on their purse.

The third problem was how to introduce the question of shifting to his mother without creating suspicion. Once that was done the rest could take care of itself. At length a bright idea struck him. For two or three days he made an effort to keep awake.

'I can't sleep once I awake. The children's crying disturbs me,' said he to Munira and waited to see if she suggested shifting to the front building. She however tried to go to Jamila's room in the middle of the night to pacify the baby. One night he followed Munira to Jamila's room.

'Bhai, why have you come here at this time of the night?'

'I lie awake almost every night after one or two o'clock.'

'You don't sleep during the day, whereas we sleep after lunch. You must be feeling exhausted.'

'If I sleep in the day the whole office sleeps. Do you know what's the condition of the business now? No proper account of the income is kept, rents are not collected regularly and expenditure is more than income. This is all due to my trusting them. Unless I sit on their heads their mismanagement will ruin us,' said Kabeer as if he was greatly absorbed in the estate affairs.

'You used to sleep like a log even when the drums were beaten.'

'Those lucky and carefree days are gone. Now the slightest noise awakes me,' said he.

'Close the door of your room just as Ammajan does. She rarely hears their cries. You too used to do it last year.'

'I hear her speaking in your room in the middle of the night sometimes.'

'Oh it is very rarely she comes here, when all the three began to howl! God knows, Bhai, how worried I am about you, and do my best not to disturb or cause inconvenience by my presence' said Jamila despairingly. She presumed that her brother was hinting that she should leave home. As there was a rumour of Nazni's return he wanted rooms for her and their son.

'The child is a mountain. Mohammed should go to it. Instead of making him keep quiet we should adjust ourselves to suit him.'

Still she could not guess his motive. Who could ask the master of the house to leave his home and go away?

'Bhai, this is your home. You have every right to be comfortable. We are a nuisance to you. Confinement is the only excuse for which I can come home to see you and Ammajan,' said she feeling very unhappy.

'Jamila, it is your weakness. If I say that I can't sleep you think that I don't want you here. Instead of suggesting something useful to both of us, you make your life unhappy. Even if you don't want to come here I shall drag you out of the prison every year,' said Kabeer.

Munira was attending to the baby in the children's room. The shrill cry of the baby awoke them all. They began to talk loudly and clap to pacify the crying child. The noise brought Zuhra out of her den.

'What is this? Everybody is up as if it were Shababarath.'[2]

'Whenever the baby cries the other children begin their sing-song. He does not sleep soundly in the night. I feed him whenever he gets up to make him quiet but he vomits and cries,' said Jamila.

'Give him a pinch of bhasm.[3] Put a dot of kajal on his right cheek before you put him to bed. He is fair you know, and people are jealous and cast an evil eye.[4] Even if they don't happen to see him evil nymphs hover about the child's room in the evening. It is always better to be on the safe side.

Don't forget to burn some broomsticks with spices and incense.[5] Rub a bit of the burnt ashes on his cheek every night,' said Zuhra.

'I do all that and more. He being the only boy you don't know what care I take of him,' said Jamila.

'Then give him a pill of morphia for sleep. You can't kill yourself for his sake.'

'When I was giving it to Looloo he was angry with me and stopped it.'

'If he is kept awake the whole night he will have nothing to say. No mother brings up her children without giving it.'

'He said children become dull and don't learn.'

'I was giving it to you and Kabeer till you were about two years old. The whole night he used to sit up if it was not given. What happened to you? Are you a dunce? Didn't he learn? Don't tell him about it but keep the pills with you and administer one when you feed the baby. He talks of things which no one has heard or done. Is he going off his head? Or what is it?'

'I shall ask Akram's nurse about it. He sleeps the whole night without the least noise. You say he has stomach trouble. That may be the cause for it,' said Kabeer.

'Every word he utters is preceded either by the name of Doulath Khan or Nazni. Their deeds and thoughts have become his kalima.[6] He wants to ask the nurse for it as if we have not reared children. He wants to disgrace us before them. If she does not give it to him he may begin giving him brandy. Those godless wretches have brought destruction to our house. It is beyond anybody to put a baby to bed without a sleeping dose,' said Zuhra.

Since he was remarried Zuhra had often used harder words, but now he thought it was his chance. He had to hit hard while the iron was hot. Apparently he lost his temper and said, 'Tomorrow I am shifting to the front building. Everyone takes advantage of me. I will die if I keep awake night after night. After all this sacrifice what do I get in reward? Nothing but rebuke, insult and sarcastic talk.' He got up to go to his room.

'You are serving everyone at your cost! There's no greater truth. Think of the lakhs of rupees spent for his marriages.[7] The enormous amount of money spent in running this house and I working from morning to night in preparing things he likes. You ungrateful wretch! God's punishment will fall on you,' said Zuhra.

'I am fed up with all that you have done and have been doing for me. In this house everything is done to suit others and I am made a scapegoat. I don't want to have anything to do with anybody. I shall make arrangements for myself. Don't prepare any food for me hereafter,' said Kabeer.

Jamila's doubts were confirmed. Her brother was angry because of her children. She determined not to come to his house any more. He had been sympathetic so long as he was not remarried but now the interest of his wives was supreme. As he went away she began to cry.

'Bhai, don't go from your house. I shall go back tomorrow without delay. I did not think of you and your comfort but I thought of mine. I was selfish,' cried she and held his hand tight to prevent him from leaving the room.

'Why do you cry? He wants to boss over us. When he starves he will realise our sacrifices. So long as I am alive this house is yours as well as his. I am here to give you comfort,' said Zuhra.

'Don't cry, Jamila. I am rooted out from this house. You have nothing to do with my grievances. On the other hand you have been my sympathiser. You make me feel at home. The hotels are not destroyed. I can have anything I like there. Mother, I will neither starve nor come back to you,' said he.

He snatched his hand away and left the room. Zuhra was surprised and shocked at the attitude of her only son. She felt that her behaviour towards him had not been right and she had to recognise the position in the family. The teaching of her sister-in-law to put her foot down and control both son and daughter-in-law had proved a mistake.

'Bhai is unhappy. He told me once that you are changed and insult him before his wife. His wife's people laugh at his loss. We at least should try to be kind to him. Without it his life will be a misery,' said Jamila.

Zuhra realised the truth of every word. They were like daggers to her heart.

'We have to co-operate with him in adverse circumstances. He has no peace of mind. If we don't understand his feelings who will?' said Jamila again.

'He is either moody or impertinent. He keeps away from me and he is indifferent, which makes me lose my temper,' said Zuhra thoughtfully.

'You must let him have his own way. Let him shift to the front building. We shall insist upon his having his food at home. He is a married man and a father. We can't treat him disrespectfully in the presence of his wives.'

'He is up to something. His wife was not here yet he lost his temper. Perhaps he does not want to live with me but he can't say so to my face. I live only for him. My life without him will be impossible,' said Zuhra excitedly.

'I don't think he wants it. All his life he has been very considerate and obedient to you.'

'If I allow him to live in the next house he will go astray. There will be no one to check him.'

'He knows best what is good for him. Our interference will only drive him out of our reach. When Bhabi comes home he is sure to return to his old rooms,' said Jamila.

Zuhra sat down for some time resting her chin on her left palm. Munira brought the sleeping baby to be given to Jamila. The mother-in-law who was feeling tired left the room.

The next morning Munira overslept and the cook was slow as usual in preparing the breakfast. Kabeer left the house without a word to anybody. Zuhra came to know of it and when the breakfast was ready she sent for him. He refused flatly to come. Jamila advised her to send his breakfast to the front building.

It was a wise plan. Kabeer had openly said he was not going to have food prepared at home yet he felt the difficulty of getting it from outside. It would let people know of the disagreement between him and his mother. He ate everything that was sent with entire satisfaction at the success of his scheme. After some time the servants came to remove his bed and other necessities. No one objected or prevented them.

He kept aloof for some days. This of course agitated Munira but what could she do? When he did not come to see his own mother and sister where was the sense in feeling anxious for him? Jamila felt wretched and planned to go back but thought of informing him of it.

'I am going home next week. I have asked him to come to take us,' said she indifferently.

'My fight is not with you. You are the one source of comfort at home. Your people will take you to task if you go before time.'

His scheme had gone well. Why should he annoy her and send her back before three months after the delivery? He made her understand that he was happy for her to stay. He even brought presents for her children one day. He had his dinner with her that night and slept in his old room.

'I have had a talk with Faiz Mohammed,' said Mustafa one day to Kabeer.

'What did he say?'

'One of his conditions is a block in our way.'

'What's that?'

'He wants the mahar to be paid in advance. It may be in the form of cash or a property to be registered in the girl's name before the marriage.'

'Because...I will not be able to maintain her! Tell him that we are not fakirs.'

'He is afraid of your two wives and prefers an official bachelor.'

'My wives are not marrying her. They know nothing of it. You ought to have told him there was only one. The other is only a servant.'

'When I said it he laughed at me and said that she is going to be the mistress soon with her child.'

Kabeer was perplexed. Munira's conception was known to Zuhra who had warned her not to reveal it to Kabeer.

'Is she getting a baby? Well, we shall think of it afterwards. Tell him so long as the rider is strong the mare will have no fear, and his attitude will create suspicion in my mind. It is not good to sew a bitter seed in a field after the hard labour.'

'I said many more such things to no effect. He definitely asked me to drop the matter if I can't settle on his conditions.'

'Then try in other places. We can't be dictated to by the woman's people.

'We can't be sure of all that we want in other places. It may take years to find a suitable girl. Our choice is not direct; we have to depend upon a third person, and draw our own inferences leaving a big margin for feminine fancies. The mahar is inevitable and it makes no difference if we pay in advance. It is the transfer of the building: the rent will be realised by us as usual.'

'How much does he want?'

'He demanded twenty thousand. I brought it down to ten. The corner cottage will serve the purpose.'

'How much does it cost and what's its rent?'

'Formerly we used to get fifty but now in its dilapidated condition we are getting thirty five.'

'She will have enough to live upon if she dislikes living with us.'

'He is also giving her a house or a shop. He is bent upon performing a simple marriage. You'll get the rent of her building too.'

'It means a rope will be given to her to hang me.'

'Let us not think of the dark days at the threshold of a happy occasion. No Muslim woman will separate from her husband.'

'When do they want it?'

'Any time you please.'

'Doulath Khan's family is in Kashmir now. Let it be done before their return, and ask them to keep her there till I find a suitable time to bring her home. By the by how much do we want for the marriage expenses?'

'They are doing it simply. We need not spend much.'

'I sold the three-cornered field as it was unlucky to keep. We shall manage within the amount.'

'Oh, that is more than we need.'

Mustafa and Kabeer did the purchasing and a few hundreds were given to Faiz Mohammed to buy other paltry things on behalf of the bridegroom. Kabeer kept everything he bought under lock and key in his office. His friend was requested to send his mother and wife to Faiz Mohammed's house to play the parts of Zuhra and Jamila. The marriage was simple and private. Faiz Mohammed had invited a few close friends but Kabeer invited nobody.

The lunch on the marriage day and dinner for a week continuously sent by Zuhra were enjoyed by the office servants on Kabeer's instructions.

After the marriage Kabeer was very kind and considerate to his sister and mother. He often visited the zenana and stayed there for a long time. Sometimes he had his dinner and even slept in his old room.

'Have you noticed the change in Bhai? He is his normal self again, because we allowed him to have his own way. We must try to keep up our changed attitude towards him,' said Jamila one day to Zuhra.

'I am not at all satisfied with him. He seems quite different to me,' said Zuhra.

One day Jamila received a letter from her husband. She was perplexed by its contents. She tried to associate the events at home with what it said, but failed.

'I received this letter from him today,' said she to Zuhra.

'What does he say?'

'Here it is. I brought it to read to you.'

'My dear Jamila,

Ahmed came here the other day and said that he was knocked out by your brother. The poor fellow is extremely upset and dejected. He has been engaged to a girl for a long time and the marriage was postponed on account of the heavy mahar they demanded. He says he was almost in love with her as she was beautiful, accomplished, a beautiful singer and player on the harmonium and able to manage an estate. How did your brother wangle her for his second wife whereas poor Ahmed failed to have her for his first? I wonder what sort of life she will live in your mother's house. Her talents will be killed by not being used. Kabeer is a lucky chap, congratulate him on my behalf. He did not care even to inform me of it. I should not hide my feelings towards him. He must have spent an enormous amount to possess her. I was anxiously waiting for your letter to hear more details but it came to me as a great surprise. You mention nothing of the happy activities in which you are taking part. Your letter is of later date yet nothing is said in it. Is it due to your fear of myself becoming a polygamous husband? Or is it because you thought I was not important enough to know of it? I shall come soon to bring you and hope the baby will be well enough to travel.

Yours ever,

Mehar'

While reading the letter, Jamila omitted two sentences where he had mentioned her mother's house. Zuhra heard it very silently.

'Our purdah system is a blessing. If he had seen Munira he would not have called her beautiful. Let him think that Kabeer's wives are praiseworthy,' said Zuhra.

'He says that the father demanded a big mahar. Munira has no father.'

'She has an uncle who must have demanded it.'

'He did not ask us.'

'They demand this and that with poor people. Your brother's wealth is enough to make them compromise with his name.'

'He says she is an accomplished girl and could run an estate.'

'There's no doubt about it. A woman who turns out such a lot of work at home can easily manage an estate. Don't you hear her singing? Why are your daughters mad after her if not for that?'

'What shall I write to him? He thinks we look down upon him and so did not care for his opinion.'

'Write to him that the information received by him is not quite true. We are greatly disappointed in his second marriage. We have kept it a secret. I had asked you not to tell him,' said Zuhra.

Jamila was still dissatisfied. She could not understand what her husband had written. But there was nothing else to suspect so she had to believe. She could not show the letter to Kabeer as her husband had expressed a bad opinion about her mother.

'Bhai, do you know what people say about Munira?' she asked when she saw him next. 'They say she is beautiful, a singer, an organiser and what not, but you condemn her.'

'If they saw her with my eyes they dare not say anything else,' said Kabeer indifferently, little knowing about whom it was said and who had said it.

Chapter XI

Maghbool Kabeer's third wife, was a beauty according to the feminine estimation. She was fat but well proportioned, and of medium height, the broad chest and comparatively slim waist making her figure very attractive. The broad, high forehead, with long nose, thin red lips with rosy cheeks, quite big almond-shaped eyes with dark, curved eyebrows, long lashes and the natural jet-black curls dressed round the forehead would have been a very good model for an artist.

She was an institution in herself. Her mastery over the Urdu language had made her crazy after papers, magazines, romance and poetry. She had a natural bent for music and had learnt many songs from the radio, pictures and even from beggars. Her rich voice had given them a feminine touch and sweetness. The whole family admired her singing and young girls and boys crowded the room to hear it. She made it a point to sing after the streets were quiet. Her father was fond of it and found solace in it after his day's hard work. Maghbool knowing of her father's liking used to try to learn something new and thrilling almost every day.

She was a good organiser and an economical manager of the house. From the day she took over the management she saved several hundreds a month. She kept accurate accounts. Her father often said that she was a son to him, his secretary and his right hand.[1] She was active and hated to while away her time. Needlework, designing and painting were her hobbies. Everything she did was self-learnt, and she did it so exquisitely that an expert in that art would say that she had reached a fair level of perfection. There was nothing that she could not do and whatever she did she did beautifully.

Getting one's children married is the primary duty of parents; they are held responsible by God if they leave them unmarried. As a rule the unmarried man is the breaker of law, but a girl can under no circumstances be left a spinster. If unable to get a suitable husband of proper age for her, parents have to give up the search for a qualified man and hand her over to a blind or a lame man. This idea had put terror into the hearts of girls and their parents, and in view of the ill consequences of failure they often yield to the first offer. The idea of marrying and separating from her had always been painful to both her parents. Her father often said that she would not be separated by marriage or he would part with her only when he secured the best man in the world. But all offers that came to her were either from poor officials or rich widowers. He despised the former and hated the latter. A high official would consider it beneath his dignity to get himself married to the daughter of a tahseeldar. Besides how could such a one come to know that here was such an invaluable hidden gem?

When she reached the age of twenty unmarried, her old lady relations began to look down upon her as a hideous being whom no man had condescended to recognise. Some of them found fault with her beauty and some said she could not get a husband because she came third in the family. She was a sinner and each breath of hers was equivalent to a curse. They would not be surprised if some terrible thing happened to one of the parents for their sin. They remarked sarcastically that she had wasted her age, energy and beauty which would have been advantageously used in wifehood and motherhood. Tired of taunts and the ceaseless remarks by the ladies at home her father resolved to get her married. As he could not get a man of his choice he determined to give her to a man who did not care to marry but valued money. Her savings with him had come to ten thousand rupees and he did not like to make use of it. He wanted to give her a big surprise in her marriage present. Poor man, if he had announced the gift he would have secured the best husband for her.

Maghbool's idea of life was quite different from that of other girls. Her vast study of romance and her passion for music had put before her an ideal married life. It meant to her a heaven on earth under the protection of a man who would be all love and would care for her desires, comfort and even whims and fancies—a selfless man as depicted in love songs. The admiration and regard given her at home had developed a high sense of self-importance and self-respect in her. She believed that God by bestowing upon her unique gifts had reserved for her a superb life. He had meant her to be something in the world, and that part of her life was awaiting her after her marriage when she would be freer to make use of her talents.

When the talk of her marriage was going on at home she did not hide herself in a corner and leave her fate to the mercy of others. Unlike other girls she overheard every word about it. She condemned all those who supported Kabeer's proposal and could not understand how they could be blind to the consequences. She pitied those creatures who could not see beyond their nose, and had a strong confidence in her father's power of judgment. She thought that he would never be contaminated by the influence of the lunatic ladies at home. How could he, a sensible man, agree to make a prey of her to this three-headed dragon who had nothing to give her for all that he would take from her?

One day she managed to hide herself in a place from where she heard her father talk with her mother. To her surprise he was not an exception and was of the same mind as his better half. The shock had a paralysing effect on her.

She stealthily went to her room and was lost in thought. Why had he not accepted the previous offer of Ahmed? Was it because he was not so well off? What more would she get by being the wife of a rich man except richer food and clothing? Would they give her entire happiness in life? Are they the only means of happiness? Are there not men and women living happily without those solaces? Could she not have tried to be happy with the frugal food and scanty garments given by that one master? Was it possible for her to please four masters, her rivals, her husband and her mother-in-law? Why had he demanded a heavy mahar from Ahmed? Was it to keep up his name and prestige? Or was it to safeguard her interests? How many men pay it? Not even one per cent. How many get it excused and then show their true colours? Will it make him a saint? Are not limited means to a certain extent a hindrance in the free play of one's instincts?

Maghbool's hopes in her father were shattered. She was miserable beyond words. She found herself among heartless people who were anxious only to get rid of their responsibility and to please society. She confined herself to her bed and gave up all her activities. When food was brought to her she made the servant eat it and take back the empty plates.

She thought she would express her dislike for the man and so escape the calamity. Whom to say it to and how? It meant a revolt against the established dogmas. She would be treated as a leper by everyone. No one would marry her if she was known as a rebel. She pictured herself married to lame and blind men. An awful fright entered her mind and she felt a palsy had smitten her. She thought that her refusal would be a sin against her God-sent parents. Would not that life be a worse torture than merely being one of many wives?

Should she let sleeping dogs lie and yield? A girl of so pushful a nature could not be passive. A ray of light shone in her mind. She would go to her widowed aunt and beg of her to break the engagement. Many times she went to her aunt's room, but she could never bring herself to utter the fateful words. At length she gave up the idea as hopeless. She was so worried that she could not sing. Her father sent for her to sing, but she gave an excuse. He thought she felt shy to appear in front of him, and was sad at her coming separation from them. One day he became impatient to hear her sing and went to her room and compelled her.

'Don't desert us so soon, Maghbool. We too have a claim on your gifts. Do oblige us now and then,' said he.

Maghbool took the harmonium and played a sad song which she had composed herself during her days of seclusion:

Life is hard and harder for the ill-trained
The world is dark and darker for the ill-omened.
Social customs and dogmas are worshipped,
Human feelings and interest are suppressed.
The world moves with the rising tide
And even the dear and the near ones ride.
Might is right and the mighty survive
The weak who yield and do not strive.
The sufferers are tormented and tortured
Even Death takes delight in their torture.
Death scorns and condemns his admirers
And humiliates himself and cringes before his haters.
O Death, do not anguish and distress the happy ones
To fulfil one's hopes is the noblest action.
The cheerful ones do not need you,
The sufferers invite and welcome you.
Their only resource is to escape with you,

Their wounds are healed only by you.
Do not turn your face from your aspirers,
Do not force yourself upon your haters.
Be just and respect yourself
And come to me, an adorer of yourself.

Faiz Mohammed was absorbed in listening to the sad tune and did not notice the words.

'You are playing something new today. It is so sad and pathetic that it brings tears even to the hardest soul. Do sing it again, you will make me wiser,' said he.

Maghbool opened her mouth to obey him and felt a big lump in her throat. She made an effort but it only brought tears to her big eyes. She looked at him lovingly and said,

'Abba, I can't. However I try to please you it is beyond me to sing.' She began to cry noiselessly and left the room. Her father was moved but was unaware of the cause of her unhappiness. At the same time he admired her sense of gratitude towards him. People would not write poems on the love of home, he thought, if it was not really dear to them. The girl was so sad because she had stayed at home so long.

A ladies' tailor was announced to make blouses for the bride. Her aunt went to Maghbool to take her for measurements.

'The tailor has been waiting a long time, come and be done with him,' said aunt who was excited with the numerous activities going on at home in connection with the ensuing marriage.

'Measurement for what? Is it for my shroud? I shall give you a nice pattern for it,' said Maghbool.

'Girls should not talk like that. What will people say? Who does not get married? Girls are born to be separated from their parents one day or the other. You were lucky to be with them for twenty years. At the time of happy events you should not mention ill-omened names. Be thankful to God that your marriage is performed by your parents. Think of the orphans who cry their hearts out at their marriages because they are not lucky enough to have their parents to see their great day.'

Custom says that one must not embrace a widow, but Maghbool cried to her heart's content on her breast. She went mechanically to the tailor and after the measurements had been taken secluded herself in her den.

A girl friend came to see her one day and finding her extremely sad said, 'What's the matter with you, child? You are sad beyond words. New life should not be commenced with tears.'

'Tears are ahead of me for life, so I want to get used to them.'

'Marriage does mean sorrow.'

'Mine means more than that. It is a gallows waiting for a murderer.'

'But why? They say he is very rich.'

'They don't say other things about him. I mean his wives and children.'

'Oh goodness! Not wife but wives! Why did you not tell your mother secretly that you don't want him? She would have taken the blame herself and rejected him.'

'The idea has tortured me day and night, but how to say it? I found them all bent upon pushing me into the sea.'

'Shall I do you a little service?'

'If you dare do it you will make me grateful for life.'

The girl left the room with enthusiasm to do a good deed, but being snubbed by everybody returned dejectedly.

'Your mother asked me not to spoil you anymore. I told her that I went to her to plead on your request.'

'What did she say?'

'Shall I tell you the exact words?'

'Do, please.'

'She asked me to tell you to shut your mouth and be contented with God's will. If you say anything more in that connection she will thrash you with a broom to serve you right. She added that she waited for twenty years to get a good man. You are unlucky and all her attempts failed. She can't wait even a day more as the other girls will pass the marriage age and will bring disgrace to the family.'

'Didn't I tell you the futility of it? All of them are bent upon killing me. No human power will change them.'

Maghbool, with no food, no peace of mind and no rest grew pale as pale could be, so much so that she fainted on the takhat at the time of the jalva. In consequence Kabeer had to wait till very late in the night and so slept. When she came to her senses Faiz Mohammad took her to him and made a short speech asking him to make her life happy.

'I fell in love with you before seeing you. Now I adore you,' said Kabeer to Maghbool, and waited for an answer.

Maghbool had hated him right from the day she heard of his numerous wives. His words rang like a death-knell in her ears. His very touch seemed like a snake-bite. She would have abhorred to answer his questions and was thankful for the custom which forbids a bride to talk or look at the bridegroom at least for three months and his people for six. He could not be vexed by her silence and ill-treat her. The law was on her side.

'I sacrificed everybody else for you. I discarded them all before I came to you,' said he again. No answer. He was surprised. Nazni had begun to speak from the third day.

'The praise of your beauty and of your skill made me mad. I was dying to see you and to call you mine, but now I feel my love is one-sided,' said he again.

How could he pronounce such loving words? Perhaps he wanted to make up for divided regard and lost love. Could she use such endearing words to him when her mind was prejudiced?

'I gave you your mahar in advance,' said he again. 'It is enough proof of my love for you. I put no value on money where your happiness is concerned. You can buy lots of things out of the rent. You need not ask me or my mother for your petty needs. I gave nothing to the other two except what they got at the time of their weddings. Of course they do not count in our life now. One is only a servant and the other is a ghost. You are above them.'

It took her a long time to make up her mind to speak to him. Whenever she tried she found harsh and sarcastic words coming to her mouth. The ladies at home asked her what he said. She repeated his words. They were thrilled. Such a rich man to love her so dearly! Sometimes they asked her what she said. She told them that she had not opened her mouth yet. They were annoyed and said any other man would not have seen her face again.

'Are you still angry with me? What have I done to deserve such a severe punishment? Do you know what happened to me when you fainted? A little more strain would have killed me there. My whole body was shivering with fright. When your father brought you I was unconscious of his presence.'

'A beggar's anger does no harm to others. She is punished instead of punishing others. I was under a false impression that extreme sorrow drives away sleep, but you are lucky. A good sleep releases one from suffering and makes a man feel fresh,' said she in her first talk to him.

Kabeer at once knew where to put her. He could not deal with her in the same spirit. He must change his attitude.

'It was not sleep, I fainted. But being stronger than you I could stand it better. By the by, why did your father get the house registered in your name before he gave his consent?' said Kabeer. The matter of the house had been on his mind a great deal. He could not help but let it out.

'Did he do so? I have no idea. He must have done it on purpose.'

'Is it because he had no confidence in my love?'

'One can create confidence in others by one's selfless deeds. People without living together cannot have confidence in one another. Naturally he could not have it in you.'

'He ought to have known at least that if a man married a third time he usually becomes his wife's slave. He ought to have confidence in your unique powers, which will make any man give not only one house but all that he possesses. He did not have the magnanimity of heart.'

'He is not an ordinary man. You can't judge him so easily. Should he not have thought so much for me after the harm he did for me?'

'Yes, yes. He did you great harm by not trusting my sincerity. He tried to make trouble for both of us. My love for you is like a vast ocean, where all particles are washed away. Nothing can prevent the movement of its surging waves. In spite of his meanness I complied with his request,' said Kabeer and was proud of his ingenuity.

Maghbool felt like laughing but controlled herself. She wondered where to put him, with the lunatics or in the category of the highest type of rogues.

Kabeer had to please too many masters. When his sister wanted to go back home before the due date he stayed at home to effect a reconciliation with her. He had his dinner and even slept there. Then he wanted to bring Nazni home and had to follow the same procedure. Whenever such necessity arose he neither sent word to Maghbool nor told her of his plans beforehand. She did not ask him for the reason of his not coming and thought it was beneath her dignity to do so. But one day her patience reached its limit.

'Did the ghost or the servant influence you to stay away? Everyone was waiting for dinner for a long time. You at least ought to have sent word to me,' said she.

'My sister was disheartened with my cruel treatment of her. I was trying to clear her misunderstanding. It took a long time and it was time for dinner. They forced me to have it with them. After that I felt too lazy to stir out of the house. Although my body was there my soul was with you and your picture was in my heart.'

'I see. Didn't you tell them that you had to come here?' she said sarcastically. She knew that he had married her without their knowledge.

'None of them know of our marriage. They are very jealous people and would not have allowed me to marry you. I intend to tell them of it. I shall do it after my sister goes. Then I shall take you there and we shall never pass a day without seeing one another.'

'So I am only your mistress and do not deserve any recognition by your people.'

'You are my mistress,' said he, 'the queen of my heart and everything in the world to me. Usually love begins after the marriage but ours began before it. That shows our marriage was registered by God and heaven. If people recognise it or not what do we care? It is all God's work. I must be grateful to Mustafa who found you for me. He must have got an inspiration. Our marriage is sacred.'

'Are not all marriages sacred? Are they not based on selflessness and all kind of sacrifices for one another? It is said that a man and a woman have to be fated to live together, but some are destined to live with three or four.'

'Marriages performed by two loving persons are holy. Not others. The elders choose and do everything so the chief person concerned has nothing to do but yield.'

She often gave him a headache by her complicated questions. She always weighed her words before uttering them. She was a strong supporter of her parents and would get cross if he spoke lightly of them.

'Although our marriage is sacred you have no courage to announce it. One should be proud of having done a noble thing. You want to take me in by the back door.'

'I shall take you by the front door. When once my mother comes to know of it we will have no fear.'

'Will the ghost be there when I go? Of course the servant will be there to work for us. By the by did the servant get her baby?'

'Don't pronounce the names of those wretches. The very mention of them gets on my nerves. Life is short but full of miseries. Let us be happy without creating unnecessary unpleasant feelings. What do we gain by such talk?'

'Their names make me mad too but I thought you felt pleased with them. As you know, now and then you get into a mood to please them. Now I see you really don't like them. I read in a book that man has double teeth like an elephant. People have the audacity to write such rot and send it to be printed. What I don't like, you too despise, so where is the hidden tooth?'

'I discarded, rejected and despised them all when I married you. Even supposing I talk to them sometimes it is only to keep a smiling face on them. Otherwise they will curse us. A disappointed woman's curse had destroyed many a man. I don't care if they only do it to me but if they do it to you to destroy my happiness I will be helpless.'

'So one's love has a quality of change. Does it change with the winds?'

'Love is an ocean. It changes and yet it is the same. The tossing of the waves makes no difference as it is temporary. One should take the rise and fall of the waves as outside enjoyments. Love in the early stage of life is not constant and it is mere child's play. There is no strong sentiment or attachment for one's object.'

'I see you speak very humorously. Your love for me is a product of old age. So there is no fear of its change. Don't they say that love comes only once in one's life?'

This was a hard question. The answers he had contemplated for days together were exhausted. There was no ready reply so he pretended to snore. Maghbool looked this side and that in the room to discover if there was a third person to overhear their talk, but how could there be?

Chapter XII

A telegram from Mehar Rasool, Jamila's husband, was received to the great excitement of the whole family. He was coming to take his family home and someone had to go to the station to receive him. Kabeer was sent for by Zuhra but no trace of him could be found. Mustafa, questioned, said that he had gone to visit the tenants, and then hurried to inform Kabeer of the agitation at home. In spite of his multifarious engagements Kabeer found time to go to the station.

'You are a lucky fellow. Luck smiles on you almost every year by bringing you a fresh, new stock whereas others rot for years. Before the congratulation for the first marriage got stale you created an occasion for their renewal. This is one of the ways of becoming prominent. If you had informed me mine would have been the first. How did you wangle that coveted girl?'

'Which...which one...who told you?' gasped Kabeer.

'You've just married Faiz Mohammad's daughter, haven't you?'

'Yes—but there is another.'

'That is your first wife for whom you were giving your life.'

'No, mother brought one.'

'Then the recent one is your third wife?'

'Yes.'

'You seem to have aimed at capturing the whole feminine world on the pretext of Tabligh-e-Islam,'[1] said Mehar.

'Whatever may be the purpose, mother brought one from the slums. I was fed up with her so I married the one you speak of.'

'So the first one does not count even numerically?'

'We are not speaking of her now. She is there. Where else can she go?'

'So Faiz Mohammad's daughter is your favourite now. How long will your sentiment for her last? Till you get a fresh hand, I suppose,' said Mehar.

'How did you know of it? No one knows of it here.'

'Are people blind, deaf, and dumb? They are more interested in such things than in anything else, and such tidings travel faster than any means of conveyance.'

'You live so far from us. Who told you in that village?'

'Don't let your imagination run away with you. The world is very small. Today, distances don't count but one's gain or loss is steadily kept in view by everybody.'

'That does not matter. Neither Ammajan nor Jamila knows of it.'

'If the ladies of your house do not know of it, it does not mean that all are kept in the dark. Your gain had been Ahmed's loss. Naturally, the subject has been discussed in detail by many men,' said Mehar.

'Was he trying there?'

'Didn't your sister tell you about it? I wrote a letter to her.'

'She has not told me. It is surprising.'

'Then the mother and the daughter are hand in glove and are plotting to catch you unawares.'

'There has been no change in them. On the other hand, they are more considerate and obliging to me these days.'

'You can't judge them by that. Their regard for you may be out of policy.'

'I have noticed their affected behaviour is temporary, but this is sincere.'

'How have you managed to keep it secret so long?

'I stopped the visits of all strangers both male and female and left the bride in her father's house. I shifted to the front building. I get my food and sleep there so no one knows of my activities.'

'Do you ever go to your first wife? Does she know of it?'

'She was in Kashmir. After her return I saw her twice and found her her natural self. She is a woman of few words, always passive like a lamb and indifferent to consequences.'

'You have proved a big scoundrel. I can't imagine myself in your position. But one thing I unhesitatingly say, that you have made a mess of your life and have wantonly destroyed your happiness. True happiness does not come by double-dealing. You will have no real sympathiser in life.'

'Don't mention it to Jamila. I want to say it myself to Ammajan. Let her not know through another source. My position in the house will be awkward. No one will trust me.'

'Your action has belied their trust. You can't expect roguery and trust to go together.'

'There is a time for everything. Mother is not ready to face an expense of several thousands. She will die of heart failure. I must gradually bring her round to my point of view.'

'You lack moral courage. The direct way of doing things is happier,' said Mehar.

'Let it be whatever it is, don't tell anybody at home. Do oblige me. You will not repent it.'

'Okay, I shall try not to let you down.'

They came home. Kabeer was nervous. He had no confidence in his brother-in-law, yet he could do nothing else but trust his goodness. He determined not to go to Maghbool during his short sojourn, and to meet Mehar often to remind him of his promise.

'So your new sister-in-law is from the slums?' said Mehar maliciously to Jamila.

'She is just the head-cook. Everyone treats her like a servant. Mother was deceived, poor Bhai was upset and even now he hates to see her face and lives in the next house. She is more mother's servant than Bhai's wife.'

'Does he live in the office because he can't bear to see her? Is he doing the right thing? He married her and has her in his house, yet he lives outside. What an innocent creature you are!'

'Why, what of it?' said Jamila.

'Oh nothing. Is she so ugly that he is driven out of the house?'

'Ugliness is not the word for it. Peep through the window. You can see her walking up and down with things. You have seen the cook so any other person than she is the newcomer.'

Mehar very patiently began to peep through the window now and then. Munira knowing the presence of a second man at home had reduced her activities. She confined herself to the kitchen and made the cook fetch and carry things. In spite of his vigilance for two days he was not able to see Munira. Finally Jamila and Mehar made a plot, the latter to bring her somehow or the other opposite to their room. Jamila started putting beds and clothes in the sun and asked Munira to help her while Mehar peeped through the keyhole of his room.

'Baba, I am going to tell Munira,' said his little girl, who had entered the room through the bathroom.

'What do you want to tell her?' said Mehar puzzled.

'You saw her through the key-hole.'

'Who is Munira? I was repairing the lock because I could not close the door,' said Mehar holding the knob and twisting it nervously.

'I know what you did. The lock is all right. See how nicely it is locked. You are telling lies.'

'Bi Bi, Baba saw Munira through this hole,' said the mischievous girl when Jamila re-entered the room.

'He is not a bad man. Only bad people look at women. Don't you know that God puts melted lead in men's eyes if they see women? The hole is very small. You can't see through it,' said Jamila perplexed.

'When I play hide and seek with Lulu I see her through it. I know what Baba did,' was the persistent answer.

'I was cleaning the lock of the door.'

'Your hands were at your back and your eye was on the hole. You did not clean it. I know what you did,' said the girl.

Jamila was in a fix. If the people of the house came to know of it they would think ill of her husband. There would be enmity between Kabeer and Mehar for life.

'Who will see a servant? Don't tell lies. If you say it to anybody at home I shall slap you and never bring you here,' said Jamila.

'I did not tell a lie. Baba did it,' said the bold child, and ran away. Jamila attempted to catch her.

'Don't strike her. You will make matters worse. The key-hole was full of cobwebs. I cleaned it and before I had a glimpse of Munira the little devil dashed from the back and shouted,' said Mehar.

'You ought to have closed the back door. She was playing in the opposite room. I had an intuition of it. So I came to see. Never mind. Munira is not respected by Bhai. Otherwise he would not have excused you for anything in the world.'

'What a monster she is. No wonder he hated to live in the house and as a revenge married Ahmed's would-be wife.'

'Was Ahmed trying to marry Munira?'

'What a simpleton you are. Will Ahmed marry a woman from the slums? A bachelor and a man of position was after the most accomplished girl.'

'Has Bhai married a third time? Ammajan and I had a discussion about your letter, but I was not at all convinced when she said you meant Munira.'

'I am forbidden from making mention of it to you. I never dreamt that your own brother, for whom you would give your life, had kept you in the dark. I was annoyed with your letter not knowing the truth. It is the way of the world. The innocent and frank are distrusted and the rogues and hypocrites are worshipped,' said Mehar to create more confidence in her for himself.

'Who will believe Bhai doing these things? He is so modest and never talks of women or marriage. Has he really married without our knowledge? I knew nothing even of Munira's marriage till I saw her at home. I had a fight and took some time to reconcile with him.'

'That is what I say. Sometimes just to tease you I talk of remarriage and you call me names, whereas Kabeer does not talk but acts slyly yet he is an angel to you. He has married a young, beautiful and rich girl, the daughter of Faiz Mohammad, Thaseeldar.

'What a traitor Bhai has turned out! How familiar and sincere he is to us, who would expect such a thing from him?'

'Yes, only such people get on in the world,' said Mehar.

'How long will their treachery last? One day the evil must be detected and the doer is punished.'

'Who punishes them? On the other hand they are flattered and respected.'

'If no one punishes them their own conscience is enough. People after all are sensible. Will I have any respect for him hereafter?' said she meaningly.

'He has kept it a secret and wants to reveal it himself to your mother, so we had better not get involved in the conspiracy. In what way will we make matters better by informing her? I promised him not to tell you but there is nothing in my life that you don't know.'

'Ammajan is already suspecting some such thing. She said that there is a big difference between the former and the present income. If she is kept in the dark he will squander the property.'

'We will be creating a misunderstanding between him and ourselves. He can't waste the money without giving you your share. We will file a suit against him. To keep a nominal friendship with him and be cautious so far as our interests are concerned is wise.'

'That's what I can't do. If I entertain ill-feeling towards someone I hate to see him. I wonder what will happen to Bhabi if she knows that he has married a third time and has a young woman. I consoled her by saying that he has got only a servant in Munira.'

'Our own worries are quite enough. Why should we bother about others? We can't repair the fate of Nazni by our sympathy.'

Mehar was an ideal man to Jamila. In comparison with Kabeer her admiration for his wisdom and fidelity knew no bounds. She made up her mind to keep his promise and not to inform her mother about the matter. Difference had to come between them over her share of her father's property, and it was sensible to do it tactfully.

'I think things are going from bad to worse. You have to be very careful in money matters,' said Jamila to her mother before leaving.

'What makes you think that?'

'Nothing in particular. I thought of the difference you spoke about in the income. Bhai is so careless and leaves things too much to others. The servants may deceive him,' said Jamila.

'I am suspecting Kabeer's sincerity. He is quite changed. Leave alone the servants cheating him, he will deceive himself and will deprive others of their happiness. A person with that attitude of mind is liable to do anything. He is self-deluded and puts the blame on others,' said Zuhra.

Jamila was satisfied with the hint she had given and also with her mother's answer. The day she was leaving Kabeer stayed at home and tried to be very loving to her and her children. She was cold and avoided him. He accompanied her to the station to find out if she had come to know of his secret but in vain. Even Zuhra seemed to behave a little queerly. She was thinking of the money.

'I think a sort of magic is going on in our affairs. No two things tally. The worst thing is the enormous difference in our income,' said Zuhra to Kabeer one day.

'How could our income be the same as before after selling so many things?'

'How many houses did we sell? Only one at the time of your wedding. The difference I speak of is after that.'

'Ammajan, you don't understand the situation. The present arrangement is not mine. It has been going on from father's days. My interference in the established affairs will only upset the whole organisation so thoughtfully managed by him. We have to trust our servants as they are more experienced than myself,' said Kabeer very sentimentally.

'So long as they were trustworthy we did respect them. They can't expect to enrich themselves at our cost. The difference is very big. If we don't deal with them seriously now we shall be left beggars after some years.'

'You destroyed my home and drove me mad. I had neither peace of mind nor happiness in life. Now I have made my life with unsurmountable difficulties and feel myself in a position to look to other things. Once I find out the culprit God knows how I shall deal with him.'

'For the last four months I am not receiving the rent for the corner house. They say nothing when I ask for it. It was reduced from fifty to thirty five and now to nothing. Are they all a pack of rogues? What are they?'

'Oh, wait a minute. Now I remember. Something very strange was said about that house. They say it is haunted. Some years ago a woman died there. It seems every night without fail at twelve she cries. If by chance any child happens to hear it the very next day it falls ill and dies. I overlooked it and made the staff get the rent by hook or by crook, but how long can we cheat people? Now no one rents it and they even refuse to live there free, said Kabeer very sadly.

'People used to live there for years and they called it a mubarak ghar.'[2]

'All that was happening before that wretched woman died. After that tenants leave the house without our knowledge. Now it is completely dilapidated.'

'The house which used to bring in a regular rent has come to that. You depend too much upon workers and second-hand information. Why don't you go to the tenants and have a talk with them?'

'What respect will people have for me if I go from house to house as a rent collector? Ammajan, you don't know what you ask.'

'Pride goes before a fall, and yours is the symbol of our ruination. Well, that is the story about the most popular house. What had happened to the three-cornered field? We ought to have got two thousand rupees six months ago, along with the rent of the other lands. Has a miracle occurred to it too?'

'Yes, there is a story behind it. Last year a python devoured a farmer and after that incident no one is willing to cultivate it. It will be some years before the villagers forget it. Keeping such lands is foolish. We must sell them all and buy shops in the city.'

'You dare not sell any more property. Jamila's husband will file a suit for her share. It has to be transferred from one generation to another.'

'Money is meant to make one comfortable and happy. If it does not serve the purpose it should be thrown in the gutter. Kharoon possessed a treasury equivalent to the wealth of the world and yet died the most miserable death.[3] Who enjoyed it after him? Misers hoard wealth and the wise make use of it in their lifetime.'

'We must thank our lucky stars for having enough to satisfy our needs. You have to think of the future and of your children. If he had not left the property what would have happened to you?'

'Yes, live in misery thinking of the future. Your ways of life are quite different from ours. My life had become unbearable while trying to adjust myself to please you.'

'Your ways and mine!' repeated Zuhra. 'Have you gone out of your wits? You are a changed man. You have neither home nor interest in its members. For name sake you shifted to the opposite house and whenever I send for you they don't tell me where you have gone.'

'I am not a woman to confine myself to the four walls of a room. God has made man free to do what he likes and a woman dare not deprive him of his privileges.'

'Don't talk nonsense to me. You are not speaking to your servant. You will know what will happen to you if you do what you like,' said Zuhra sternly.

'You are my mother. I pay you as much respect as you deserve. Neither more nor less than that,' said Kabeer furiously and left the room.

The very next day a car stopped in front of the door. Zuhra was near the kitchen for her morning round.

'Somebody has come. See who it is,' said Zuhra to the cook.

'Bring a curtain,' said Kabeer to the cook.

'Master wants a curtain. He has brought a beautiful woman, I saw her peeping out of the car,' said the cook, panting with excitement.

'Kabeer has brought a woman! It must be Nazni. He would not have done it without informing me.'

'It is not Nazni Begum, but a young girl who looks like a bride. I think she is his new wife. Both of them are whispering and smiling very lovingly. He never spoke to Munira,' were the relevant and irrelevant sentences uttered by the cook.

'Don't talk rubbish. Who asked you to pass your remarks? This is how people scandalise!' said Zuhra who was standing in the quadrangle. After hearing the arrival of a new person her hands went mechanically to her head. The fingers combed the hair and automatically they came down and set right the creases in her sari. She looked smart and was prepared to receive the beautiful woman.

'Greet Ammajan,' said Kabeer to Maghbool, who with a frightened face and a heart broken to pieces bent down to touch Zuhra's feet.

'Who is she?' stammered Zuhra.

'Who will come with me to my house?' Kabeer said.

'Who will come with me to my house!' repeated Zuhra.

'Have girls become so cheap and immodest as to follow men?' said she again, gazing at the kitchen. Perhaps her sympathy with Munira directed her eyes to see if she was also one of the spectators of the drama.

'No girl follows a man unless he marries her,' said Kabeer slowly while Maghbool was looking at her mother-in-law, who after a glance at her had averted her face. Zuhra with a jerk turned and walked back to her room.

Munira, standing behind the kitchen door, had listened to every word uttered. She was admiring the beautiful woman by the side of her husband. She did not know whether to cry or laugh at his fantastic way in bringing home a new wife. She felt proud at having married respectably with the knowledge of her mother-in-law. Her dog-like faithfulness to him prevailed over her sentiment and her right of wifehood. She decided that it was her duty to love them both and serve them.

Kabeer did not like to follow his mother and beg of her to excuse him. He had learnt to keep up his dignity before his wives. He took Maghbool to his old room and told the driver to send her belongings there. The furniture was waiting outside for him. He had the bed and dressing rooms arranged at once.

Maghbool felt insulted and was depressed beyond words. She sat with her chin in her palm, as a person leaves herself to be tossed by circumstances.

'Don't worry,' said Kabeer. 'I shall bring Ammajan round. If she does not come to her senses and treat you kindly I shall keep you in a separate house. She knew nothing of our marriage. When she saw you unexpectedly she was surprised and did not think how she was acting. I shall make her understand that if she wants to see me alive she must make you happy.' He left the room with a gentle touch on her pink cheek.

Munira kept a keen watch on them. She felt sad to see Maghbool unhappy. When she saw Kabeer go to his mother's room she ran from the kitchen to Maghbool's room.

'What's your name?' asked Munira panting.

'Maghbool,' was the curt answer. She wondered whether the speaker was a servant or a relative of Kabeer.

'It just suits you. You are a real Maghbool.'

'Am I? It is very kind of you to say so.'

'If I were as beautiful as you are I would never have been sad.'

'You seem happy without it. Good looks don't make a person happy. Are you pleased to see me?'

'After seeing you from the kitchen window I was dying to make your acquaintance. I was simply longing for him to leave the room,' said Munira.

'Why didn't you come when he was here?'

'I feel nervous in his presence. I never go to him when he is with other people. Even if I go there he never looks at me and he gets angry with me afterwards.'

Maghbool understood that the ugly woman in front of her was Kabeer's second wife, whom he called a servant. The poor thing seemed to have no idea of jealousy.

'What do you do all day?'

'What do women do except cooking, washing and stitching? When his sister was here I had a lot to do.'

'Do you feel happy?'

'I feel unhappy if there is no work. Are you married, or have you run away with him?'

'Do Muslim girls do such things?'

'Oh yes,' said Munira knowingly. 'There was a beautiful girl near our house. Once she was peeping through a window when a man was passing by. He noticed her and bribed an old woman to bring the girl to him. The old wretch visited the house on some pretext and told the girl there was a nice tamasha she would take her to that night.[4] She took the girl and handed her over to the man, and she has never been heard of since. The father was furious and wanted to kill himself and the mother died of sorrow.'

'You can't strike all girls with the same whip. That girl may be from a poor family.'

'Yes, she was. When were you married? Who came for your marriage? For my marriage Ammajan herself came,' said Munira proudly.

Maghbool hesitated. Her husband had kept it a secret and she did not know what he would want her to say. She cursed herself for being the victim of double-dealing, and being looked down upon by everybody.

'I don't know,' she said with a deep sigh.

'You don't know the date of your own marriage?' Munira exclaimed. 'I was aspiring to get married and I counted the days on my fingers. Is it months or days since you were married?'

'I don't remember anything about it.'

'Never mind. We shall be friends. All these days I have been alone and there was no one to talk to. What can you say to Ammajan except answer her questions? I have someone to talk and laugh with. I am glad you are here.'

'I shall be pleased to be with you. You are very kind to me.'

'You are joking. No one here has told me that although I love and serve them all. I think he married you four months ago,' said Munira.

'How do you know?'

'One day, without any cause, he picked a quarrel with everybody at home and went to live in the next house. For eighteen days he did not enter the house. Everyone was worried and I did not know what to do. I cried every night. Now I understand why he did it.'

'Does he not live here?'

'No, he comes once a day to see his mother. I see him coming and going through the window. Sometimes I see his face and other times only his back.'

'If he does not care for you why do you see him and die for him?'

'I feel miserable if I don't see him at least once a day. Let him do what he likes but I don't like to do the same to him. God has made him a man. Because of my sins He created me a woman. During these four months he had his dinner twice with his sister and mother and slept in this room on that bed. Your cot is very nice. It is better than his first wife's.'

'Where is it? Have you seen her?'

'No, they say she is like a hoor.[5] It is in the opposite room. His sister had been using it. I don't like to leave you alone, but I must go to see to the food. Shall I bring you lunch here?'

'Don't worry. I don't feel hungry,' said Maghbool.

She was pleased with this simple talkative woman. She felt that she could while away her time in her company. Her philosophy of married life seemed queer to Maghbool. She thought if she had to live in that house she would have to follow Munira's example. Could she do it? Could she suppress her feelings?

'Oh hopes, how hideously you differ in realisation!' said she to herself and lay down on the bed.

'From the day you brought the negress home I was wild with rage. I scorned everybody and everything in the world till I found a woman to my satisfaction,' said Kabeer to Zuhra.

'You behave as if you had no beautiful wife. Bad enough acting like a coward, you want to justify your roguery by a lame excuse. If you wanted to marry a third time why didn't you say so?'

'Because I knew I would not be allowed, and you would have brought a woman of your choice.'

'I know you now. I was under a wrong impression. I took you for what you seemed,' said Zuhra.

'I am fed up with this life. I shall kill myself, then everybody will be happy. No one cares for my happiness and no one has eyes to see my sufferings.'

'We sympathised with you and did our best to make you happy. If you were destined to live with an ugly woman it was not our fault. For all my sacrifices I am made a monument of wickedness and the most selfish creature,' said Zuhra.

'If my own near and dear ones can't get on with me and my devotion to my mother has resulted in this it is better for me to end this life. I don't want to live any longer. I don't want wives and children. Let them all be widows and orphans. What do I care for them when I am going to the grave?' said Kabeer emotionally.

If there was anything in the world that could melt Zuhra's heart it was the idea of Kabeer's death. She was already apprehensive that Akram having being born the same day and time as Kabeer was a bad omen for him. She was tortured by the idea but being afraid of its coming true never expressed it to anybody.

'Don't talk of death and the grave,' said Zuhra, deeply moved. 'Let those expressions go to your enemies. What is over, is over. For whom am I labouring here if not for you? If I had not allowed you to marry again it would have been in your and your children's interest. You'll find out how difficult it is to keep more than one wife. I won't live much longer to plague you. I pray day and night for your long life and happiness. If you live happily even my bones in the grave will be pleased.'

'Everything in the house is left to you. I have nothing to do with it. If I attend to domestic duties the outdoor work and the care of the property will suffer. I have no more desires in life. I shall be ever obedient and grateful to you for all that you have done for me,' said Kabeer equally moved.

'I solved the problem very easily. My love for you gave me resolution and tact to deal with it. Ammajan will be very kind to you hereafter,' said Kabeer to Maghbool.

'I hope so. Munira has been here.'

'Why did you allow her here? Her place is in the kitchen,' said Kabeer.

Maghbool felt pain in her heart to see the attitude of the man for whom that woman had such disinterested devotion. Could she expect anything better?

'I did not see anything bad in her.'

'Perhaps you did not look at her face and teeth.'

'I did, but did not care for a thing for which she was not responsible,' said Maghbool slowly. Though she felt sad for her rival she did not want to make him love her more.

Chapter XIII

Doulath Khan was confined to bed for some weeks after his return from Kashmir. The cold climate had been too much for his poor old limbs. Crowds of friends came to make enquiries after his health. One of them was an intimate chum, Zakir Hussain, a man of communicative nature, who had made friends with many of the leading people of the place. Unfortunately for Kabeer he had happened to be present at the time of nikha. When he heard of Doulath Khan's return from the hills he went to him to tell his friend of the roguery of his son-in-law.

'There is no end to dishonesty, selfishness, treachery and ingratitude in this world,' said Zakir Hussain emotionally. 'The greater the rogue the more prominent he is. A man in the good old days was frightened to death to be called a sinner. Now sin is an art appreciated by friends and applauded by relations. No trace of the modesty, honesty and straightforwardness of our days is left in this worthless world. God should close our eyes before showing us any more of their treacherous doings. One's own friend and son-in-law's ingratitude towards his benefactor, a living saint, has come to light. It is said in the future one's own children will be traitors. We should not live to see those days,' he added.

'Who is that living saint?' asked Doulath Khan calmly.

'Who can it be but you?'

'Oh I see! You have not understood me well. You are blind to my shortcomings. There have been many instances wherein sons and daughters have acted treacherously to their parents. You need not wait to see those days. The world would be monotonous without such elements. People of a complex nature are both constructive and destructive. The former because they warn more conscientious beings against involving themselves in complications, and the latter because the inevitable nemesis sets an example to less experienced men. In the present world changes are so rapid that we are too old to cope with them. Hence they are hideous to us. Has there been any particular instance worth mentioning?'

'Your son-in-law has married your friend's daughter.'

'He did not marry my friend's daughter. Moreover it is an old story. It is almost a year since he was remarried.'

'The event I am speaking of is recent. It took place when you were in Kashmir. I attended it.'

'You are mistaken. My going to Kashmir was in that connection. After his remarriage my daughter was seriously ill. I took her there for a change. I believe he married an ugly and poor woman and treats her like servant.'

'Whose daughter did he marry then?'

'I don't know the details, but this is certain that she comes from an unknown family.'

'I know the history of the girl he married now. She is beautiful, rich and accomplished. When Kabeer saw me at the time of the nikha he did not know where to look. I was staring furiously at him, otherwise he would have asked me to keep it a secret.'

'Didn't you say he married my friend's daughter?'

'Yes, Faiz Mohammed's.'

'Faiz, the Thaseeldar,[1] the wretch used to be here almost every day before I left for Kashmir,' said Doulath Khan perplexed but with apparent serenity.

'The blighter owes his position and wealth to you. The minute your back was turned he showed himself in his true colours. I happened to pass his house that day and on seeing the commotion I went inside. I could not believe my eyes seeing Kabeer on the bridal seat, but I sat down opposite him till the nikha was over. Then I slipped away.'

'No wonder the poor wretch has not been here so long. He had no courage to show his face. I am not so much surprised that he got his daughter married without informing me, but that he made her a third wife. He had given me to understand that he cared more for the happiness of his daughters than their marriage. I wonder what made the fellow act like a lunatic? Was it Kabeer's wealth? I shouldn't think so. After Kabeer's second marriage he told me one day sarcastically that he would never give his daughter to every Zaid and Bakar just because he had some money.'

'He has not been blind to his daughter's interests. He got a house worth fifty thousand registered in her name before the marriage was settled. He himself gave her a dowry of ten thousand, not in the way of jewels but cash deposited in her name in a bank.'

'So he made her economically independent.[2] Now I understand why he was indifferent in the choice of a son-in-law. He made it a business. I spent a lakh of rupees on the marriage of my daughter yet I left her in a helpless condition. He is superior to me in his practical knowledge of the world.'

Zakir Hussain was astounded at Doulath Khan's calm. He would have raved and created a commotion in the whole family and made his daughter divorce her husband; but Doulath Khan appreciated the wisdom of Faiz Mohammad. Zakir Hussain had come fully prepared to light a bonfire in his friend's family, but left him convinced of his way of thinking.

After his departure Doulath Khan pondered over the situation. His son-in-law had brought home two more wives regardless of the happiness of his daughter. He stopped seeing him after his second marriage. His indifference to his wife was clear. Should he inform his daughter of Kabeer's third marriage? She would only cry and fall ill. He thought of no one in the family with whom he could consult and share his burden. He could neither convince the ladies of his ideas nor make Nazni discard her husband. He thought it would be better to leave things to take their own course.

Nazni's elder brother had been transferred to a distant district. He often wrote and invited his sister to his place for a change and to prevent her from going to Kabeer. Maghbool's arrival at home compelled Kabeer to make another serious effort to bring Nazni home before she came to know of his third marriage.

'He told me if I don't go home soon I will have to repent it,' said Nazni to her mother.

'The harm a husband usually threatens his wife with had already been done. What more can a woman have than a rival at home?' said her mother.

'He said he would not come here any more. I asked him to take Bavajan's permission and take me with him. He said he has nothing to do with anybody in the house. He is his own master and will care for no one,' said Nazni crying.

'Now it has come to that it is better you should go. If you refuse the result will be separation,' said the mother. Nazni cried bitterly.

'Crying will not make things any better. You cried for a whole year but you had to go in the end. When a woman enters married life she has to be ready for anything and everything. Why do the parents cry at the birth and marriage of a girl if not for her misfortune and the sufferings she will have to undergo in the world?' She left her weeping daughter.

'Nazni is going to her husband's house tomorrow. We must prepare thosha to be sent with her.'[3]

'It will bring no good luck to her. You sent many from the day she was married but it was no use. If she must go let her be ready without it to face the consequences.'

'Thoshas are sent to quiet the barking dogs. Old customs are based on reasoning and have been followed advantageously for ages. We prevented her from going there for about a year. Now he has given her an ultimatum. He will come here no more.'

'What will she lose by it?'

'What will she lose?' repeated the wife. 'She will lose the world. What will she gain by not going except misery and disgrace? Marriage is not a business to think of advantages and disadvantages. It should be made a matter to give and never expect to take. She is his property. We have no right to it. The longer she keeps away from him the greater will be the breach between them and consequently the relation between him and the other woman will be closer.

'The presence of a discarded woman will not change his heart. She is to him like a dropped tear. He will still be at liberty to love the ugly woman or to bring home another pretty one even when your daughter is with him. A woman who only yields and has not learnt to assert herself and resent wrongs done to her is only a puppet who is pitied but not respected. Pity is soon converted into scorn. I wish the punishment could be inflicted on you instead of on that innocent girl.'

'How grand it would look with your false teeth, grey hair and aches all over your body if you brought a new wife to inflict punishment on me!'

'Impulsive woman. You can't understand anything beyond your affairs. I meant that you are more responsible than she is for having caused complications in her life. On account of your doings she had to suffer.'

'As if I am not concerned with her sorrows. Why don't you speak out and say what you want her to do? You behave as if she matters nothing to you,' said she sarcastically.'

'You and I can't change her destiny. The consequences good or bad of one's doings are inevitable. It is the irony of fate that the innocent suffer and the criminals escape immediate punishment. There is no use repenting when it is too late.'

'I remember when he was remarried you sided with him. Now all of a sudden what has made you so depressed? It is beyond a woman's power of understanding to judge man's nature. It is one thing one time and something else another.'

'According to your logic a woman is very constant. Nazni is a woman and a mother. Our duty is only to aid her in her decision,' said he.

'He is indifferent to her and unfriendly towards us. He does not even care for you and flatly refuses any obedience to you. For all our sacrifices we got nothing but ingratitude and disrespect.'

'No son-in-law is ever grateful to his parents-in-law. Every young man enters married life with an expectation of a world of no worries where the parents-in-law satisfy all his needs. Such a high demand can never be satisfied. Discontent commences, grievances increase, hatred for the source which seemed very lucrative results. Your son-in-law is no exception. A man entering a new life increases his responsibilities and needs with the enlargement of the family, naturally he feels himself at bay. Send her if she is willing.' He made himself busy with a paper. His wife had to leave the room.

Nazni came home escorted by her uncle and Akram's ayah. The former after sending all her belongings inside the house left at once. Kabeer had gone out. Nazni went to her mother-in-law and after paying her respects stood there very modestly.

Zuhra had found Maghbool haughty and proud and now felt an unwonted sympathy for Nazni. Whenever Maghbool was checked she frowned and disappeared, or answered back. Maghbool did not make it a point to visit her mother-in-law every morning to pay her respects. Any time during the day when she saw her she wished her good morning but not politely. Zuhra disliked her, but there was no remedy. Her son was changed. She could not say anything against his wife. Once he frankly told her to change her behaviour towards his third wife. Nazni after standing there for some time turned to leave.

'Your indifference and foolishness have been the cause of your destruction. I used to ask you not to comb your hair standing as it meant an invitation to a rival. You brought a curse on your life by your own actions I pity you and hope at least you will come to your senses now. Come to me for help whenever you need it and don't run to your parents for consolation.'

Nazni thought of Munira and looked at her mother-in-law with eyes that craved for sympathy. She walked towards her old room. The cook seeing her going to Maghbool's room ran after her.

'Bi Bi come this way, that is not your room,' said she. She was fond of Nazni.

'Why, what has happened to our room?'

'Don't call it yours any more. It has been occupied by a person superior to you. This is yours.'

'It is dark and stuffy. I shall die if I live there. You said she lived in the lumber room.'

'It is not the ugly one but another who has taken the best in the house. Master himself took her there and arranged all her things. You have not one rival but two.'

'What! There are two? I am put between two dragons to be devoured! Show her to me! I shall strangle her to death and burn her body to ashes! How dare she use my things having come to my house to lick my paw?' raved Nazni. Controlling her tears with a great strain she staggered to the room meant for her and sat down on her old bed.

'Strangle her to death,' repeated the cook.

'If she only opens her eyes to stare at you you will die a hundred deaths. Even Begum Sahib is afraid of her. Master is simply a slave and anything she commands is done immediately. Even if she wants a tiger's milk he will spare no effort to fetch it for her. She has given him a pill to make him mad after her. You just wait and see how they behave,' said the cook.

This was a heavy blow to Nazni. She could not control her tears. She turned her head to hide them and they rushed profusely. She got up from her bed and went to Akram who was pulling and dropping things from the dressing table. The cook was a foolish friend and was agitated with the mischief she had done. She tried to pacify her victim.

'Don't cry, Bi Bi, I shall be with you in weal and woe. You, Begum Sahib and I are one party. We three can drive her away from here. While you have been away Begum Sahib has praised you. If you win her, master becomes your slave.'

'If you had told me of a newcomer I would not have stepped into this house. Send for a conveyance from my father's place. I shall leave before he comes.'

'If I were you I wouldn't leave the house. If you go away their way will be clear. That is what they want. You are the first wife and the mother of the heir to the family property. You have to be on the spot and keep everybody under your control, not only for your own sake but also for your son's. Your enemies will be benefitted and your son will be a beggar if you run away Bi Bi. You have to think of your moon-like offspring.'

Nazni sat down despairingly and tried or pretended to play with Akram and his toys, while the cook and the ayah made her bed and arranged her things.

Maghbool knew by the commotion that her rival had come home. She heard Akram's prattling, and was inclined to see him, but remembering that he was her rival's son refrained.

Munira was excited and would have gone to make acquaintance with Nazni, but she was indisposed. She was jealous towards none, and thought that everybody in the house was superior to her and it was her duty to serve and please them. She liked all children. The shrill voice of Akram thrilled her. She peeped through the window and asked the ayah to bring him to her. But a glance at Munira made Akram scream. She picked him up and tried to divert his mind, but he slapped her and roared. The ayah took him out of the room. He seemed frightened and continued to cry.

Kabeer came home and tried to pacify Akram, but he cared for nobody and nothing. Zuhra lost her temper.

'What a spoilt child he is!' she cried. 'They have made him good for nothing. Stop that manhoos wailing.[4] He is starting his life with weeping. Let it be a bad omen to him. Take him out. It gets on my nerves.' Zuhra remembered Akram's birth and the risk to Kabeer's life.

Nazni overheard from her room. She did not like to go to the scene though her mother-in-law's words were daggers to her heart. She wanted her husband to come to her first to welcome her. His third marriage and his keeping it a secret from her had made her distrust him.

Kabeer did not expect Nazni that day. Her unexpected arrival perplexed him. He needed time to prepare himself well to explain and justify his action in bringing home a third wife. Moreover he noticed both Maghbool and Munira were keeping a keen watch on his movements. If he went to Nazni's room first it would only create jealousy. He should show preference to none of them and inform none of his visit beforehand. He left home on the pretext of taking Akram out. His departure did not displease Maghbool. Munira's anxiety was only to see whom he preferred of her two rivals.

Kabeer returned home just at dinner time with lots of toys, sweets and fruits. He knew the things Nazni liked and bought some for her too. Nazni smiled when she saw them as they expressed his preference for her. Her rival could not be jealous as they were brought for Akram.

Zuhra was furious to see packet after packet being taken to Nazni's room but she did not question her son as to the money spent on them or from where he got them.

Kabeer knew his mother was displeased and a stay was not advisable. He asked the ayah to keep Akram in the room till he got used to the new environment, ordered his dinner to be sent to his office, and left the zenana.

In his estimation Maghbool came first, but the immediate question was the reconciliation with Nazni. When the whole house was quiet he unlocked the wicket gate leading to the zenana and went to Nazni's room. He found her in bed crying, her eyes, nose and cheeks red and distended. She lay passive, as if dead.

'It is said a person is rewarded for his good deeds,' he began, 'but mine always bring me punishment. The more I try to please you the more enmity and disregard I get from you. I don't know how to serve you. All my attempts have been a miserable failure. You asked me to get a decent girl, so with the utmost difficulty I secured one worthy to be your companion. Your loneliness at home drove you out of the house often. Now there is a woman of your age and status. Make friends with her. Both of you can work and live together as sisters. I don't come in your way. I made a pleasant home for you and separated myself to live like a sanyasi in the office to work and bring money to satisfy your needs.'

'You brought one as a servant and another as a companion. What will third one be? I don't want your house or your companion. I shall go to my parents. I came here against their will. If I knew that you had brought another woman I would not have come.'

'Is your love so small? It vanishes just because I did something. You used to profess that you could give your life for me, and that you hated to live without me. Now you want to live away from me. Can you possibly live in the same country separately? Now you have a servant and a companion. There is no need of anybody. I assure you this is the last one.'

'I don't feel as I used to. I don't care for my life. I might live or die after going from here. When I am not happy what do I care for other things?'

'Women are blind and always create misery for themselves. They never understand the right thing and never judge correctly. They are rightly called naqis ul aql.[5]

'Woman is not cunning. She is always straightforward. No one gets lost on a royal road. With a man no one can understand where she stands. Who knows what is going to happen tomorrow? Who else may not come?'

'There is no need of any doubt for your future. It is foolish to make your present life miserable with your imagining. If I die tomorrow all your fears will be baseless. I think you would prefer to be a widow to an extra person at home. You are such a good-natured woman that even your enemies adore you. She has come to your house as a guest and craves for your mercy. If you are generous to her God will bless you. If you can't live with one person how can you expect me to live with robbers, murderers and rogues to earn money for the family? That is why God has given superiority to man over woman. Imagine yourself in the place of a Nawab's wife. What wonderful love she must have for her husband to tolerate hundreds of rivals.'

Nazni's temper calmed down with these wise words. She admired his superior sense and took every expression for gospel truth. There was no alternative. She had to yield and adjust herself to the circumstances

Maghbool was alone in her room. Having heard somebody's heavy footsteps in the quadrangle she put out the light of her room and peeped through the window. She saw Kabeer entering Nazni's room. She was taken aback. But she could not let him know that she had been watching his movements. She switched on the light, fished out her music books and sang softly all the sad songs she knew till she felt sleepy. She laid herself on her bed and tried to sleep. Her eyes were closed but her mind was alert. She heard somebody sobbing. She jumped from her bed and opened the door. The voice came from Munira's room. Her despair gave place to pity and she resolved to help her. There was a light in Nazni's room. She hesitated to pass it and risk being seen, but sympathy drove her on. She went on tiptoe and found Munira walking up and down her room.

'Do you want anything? I have come to help you.' Munira could not believe her eyes. None of the family had ever done such a thing.

'Is it really you, my angel? How did you know I was unwell? You are not a human being, you are above them.'

'Don't look so aghast. Don't be surprised but tell me what you want. I have come to serve you.'

'You can't do it. I want the help of an old woman.'

'Shall I wake up Ammajan?'

'Will she stoop to dirty work? It is useless to approach her. She does not like to be disturbed in her sleep. This evening I told her about it but she gave a deaf ear.'

'Shall I wake Akram's ayah?'

'Yes, she would be of great help to me, but how will you go to her room? See if the bathroom door is not closed. You can enter her room easily.' Munira talked only with great effort and sat down.

The old ayah knew a little of the job. She passed as an expert in her locality. She was sympathetic and often rendered help to the needy. She came and examined the patient.

'Go and make some water hot,' she said to Maghbool. 'Your presence now is not needed, come into the room when I call you. Go, soon, and close the door behind you.'

She was soon at work, and within half an hour the ordeal was over. God is helpful to the uncared-for.

'It is a nice little boy,' said the ayah.

Maghbool heard the cry of the newborn and ran with the hot water.

'Here is the water.'

'Wait a minute. Don't come in. I shall call you soon'

After attending to the mother's needs the ayah called Maghbool inside and both gave a bath to the baby.

'A newborn baby is crying. Is it your second wife's?' said Nazni to Kabeer.

'It may be. Why do you bother about it? Let us not make our happy hours bitter by unwanted notions.' But in his heart of hearts, Kabeer was anxious to know whether it was a girl or a boy. Akram woke and called the ayah and not finding her there began to cry. Nazni went to him. The ayah came running.

'Where had you gone leaving him alone?' said Nazni.

'Your rival got a baby. I was attending to her and before I had finished my work I heard Baba crying so I came.'

'What did she get?'

'A boy, nice and strong.'

On hearing the ayah's talk, Kabeer entered the room and heard of the birth of a second son. He felt proud.

Maghbool was still with Munira making a bed for the baby out of rags gathered for the purpose.

'Did you not make clothes for the baby? The poor thing is wrapped in a big torn shirt. See how he is shivering,' said Maghbool, putting him on the bed.

'Among our people we never do it. Whenever such a thing is attempted the child dies either before birth or soon after it,' said the mother.

Maghbool did not know what to say to such an ignorant creature.

'Do you want anything more?' she said.

'My throat is parched. Can you give me something hot to drink? Oh you will save my life!'

Maghbool left the room and in ten minutes brought a hot cup of coffee. After drinking it Munira felt herself in a strange world.

'The coffee has worked on me like ab-e-zamzam.[6] I have done nothing to you to deserve any kindness from you. All rich and beautiful people coming from high families ill-treat the poor and ugly. All of them here expect everything from me but return nothing. Although you are one of them yet you are so different from them. You are an angel on earth. God has sent you to set an example to these people. When I am well I shall serve you to the utmost of my ability. I would not mind even to make slippers for you out of my own skin,' said Munira.

'Don't talk, you will be thirsty. Doctors do not allow women in your condition to speak. I feel happy to help others if they want any aid from me. I shall come to you every day to look after you and the baby.'

The baby was wet and it began crying. Maghbool, without minding her expensive clothes, sat down and took him on her lap. She had often handled little ones in her mother's house.

'Each time he wets the big cloth you have to expose him while changing and he will catch cold,' said Maghbool.

'Put a rag under his waist. You can make him not to feel the cold cloth and you need not change the big one.'

'The big wet shirt will be under him. You should not make children sleep on a wet cloth. The wetness will cause him to catch diseases that come with chill. Moreover the gasses are bad for him,' said Maghbool.

'That is what they do and nothing happens to children. After all they do that for twelve days,' said the ignorant mother.

'I don't believe in what you say but there is no alternative,' said Maghbool.

Munira was admiringly noticing her beautiful rival sitting by her and lovingly handling the baby.

'You don't hate to touch my clothes. The people here either kick or push them with a stick. Once I had left my sari in the bathroom Ammajan called me to remove it. I was busy in the kitchen. When I went there I saw her pushing it with a long bamboo. I am treated here worse than a servant. The cook at least gets her pay. I get nothing except old torn rags. Even those old clothes when I wear them they say I use them roughly. Once Ammajan said that there is a pair of scissors in my body which cuts everything I wear. You spoil me. You make me expect better treatment, and that will make me feel unhappy. Leave me to myself. I have to live according to my destiny. I am not your equal. Don't come to me. You will be disgraced with the people of this house. I feel happy to see you. Can you come in the night when everybody is asleep? Listen, the lizard is endorsing all that I said,' said Munira with tears in her eyes.

'Let others do what they like. I don't care for them, nor am I inclined to imitate them. I shall do what pleases me. Why should I be afraid of them and come in the night? I shall come to you whenever I feel like seeing you.' Maghbool gave the baby hot water with sugar.

'What are you giving him?'

'Hot water and sugar.'

'We never give water to children till they are two years old. They get convulsions and die. Water is very bad for them,' said the mother with a shudder.

Maghbool was confused with these ideas of her rival. Was she thinking that she was trying to kill him? Had she to do things on her own while helping her or obey her mechanically?

'I have seen my mother doing it and they give it in hospitals. Nothing happens. Don't be afraid. I shall look after him. I brought up my youngest brother, as my mother was seriously ill after his birth. Look how quickly he is sleeping.'

The sincerity and the disinterested help rendered by Maghbool had given Munira confidence in her.

'I will have no time to look after him. You have him as your son. I will have to leave him alone here or take him to the kitchen.'

Maghbool smiled at the idea. She was not displeased as it would keep her engaged. She felt exhausted having no sleep the whole night.

'Shall I go to sleep? I am feeling giddy.'

'Do go. The baby is fast asleep and I am feeling sleepy too. I don't know how to thank you for all that you have done in saving two lives. I pray to God to give you a beautiful son as a reward for your good action,' said Munira and asked her rival a second time to go and sleep.

Chapter XIV

After the heavy work, Maghbool went to her room exhausted. The selfishness and heartlessness of the people of the house made her feel in an alien world, from which human feelings had been excluded. None of them was bothered to know what was happening in the house. The commotion and even the crying of a newborn child did not make them leave their cosy beds. She heard Nazni and Kabeer talking when she was in the kitchen but they gave a deaf ear to the wailing of both the mother and the child. This house seemed to personify that indifference towards others caused by wealth and ignorance. If the treatment of a member of the family was such, what would it be to their neighbours and strangers? She tossed in her bed for some time and then fell into a sound sleep, and overslept.

Kabeer came to her room at about ten o'clock in the morning. In her half-sleep she felt that he was standing near her bed but her dislike for him prevented her from opening her eyes. She heard his steps going away. She was now wide awake but felt too tired to get up. Her mind was wandering on the road of life in a polygamous house, where human beings conform to artificiality, and sincerity seems out of place.

'Oh, life! How glorious you seem in theory, how hideous you are in practice! You are nothing better than a horrid disease that consumes one's youth, eats up one's days and nights and leaves one wretched. You profess virtues and in practice you necessitate vices. Why this disparity between principles and execution? Those following theory are condemned and discarded and those practising vices are prosperous. What is the criterion of life you set before ignorant humanity? Should I follow the well-recognised, hypocritical method of getting on, of self-interest? No, I would rather suffer and die than distort my character.' This was her resolute soliloquy which is the bliss of solitude. She was still in bed, and her tears were now falling profusely.

'Munira Bi got a baby last night,' said the cook, entering the room, 'and so she has a good excuse to stay in bed. I wonder how many days she will stick to it. We people get up to work from the third day. Coolies work from the same day. She belongs to our class and will resume her duties from the day after tomorrow. If we don't give her proper food and in time she will be forced to do it sooner. What work does she do there? Just sit and stir a pot with a spoon. All the heavy and difficult work I do, making her sit down like the goddess of fire near the oven. Even then she grumbles at me. I know how to serve her right. She is in my power now. Begum Sahib has sent me to you to ask you to take over her work. Just for name sake you come to the kitchen. I shall do everything for you. After eating all those sweets you have given me now and then I would not allow you to work hard.'

'I am not a servant here to cook. Why does not your Begum Sahib ask Nazni to do some of the work? Go and tell her that unless she divides the work equally between us I shall not step into the kitchen.' Maghbool could very well have cooked if she had wanted to, but her jealousy towards Nazni made her protest.

'Nazni Begum comes from a very rich family and in her whole life has never been inside a kitchen. She is the first wife. You can't treat her like your equal. All subsequent wives have to serve her and her children. Moreover she has not been well and is just recovering from her illness. No one would have the heart to ask her to sit near that burning fire. If master hears of what you say he will murder you. You don't know how he worships her.'

'Go away from here, you idiot! Do you know whom you are speaking to? Don't show your face any more to me,' said Maghbool angrily.

'Then you cook the breakfast and lunch. Akram's ayah will do the tea and the dinner. I shall ask Begum Sahib to agree to that.'

'When did you become the dictator of this house? Don't tell me what I have to do. I know what is good for me. If the ayah cooks for Nazni my servant will to it for me.'

'Your servant! Good heavens! A woman coming here without marriage talks of servants. A servant for you! Who will pay her? A servant without salary! Has anybody heard of such a yarn?' The cook left the room.

It was a long time since Maghbool had come to her husband's house. She had never yet been asked to work. She did the cleaning of her rooms of her own accord. Sometimes she had helped Munira in serving meals. Now on account of Munira's seclusion the work suffered and none of the meals were served in time. The ayah looked after Nazni's and Akram's needs, and the cook carefully attended to those of Zuhra and Kabeer. The only sufferer was Maghbool. It was past twelve, and no one had spoken to her about breakfast. She had made up her mind not to work unless she was treated respectfully. If her mother-in-law had asked her to work she would have gone in spite of herself. Zuhra disliked going to the rooms of her daughters-in-law. She expected them to go to her and get her orders.

'Your father has come to see you,' said the cook, re-entering.

'My father my dear father has come to see his unlucky daughter! It is the first time he has come to this house. It is ages since I saw him and now he has to see me in my nightclothes. Look at my face and hair! It does not matter how I look. Go, bring him soon. Let him not wait outside like a servant.'

Maghbool had quite forgotten the insolent behaviour of the cook an hour before. She stood nervously to receive him.

'What has brought you to this condition? Had I to live to see you so haggard, pale and unhappy? What has become of your cheerfulness? Have I to hear you crying instead of listening to that rich nightingale voice,' said Faiz Mohammad holding his daughter to his breast. 'Why are you crying, Maghbool? This is a cold reception to your father, who adores you,' said he again, extremely moved.

'You have let me cry the whole of my life,' she sobbed.

'No, you don't mean that. You are hasty, you are thoughtless, my dear child.'

'It is due to your doings I am ungrateful to you. Knowingly you pushed me into a well,' said Maghbool desperately.

'You mean I gave you in marriage to a polygamous man? He has wives for name sake. You can't judge him in such a short time.'

'You gave me to a man who had no love for me and did not need me. How can I get on with him? Where there is no love disagreement and misunderstanding creep in and life becomes unbearable. Even the sincerest service will seem a disservice to him. You have destroyed the lives of three helpless creatures. The curse of my rivals will always haunt my happiness, and their jealousy will make my daily life a misery,' said Maghbool sitting by the side of her father, who was caressingly stroking her curly hair.

'Plurality of wives is not uncommon. Are all such women unhappy? People say rivals live more happily than sisters. Women quickly adjust themselves and create a happy world of their own.'

'Yes, those who have no power of thinking live like machines. My rival Munira is treated worse than a dog here, yet she is not unhappy.'

'Thinking women don't make good wives even with a monogamous man.[1] When a woman begins to think for herself she gives less regard to her husband's comforts. She must have implicit faith in him if she wants to make her life happy. Marriage is one of those things that are not proved at all by reason. Submit to him like a child and be happy.'

'So a woman is lifeless, feelingless and respectless?'

'She is respected by revering her husband. She becomes lively by making him happy. She feels as he does. When he is sorry she is sad. When he is happy she is cheerful,' said Faiz Mohammed, hiding his smile from her.

'She is his shadow, in fact. She goes to heaven by serving him. She is respected by disrespecting herself. Where does she come in his life? What is her position in his house? May I know?' was the haughty reply.

'She is the queen, the ruler, as well as a servant of her house.'

'When there are three queens where is her house? Two kings in a country can't rule and be happy. How can three queens rule in a house?'

'I am not responsible for the destruction of your rivals' lives, am I? Your husband did the crime wantonly,' said Faiz Mohammed to change the topic.

'You can't escape the blame so easily. You knew he had two wives, and that he was lying when he said he had nothing to do with them, yet you agreed to his offer. If he is directly responsible for it you are indirectly. Between the two of you and for no fault of mine I have to suffer the consequences.'

'Maghbool, the only thought in my mind was to get you married and get the suspicious name of a spinster wiped off. I realised the extent of my folly only when I handed you over to the man. I am not entirely responsible for it. I was intoxicated by the influence of the ladies at home I was blind to all the other complications.'

'You gained experience at my expense.'

'Yes. But I have not been as foolish as other fathers. I have had your interest uppermost in my heart. I made you economically independent. The knowledge of that will prevent him from doing any disrespectful action towards you. He will think twice before he separates from you as it means a disgrace to him.

'That is one consideration, but it will make matters worse. Even when I live with him he will think of my money and not of me and my needs. It will make us feel like two equal powers that repulse one another.'

'You wouldn't have lived unmarried all your life? A woman's life without a mate is empty. A Muslim woman, confined to the house, has no other way to make use of her energy than married life, which is the only recognised goal for her.'

'That does not mean that she should be given to any man just so that her father can get rid of his responsibility. With all your efforts you have made me hypocritical and selfish. I am true neither to him nor to myself. It is a sin to live with a man and not to be sincere to him. I see nothing good in him. His very presence is repulsive and even his loving words convey no meaning to me.'

'Nonsense!' said Faiz Mohammed tersely. 'You will have to change your attitude towards him. If you persist in your present behaviour his regard for you will gradually disappear. It is against Islam to return evil for good.'

'He lives the same unnatural life by keeping up a sort of show to every woman he meets. He can't meet them all at a time. When he meets one he is afraid of the other two.'

'You know more about it than I do. Why didn't you refuse to let him marry you? You are doing a wrong thing in disliking him after accepting him as your husband. You are partly responsible for the shipwreck of your own life. If you had taken the initiative everybody would have yielded to you. Your voice in the matter was essential. Your silence made me believe that you were willing.'

'I did ask mother through a friend, but being snubbed I had no alternative.'

'There you are! You approached the wrong person for it. Now the question is not to discuss marriage but how to make your life happy in adverse circumstances. Conservative men say the love of a polygamous husband is like that of a father. He seems to be indifferent, but it may be due to his interest in their well-being.'

'It is absurd to compare a husband to a father. The coming of children is not in a father's power, whereas marrying other wives is due to his dissatisfaction with one wife, or his lust. A father's love is disinterested and that of a husband is selfish. A father is grieved at the suffering or death of a child, whereas a husband's imagination begins to work on the replacement of his dead wife. The life of a child and that of a wife are not at all alike. A woman being transferred from a semi-prison to a real one has no aim in life.'[2]

'In that house your parents kept you under control, and here it is your husband,' said Faiz Mohammed smiling.

'My parents were not unsympathetic or critical or intolerant. Here every action I do is criticised and every word I utter is taken in a wrong sense. In spite of all efforts to please them I am looked down on.'

'A woman enters married life with the emblem of self-sacrifice in the service of her husband and his family.'

'Self-sacrifice is not the word for it, but self-effacement in the face of ingratitude and dissatisfaction. The more serviceable she is the greater is the demand for service, and fault-finding.'

'Yet she can make the best use of her life. No person in the world can be happy unless she forms her own world according to her taste and duty. It depends upon you to make your own life happy, and that of your rivals too. After all you know much more than they do. Fit yourself into your surroundings with a fair mind. Types of lives differ as human beings do. The glamour of married life dwindles after some time. A woman lives on tenterhooks either about a rival or from seeing the man having illicit connections with others. Wisdom lies in adaptation to one's circumstances.' Faiz Mohammed was surprised at the intelligence of the girl who had lived like a dumb creature in his house. At heart he agreed with all that she said, but he could not let her discard her husband and live alone.

It was about three o'clock in the afternoon. No one had called Maghbool for lunch. She felt hungry and went to the kitchen to see if there was anything left for her. She found some cold, greasy curry and rice in the pots left in a corner. She washed a plate and served a spoonful of each of them and tried to eat, but the cold grease was insipid. She drank some water instead. She remembered her promise to Munira.

'Have you had lunch?' asked Munira as soon as she entered her room.

'Yes, I am coming from the kitchen. How are you feeling? How is the cruel world with you?'

'I have been thinking of your food the whole morning. When I am all right I shall make it my duty to see to your comforts. I feel quite well except the cold. I feel benumbed. If I begin to work I will feel warm. Sitting near the fire will cure all my trouble.'

'No, no, you should not get up from your bed for ten days. Don't bother about me. I am all right. My father came to see me and on hearing the circumstances at home has promised to send a servant for me. I shall make her work for both of us.'

'Ammajan wouldn't allow you to have her, I believe. Nazni Begum was not allowed that privilege.'

'She is allowing an ayah for her.'

'The ayah is for Akram. This morning she was grumbling at her. She is sure to sack her soon. You get his permission for it beforehand.'

'I thought of the servant for you. I can manage without her. Let her come. We shall see what Ammajan says. Have you had your lunch?'

'I, a God-forsaken person, can't dream of having all that I want. I have to work hard for my board and lodging here.'

'Not when you are bedridden. Every one of them had to give what he or she took when you were well. Good and kind people serve their servants when they are ill. You are not a servant.'

'I am poor, so I'm equal to a servant.'

'Are you not his wife? Didn't he marry you?'

'No, it was only a nikha.'

'Nikha is the essential part of a marriage.[3] All the other ceremonies were invented by women. Your marriage is more in accordance with the Islamic rule than ours. So you must be respected more than all.'

'Poor girls are brought by nikha to serve the married wife. It is my qismat.'[4]

Maghbool did not understand her rival. Her ignorance was indeed bliss to her, and it would be folly to make her wise. By putting new ideas into her mind she would make her life miserable. To change the subject she said, 'I heard the baby was crying for a long time. Why did he?'

'He has been crying every second minute. Children cry to foretell coming events. He started it the very first minute of his life. If it is for my death I don't mind, but if it is meant for my widowhood I hope to heaven his prediction proves false.' Maghbool felt like laughing but controlled herself.

'I wanted to come to see him but my father was with me for a long time. Has Ammajan come to see her grandson?'

'Yes, she did enter my room the first time and looked at the baby from a distance, holding her clothes above her ankles as if he and I were outcaste and nearness to us would soil them. She neither touched him nor expressed her pleasure. She did not like me being confined to bed. The only thing she expects from me is to work—day and night—eat whatever food is left over, and not to ask for clothes or money.'

'Has he come to see his son?'

'No. He was displeased with my pregnancy from the beginning. He treats me like a keeper and is ashamed if people know of me. Naturally he would hate to have a child from me.'

'How do you know all that?'

'Can't I understand that much?' said Munira, shaking the pillow of the crying child.

'Oh, goodness! There are red ants all over him. No wonder he has cried the whole day. Look! His body is covered with a rash. This wretched room has no windows. You could not see the ants because of the darkness. Why don't you keep the door open? Maghbool took the baby on her lap and removed the wrapper from his body.

'Something is biting my feet too,' said Munira.

'Oh God, there are white ants under your bed. They come because of dirt. I am sure the ayah did not clean the place last night. It ought to have been washed well this morning,' said Maghbool, bending and lifting the mattress.

'White ants never come to living beings unless they are permitted by God,' said Munira. 'They have come to do their duty towards me. Sinners' bodies are eaten up by them before death, whereas good people's are protected by God even after their death. I am a sinner and this is the proof of it. I don't know my own crime. I always try to please others and never talk ill of anybody and pray to God five times a day for the forgiveness of my sins.'

'They may come up under baby's bed if you don't change the place soon,' said Maghbool.

'No, they can't reach him. He is innocent and his body is protected by angels. Look how he is staring at them. They are with him day and night.'

'The white ants come through the wall and your bed is close to it. There is nothing like sin and sacredness to them. It is all your imagination. I shall change your bed and put it at a distance from the wall.'

'But it should not be in the middle of the room.'

'Why not?'

'That is the way they put a dead body before burial.'

'Oh, I see. I shan't put it in the middle. I'll leave a space of two feet from the wall. Don't get up. No, no, you should not stir from your bed. I shall call the ayah to help me. Wait till I get another bed ready.' But to her surprise Munira stood up holding the wall, without caring for her entreaties.

'I have no other bed. I brought nothing except a small carpet with me. Ammajan gave me our father-in-law's sacred bed which she had preserved so carefully. Was it not very good of her? Sometimes she is very kind to me,' said the patient, still standing. Maghbool did not know what to do with the mad woman. She put the baby quickly on a cloth and began folding and shaking the bed-clothes.

'How do you sleep on it? It is all in lumps, and it stinks. You would not have used a sick man's bed?'

'There is nothing in it.'

'There are germs which can't be seen by us.'

'What is that?'

'They are a sort of very small insect which can be seen only by a microscope and they create diseases.'

'If a kira creates disease why should there be God and qismat?[5] A person suffers from the disease he is fated to. I don't feel the unevenness. The minute I lay my head on it I am off. I awake only with the sound of the azan.[6] I can sleep soundly even on a stone.'

Maghbool killed the white ants with a broom, spread the bed again, and helped Munira to lie down on it.

'Have you had lunch? The food by your side seems untouched,' said Maghbool after putting the baby on his bed.

'My lunch yesterday afternoon was my last meal. I cooked the dinner with great difficulty and left the kitchen without having my dinner.'

'The cook did not care to bring it for you?'

'She did not even ask me if I wanted it. She must have taken home all that was left.'

'Didn't they give you breakfast?

'Only two meals are given to a woman in my condition. They usually give toast and black coffee, but the cook brought raw rice and coffee. I wonder how the people of the house ate it. My mother used to say that nothing upsets a woman's stomach during the days of confinement as much as uncooked rice. Was it boiled when you had it?'

'It was all right.'

'Touch and see what she gave me. It is just half boiled. Did she purposely bring it for me?'

'I shouldn't be surprised. She said something like that to me. Don't eat anything she gives you.'

'I feel ravenously hungry.'

'I shall get you tinned food from a shop. You can keep it for days. My cousin is coming here this evening.'

'How is he related to you?'

'He is my mother's sister's son and is younger than myself. We were brought up together from childhood. My aunt lost her husband a year after her marriage, and my mother gave her shelter and brought up her son.'

'We observe purdah in front of cousins because of their marriageable relationship. After seven years of age we don't go before strangers, and after ten before all relations, except uncles if they are our brothers of mother or father.'

'We do the same, but this cousin is treated like one of my brothers. He is still a student.'

'What does that mean?'

'He is reading in a college for B.A. He comes so late in the evening because his college is very far from here.'

'That is a very big examination, is it not? He will be very rich, richer than your father. One boy in our neighbourhood passed it and got a job at forty rupees. He became so proud after that he did not talk or look at other people. He called all the old men of the locality damn fools.'

Maghbool smiled at the fantastic information and began to feel a desire to escape.

'Shall I go to see if he has come?'

'From where will you get money to buy food? They won't give it to you if they know the reason.'

'I don't ask those beggars for anything. My father brought the rent for my house and said he would send the interest of my ten thousand rupees deposited in a bank in my name.'

'How disgraceful! Then all the men know your name.[7] It is only bad women's names that come to the notice of men. What is the use of living in purdah when your name is pronounced by strangers? You have lost your gosha and your virtue. What is the use of living when one's name is spoilt? What will Ammajan and he say? He has every right to divorce you for that, but don't let anybody know of it. Is the house in your name too? Who gave it to you?'

Maghbool hesitated to reveal that she was not aware of her husband's view of the matter.

'My father told me that I have a house and the rent is fifty.

'Then your father is richer than Nazni's! But you never told me about it. You are kind and work for me like an ordinary poor girl!'

Chapter XV

Submission, subjection or servitude as it is variously called has its own significance as far as the feminine world is concerned and is very effective in making man favourably minded towards a woman. It creates pity for her and quenches the fire of his passion. It is applauded by members of both sexes. The greater her submissiveness and her ignorance the greater is the self-importance felt by him. An unfortunate woman devoid of this unique quality is only tolerated if not scorned.

Maghbool's frankness, respect for right and hatred for wrong could not go forever without surrounding her with enemies. Zuhra despised her inwardly and awaited a proper opportunity of poisoning her son's mind against her. Kabeer bore it patiently during the days of her bridehood—which converts even a tyrant into a saint—and till Nazni came home. Nazni's lack of confidence in herself and undiscriminating belief in Kabeer's words and deeds flattered him. Consequently he began to reflect on Maghbool's behaviour, and experienced a growing dislike for her. A person is humoured so long as his faults are not brought to his notice. All sweet and soft speakers have a cunning world of their own and impose their spell on those that come across them. Each meeting with Maghbool had overstrained him beyond words and the preparation to face the ordeal was too much for his poor nerves. Coupled with this her indifference to whether she enjoyed his favour or not had made him resolve to keep aloof for a time, to bring her to her senses. He feared his other two wives might be spoilt if he encouraged her. The only solution was to behave indifferently towards her, and this he immediately put into execution.

Maghbool also was heading towards the same goal. Her aim in married life, which she had cherished during the long years of maidenhood, was changed. It had become meaningless to her. The old fanciful sentiments had given place to an idea of making life possible in these adverse circumstances. Even her parents had advised her to make her life and that of her rivals happy. She could not be happy without being of one mind with her husband. A common purpose and mutual respect mitigate all sufferings and supply patience, energy and means to surmount them. In a life where the purpose of both was at sixes and sevens happiness was a dream of the past. To make others' lives happy was beyond human powers, but she could make her life useful to them. She should forget that there was such a thing as self. Her mother-in-law sent word to her to work for Munira. Should she wait for the allocation of work between herself and Nazni, or start working alone? Jealousy prevented her from taking the initiative. She recollected Kabeer's remark that he married her to rule over the other two, and waited for its ratification. The world will be a domain of saints if jealousy is eradicated from it, she said to herself.

Zuhra was wise in the choice of her room as from it she could command the movements of those who entered or left the house.[1] She had arranged her bed in such a way that she could see the visitors clearly through the curtained window without being noticed by them. She kept a keen watch on Azeem's (her cousin) entry into Maghbool's room with a small parcel every evening. When Maghbool sent for eatables for Munira he brought things twice, and big parcels too. Zuhra's curiosity was aroused. Why should he be so considerate to her? After all she is only a cousin. What will people say if they see him carrying bundles and packets to the house? She intended to go into the matter and nip it in the bud. She passed by Maghbool's room unseen by her and heard her talking and laughing with Azeem. A virtuous woman will never laugh in the presence of a man, and still less will she sit with him alone. No two members of opposite sexes are expected to be in any place without a third person, and if they are the place is taken by a devil, a creator of mischief. She thought there was something wrong somewhere. No wonder Maghbool was never seen happy in the presence of Kabeer. She knew that such ideas are more effective if they are put indirectly. She had already cultivated the ground by describing Maghbool's indifference towards home duties. She was waiting for a fall of rain to sow the seed and it would not take long to sprout from well-nourished ground.

The cook had worked alone hoping Munira would resume her duties on the fourth day, but finding her still in bed stopped at home. Maghbool would help her occasionally in serving meals. There was no extra work on account of Munira as she ate tinned food and the coffee was made and brought by her kind rival.

'The cook is sick and has sent a messenger to ask for leave,' said the ayah to Zuhra.

'What is that to do with me? Ask those bhainsain (buffaloes) to take on her duties. The poor woman worked these four days and the overstrain has tolled on her health. Do I look younger than they to your eyes?' said Zuhra.

'Begum Sahib, it is not my duty to order the mistress to do this or that. The messages are brought to you and orders are given by you, so I did it,' said the ayah, who disliked Zuhra intensely.

'Has anybody heard the tale of woe of a house consisting of three strong young women sitting in perfect idleness and growing flesh to fatten the white ants? Why do they protect their bodies in that way? Can there be any worse kind of ingratitude than to eat our food, live under our shelter, and yet grudge to work for us? We feel shy to eat the food cooked by others, whereas they take pride in it. What was considered by us a wrong thing has been taken for granted as a right one by them. If they are incapable of taking indirect hints they should be cudgelled and made to understand their duties. Ask them to leave their thrones and come to the kitchen, as they are not brought here to rule but to serve. Go, send the messenger and inform your mistress of what I say.' The ayah listened to the eloquent speech with unconquerable patience.

'They have been doing the work of beevies and you want to make them pakathies.'[2]

'Get you away, nalaiq and give them my command,' said she furiously.[3]

Maghbool overheard the bitter remarks about her life in the house. Before the ayah entered her room she left for the kitchen and began the work of washing with a heavy heart. She was angry with herself. The remarks made no difference to Nazni. She was as comfortable in her bed as if nothing had happened.

Munira listened to the talk, and heard her rival's footsteps and the sound of utensils in the kitchen. She stood up and peeped through the door, and was oppressed with sorrow when she saw Maghbool light the fire. She sat for some time hesitating. She knew perfectly well that her mother-in-law would not like her going into the kitchen before she had a bath on the twelfth day,[4] but gratitude felt for Maghbool's selfless work supplied energy and a firm determination to help her. She darted from the room to the kitchen in three long steps, leaving the baby alone. With its mother's overflowing milk it was a patient child.

'Oh God, why did you come here? You will kill yourself,' said Maghbool, excited, but with delight to see her there. She felt so light that she could do the hardest work for ages with her.

'Why did you come? I came here for the same purpose. I could not stay there after hearing what Ammajan said about me.'

'It was not meant for you. You have good cause to sit there and do nothing.'

'I wanted to help you too as I could not possibly be in my room while you were doing the nasty work with those snowy white and delicate hands. You will lose your lovely complexion sitting near the fire,' said Munira, pulling Maghbool away. 'Don't tell anybody that I cooked the meal. Even our talk will be overheard,' she said again.

'Why?' said Maghbool surprised.

'Because food is a sacred thing and it will be polluted by my touch and will make the consumers unholy.'[5]

'How funny! What is there in your hands to take away its sanctity? My objection is not that but for health. It is very sweet of you to think of me. I love to have you here, but I should not be selfish.'

'Soon after the cooking is over I shall go back to my room. I am quite all right. There is nothing wrong with me. I have been sitting up from the very first day and I can sit here with advantage as the fire will keep me warm.'

Maghbool felt doubly strong to work so she did not compel her to go back. Both of them prepared the breakfast and were scared to death lest Zuhra should appear in the kitchen. Her burst of anger had made her inactive. They waited a long time for Kabeer to have his breakfast first. Anything cooked should first be eaten by man, the sacred being, as it increases by itself. After the earning member has had his fill the women may eat. Even Maghbool held this opinion.

'I shall remove the upper part from each dish and keep it separate for him,' said Munira. 'In such circumstances I used to give the first helping to a fakir but today I heard only women begging. You have yours after his share is removed.' She was feeling more for her rival than herself.

'You don't worry. I shan't die if I don't eat,' said Maghbool who was bent upon self-destruction.

'I don't feel so tired working as waiting. It is disgusting. We can neither have our breakfast nor start cooking lunch.'

'He is always like that. He never comes home in time for meals. He wants everything steaming hot and does not like it warmed. He says warming spoils the taste and it must be just cooked,' said Munira who had undergone untold discomfort in the house.

'But what does he want us to do?'

'He wants us to cook just in time. The dishes should be neither overcooked nor stale. And he wants them to be brought as he goes on eating, into the bargain. A quarter of each should be taken at an interval of ten minutes so that the fat should not be thick and hard.'

'Why does he not buy dishes that can keep the curries hot till he finishes his meal instead of making the poor wretches run to his room a hundred times?' said Maghbool, who in spite of her determination not to question or reason but obey implicitly and die, could not control herself.

'How can a dish keep anything warm without fire?'

'There are dishes specially made for the purpose. Boiling water is filled under them and so long as the water is hot the things kept on them are warm. Here he is entering his mother's room,' said Maghbool who was standing near the door lest one should come and find out Munira's presence in the kitchen.

'You have to serve his breakfast.'

'I can't and don't want to.'

'Call Akram's ayah. But I must leave the kitchen before she comes.'

'She has gone out with him,' said Maghbool who would rather have done the hardest work than send her from there.

'As soon as he enters the house the food must be ready. Otherwise at the very outset his temper is irritated and even the best food does not please him. Go soon or else your labour will be lost,' said Munira and left the kitchen stealthily.

Maghbool was still hesitating to carry the tray. A false sense of dignity to do a thing which she had never done in her life prevented her.

'Maghbool, bring his breakfast. He has been waiting here for hours,' said Zuhra.

'Why? Where is the cook?' said Kabeer, who knew nothing of the new arrangements. His feelings towards Maghbool were not hostile, though he put on a forced seriousness.

'She is sick and is on leave. The poor creature had to work hard. If someone had helped her these four or five days she would not have overstrained herself.'

'She ought to have sent a substitute.'

'She is also a human being and is bound to have ailments. When she was healthy she served us well and when she really needs rest we should not grudge it. Sending a substitute means an extra expense for her. Let the women at home work for a bit. They are lucky to be destined to come to our house. If they had gone elsewhere they would have worked till they looked like charcoal. Sitting idle will make them wicked. An idle brain is the devil's workshop. In our days no woman was allowed to sit idle even for one minute. Hence the men of those days lived a carefree life as far as women were concerned.'

As usual Kabeer was contemplative. Whatever she said went deep into his heart. He thought that her idea of making women work was a wise one. They were bound to go astray having nothing to do. Yet his better sense prevailed.

'Cooking is a drudgery. Servants are used to it. There will be no difference between a mistress and a ward if we treat them like menials. Moreover people will talk ill of us because men of our status have numberless servants.'

'Cooking and feeding are the only sacred duty for women. It has been in vogue for centuries. A house where the mistress herself does not cook is worse than a hotel. Ninety per cent of them do it willingly. Women are women whether they are rich or poor. The only difference is of age. A woman who works keeps her health, vigour and youth longer than these idle mischief-mongers. If they live to my age they will be bedridden. You will have to serve them instead of being served. Have you not seen many unlucky men carrying bottles of qarura early morning to hakeems?[6] Who are they if not lunatics like you?'

The picture of men carrying such bottles flashed upon Kabeer's inward eye and it made him shudder. He felt gratified that God had given him a mother who was experienced, wise and farsighted. He thought he would be safe if he left all home duties to his mother. His hands were full with the affairs outside.

While mother and son were talking Maghbool was serving the breakfast.

'Hide his shoes somewhere. I hear Akram's voice. He might play with them and put one over the other. That ensures the start of a fresh quarrel in the house. We have led a very quiet and peaceful life. The very word quarrel makes me tremble,' said Zuhra to Maghbool who was passing by the door. She obeyed immediately and brought them back when Kabeer was going out. He lived in four places, with his two wives, his mother and in the office. His belongings were left wherever he sat or slept. One had to keep an eye on them and supply them when needed.

From the day Maghbool came to Kabeer's house the last thing she did before going to bed was to make milk hot for him and the first to make his bed and coffee. As he did nothing in time the times for these too varied. He often wanted a hot water bottle to keep himself warm in the night and massaging his body till very late in the night was an alternate duty of his wives. He had got it firmly fixed in his mind that his wives were there to look after his needs and he need not forgo any of them. A wife who was not made to do these things from the beginning would not be under his control. This also showed how much she respected him. At any time of the night he would ask her to cover him with a blanket if it was wet, or to fan him if it was hot. The minute his voice was raised she had to jump up and be prepared for the order. Any slackening meant disrespect. Hence they had arranged all their duties with the supreme object of his service. Her father's advice, 'You agreed to accept him as your husband and if you don't devote yourself to his service you will be a poor creature,' kept haunting her mind. Coupled with it her determination to be selfless if her life in that house was to be possible made her do everything willingly and not to make him wait for anything. Yet it was not an easy thing for her as he neither worked according to schedule nor was easily satisfied. He was of opinion that nothing done by others, particularly women, could be satisfactory.

Both the son and the mother sat for breakfast. Zuhra as usual commenced with fault-finding. She grumbled that the vegetable was not properly peeled, the fibre was not removed, it was not well boiled or over-boiled, the rice was smelly from not being washed or boiled too much, the grains were not separated, the masala in the curries was not fried well and the appearance was repulsive, and so forth and so on.

'Haven't your people trained you to cook? Did they live on ready-made food?' said Zuhra to Maghbool who was standing motionless and speechless behind the door. No answer coming she said again, 'Beggars live on preparations made by others. It makes no difference in their civilisation even when they get some means of living. No human power can make a beggar woman sit near the fire. Cooking teaches discipline. You seem an open-air sort of woman.'

This harsh remark was rather displeasing to Kabeer. He found no difference in the food as everything had been cooked by Munira.

'Today being the first day we shall give a margin. Practice makes perfect. The food will be better in course of time,' said he. Zuhra knew he was supporting her indirectly and she thought as far as Maghbool was concerned he needed quite a different pill.

'I hope she will be more careful. Indifference in anything is bad. My days are past. I am already one foot in the grave. I have neither any desire to eat nor need for it. My objection is for your sake. If you don't eat well how can you earn and feed so many mouths?' said Zuhra who was in no way a smaller eater than Kabeer. She was very careful in not serving anything on her plate more than a spoon at a time, but till the end of the meal no one could count the number of them.

'Bring some more feet curry,' said Zuhra to the dumb creature, who, very modestly covered from head to foot, entered the room and taking the empty bowl left it.

'She was not brought up in that way in her house. Her people are very rich and live after the Western fashion.[7] We should either send for cook or the negress to go to the kitchen,' said Kabeer who was touched by Maghbool's sad appearance.

'Day by day you become more irresponsible. Munira is still rolling in filth. If she enters the kitchen I shall starve to death. Having lived all my years an undefiled life I don't want to pollute it in my last days.'

Maghbool was just entering with the curry and heard the words distinctly. The blood in her body froze. She stood motionless with the bowl in her hand.

'What are you dreaming like a woman possessed by an evil spirit? Bring it here,' said Zuhra.

Maghbool put the bowl down and went to the place allotted for her till they finished their meal. Should she inform Munira of what her mother-in-law had said or take her help and keep the old lady in the dark? In the former case she alone would suffer but in the latter Zuhra would create a hell and all would suffer. She resolved to tell Munira what she had heard and work alone at any cost. She carried all the empty plates to the kitchen. Akram's ayah had already taken food for Nazni and herself. There was not much left in the pots. Maghbool served the remnants in a tray for her rival.

'Of course. Do you think I shall bring it before filling my stomach?'

'Five minutes ago you carried away the empty tray. You could not have finished yours and served mine in that time.'

'I did two things at a time, serving and eating.'

'Open your mouth,' said Munira.

'Why? I don't carry it all the time in my mouth.'

'No. I can tell by smelling. Breathe out,' said Munira.

'There is no smell. What you said was a lie.'

'I drank water after finishing my breakfast.'

'You cannot cheat me. I can't ask you to share mine. You would not eat from the plates returned by Nazni. That swine of an ayah takes a lot to her room and wastes it. She brings the plates and throws them down without caring for what is left in them.'

'Don't bother about me. I tell you I had some.' Maghbool had no more patience to argue with her. The idea of cooking alone was torturing her mind.

'I must go to prepare lunch. I shall be seeing you again,' said Maghbool trying to leave the room.

'I am coming too. What did they say about the breakfast?'

'Showered me with rebukes and said there was nothing good. All the same they ate well.'

'That is what they do. However you try to please them they are never satisfied. Often I used to be disgusted but to what use? A beggar's anger costs her own self. The only way to get on here is not to open your mouth. If they show you a jet black thing and ask you to call it white echo the sound. Anyway I am coming to cook lunch. By the time I finish my breakfast you try to do something there.'

'No, no, you are not expected to step into the kitchen.'

'What is the matter?'

'Ammajan said if you enter the kitchen she will starve to death.'

'What made her say that?'

'I don't know the cause but I heard it clearly.'

'Oh my poor dear, how will you do it?'

'When you are in hell you should not shrink from its heat. Let it burn me till my body turns into ashes. I shall try to do what I can. If they don't like it I can't help it.'

'Why don't they ask Nazni to work? You are in no way inferior to her. She is treated like a man.'

'Don't you know she possesses a passport in her sickness which is acknowledged by her devoted husband and her beloved mother-in-law? They not only don't ask her to work but ask me if her food was sent into the bargain. Is there any justice shown? Islam says if a man can't do justice among his wives he should not marry more than one. You are treated worse than a galley-slave and my fate is not very enviable.'

'You must fight for your rights or else they will make a paste of you,' said Munira.

'Why didn't you do it?'

'Your case and mine are like the sky and the earth. One is elevated and exalted in every respect, the other is only a lump of dirt. So there is no comparison between you and me.'

'Let them destroy and burn me till they can do no more.'

'When you are being burnt you must burn those who rule over you.'

'No I can't. I shall burn myself like an iron piece but unlike it I shall not harm others. I shall not grudge to cook Nazni's food while I do it for everybody else.'

'They neither allow me to go to my mother's place nor permit anybody from there to come here. There are myriads of women servants in our locality. I would have asked to send one.'

'Don't worry about me. God will provide some way for me, or He will give me enough strength to face the situation patiently.'

Maghbool went to the kitchen. She was dismayed when she looked at the heavy work before her. It was past twelve and she felt ravenously hungry. The pots were empty and there was nothing else to eat. She drank water till she filled her stomach and resumed the work. Tears were blinding her, but it was beyond her with all her efforts to control them. The spices which she was grinding were becoming watery. She lifted her head to wipe the tears and saw a woman with a letter.

'Are you Maghbool Begum?' said she.

'Yes, I am that unfortunate being.'

'Here is a letter for you from your mother. She has sent me to work here.'

Maghbool read it and was at a loss what to do. She dared not ask the woman to work without the permission of her mother-in-law. She had no confidence in her generosity. Her distress made her think of her husband's mercy. She would be satisfied with her lot if he rejected it.

'Go to the opposite building, ask for master and show this letter to him,' said Maghbool.

Unfortunately the woman did not conform to the principle of seeing the mother-in-law on such occasions. She left the house without seeing Zuhra who had seen her enter the house. This naturally vexed her and her dignity was wounded. Why should she be there if people acted as they liked in her own kingdom? This was added to her many grievances against Maghbool. She thought she would be a vile creature if she did not punish her for her impertinence.

The woman gave the letter to Kabeer. He was pleased with it as it answered the vital question which his mother would raise over the appointment of a servant. It clearly said that the servant was known for her honesty, hard work and efficiency as a good cook and her salary would be paid by Faiz Mohammed.

Kabeer entered the zenana followed by the newcomer.

'Who is this nasty woman' She walks in and out on her own as if she were the mistress of the house,' said Zuhra as soon as her eyes fell on her.

'She is a good cook sent by Faiz Mohammed.'

'I don't want anybody. I have had enough of them. We have a cook. We can't dispense with her services.'

'Let us give her a trial. If she proves satisfactory we can sack the old one. She is becoming very talkative nowadays. You have often said she was very extravagant.'

'No servant can be economical. If you think of expenses you must make your wives cook. A servant takes her share twice, one without our knowledge and the other with it. On the top of it her pay is a drain.'

'We have nothing to do with her pay. He has taken that responsibility. What will he say if we send her back immediately?'

'I don't want to have a person who wants to rule over me.'

'What did she do?'

'She came in and had a talk with your wife and has come back with you as if I am nobody here.'

'Being a new person she did not know that you are here. Moreover it was the mistake of the mistress who had to send her to you instead of me. The servant is not to blame.'

'Unless she admits her impertinence and make amends for her audacity she will not be allowed to work here.'

Kabeer turned to the servant to give her a sign to do it but she was already disgusted with the job and was on the point of leaving the house.

'I have not come here to beg for a job. I was sent for a hundred times from the place I was working on a promise of a higher salary. I have never stood this sort of humiliation in all my life and I have worked under respectable people,' said the servant.

'Did you hear what she said? She calls you a disreputable man. She has come to beg but behaves as the mistress. Take away your wretched face from my presence,' said Zuhra tartly.

Kabeer stood hesitating. A shrill cry was heard from the kitchen. Maghbool while straining water from the boiling rice slipped the lid off the vessel. The boiling water spilt over her hands and feet and made her scream. Munira ran from her room to the kitchen and poured cold water on the scarred hand and feet. The new servant forgot her resentment and went to the kitchen to see the matter. Kabeer, in spite of his will not to show curiosity, dragged himself to the spot. Zuhra also condescended to reach the place not so much for clemency as to discover a new cause for grumbling.

'What a clumsy woman you are. Even a girl of seven years can cook ordinary rice. What a waste! The whole pot of rice is thrown on the ground. Did you grow that huge body playing marbles and kites? Even a man will prove a better cook. You are a disgrace to womenhood,' said Zuhra to the poor writhing creature, and turning to Kabeer she said 'She has done it purposely. No one will ask her to cook if she gets her hands burnt. If she cared for your money she wouldn't have the heart to waste such a lot of rice. It is at least two seers. We hardly need half the quantity.'

Kabeer thought it was the best opportunity to strike the iron.

'Go and apply cold cream on the blisters,' said he to Maghbool. 'Start cooking lunch. I am feeling hungry,' said he to the cook.

Munira seeing Zuhra's temper rightly guessed the royal gale would turn from Maghbool to herself and slyly slipped away with two big potatoes, and Maghbool followed suit.

'Is this the time to say all that? One sympathetic word would minimise her sufferings. Poor thing, so patiently she is bearing the pain,' said the servant.

'You shut your mouth. You have lost nothing so you feel nothing. Our money is wasted so our hearts burn. Before you start cooking put all the things out, wash the kitchen and after washing them bring them inside,' said Zuhra.

'Why all that fuss?' said Kabeer.

'Didn't you see the zachcha (woman after giving birth) in the kitchen? One can't cook before the purification is made,' said Zuhra with an idea of enforcing her will at least in that way. The proposal to send away the servant had been defeated automatically.

'Do all that Ammajan asks you,' said Kabeer, and left for his office.

Zuhra stood there to see whether the servant would obey her. When half of the pots, planks and other things were taken out she left.

Chapter XVI

Maghbool was alone and restless in her room. The cold cream had no effect on her burns as it melted and left them dry. She needed something that would keep them cool. She knew no medicine to apply and was crying noiselessly.

Munira knew that she required immediate attention. Her experience had taught her crude but effective medicines. She had carried some potatoes from the kitchen and was waiting for Zuhra to clear away from the quadrangle when she hastened to make a fine paste of them. She did it with so much alacrity that even the servant in the kitchen was left in the background. Zuhra was surprised at the noise of grinding and peeped through the window. She guessed what Munira was doing and said to herself 'Who will call this devil an invalid?'

Munira came to Maghbool with her preparation.

'How are you? Are the burns any better with the cream? I feel as if those sores are on my heart. This is a simple medicine but will do you a world of good. You will feel its effect within five minutes. Stretch yourself on the bed. I shall apply it.'

'It looks so dirty. What is it?'

'It loses its efficacy if you know what it is made of.'

'Do whatever you like. I leave myself entirely in your hands. You are the only real friend I have in this house. Oh, how nice! It is cooling. I feel much better. If Ammajan sees you making this fuss over me she will boycott you as a leper.'

'Don't bother about me. I am a leper already. She is confined to her bed, her throne I mean. She will descend from it only when lunch is ready. By the by, from this morning I have been wanting to tell you something funny I saw yesterday. When Azeem was in your room I noticed Ammajan standing behind your window and listening. As soon as my eyes met hers, she bent down, took Akram's ball which was lying there and went away to her room.'

'Perhaps it was the spirit of economy that made her take care of it.'

'Oh no. If that was the case she would have called the ayah and scolded her till she shed tears. I am sure there is something fishy. She wanted to overhear what you two were saying.'

'How mean of you to think that about an honourable women! No respectable lady will stoop to that humiliation. From our childhood we were severely punished for the evil of carrying tales or listening to other people's talk.'

'I have seen many old women doing it. They have every right to do it in the interest of the family.'

'What do you mean by in the interest of the family?'

'When a young man and woman talk and laugh it is the duty of more experienced persons to keep them aware of the natural and harmful consequences. Familiarity between members of opposite sexes is always a bad thing.'

'This cousin of mine has all his life made it a point to make people laugh. When he was in school he used to make us all roar with laughter and now he's a college student he is not reformed. When you hear how they tease and irritate their lecturers you can't but laugh. I used to laugh and laugh till I looked red in the face. I look forward to his coming as he knows the art of making people cheerful in no time. If you could have come in you would have laughed till your stomach ached.'

'God forbid the day when a stranger would make me laugh. If once I did it I would be destined for hell.'

'How funny! Laughing is not a sin.'

'You are yet a child. As a friend I ask you to be careful in the future. Don't laugh loudly. You give room for suspicion. I was glad to see the door left open.'

'It never struck me that the door had any significance. It is often banged by the wind, but Azeem was careful to keep it open. Once he put my slipper against it. I was furious with him.'

'God's all-knowing hand helps us without our knowledge and spares us from miseries.'

'Why should anybody suspect me? After all I am a married woman. I have reached majority and know what is right and wrong.'

'A woman is not above suspicion and safe till her death and three days after it. There have been cases when women have been molested in the grave. That is why the Brahmins burn the dead bodies.'

'This is an awful world. We don't know where we stand. We were encouraged to laugh freely and my father said that it keeps a person healthy and lengthens life.'

'Old people never laugh, so if they see others doing it they invent hideous ideas.'

'Have we to cry all our lives?'

'Not exactly that, but be serious and reserved. It is not only dignified but also keeps a woman cautious of her virtue. I am telling you all this because, who knows, Ammajan's sly observation may have a wicked motive? She might poison his heart against you.'

'Azeem comes here only for fifteen minutes and that too when mother compels him to bring sweets and papers for me. She knows I love them.'

'You should not love any object in life except your husband.'

'Oh goodness, then say I like them.'

'His bringing sweets too can have a bad meaning.'

'I give them to him when he comes to my room. He likes them very much.'

'That is not the way of doing things. The packet should be given to Ammajan. She should open and distribute it to everybody at home. Then it does not mean he brings it with a wicked purpose.'

'But my mother sends so little, just enough for my tea. I make three shares for you, him and me.'

'What does he say about it?'

'Once or twice he asked me from where I got it. I told him. He likes Azeem and praises him.'

'Does he? I hope everything will be all right.'

'But why should she do anything mean?'

'What is mean in that?'

'Standing behind the window and listening when she is supposed to be in purdah.'

'She did it in her home. She has every right to save him from harmful consequences. If she had confided in me or if I had more regard for her than you I would have encouraged you to fall in with her design. I have come across many instances of mothers-in-law. You can't deny that she dislikes you, and she is formal with me because she sees us often together.'

'What shall I do? Shall I tell him all that you have said?'

'Oh no, no. They will kill me. Try to keep on their good side. Now and then tell him about Azeem and what he says, and watch his reaction. If he dislikes his visits stop Azeem from coming to you. Baby is crying. I must go. I shall come back with a fresh paste.'

The new cause of worry agitated Maghbool. She lay in bed considering her future actions. Could humanity be so base as to derive imaginary evil out of nothing? How could anybody say anything against one's own conscience? Islam professes to hide the failings of others even when they are seen and known as facts. Is it Islamic on the part of a respectable woman to make a baseless accusation?[1] Munira was helpful and sincere, but her ignorance and upbringing were bound to create such ideas in her. She should take advantage of Munira's goodness and overlook her defects.

Kabeer was not unmindful of Maghbool's accident. A cursory glance at her blisters and her painful writhing had stirred his nobler nature to life. On the pretext of going to office he went straight to a doctor and bought medicine from a shop. He dared not take it with him and tell Maghbool how to use it. He wrote the method of its use on a piece of paper and inserted it between the cotton and bandages lest it should be seen by Zuhra.

A servant came with the packet, called out the cook, handed it to her with an instruction that it was to be shown to Zuhra and to be given to Maghbool. It was an unpleasant duty for the cook to act as a mediator between men and Zuhra. The latter opened the parcel, examined every bit of it and recognised Kabeer's handwriting.

'What are all these bottles, ointment, cotton and bandages? As if someone were seriously ill and dying? Who sent it?'

'Master sent it to be shown to you and be given to Maghbool Begum.'

'I see. This is the office work he was making a fuss over before he left. He must have squandered money on it. Give it back to the servant, ask him to return it, and tell him that Unani medicine has been applied already and she is well.'[2]

'It has been bought from a big shop. What respect will they have for master if he returns it?'

'Ask the servant to go himself and return it. Even if he takes it back with some annas less it does not matter.'

'The servant is gone already.'

'Who asked you to send him away without my order? She gets herself burnt at a time when no hospital works and people are forced to spend money uselessly. Where was the need for it when she has been already attended to?'

'Begum Sahib, such cases are not treated at home. In Nawabs' houses doctors are sent for and nurses are appointed to look after the patient. Ordinary people are sent to hospital. A small burn can be cured at home. I know the medicine applied. It wouldn't cure but keeps it cool temporarily.'

'I have cured more serious ones than this.'

'If you had looked at the burns carefully you would not have said that,' said the bold servant who from the first day had established her position.

'Send Nazni here and you go to the kitchen.'

'Read this,' said Zuhra to Nazni, giving her the note.

'It is the direction for using the medicine.'

'Is it not in his own handwriting?

'Undoubtedly it is.'

'He hides it in the bandages so that I may not see it, as if I am her enemy. If I prevent him from squandering money is it to take the whole property to my grave? He will be a beggar after me. These days of comfort and luxury are short.'

'When he has given her a house worth ten thousand and sold a piece of land of equal value for her marriage this is an insignificant expense,' said Nazni, whose jealousy was touched to the quick.

'He did not give it to her. It is in a dilapidated condition and is haunted.'

'It was registered in her name before the nikha took place. It is rented for fifty rupees. She gets it.'

Zuhra thought her ignorance of the matter would lower her in the eyes of her daughter-in-law.

'Yes, I remember he told me about it. I forget things very soon. In course of time, I may do it with my meals as my grandmother used to do.'

'I believe he did it without your knowledge and has kept it a secret. My father told me about it and asked me not to say anything about it to anybody.'

'How did your father know?' said Zuhra, changing the topic.

'He knows Faiz Mohammed very well.'

'How things leak out. We wanted to keep it a secret from your father. There is no privacy in the world.'

'My father wasted lakhs of rupees on my wedding, but her father made a property for her.'

'She has only that, but you and my son have a right to the whole property. Now and then come to me if you want any help or if you get any information worth mentioning,' said Zuhra and told her to ask the cook to take the medicine to Maghbool.

Nazni was frightened at having let out the secret. She thought that Zuhra knew it as she did not express any surprise. On the other hand she was supporting Kabeer.

Zuhra's anger knew no bounds. Her own son in whom she had all hopes and for whom she was giving her life had acted treacherously. Had he really done this? How could she know it was a fact? Nazni's jealousy must have made her invent the story, but the question of the house and the land had often been discussed. He always gave her lame excuses for the defalcation. She said to herself that there might be some true in it. There is no smoke without fire. This was an addition to the numerous grievances against Maghbool. He had brought her at great cost and had given her a rope to hang him. She thought over it and concluded that an antagonistic attitude towards him would only make the matter worse.

When the medicine was taken to Maghbool's room Munira went there.

'I don't think Ammajan was up to the mischief I guessed at. Even if she was she has not poisoned his mind or else he would not have bothered to send the medicine,' said Munira while bandaging Maghbool's left foot, which was now a frightful sight. This changed Maghbool's unfriendly spirit towards Kabeer. She thought that he was not altogether devoid of human qualities.

Kabeer, well prepared to face the tyrant and little knowing the complication created by Nazni's simplicity, came home. He knew very well the art of winning her heart. As soon as he entered her room he threw his turban aside, breathed a heavy sigh, sat down with a thud as if he had no control over his limbs and began to wipe away perspiration with a kerchief. These signs of exhaustion made a quick appeal to her maternal heart.

'What has made you so tired? If you run about in the hot sun to doctors and shops you are bound to exhaust yourself,' said Zuhra.

'I went out in connection with rent and revenue but I met Faiz Mohammed on my way. He asked me about her. I told him she had met with an accident. He bought some medicine for her. Did the servant bring it?'

'To suit your whims and fancies how magically things are done for you!' said Zuhra sarcastically. 'Such incidents fit to adorn fables! Your houses produce evil spirits and cause the death of human beings, your lands grow snakes and kill the cultivators, your father-in-law drops from heaven when you need him and buys medicine which you did not want.'

Kabeer felt as if a bolt had fallen on him from the blue and he sought for his kerchief and began to blow his nose violently. Zuhra knew the effect of her revelation of his secret on him so she changed the subject.

'No woman can be called a good cook without tasting the warmth of fire. Often such burns are cured without the knowledge of men. In this house everything is upside down. A world of fuss is made over a scar. People are informed from one end of the town to the other as if an honourable thing has taken place. On the other hand that woman ought to be ashamed of herself for her inefficiency and you ought to feel it in the same way.'

'I told Faiz Mohammed because if he came to know of it through a third person he would think I intentionally hid it. I told him there was nothing serious and we will look after her carefully.'

'Yes, that is the only thing left for you now. Shave your moustache, put on her dress and become her nurse.[3] You have brought yourself to that condition,' said Zuhra, checking herself from even franker expression.

'He wanted to take her home till she is completely cured. I said that to avoid it,' said Kabeer.

Kabeer was silent for some time. He thought that someone had informed her of his double dealing. There was no doubt about it. Whoever the culprit was he would kill him or her as he would a dog. What should he do? Should he still act hypocritically or tell her plainly the necessity that forced him to do it? He made up his mind to wait and find out her informant, and meanwhile if Zuhra herself told him about it straightforwardly, to tell her the truth. Lunch was announced and both went silently to the dining room.

'She seems a good cook. We can stick on to her,' said Kabeer to break the silence.

'Munira is a better one. She will resume her duties after twelve days. This one can be a helper,' said Zuhra. Dead silence continued throughout the meal. Zuhra left the room soon after she finished. Seeing Zuhra go out the cook entered.

'How is she? Did you apply the medicine?'

'She is much better and is having a nap,' said the cook, who had worked in many joint families.

'Look after her well. I shall pay you something besides your salary. Keep me informed of her progress.'

'I shall do my best. You need not worry, master. The medicine you sent is an excellent one for burns,' said the cook.

'Was there any visitor this morning for Ammajan?'

'No, master, the only person who came was the servant with the medicine.'

'Was anybody speaking to her in my absence?'

'She asked me to send Nazni Begum to her and they were talking for a long time,' said the cook, and hearing Zuhra's footsteps bent down, took the empty plates and left.

'What were you jabbering about here?' said Zuhra.

'I went to bring these,' said she and without stopping went to the kitchen.

'I told her that she is satisfactory and will be kept on,' said Kabeer, who met his mother on his way to her room in order not to create any suspicion in her mind.

'I left the room in a hurry to finish my duties before confining myself to a corner till eight or nine in the night,' said Zuhra.

'Why should you? What is happening today?'

'Nothing particular today. I am speaking of every day. You are absorbed in outdoor work, little knowing what takes place at home. Azeem comes whenever he likes and stays till late in the night. It is not difficult to stick to a corner especially when one likes to get a little fresh air in the evening. Poor Nazni too is sailing in the same boat with me,' said Zuhra.

The doubt created by the cook about the informant was confirmed by his mother's sympathetic reference to Nazni. How did she know of it? She never told him about it even indirectly.

'The window and door of her room may be kept closed,' said Kabeer, coming back from his reverie. 'Yet one's own conscience can't be clear when one knows a stranger is sitting within the four walls.'

'He comes after the college gives over. Perhaps he needs some rest before he starts on another strenuous ride back home. His house is pretty far from here,' said Kabeer looking towards Akram who was dressed to go out. The ayah was getting herself ready leaving him free. He came running to Kabeer, examined his watch and heard its ticking.

'Baba, my watch is no good. I want one like yours. Listen, mine does not work. Give me yours,' said he to Kabeer, who knew it was a toy watch yet to please the little fellow bent and listened.

'It works if you shake it,' said Kabeer.

'But it stops after some time.'

'If you try to be a good boy I shall buy a nice one for you.'

'I want buttons like yours. See how they shine,' said Akram, examining the gold buttons with costly stones which were Kabeer's wedding present.

Zuhra's temper was rising but she controlled herself with a great effort. She was of opinion that when a particular thing on a person's body is liked by others it should be given to the admirer or else the wearer's life is cut short. She could not ask Kabeer to part with the watch and the buttons as she did once his new silk shirt. Both of them were very expensive.

'When you grow big and get married your mother-in-law will give you such buttons,' said Kabeer. The reply was not very pleasing to his young heart. Akram looked this side and that and his eyes fell on the stool on which a goblet full of water and a glass were kept. He ran towards it.

'Don't touch it! You will break it,' shouted Zuhra.

'I want cold water to drink,' said Akram, trying to pour water into the glass. He tipped it too far and the water rushed over his face. He dropped the glass in fright. It was a relic of the house as it had been used by Kabeer's father. Zuhra would not have parted with it for a hundred glasses.

'Oh pig, scamp and rascal!' screamed Zuhra, and gathering all her energy rushed at him with a stick and thrashed him.

'Do you see what you'll get if you disobey?' said she again, still beating him.

'Say you will never touch the goblet and will obey me,' said she again. No reply coming she dragged the howling child to a corner and made him sit down in his wet clothes.

The ayah was still busy in satisfying her needs. Nazni could not stay in her room. She came forth hesitatingly to know the cause and stood staring at the little criminal, who began roaring again, expecting help from his mother. But even the ayah would have been of more help than that pathetic picture standing before him.

'Go away from here,' said Zuhra. 'He is becoming a truant and is beyond control. I am asking him to say that he will not disobey me but he refuses to open his mouth. Let him cry till he begs pardon.'

Nazni had no alternative. She was nervous after the morning affair. If she did anything to displease Zuhra she would probably inform Kabeer what she had said. She stood expecting help from her husband, who however was also silent.

'I manage the child day and night. If he is left for five minutes he is brought to this condition. The poor baby is shivering in his wet clothes. The new shervani and the pyjama are solid with the dust,' said the ayah entering the room.[4]

'Stand aside. Don't touch him. You are only a paid servant. You are here today and will be sacked tomorrow. We are his well-wishers and his interest is close to our heart. If he is spoilt we will be pained to death and not you,' said Zuhra.

'Ayah, please take me with you, take me,' sobbed Akram.

'If you don't want me to console him in his distress I shall leave the place. I have nothing to do here,' said the ayah, vexed.

'Take yourself away, be gone, good riddance! Who is preventing you? You will not take away our fate. Next minute there will be a better person than you,' said Zuhra.

The ayah turned to leave the house, but a shrill pathetic cry stopped her.

'Ayah, don't go! Take me with you. I shall die!' cried Akram bitterly with raised hand. The sad picture would have melted a heart of stone.

'What shall I do, Baba? If I did not love you more than my honour I would not stand another minute in this place,' said the ayah and went to Akram.

'Darling, say that you will not touch the goblet any more,' said she, wiping his face with a kerchief.

Kabeer thought the ayah would handle the situation more tactfully than he or Nazni and left the room without a word. Nazni, who had stood like a statue in his presence now went to the distressed child who was getting hiccups.

'Shall I change his clothes, Ammajan? He catches cold quickly,' said Nazni.

'Do it, and let him sit there till he apologises.'

'Go and bring his warm clothes,' said Nazni to the ayah.

'I have never seen such heartless people in my life. They will not mind killing the child on the plea of discipline,' said the ayah going out of the room.

'Did you hear how haughty she is? When a servant assumes the attitude of equality she should never be kept at home.'

'Yes, she is very impertinent in that way. Even if I hit Akram she begins to grumble at me. He is such a self-willed child that I can hardly manage him for ten minutes. I shall send word to my mother to look for a decent one.'

'Do it soon. I don't want to have anything to do with that wretch,' said Zuhra, and resumed repetition of God's names on the rosary.[5]

His mother's nearness, her gentle strokes on his head and face, and her kiss made Akram forget his obstinacy. He put his arm round her neck and his head on her shoulder.

'Bibi, don't leave me here. I don't like granny. Take me with you when you go,' entreated Akram pathetically.

'If you obey my one request I shall do anything you like,' said Nazni, who remembered her mother's method of bringing round naughty children.

'Tell me what you want. I shall do it,' said he, controlling the hiccups.

'Say to granny that you will not touch the goblet. You broke that pretty glass.'

Akram looked at the stern face of the old woman. It was a repulsive sight to him. He turned his face and put it back on his mother's shoulder.

'Say it, dear, you can go to your room and you can go out. I shall ask the ayah to take you to the merry-go-round,' said Nazni again. Akram whispered the words in her ear.

'Say it loudly. Granny did not hear it. Louder, louder, louder, still.'

The ayah returned with warm clothes and without looking at Zuhra gave them to Nazni.

'Shall I take him to my room, Ammajan?' said Nazni appealingly.

'Yes, you change his clothes. Let the ayah clean my room. It is in a mess.'

Nazni gave a sign to the ayah to do so, but she followed her heedlessly.

'Nazni Begum, take the account of Baba's clothes. I am not staying here any more.'

'Ayah, don't make me more miserable. If you leave me you will hear no more of me and my child,' said Nazni, greatly perplexed. She could not force her to stay and she could not think of the idea of minding Akram.

'Even supposing I try to tolerate her ill-treatment of me I can't bear the sight of the innocent child being beaten. Not a day passes when he is not flogged. He loses weight, keeps on crying in his sleep and gets frightened at the very sight of your mother-in-law.'

'Knowing all that you can't leave him. Have pity on him, if you don't care for my comfort.'

'I am not going to clean her room.'

'Don't bother about that. I shall do it.'

The ayah and Akram went out. Zuhra saw them going and her blood boiled.

'Where is that woman? How long does she want me to sit among the rubbish?' said Zuhra when she saw Nazni enter her room with a broom and a cloth.

'I sent her with Akram as it was getting late for him.'

'You don't know how to control servants.'

'This one has been spoilt from the beginning. When I get a new one I shall keep her under strict restrictions,' said Nazni. After cleaning the room she left.

Zuhra said her evening prayer and sat with the rosary. Kabeer was anxious to see Akram. He bought the watch he had promised him, went straight to Akram's room and gave it to him.

'I hear a man's voice in the house,' said Kabeer to Zuhra.

'Which man will dare enter the house except that dare-devil Azeem?'

'He seems late today.'

'Every day he is late. Our Maghbool is a funny girl. The whole day she was in bed lifeless. Now she is talking and laughing and perhaps eating the sweets he brings.'

'I don't hear her voice,'

'Perhaps she knows of your arrival.'

Kabeer went to Maghbool's room. Azeem was standing ready to go home. As soon as he saw Kabeer he bowed and wished him good evening very politely.

'Today was my busy day. I had no intention of coming here but was compelled to the point of being driven. Some special preparation was made and I had to bring it. I am glad I came. We did not know of Apa's accident.'

'I had no time to send word. But it is nothing serious.'

'Yes, she told me that and added you brought her some wonderful medicine which made her feel okay,' said Azeem, and left.

'Are you really feeling better?'

'Yes, much better. Thanks for your kind thought of me.'

'Someone has been playing mischief between me and Amma. She knows of the house I gave you and the land I sold for your clothes and jewels. Did you say anything to anybody here?'

'I told Munira, but I did not say that you gave them to me. Ammajan is not on good terms with her.'

'I believe the ghost was talking to her for a long time. How does she know of it?'

'Her father and mine know each other very well. He might have told her.'

'But she did not tell me.'

'She must have done it to get on the good side of Ammajan.'

'I must wait and see who has really done it.'

'Please see what mother has sent today. She forced him to bring it.'

'You did not even open it.'

'I never do. What will he think of me if I act greedily before him? I being his elder sister should try to keep up my dignity.'

'I am finishing everything, it is so delicious.'

'I don't feel like eating anything tonight. If you don't eat it all, it will have to be given to the cook.'

Kabeer needed no coaxing to do his duty. He left the plate empty.

'It was very good of Azeem to come here, with all his numerous activities,' said Kabeer.

'He is mother's protégé and has no alternative. My aunt and he have no one in the world and nothing to depend upon.'

Kabeer did not like to sit there any longer lest he should vex his mother. So bidding her good night he left.

Chapter XVII

Zuhra was very persevering if she had made up her mind. Although her body was flabby her will was iron. Her mind was active in planning a scheme not only when she was engaged on her daily duties but also when she prayed and recited on the rosary.

When Kabeer went to Maghbool's room in a temper she was sure that he had caught Azeem and Maghbool red-handed. Even supposing a suspicion had occurred to Kabeer, Azeem's courteous behaviour, his indifference towards Maghbool, his hurry to go home and the effect of the rich sweet replaced it by confidence and respect for both. He returned to his mother as peaceful as he was comfortable. Zuhra thought the dunce needed a bigger and bitterer dose.

'Old people used to say that the birth of a child and the coming of a new person in a home were of good or bad omen. From the time you married your third wife there has been loss after loss. Since you began negotiating for her marriage you will find the house and the land have been lost to us. Three is an inauspicious number both in living beings and inanimate objects. What people generally do when they are forced to deal with it is they either reduce or increase the number.'

'Someone told me at the time of the wedding that she was the third in the family and many good offers were withdrawn on account of it.'

'Yet you married her. If you had taken your mother into your confidence you would have saved all this monstrous loss.'

'Experiences are gained only through suffering. A poet has said that henna produces its effect only after being ground and used on the palm.'[1]

'There are many who gather experience by mere observation. It is not necessary that a person should be afflicted to be wise. That property is still a problem to me. The old cook said it was rented out, but I am the last person to believe what others say.'

'Yes, it has been rented and we will be getting the rent from next month,' said Kabeer.

This allayed Zuhra's anxiety. She thought that Kabeer would take the house back from Maghbool.

Maghbool's burns were getting better, gradually. Kabeer's kindness and the cook's information of his talk to her about her welfare dissipated her spirit of non-cooperation. She believed that life for everybody is not poetry and it cannot be as it is the result of action and reaction of antagonistic elements. Happiness in life should not depend upon goods but upon thought. It was her thinking that would make her life poetry or prose. When both are possible why should she not select the easier path?

She now often went to the kitchen and helped the cook. She went to her mother-in-law, mended her old clothes and stitched new ones for her. She helped her when she had her head bath and was very particular in getting hot water five times a day for wuzu.[2] She tried to be good to Nazni and Akram, who took a sudden fancy for her music. He sat absorbed when she played and asked her to let him use her harmonium. She taught him the fingering. The shrill sound produced by his touch thrilled him. He was proud of his new art.

'Bibi, I play the harmonium. You don't know that,' said Akram one day to Nazni.

The relation between a mother-in-law and a daughter-in-law is a mystery. An elementary knowledge of human psychology certainly helps in gauging it. It varies as human nature is different, but in general a sort of semi-rivalry exists between them. A mother loves her son with a motive of love and be loved. She cares for him with the expectation of being cared for when he is strong and holds a position in life. She thus develops a sentiment in him of hero-worship for herself. Her regard for him also varies according to his capacity, intellect and position in life. She does try to bring a third person in between herself and her son as it has to be done, but she finds to her regret that the newcomer excels her in many respects. The young man finds the wife mentally more alert, physically active and her ideas and principles nearer to his than his mother's. He finds her more of an entertainer, an interest creator and a satisfier of his needs. Naturally he begins to care more for her feelings, happiness and comfort. The mother-in-law should sacrifice her interests in consideration of both the son and the daughter-in-law. Self-sacrifice is a feat of which only moral giants are capable and very few women are moral giants. Hence it is usually a case of mere tolerance on both sides. The spirit of give and take and that of forget and forgive which are so essential in human life do not seem applicable in that relationship. After a couple of months when sentimentalism for married life begins to dwindle and both man and woman begin to face facts in life the mother-in-law carries the palm being more experienced and influential.

'Today you have to go to the mazar of Peeranepeer,'[3] said Zuhra to the cook one day.

'Begum Sahib, it is a work to be done by men. The village is six miles from here. The dinner is to be cooked, I may not return in time.'

'Even if you return a little bit late it does not matter. There are others to look to it. I can't speak to male servants to explain what I want. I always send a woman there.'

'Women are not allowed to enter into the mazar.'

'Don't give lame excuses. Hundreds and thousands of women go there, speak to men, describe their needs and get the fatiha performed through them,' said Zuhra.

The cook wanted a change. From the day she came to work she had not left the house even for five minutes.

'In what connection have I to go? Is it a thuhfa[4] to be taken for the murad[5] which is fulfilled?' asked the cook.

'No, no, to pray for a murad. Two of our properties have gone out of our hands. We want the pir to transfer them to us.'

'You have to tell him what the properties are, and who took them, or else how can the pir fight with the enemy and get them back?' said the cook.

'There is no need for all that. You just give them Kabeer's name and say that his properties are taken by others and he wants them back,' said Zuhra, and gave the cook a five rupee note for buying flowers, sweets, incense and to pay some money for niyaz.[6]

No one knew of the cook's absence till seven in the night. All of them were busy with their routine work. Munira was occupied in stitching clothes for her son, Mahmood. The days of putting on rags were over. Zuhra had given her some spare pieces of cloth and so had Maghbool and Nazni. There were lots of pieces and she could make from them clothes to last for a year. Zuhra had asked her not to cut small kurtas and destroy the pieces but make them as big as she could. If they were too big she could put tucks or use them as a big garment covers the child's body well. If it is loose a child can move its limbs freely. Munira religiously followed the instructions. A few of them were made by Maghbool with fancy work. When these were shown to Zuhra she said that they were suitable for Moharram's jalali and asked Munira not to use them as she would make him an object of laughter. Munira disliked the objection and kept it a secret from Maghbool.[7]

It was half past six and there was no sign of the cook.

'The unusual silence in the kitchen today surprises me. Are we going to have a big dinner from outside?' said Munira to Maghbool who came to her room.

'Wonders never cease. Who knows what is happening? Our tea was stopped. Fortunate beings never forgo their needs. Ammajan takes hers all right,' said Maghbool.

'If the dinner is not ready when he comes we will be taken to task.'

'In what way can we be held responsible for it? If someone had told us the reason, had asked us to cook and if we had disobeyed the orders then he would have a right to be angry with us,' said Maghbool. Azeem was announced so she left for her room.

'It is seven o'clock and no dinner is cooked. Are we invited out?' said Munira to Zuhra.

'Invited, invited? Sharpen your teeth to eat lumps of meat, shameless creature,' said Zuhra, who was vexed because Munira noticed the absence of the cook so late. She was getting angrier every hour, as the daughters-in-law were so indifferent to home affairs.

'There is no sign of the cook,' said Munira.

'She is gone on business.'

'If we were informed of it we would have cooked the food.'

'Had I to come to you or you to come to me and get the information? Have you no eyes to see the kitchen door is shut? From when did you become the queen? From the time you got the baby, I suppose. You wretch, don't forget I brought you out of the gutter,' said Zuhra.

Munira felt like crying but controlled herself.

'Please tell me how many curries and what kind are to be made. It is getting late.'

'It is a wonder you thought of it. What can you cook at the last minute? Let it be late, let him come and see what obedient and loving wives he has,' said Zuhra.

Munira was disgusted with the argument, but she dared not go and start cooking what she liked. She stood humbly as a penitent. This cooled down Zuhra's anger a bit and she told her what to cook. Munira rushed to the kitchen, lighted four ovens at once and started cooking. The cook after describing her experiences at the mazar to Zuhra returned to the kitchen. Maghbool also joined them after sending Azeem away.

Kabeer usually came home between nine and ten for dinner. But unfortunate coincidences never cease. He came home soon after eight having a secret plan of going to a late show at the pictures with his friends, who had to call on him, after nine.

'I am very hungry. I want dinner immediately,' said Kabeer to Zuhra.

'If you are prepared to eat raw rice and meat you can have it at once,' said Zuhra who did not know whether the food was ready or not.

'Why, the new servant is very active,' said Kabeer, surprised at the mother's temper.

'She wanted a half day off. I allowed her to go in view of the hard work she has done all these days. She returned just five minutes ago and is cooking.'

'What on earth do the women do at home? Could they not prepare one meal in an emergency?'

'A bad workman quarrels with his tools. You have spoilt them from the beginning and all of a sudden if you want their services God alone should come down to make them work. Who are the women you speak of? One is an invalid, the other is a zachcha, and the third is an unruly colt.[8] Entertaining her cousin is more important to her than her husband's food. She knows he is Nandi ka bail who knows neither this side nor that but nods for both,' said Zuhra to pour oil on the burning fire.[9] The personal condemnation naturally raised Kabeer's temper but he could not be angry with his mother.

'Did he come today? I understood he had stopped coming daily.'

'Which day is it that he does not come? He left by the back door just when you entered by the front. I am of the strong opinion they keep a watch for your arrival. As soon as you enter he leaves,' said Zuhra.

There seemed a certain truth in Zuhra's statement, as the other day when Kabeer went to Maghbool's room Azeem was going out.

'Our women are strange creatures. They are indebted to us for everything in life yet they worship only their maternal relations. Nazni's ways were quite different. Her visitors were her own brothers. There is a world of difference between visitors and visitors,' ended Zuhra with a significant laugh. 'I am just giving you a hint in your own interest. Keep it in your mind as such matters end in life and death. The stricter the secrecy you keep about it the better it is for your name and fame,' said she again.

Kabeer's blood was boiling, and there was no sign of the food. The women were openly insulting him by making him wait. Coupled with this a tinge of jealousy had been created in the corner of his heart.

In the kitchen no one knew of Kabeer's arrival. All the three were so busy that they hardly tried to hear him talking. Moreover he did not speak much. Women are very generous with their words, and what is in their heart is on their tongues. They were not working like dumb creatures. The cook was a chatterbox and was very dramatic in her expressions. She explained her experiences with due exaggeration and made the other two laugh. Maghbool who had a naturally loud voice shrilled in the kitchen.

'Did you hear her laughing? Oh, that is nothing compared to what she does at other times. I am sure she is laughing because she has kept you waiting here. She is elated at it,' said Zuhra again.

The happy laughter when Kabeer was both angry and sad was not an appropriate incident and it got on his nerves. His patience reached breaking point.

'Fatima Bi, what are you doing? Bring my dinner soon,' shouted Kabeer to the cook.

His shout came like an electric shock to all of them. They rushed to arrange the trays.

'He seems angry. You go to him with a smile and cool down his temper before he sits for dinner,' said Munira to Maghbool, who was bent upon doing any service in the house. Maghbool ran with a dastarqan, spread it and laid all the other necessaries on it. She ran back and brought a tray full of dishes. When she was arranging them both the son and the mother entered. She stood up and smiled expecting an appreciative word for her alertness in serving the food for a man who needed it before time. But to her surprise there was a frown on his face and he did not look at her. She knew he was angry, but with whom was he angry? Perhaps his outdoor duties had worried him. It was by no means anything she had done. She had run with the dastarqan as soon as he called the cook. When she brought the second tray she kept her eyes down and set out the articles in silence.

'Why was the dinner not served when I came home?' said Kabeer sternly.

'You asked for it just now,' said Maghbool in a trembling voice.

'If you had eyes you would have seen me half an hour ago.'

'The cook had disappeared.'

'You were not dead.'

'I did not know that I had to cook.'

'You know many other things and do them with pleasure but did not know I needed food. Did you imagine that I live on water and air?'

'No one asked me to cook.'

'Shut up. Don't talk nonsense. I know the cause.'

Maghbool stood staring at him. A film covered her eyes and she saw nothing of him.

'Even if she knew it she was not free to cook,' interrupted Zuhra.

'Remember if you behave indecently you will be kicked out of the house as you stand,' said Kabeer.

Maghbool was trembling in all her limbs with surprise and fear, and her tears were uncontrollable. Instead of going to the kitchen to bring the remaining things she went straight to her room, closed the door, threw herself on her bed and cried.

'Did you hear the door bang? It means if she could she would have broken your head with that force. Instead of taking your resentment obediently as it was for her own good she is defying you. She did not care for your food. Any other person in her place would have stood and asked courteously if you needed anything more. We don't treat even a beggar in this way when he eats,' said Zuhra.

Kabeer could not take one morsel more. He went straight to Maghbool's room and finding the door closed kicked on it thunderingly. Maghbool ran and opened it. As he entered the room he took off his shoe and struck her with it over the head. She put her hands up to prevent another blow. Another came with a heavy thud on her slender hands and fingers. A third and fourth fell in quick succession, and broke her bangles, and her wrist started bleeding. The sight of the blood made him stop, and he went back for his dinner.

The cook had taken the rest of the things to the dining room and was waiting for his return.

'If Begum Sahib had not compelled me to go to the mazar for fatiha all this would not have happened.[10] The poor girl is just recovering from her burns,' said the cook.

'Don't tell lies. You took leave to go and now you put the blame on Begum Sahib. All of you are a pack of liars. Go away from here,' said Kabeer.

'You served her right. When a woman forgets her duties she should be reminded of them by gentle means. If she is so obstinate as not to heed she should be dealt with more forcibly. The whole day she keeps on writing. I wonder to whom she writes? Her playing the harmonium is another thing that shatters my nerves,' said Zuhra again when they had resumed dinner.

Kabeer was quiet. His energy was exhausted in the strenuous feat and his right hand was aching with the strain. His friends were announced. So he left home, disheartened. His eyes gazed at the picture, but his heart was sad. He himself did not know why he was so upset. Was he grieved because he had ill-treated Maghbool? Was it jealousy that put him off? After a second thought he found the latter idea was meaningless. He reflected over his personal experiences with her and came to the conclusion that she was a woman of strong character. His cruelty might lead to her separation, he thought. She could live comfortably with the means he had unwillingly provided for her. He would lose both a woman and her income. He made up his mind to go to her after the picture and be reconciled with her.

Munira was on pins when Kabeer was beating Maghbool and ran to her the minute he stepped out of the room. She found her on the ground, her clothes stained with blood. The heavy blow on the head had made her swoon.

'Maghbool! Maghbool! It is me. Open your eyes. I have come to repay the sacred debt I owe you,' said Munira.

'My throat is parched. Give me some water,' said Maghbool faintly.

The kind sympathiser gave her water, dressed her wounds, brought her dinner and tried to feed her with her own fingers, but a sensation of nausea prevented Maghbool from eating. Munira made hot coffee and forced her to drink and left her to herself.

'I was extremely hungry and was in a hurry to go out. When I was dying with hunger you were laughing at my loss. Just imagine yourself in my position. You would treat me leniently,' said Kabeer to Maghbool. 'I am sorry for what I did,' said he again, looking at the bandage on her hand and the plaster on her head.

There is no stronger weapon to tame nature to the point of self-disrespect than the sense of dependency. Maghbool thought that it was time for her to show her mettle and not to return evil for evil.

'I did not know you were at home till you called the servant,' said Maghbool.

'If the food was ready there would have been no cause for my anger.'

'It was ready and was served immediately when you asked for it. The cook had gone and we did everything in such a hurry.'

'She took leave. Should you not think because of it I should not suffer?'

'She was sent to the mazar by Ammajan to pray for the return of her lost property. We were not told about it till Munira went to her to enquire about it. Just then Azeem came after one week. I had a talk with him for two minutes and sent him away and went to the kitchen to help. The cook was describing the funny ways how she prayed at the mazar and made us laugh.'

'Did you not laugh because you made me wait?'

'I should have felt ashamed to do that, and would have cried to know that you were hungry and I was of no use to you.'

'Don't worry. What is over is over. Forget and forgive it. These are only tiffs between man and woman and they don't last long. Is there anything to eat? I feel like eating.'

'I stopped Azeem from coming daily and bringing sweets. He comes only on Sundays if he is free.'

'Why did you do that?'

'I don't know why. Just like that.'

'That is all right. People will think we starve. You and your mother send things from home. By the by, what do you do with the money you get?'

'I buy papers, magazines and other things I want. This month the cook's salary is paid out of it.'

'All those things wouldn't cost much. How much interest do you get on your dowry?'

'Father bought some shares so I get fifty. I used to get twenty-five.'

'So you earn a hundred a month. That is better than many men do. You must have saved a lot.'

'Yes, three to four hundred rupees, but Azeem has already found an outlet for it.'

'How?'

'He is so much fascinated with my rubaiyat and ghazaliyat that he wants them all printed in the form of a book,' said Maghbool.[11]

'Nothing better to do? A woman without getting her name in print has much to do at home. Such ideas will take away your home interest. No one will buy even one copy of it, the money will be wasted and people will come to know what sort of person you are and your infatuation, as all poems in Urdu are love poems.'

'You have not read mine. Not even one, to tell the truth. They are on general subjects such as sorrow, loss, pain, the suffering of the destitute. My father read some of them and thinks that they will bring wealth to our people.'

'I have not seen a better self-advertiser. A woman enclosed in the four walls always thinks what she does is the only thing worthy. She is the best person in the world. Earning money out of it is only your imagination. Who will care for your poems? The world is full of rubbish and no one bothers to waste his time on reading when he is busy in the life and death struggle to make both ends meet. Ask your father to return those four hundred rupees.'

'I have already given him permission to use it for the publication. There are so many people interested in it. I am pleased too. Don't try to deprive me of my little pleasure.'

'I see your point. You mean that your life here is a misery, so you want to have pleasure in that way. You do things on your own accord or to please others. Where do I come in your estimation?' said Kabeer fretfully.

'When you married me you definitely told me that I could spend the money in any way I like to meet my petty needs. That made me act independently.'

'It was not meant to be wasted but since you live with us it had to be spent in the interest of the members of the house. You care more for your name.'

'If you don't like my name to be on it I can easily ask them to change it to Azeem's.'

'Yet you insist on getting it done. You prefer to ruin us and at our cost make someone's name. You don't know how to make your own life and you dream of doing that for others.'

'That is quite a different thing. Since the order was placed long ago it is not fair to recall it. Those who are interested in it will have no respect for us.'

'Here is a living example of the precept that to give money to a woman is to give a dagger to her. I have to bluff Ammajan every day on something or other about the house and face her anger, just to enable you to throw away the rent heartlessly.'

'In that case give her the rent.'

'That will make the matter easier. You will still have your father's fifty rupees,' said Kabeer, but he could understand how his wife could call him her lord and yet not trust him. Why should she desire to have the house and the money in her name? If she really loved him she ought to have transferred the things to his name. He knew that Faiz Mohammed had arranged the matter so carefully that even she could not do it against her father's will. But why should she care for her father once she was married? He had nothing further to do with her. If she were loyal to him she would have quarrelled with her father and entrusted her fortune to her husband.

Such ideas often haunted his mind, and his love, which was already in a mist, disappeared altogether. He showed more regard and attachment to Nazni. At the time of feasts he bought clothes for every member of the house including servants, but not Maghbool. He was more generous to servants than to her. Their faults were pardoned and the least mistake of hers was exaggerated, criticised and condemned in front of everybody. She had to give him the rent of her house, but sometimes if it was delayed or a part payment was sent the blame was not on the defaulters but she was distrusted.

The open insults, rebukes and disregard of Maghbool by Kabeer melted even the stone heart of Zuhra. Her animosity gradually decreased. Once she actually said, 'Why don't you bring something for her too? Where will she go to get her needs satisfied? She is behaving very well, so we must show her some consideration.'

'She has enough money to buy what she needs and to spare. She is worth several thousands and wastes her income on others,' said Kabeer.

Maghbool noticed it all but was heedless of her personal interest. Her needs were few and she was easily satisfied. She always felt that she had all she needed in life and she was rich without them. She often spent her money to please the members of the house. In spite of all her sacrifices she found that no one was pleased.

For weeks he never showed his face to her. She tried to console herself and often said to herself that his slovenliness and his unshaven face and his costly but dirty dress would make her more angry so it was better he kept aloof from her. Whenever he did show himself it was with a fresh quarrel to burn her heart.

Chapter XVIII

Ahome in a child's life is a world in miniature, where his needs, intellectual, social, moral and physical are satisfied. It is a place where the solid foundations of his character, education and personality are laid and his instincts, emotions and interests have fair play. It is a place where love, sympathy and forgiveness prevail and punishment, condemnation and competition are minimised. His fancies and whims are humoured and his sense of self-importance is kept up to the maximum.

Such an ideal home is rare in a country where parents are enslaved by dogmas, customs and a false sense of dignity. A child usually is taken for a puppet and is supposed not to have feelings, interests or self-respect. He is expected to act whenever the string is pulled and otherwise to be a mere spectator. The string is ever to be strong; if by long use it wears out and becomes looser in its action the movement of the puppet should not differ. He is a plant in the hands of many unpracticed gardeners, each one of them trying to trim it to look smart at every stage of its growth, one plucking the ill-looking stem, the other an unshapely leaf and another making it straight. Thus its natural and free growth is stunted. Often his body is developed at the cost of his spirit and will. Suppression of the emotions does not in the least mean their death, but their explosion in a wrong direction. They are the pivot upon which life rotates. If one has no chance for their free execution one looks for and creates a world where imperatives are absent. Hence a child's life in a repressive environment is dual and in the absence of high and noble ideals evil ones are adopted.

Akram was intelligent energetic and mischievous from his infancy, and was therefore very troublesome at home. Nothing could be kept within his reach that was not destroyed, and no child could he play with without making him bleed. So he was made to spend the whole day, except his mealtimes, out of the home. The ayah being an old woman was not of much use to him. She used to take him to shops or hotels in the neighbourhood and make him play with the vagrants and scamps while she prattled with the servants. The habit of spending his time out and the influence of his associates led him towards a wild life. Brawling or coming home with a black eye was not an uncommon thing. Complaints from parents and shopkeepers were often heard and the damages paid.

When Akram was four years old the ayah was no longer needed and she was engaged for Nazni's second child. Akram was admitted into a school where he found himself in an alien world. He disliked it, but with compulsion he did go there. Progress was slow as he was detained in every class.

As he grew bigger Zuhra stopped her daily evening corporal punishment and handed him over to Kabeer who thrashed him till he bled. Both home and school were cruel to him and he craved for a kinder place. Nazni was not able to understand his needs, and the most she did for him was to cry with him and describe her own sufferings. She often begged Kabeer to send him to her mother's house where he could be better looked after but her request was flatly refused.

If human nature is greatly in need of something it is sympathy which heals the wounds caused by the ill usage of the world. Akram's childhood friend was Mazhar. Whenever Akram was ill-treated at home Mazhar took him home, and when he was not given food as a punishment for his bad behaviour his friend fed him. Mazhar's mother and sisters were very good to Akram. They did not observe purdah before him as he was yet in his early teens. Akram felt happier in the company of children of his own age, which privilege he was denied at home. Mazhar had three good-looking sisters, the eldest of whom was ten years old, the same age as Akram. All the ladies liked him so much that if he did not go there for some days they used to send for him. His long acquaintance with the family developed into an innocent liking between him and the big girl named Asmath. She often felt anxious to see him and talk to him.

'I feel happy when you come home. Do come to us every day with Mazhar,' said Asmath to Akram one day.

Akram had been Mazhar's classmate in the beginning, but his failure had made him his junior. Yet he went to Mazhar's house and studied there. He was given a duplicate key to Mazhar's room to enable him to take any book he wanted. When Akram was fourteen years old the two big girls began to observe purdah in front of him, but the mother still used to see him whenever she found time and often sent eatables for him with the youngest daughter who was only five. In spite of the restrictions Asmath somehow managed to peep through the window, uttered a word of welcome, and even came into the room pretending not to know that he was there and ran away immediately.

Thirteen or fourteen is the age for a girl to get married. Asmath was engaged to a rich merchant and was to be married soon, to her regret and to Akram's displeasure. Her husband was a good man and made her life a happy one, but suffering and woman are synonyms. In the second year of her married life her husband fell prey to a severe attack of double pneumonia and passed away. It broke the heart of the poor girl. She thought of committing suicide but this not being very practical she determined to aim at a gradual death. She secluded herself in a corner and reduced her food to liquids. She thus fell ill, and began to cause anxiety at home. Mazhar liked her the best of all his sisters. His worry about her often made him describe her condition in the presence of Akram, who used to listen with a pretended indifference. All the same he liked to hear about her. Sometimes he himself asked Mazhar about her.

One afternoon it was very hot and Asmath was lying in Mazhar's room which was cooler than others. Akram, as he often did, opened the door from outside as he wanted to take a notebook from the table. When he saw Asmath pale like death and excited with his entrance, he stood firm.

'Don't be sad. It was God's will. When the time for my marriage comes I shall make amends for your loss,' said Akram pulling himself together. Asmath in spite of the change in her life had a soft corner for him in her heart.

'Go away soon. If they see you in this room, they will kill you,' said Asmath in great agitation. Like a frightened child he left the room.

Human nature is such that it adjusts itself to any circumstances. This is specially true with women. They being used to tolerance, patience and suffering try to be happy in adverse circumstances. Asmath gradually forgot her sorrow, and the words of Akram frequently rang in her ears. After the loss of her husband she thought that she would love nobody in the world, but she found that any mention of Akram pleased her.

Dusk is the time when the night birds come out of their dens. Ladies leave their semi-prison and come into the courtyard to enjoy heavenly gifts. Mazhar's mother, sisters and others came and sat there for some time and then one by one went back, except Asmath. They knowing her plight did not compel her to do this or that. Left alone she went to the front door and peeped out. To her surprise she saw that Akram was approaching. Her first impulse was to run inside, but her heart would not permit her legs to do it.

'I had an intuition that I would see you today. It is exactly four months since I saw you last. I don't count how many rounds of your house I make every night I do it till I feel exhausted. I came to ask you something …'

'What is it? Tell me soon. I can't stand here talking with you,' said Asmath.

'Write on a slip of paper how you are and leave it under the tablecloth. When I come here to study I shall take it without Mazhar's knowledge.

'I can't. It is impossible. If it is discovered it will mean our death.'

'Please, please, do it! I want nothing from you except one sentence. I shall take care that no one comes to know of it. Even supposing it falls into others' hands they won't be able to make head or tail of it. Please do it till you get better.'

'But my writing will be discovered,' she stammered. Then after some time she said, 'All right,' and disappeared as quickly as possible.

The promise was religiously carried out. At first there used to be one sentence: 'I am getting better.' Subsequently more sentences followed, notes were exchanged with loving words, and verses followed suit. Thus the afflicted exchanged and in so doing soothed each other's grievances. Each supported and pacified the other, yet they never saw one another.

Akram's regular absence from home on the plea of study created a great sensation and both his mother and grandmother began to suspect him. They asked him questions directly, and not finding any clue they coaxed Mahmood to follow him wherever he went. He often carried exaggerated and made-up tales, having caught him round Mazhar's house. Sometimes he found him speaking with Mazhar's mother, or playing with his youngest sister.

'Do you know why Bhai goes to Mazhar's home? Not to read but to talk with the ladies. If he does not do that he walks round their house making tavvaf[1] of it,' said Mahmood to Zuhra.

'Akram is fast cutting adrift and becoming a truant and reckless day by day. If you don't check him he will be lost to us,' said Zuhra to Kabeer.

'He is not good at his studies either. He is detained in every class for two years and then is pushed up. We must stop his education, and engage him in business.'

'I believe he is always in his friend's house.'

'Who is he?'

'Don't you know Mazhar, who has been his playmate from his childhood?'

'His company is not bad, and his father is the proprietor of a big hotel.'

'But Akram goes there for his sisters.'

'That is a lie. No Muslim girl will be allowed to see or talk to a stranger.'

'You should not take things so lightly. There is something wrong somewhere. Otherwise a young boy will not be absent from home very late in the night.'

'You must ask him about it directly.'

'We did all that we could and being disappointed in our efforts have come for your help.'

'I can't interfere in the matter directly. If his father comes to know of it there will be misunderstanding between us. I shall take Akram in my charge.'

'That will be a sensible thing. Girls should be under their mother's control but boys under their father's,' said Zuhra.

'Is he at home?'

'No, he had his dinner early and went out. He will come after twelve.'

Next morning Akram was informed of Kabeer's intention and his belongings were sent to the office. He was given a room there and was made to look to the accounts and expenditure of the property. He had his food with his father and slept under his supervision. This restriction increased Akram's innocent desire to write to Asmath, and it became almost an obsession. Every day he wrote to her and accumulated all his letters. One day in Kabeer's absence he went straight to Mazhar's room and put the bundle of letters under the tablecloth. He did it in a hurry and without noticing how it looked left the place.

As Akram had stopped going to Mazhar's house for a long time Asmath had ceased to use his room. The same night when Mazhar was reading he found the tablecloth uneven. He lifted it and found the bundle. He opened it and read the contents. He knew they were love letters and were in Akram's handwriting, but to whom were they addressed? He went straight to his sister's room. He did not suspect Asmath as she was a widow and above suspicion. He made up his mind to look for more such letters in his second sister's box.

'What do you want, Bhai, from my box? I have nothing of yours,' said Zubaida.

'I have lost some important papers. I am looking for them all over. The children might have brought them and thrown them here,' said Mazhar.

Asmath's heart began to palpitate. She could not escape the inspection.

'I arranged my box just this morning and since then I have kept it locked. I don't keep things in it except my clothes,' she said, but her expression confirmed Mazhar's doubts.

'You will upset all my saris and jewels. It is so difficult to re-arrange them,' said she again.

'I shall keep everything intact. Don't worry, Asmath,' said Mazhar and snatched the key from her hand and opened the box. As he was removing the things one by one she grabbed a bundle from among them and held it firm in her hand saying that it contained her underwear. Mazhar left his search, asked the other sister to go out, closed the door and snatched the bundle from her hand. She began to cry.

'Bhai, I honestly tell you that there is nothing of yours. Even for the world I would not rob you of anything,' wailed Asmath.

Women's strongest weapon melted Mazhar's heart.

'Read these letters. If anybody sees them it will mean your instantaneous death. That rascal Akram took a mean advantage of my kindness to him. I fed him, gave him shelter when he was driven out of the house, helped him in his studies. In return he has planned to cut my throat. Father will hold me responsible for all this. I have either to commit suicide or murder him.' Asmath was still weeping.

'I came here not for my papers but to read his other letters. Show them to me. I can judge what he is up to. Have confidence in me and you are safe. Remember no one will help you out of this mess.'

Asmath felt a sort of confidence in him and in his support. She confessed everything and gave him all Akram's letters.

'So you wrote to him, too. How did you deliver them?'

'He asked me to leave them under the tablecloth and he did the same,' sobbed Asmath.

'I found this bundle in the same place.'

'When did he come here?' said Asmath.

'Who knows? You ought to know it better.'

'I swear I don't know anything about him,' sobbed Asmath.

'Are you not ashamed of yourself? Is it not disgraceful? Your younger sister though unmarried is more virtuous than you,' said Mazhar.

'I honestly tell you I stopped writing to him. It is almost two months since I did it. It was a mistake. It was the first and the last. I am not only ashamed of myself but I hate my very existence. Bhai, save my honour,' sobbed Asmath.

'His parents must have seen your letter so they stopped him from coming here. I permitted him to visit my room but I did not expect any mischief as the other door of my room was always kept locked from inside. I still can't understand how you could write to a stranger. Is this the result of teaching girls to read and write?'

'He compelled me to write one sentence about my health when I was ill. He said when the time for his marriage came he would make amends for my loss.'

'Did he mean that he would marry you?'

'I don't know. Those are the words he said.'

'So you met him too, you disgraceful wretch!'

'Only once for two minutes in your room.'

'He is a first rate rogue. Neither his parents will permit him to marry a widow nor will he be content with you. His father has several wives, so he will also.'

'Bhai, let the past be dead. I promise you on my honour not to have anything more to do with him.'

'Shall I burn all his letters?'

'No…yes…yes,' stammered Asmath.

'You still don't know your mind. You have yet a soft corner for him. If you clearly think of the consequences of such illicit friendship you will decide now what should be your future action.'

'Burn them all! I don't want to have another look at them,' said Asmath.

'Read them again if you want. Then I shall burn them.'

'No, no! I don't want to look at them. I hate to touch them!'

'Now you have come round and are on the highroad of honesty,' said Mazhar. He set fire to the bundle and threw the ashes out of the window. He opened the door to let his mother and sisters in.

'What has happened? What did you lose?'

'My school leaving certificate was misplaced. I remembered having given it to Asmath.'

'If we have some more persons of your memory the world will go upside down. The certificate is in my custody. Why did she cry?' said Mazhar's mother, looking at Asmath.

'When doesn't she cry? Her beloved husband is in her heart and her eyes are ever wet,' said Mazhar and left.

Next day Mazhar sent a servant to Akram's house and got the key for his room which had caused so much mischief. He now hated Akram so much that even if he happened to meet him on the way he would turn his face. His heart was in his mouth to think if Akram just mentioned it to his friends. What would happen to the family?

Kabeer was forty, measured forty round the waist. If a person with a brown complexion, beard and moustache can fall into the category of handsome men he did so. Beauty had still an appeal for him. He was not at all an unattractive figure. At the first sight of him anybody would know that there was a lot of energy and strength which badly needed an outlet.

The mania which so many people have to hoard wealth and leave it to their children has done more harm than good. It has made their children indifferent, irresponsible, carefree squanderers of the fruit of the parental hard labour. But Kabeer was not a very bad type of man. His motive was the same, but an economical way of spending money makes a world of difference. He did not drink nor spent money on women or gambling. These notorious vices have made many millionaires beggars. After all marrying two or three wives is neither a sin nor a drain. Men of strong orthodox principles who hate to have any illicit connection with women do have many wives. At the initial expense of a few hundreds for jewels and clothes a man can keep a woman at home. This wise policy is so handy and economical that it has made many men polygamous.

Leniency and loss are synonyms. Landlords in general are not fortunate in their tenants who believe in non-payment. Kabeer's tenants included both rich and poor. The rich paid up all right as they were not left in peace till the rent was recovered for the month. Where a small rent was concerned indifference on the part of the collectors and excuses on the side of the inhabitants were inevitable. The accumulation of arrears for years resulted either in their sly escape from the house or obstinate refusal to pay.

In such cases Kabeer himself intervened. Either he excused the heavy rent in deserving cases and got the house vacated, or he forced payment in installments. There was an old woman tenant who had not paid her rent for two years. Poverty and the care and protection of a granddaughter had made her bold beyond words. Often the bill collector went to Kabeer with a complaint against her high-handedness which instead of making him angry made him laugh. He often said, 'Go to her after some months. Perhaps fortune may smile on her in that time.' Years passed. Kabeer fixed a day for the settlement of the case. She was informed of Kabeer's arrival and was asked to be ready to leave the house. No one knew that she had a beautiful granddaughter.

'I have nothing to pay you, my lord. If you care more for money than human life kill me and this girl. I am doing the duty of the rich and the country who ought to make provision for such destitute people. If they are blind to their own duty someone has to do the job,' said the old woman to Kabeer, holding the girl's hand.

Kabeer could not believe his eyes when he saw the girl, who was young, beautiful, and as fair as a lily. He said to himself if she had been born in a palace she could have graced a queen's throne. She was a hidden beauty whom God by mistake had created destitute. The flawless girl stood very modestly in his presence. When the grandmother created a pathetic scene with her wailing she was touched to the quick with the sight, lifted her head with an expression of appeal in her eyes and looked at Kabeer but said nothing. Her silence was more impressive than expression. Whose heart would not melt at the sacred scene? Even a woman would be moved to help her.

'Grandma, I have excused the arrears. You can stay in the house as long as you live. As you say, it is the duty of the rich to help the poor. I shall make it my duty to support you so long as there is life in me. Take this money and make your life comfortable,' said Kabeer, handling her over a handful of rupees. The girl disappeared from the scene, to his displeasure. The old woman shed tears of happiness, raised her hands and prayed for Kabeer's long life.

'You have released me from a great sorrow that had almost killed me before your arrival. If you do one more service to me you shall send me to my grave carefree. The service I need is to give a home to this girl,' said the woman and turned to present her to Kabeer, but to her surprise she had already vanished.

'Have patience and confidence. I shall do all that lies in my power,' said Kabeer.

The promise was given in a sacred hour and no human power could change it. Kabeer left the place, but the picture of the girl was before his eyes long after the incident.

He came to his office quite exhausted and sat alone in the visitors' room. Imagination which is the bliss of solitude soon came to his rescue. 'How many more wives am I destined to have? Living together both for man and woman is a matter of fate. No one can change it as it has a miraculous way of uniting them however one tries to put obstacles in its way. A woman will not be any protégée unless her name is written on the grains she will eat. Three is an inauspicious number. From the time I married that rebel, Maghbool, everything I do has gone wrong and I have suffered nothing but loss. Why should the loss take place unless there is a supernatural hand which shapes things and warns us to be cautious? Old sayings have their own significance. We living in the modern world laugh at them and bear the harmful consequences of our audacity. I have been sustaining these losses for quite a long time to no purpose. How long can I wait before things are set right? The number must either be increased or decreased. Decreased! How?' thought Kabeer.

He shook his head, got up from the chair with a little effort, went to the table, and began fidgetting with the articles on it as if they might inspire him. He turned from the table and putting his hand on his bald head scratched it. Coming to his senses he sat down again on an easy chair and stared at the carving on the ceiling and resumed his reverie.

'I cannot divorce her. What will happen to her child? She is sweet, is she not? I can't discard her without proper reason. Once she is free she will either live an ignominious life or get herself remarried. In either case it will mean death for me. So long as I live she will not live with anybody else except myself. To increase the number is the only solution. Four is an auspicious number, otherwise Mohammed (peace be on him) would not have fixed it.[2] Who knows what is reserved for me? I have volunteered to help a helpless woman. God says if one supports a destitute person he will be blessed a hundred times. Fortune is a wheel which in its rotation lifts some and puts down others. It has been indifferent to that poor girl. If it takes a fancy to smile on her who will be benefited by if not we? This marriage definitely is not for my own sake but is meant to help an unfortunate creature. Anything done disinterestedly has its own supernatural reward. Well, this is a resolution not an intention.' Thus his daydream came to a conclusion.

He felt restless and walked up and down the room. It is easy to make a resolution but carrying it out may present myriads of difficulties. The obstacle in his way was Akram's question and Zuhra's longing to have his marriage performed before her death.

She had sent proposals to almost all the rich houses both in and outside the country but all were rejected because Akram was not employed. When the refusals were brought she had a ready reply. She said that in a house where so many members are fed one extra girl will not starve. The world has become reasonable and the sufferings of women have opened the eyes of parents.

After reflecting over the matter Kabeer said to himself that there is time for everything. When the time for the blossoming of the flowers of Akram's sehra comes no one will prevent his marriage.[3] His youth and bachelorhood are the strongest temptation to people to refuse him. He should not forgo the God-sent chance in view of this lame excuse. He had given his promise to the old woman so there was no question of hesitation. He began to smoke and as the smoke soared high an idea struck him. When a good deed is aimed at even foul means in its fulfillment are permissible.

There was a knock on the door and Mustafa entered. Kabeer was surprised. It was a long time since Mustafa had visited him after his resignation. His faith in fate was strengthened. Why should this man come particularly when he was in the throes of deciding the question? There was the supreme hand in the matter. His hesitation was due to his lack of confidence in the Almighty.

Kabeer at once confided in his visitor who not only approved of the idea but promised him to carry out his desire. This excited Kabeer immensely. Romance in early life involves unimaginable sacrifices and it is not powerless in ripe age too. After all, what is progress if not change, discard and adjust?

'There is some truth in what is said that there is a connection between hearts. You were inspired to come to me at this junction and solve the problem,' said Kabeer.

'If regards are sincere the parties get telepathic information of each other's anxiety,' said Mustafa. 'It is my duty to keep your promise and no effort will be spared in that direction. Are there any difficulties in your way?' said Mustafa again.

'No, no, none at all,' said Kabeer. 'There is nobody to object to it as everyone is absorbed in her own affairs. If I take interest in the home activities there are nothing but quarrels, jealousy, crying, sarcastic talk and woebegone eyes. One can't bear the sight of the other if I only utter one word to one of them. It gets on my nerves when I see the innocent children whipped in revenge. The house is a hell for me. I don't know what is a happy home where one forgets his worries and gets relaxation from the ills of the cruel world. I can call none sincere to me and no one whom I take for a real sympathiser. When I begin to have confidence in one to my surprise I find that she falls short of my expectations. I have made up my mind not to bring the girl to this wretched house and contaminate her in the company of those murderers. The house where she is now though small seems to have the world of peace and happiness. There I am certain of getting my wounds healed. If she brings luck who will be benefitted if not they?'

'Certainly, certainly, they are the gainers,' said Mustafa. 'I am told the girl possesses several signs of luck on her body. They will surely bring fortune to her husband, for God does not create those marks for nothing at all,' said he again.

'My way is clear. Go ahead,' said Kabeer.

He got up from the chair, opened the safe and gave Mustafa a bundle of notes. 'Buy all that is necessary for her and for the nikha. One thing you have to be very particular about is secrecy. Let it be between you and me. Let the kazi be there, and as for the two witnesses you can be one and the other you have to choose according to your discretion.'[4]

'Have confidence as to that. In these cases one's own breath can't be trusted. When do you want it to be fixed?' said Mustafa.

'This very night. Let it be any time after ten. You need not come here. I shall be there exactly at half past ten.'

'Right you are. I shall not fail in my duty,' said Mustafa and departed.

Kabeer was thrilled with the success of the day's work. He remembered the saying that each successive day should be better than the last, and the work started in the morning should be completed before it passes.

Akram's presence in the office was not very pleasing as it meant a check on Kabeer's movements. He was a shrewd young man, and when he saw Mustafa enter his father's room he thought that there was something in the air. 'Old pop is still going strong and his schemes are ever green,' he said to himself. He did not like to question Kabeer but consoled himself saying that Kabeer was arranging for his marriage.

Kabeer after seeing Mustafa off went to Akram's room and to his disappointment found him reading a novel.

'Reading novels the whole day is not good. When you feel tired of the office work you can read them. Alexander, the manager, is a very old man. Your presence there will be a great help to him,' said Kabeer. Then the two of them had their lunch. It was a very quiet business.

After lunch they went back to their respective rooms. Kabeer had a good rest after the heavy meal. He awoke just in time for the evening prayer, said his Namaz and prayed to God to take away the curse and the righteous wrath from him and grant him peace of mind and happy home.[5] The prayer being sincere floated straight away into heaven. The Merciful blessed it immediately.

Chapter XIX

The typist appointed by Kabeer's father continued his work very faithfully till one day he fell seriously ill and was advised by a doctor to take a complete rest for some months. Kabeer considerately granted him leave on full pay for the period of his retirement in view of his long and meritorious services. Here was an opportunity for Alexander to act immediately, and with the consent of Kabeer he appointed Rose, his niece, in the place. She was engaged to a ticket collector and was to be married after six months. She wanted to work not only for the time being but also after her marriage.

Rose was working in the office two months before Akram's transfer from the zenana to the mardana.[1] One day when he was sitting near Alexander's table Rose entered the room with a bundle of typed papers. Akram felt a chill all over his body and beads of anguish on his forehead. He bent down his head and began playing with an ink bottle which slipped from his hand and dropped to the floor. Rose bent to see if her dress and shoes were stained with the red ink. Finding no damage she went back to her room.

After this incident Akram did not sit at Alexander's table and just visited him when Rose had finished her work with him. He used to avoid even passing her room. If by chance he met her while crossing from one room to another he used to lower his eyes and disappear.

'You are more shy than a girl. Look at her, how erect she is and how boldly she walks, talks and acts,' said Alexander to Akram one day. He was a man of broad experience and knew how to train adolescents. He often brought simple story books for Akram and read them to him.

'I have nothing to do with her. Why should I talk to her? We are not supposed to look at women.'

'She is your servant. You have to command her and get the work done,' said Alexander.

Akram had no answer so he left the room. Rose also would go to her uncle's room for preference when Akram was not there.

'Why don't you try to be polite to Master Akram? He is shy and reserved. You should not be formal and expect a greeting from him first. You girls don't know how to get on in the world and are vainly proud of yourselves,' said Alexander to Rose.

'As soon as he sees me he turns his face and is off.'

'There is no harm in saying a word, good morning. He is our future boss. If he begins to like you he will influence his father to make you permanent here.'

'Yes, yes, say good morning and if he does not answer be snubbed. He does not even look at me.'

'His father also does the same, doesn't he? They can't help it as they are brought up in that way.

If he does not answer your greeting once or twice he is bound to do it the third time. What do you lose even if he does not do it?'

'Okay, it shall be done,' said Rose.

She made up her mind to give it a trial and began to wish him good morning and evening. Sometimes she asked him questions about the correspondence, though she knew more than he. Akram took almost a week to return her greetings, and said nothing more than that. Once she asked him something in English, and he answered in Urdu. She had discovered the cause of his shyness. She began prattling with him in her broken Urdu which made Akram laugh loudly. His natural feeling of inferiority began to decrease. He sometimes spoke to her in English. Her pleasing manner, sweet smiles and mild jokes made him quite familiar with her. His growing instinct of love and romance needed an outlet.

He began to spend most of his time with Alexander and visited Rose's room often. The transfer of monetary responsibility to him by Kabeer had no value to him all those months, but now he felt it a blessing. Once or twice Alexander and Rose invited him to have tea with them. This made him buy things from hotels and share them with them. He began to save some money for his private expenses from the daily accounts. Kabeer's trust in his economy was implicit so he neither checked the accounts nor asked him how much money was sent to the bank daily. Akram was under his eye day and night. His personal experiences and the thrifty life he led under his mother's control could never allow him to suspect Akram. On the other hand he thought that if he was not allowed to handle money at that age his desire for it would result in squandering it after him. The sense of responsibility is a hard teacher so he never thought of the possibility of the other side of the question.

'I have placed orders for two suits,' said Akram.

'You ought to have taken Granny's permission for the change of your libas.[2] She never allowed me to do it.'

'I knew it was impossible. I can never wear a thing I like,' said Akram.

'It is all right, but try to convince her,' said Kabeer, without asking how much money he meant to spend on them.

'I shall wear one and go to her. She will grumble for some time.'

'Your marriage question is decided and it is to come off soon. We have to be very careful with money. As you have control of the money you will know how much it will come to. A marriage means one lakh,' said Kabeer as a precaution against extravagance.

Akram's policy was not to argue but never to forgo his needs and desires. He wore one of the suits one evening and went to the zenana. He entered it from the back door. The very sight of him made the ladies run into their rooms and bolt the doors from inside. He heard one collective scream, 'Soldier agaya!'[3]

'Who is that shameless swine? Is he drunk or mad? Fathima, what are you doing there? Have you no eyes to allow drunkards into the house?' shouted Zuhra from behind the door after recovering from the shock. The cook was laughing. Akram stood for some time and then went to Nazni's room and knocked on the door.

'Bibi, it is I. Open the door.' When the door was opened, 'How do I look? I don't wear those shabby clothes any more,' said he.

'I don't know how you look. Have you seen Ammajan?'

'I dare not go and see her. Didn't you hear her shouting and calling me names?'

'She did not know that you had come. Come, I shall take you to her or else she will be angry with me. She must see you first and you must ask her for her opinion. Ammajan, it is Akram who came in. Here he is.'

'Hai, hai! Who is this kafir?[4] Good heavens, just before his wedding he changes his religion! How can I show my face to those people? Look at his face. It has no expression of a momin.[5] O God, that I had to live to see this day!' ejaculated Zuhra.

'I look like a gentleman now,' said Akram, dusting his pants with a kerchief, a trick which he had learnt from Alexander.

'Who gave you that? How dare you take your father for a loafer? Your dress looks as if a bamboo is wrapped with a kambal. Our costume is picturesque and artistic and unites all Muslims. On the day of judgement you will get up with kafirs and long to see the face of a momin, but it will not be shown to you. One can't think or feel like a Muslim in the garb of a Chatta,'[6] said Zuhra.

'Our teacher said that one's dress does not change one's religion. When I was at school almost all the Muslim students wore suits. You can't understand how one feels in the company of friends with that funny dress,' said Akram addressing Nazni.

'Let your teacher go to hell! What does he know about our religion? I hate to see your face for one minute more. Go and change. Give that dress to some beggar,' said Zuhra sternly, and turned her face from him as if it was a sin to look at him.

Akram was too proud to sit there and try to bring her round or go and change his suit to please her. He went to Maghbool's room.'

'How pretty! How lovely! How did you wangle to get such a sweet suit? It fits you wonderfully. Where did you get it made?' said Maghbool.

'Is it really nice? What do I know about the clothes and the tailors? Everything was done by Rose. I went with her merely to give my measurements.'

'No wonder it is so exquisite. Honestly it is flawless. She has good taste.'

'Did you hear what Granny said?

'Young men should not go by old people's opinions. Their tastes and ours differ. Take it from me that you look decent, smart, handsome and respectable. Didn't Ammajan say that when a man exposes his ankle the fire in hell starts burning for him?'

'What will happen to the English girls then?'

'Don't talk of them, they are hellish. Heaven is reserved for Momins.'

'You don't mean what you say?'

'Don't go by my opinion. I am a destined douzakhi. Try to be on the good side of Ammajan as your wedding is fast approaching. She will make him disinherit you.'

'I am not going to marry the girl she has chosen. Let her marry her herself.'

'Then whom will you marry? You can never choose a Muslim girl.'

'Why not? I shall marry one whom I like and can choose.'

'Even the walls have ears. Don't say all that, or both of us will get into trouble.'

'You just wait and see what I do.'

'Don't do anything that will mar your prosperity. Your very words make me shudder. Ask Rose to see me. I want to consult her about baby's dresses.'

'I shall bring her, but you have to see that Granny does not insult her.'

'Even if she gets angry with her she will not understand Urdu.'

'She understands it very well. When Granny begins scolding Rose we shall say that she was angry with the servant.'

'Let Rose come alone. If you accompany her Ammajan will be upset.'

'Then I shall come after some time,' said Akram.

Alexander and Rose admired Akram's suit. Kabeer did not know his own mind. He did not even guess why the change had taken place, what was his motive, what new habits he had learnt, and whether the new ways were costing him money. He often saw Akram talking with Rose but little thought that it was anything more than business talk. He himself at that age was his mother's child and his time was spent at her side.

'You are looking very smart today. Our dress makes a man look older than his age, being loose and baggy,' said Kabeer in the way of forced appreciation. 'You must be wanting to take your friends to the pictures. I don't like to send you to the late show alone. I shall ask Raju to take care of you. When you return, don't disturb me. Once I wake up, I don't get sleep again till morning,' said Kabeer. It was the night of the nikha and this solved the problem neatly. He did not like to dress himself grandly in Akram's presence. It was a private affair, but the first impression on his new bride could not be overlooked.

Akram was thrilled and needed no second order. The dinner was served and both had a little just for the name sake, being excited in different ways. Akram was thinking of the unexpected leniency of his father towards him. Was the old man planning something on the sly? So long as he got permission to go out what did he care for other things?

Soon after dinner Kabeer went to Raju.

'Take Baba to the pictures and bring him home safely. Tomorrow you will have to tell me all about your taking him and bringing him back,' said Kabeer and asked Akram to go soon so as not to lose a good seat.

Akram taking leave of his father went to Raju, took him out of the gate and to the west end of the street.

'Do you see who is the master of the property now? Father has nothing to do with it. I have all powers and can keep or sack the servants,' said Akram to Raju.

'Yes, Sircar.[7] I see it daily with my own eyes. I am ready to do anything for you. If you only show me with the small toe of your foot I shall do it with my head.'

'I want not only that but more than that.'

'Anything in the world, even if it is as impossible as getting the milk of a tiger in the middle of the night, it shall be produced immediately.'

'You talk as if you are the bravest man in the world, but I want another type of man who can command two hearts and two words at the same time. Do you understand what I mean?'

'That is nothing. Even an old imbecile woman can do it. I shall supersede the rest in our country in that line.'

'Well, guess what I am going to tell you.'

'Perhaps you want to take that missy with you and want me not to say it to master,' said Raju after some time.

'Which missy, you rascal?'

'The one who works in the office. Don't I know that much?'

Akram was puzzled. After a minute he thought that the man was the right person in the right place. Yet caution in every stage of life is indispensable. He did not like to disclose the secret to him till it was absolutely necessary.

'Who gave you to understand that rubbish? Have you seen my father going out with women? Our mussalmans will murder me.[8] What woman will come with me at this time of night?'

'Yes, Sircar, I was just joking,' said Raju meekly.

'Joking, you namaqhool?[9] Joking with your lord and master? Listen, I am going alone. You sit down here on this very spot till my return. Then both of us will go together into the house. If father asks you tomorrow what will you say?'

'I will say that I took you to the pictures, brought you safely back, and after attending to your needs I went to bed.'

'That's very good. Take this bakshish.[10] The greater the service the greater will be the reward,' said Akram, giving him a five rupee note.

As soon as Akram's back was turned Raju went straight to an alehouse and had a drink. Just as he entered he saw Kabeer walk quickly across the street. It was dark yet by the light of the street lamp he could see that Kabeer was wearing a grand shervani and the shamla of his turban was tossing in the air with the force of his fast walk.[11] Raju thanked God for his narrow escape. If he had been two minutes later he would have met Kabeer face to face.

The stimulant and the inactivity made Raju think on the surprising behaviour of both the son and the father. He was only a tool in the hands of both. One gave him his bread, but the other great hopes, and tips into the bargain. He had not got five rupees present from Kabeer all the years of his service. With whom to side? The old or the young? 'The young, of course,' came a voice from his heart. He followed Kabeer, keeping at a distance. When he halted at a house Raju hid himself in a corner formed by two houses and covered himself with the jet-black blanket he had carried to keep himself warm while waiting at the picture house. Kabeer knocked at a door which brought Mustafa to the threshold. Both of them disappeared. Raju's curiosity dragged him to the side of the little house. He discovered a ventilator with a dim light. As he could reach it he brought a stone and standing on it peeped through. He saw clearly Kabeer, Mustafa and another man having dinner, a compulsory meal after nikha. He understood neither head nor tail of the incident so he hastened back to his post.

Akram after leaving his faithful servant went straight to Rose's house. It was his first visit to her. He heard a man speaking and then her shrill laughter, so he hesitated to go inside the small gate. A dog began to bark. He left the gate and stood in the middle of the road. Rose herself came to see what was the matter but could not see him clearly. The dog was still barking so her fiancé, George, came out.

'There is someone standing there,' said George.

'Let us go and see.' Rose walked to the gate and George followed.

'Hello, what has brought you here at this time of the night? You ought to be in bed under guard.'

'I was permitted to go to the pictures but I did not like to go alone,' said Akram looking round the drawing room. The house was simple but very well kept. He was amazed at the striking surroundings and coupled with that the presence of a young man, made him dumb. He had rehearsed a few sentences on his way but he found his power of expression was killed.

'May I introduce you? My future husband George Macarthy. This is Master Akram, our master's son,' said Rose.

George extended his hand. Akram came back to his senses, and shook hands with him.

'Won't you take a seat?' said George.

George knew the visitor was nervous and he had to make him feel at home as he was his wife's future boss. He went into a side room.

'What do you really want me to do for you? You were brave in coming here, but you look so depressed. What has happened?'

'I want to take you to the pictures.'

'You mean us. Mother had invited George for dinner and we were having it when the dog began to bark. I can't leave him alone.'

'Darling, I am not coming to the pictures. I am dead tired of them,' said George from the room.

'Then do hurry, it is getting late,' said Akram to whom George's decision came as a great blessing.

'Which picture are you going to?' asked Rose.

'I have not yet decided.'

'Do you really want to go to the pictures? Let all of us sit together for some time and then you can go back home.'

'No, I have to tell father tomorrow about it,' said Akram.

'Go to the Metropole. It has Gone with the Wind,' said George coming back into the drawing room.

'I shall send my mother to have a talk with you. Meanwhile we shall finish our dinner,' said Rose, and they went hand in hand.

Akram somehow disliked the sight.

'I am very glad to see you, Master Akram. You are always welcome to our humble abode. Whenever you are free do come to us. There is no one here except Rose and myself,' said Mary, Rose's mother.

'Thank you very much. I shall try to come whenever I get permission,' said Akram.

'You being a man must be allowed to do what you like. We don't restrict even our girls.'

'We are not allowed to do anything ourselves during the lifetime of our elders. I have to get permission from my grandmother, my father and my mother. If all of them agree I have to do it and if one of them disagrees I have to keep quiet.'

'That's very bad, is it not? In our days girls were controlled in that way but not boys.'

'Our girls never step out of the house. There are some who have lived and died in one house all their lives.'

'How horrible! We should die in no time if we were confined like that. Rose praises you very much. She is my youngest and dearest. I believe her appointment is a temporary one. She wants to work even after her marriage as her husband gets only 80 rupees.'

'I shall ask father to make her permanent.'

'Did you enjoy mother's company?' asked Rose who had just reentered with George.

'Oh yes, I liked it immensely, and I don't want to miss that pleasure in the future.'

'George, change your mind and come with us. I will have to come home alone,' said Rose.

'I won't send you alone. I shall drop you here and then go home,' interrupted Akram.

Mary repeated her invitation to Akram to come again to her house. George went home. Akram and Rose went to the pictures in a taxi. They took box seats, a luxury which Akram had the fortune of enjoying for the first time. They were surrounded by officers who started the pictures with drinks. Akram wanted to imitate them and ordered two glasses of wine. For every one glass Rose drank he drank two or three, and before the interval he was thoroughly intoxicated.

'How heavenly! I wish it could continue forever and ever,' said Akram.

'What is heavenly? I think you are drunk,' said Rose.

'The beautiful scenes are godly. I feel warm but not drunk.'

'Behave yourself. What will people say? They will carry tales to your father and George.'

'Hang that George. You talk of him the whole time, as if he was your god. Who cares for my father? I am not a girl to be ordered about.'

'Have a cigarette,' said Rose to divert his mind. She was sober.

Akram ordered another glass, but Rose gave a sign to the bearer not to bring it. He was behaving badly and had control neither of limbs nor brain. She felt it would be better to leave the place before the picture was over. She took all his belongings, engaged a taxi and went first to Akram's house. When the taxi entered the road Raju who was dozing on a stone jumped up at the noise, stopped the car and got into it. He took Akram to his room, changed his clothes and put him to bed. He went to see if Kabeer had returned and not finding him there he slept in Akram's room.

'What happened in my absence?' asked Akram when he awoke in the morning.

'What happened to you, Sircar?' said Raju.

'You ask me a question instead of answering mine, you rascal,' said Akram.

'I did everything so skillfully that he knows nothing about it.'

'Well done, my boy, you deserve more bakshish. Bring my coat here,' said Akram and searched for his purse.

'You scoundrel! You robbed me of my two hundred chips and yet you are waiting for me. I shall hand you over to the police if you don't give it to me at once!'

'Sircar, blame me for anything but theft. I have been working here for the last six years. If you take drastic steps against me I will have to tell the truth,' said Raju.

This poured cold water on Akram's nerves. He had no alternative. Both father and the son overslept.

'Did you lose anything?' asked Rose when Akram went to the office.

'Lost all my money. I remember having left my purse in my cap. Now I find it nowhere.'

'Here it is,' said Rose, taking it out of her bag. 'See if the money is all right.'

'It is okay since it was with you.'

'There are one hundred and ten rupees. How much did you take with you?'

'Two hundred.'

'So you wasted ninety in one night!'

'Never mind. What is left is ours. It was well spent in view of the glorious time we had,' said Akram.

Akram called Raju to his room and gave him another five rupees note saying that he was an honest fellow and he had suspected him for nothing.

The day passed and they had dinner.

'I want to go for a short walk,' said Kabeer. 'I don't get sleep because of the rich food and sitting at home doing nothing. You go to bed as usual at ten. Young men should not keep awake later than that time. When I was of your age I used to go to sleep on Granny's bed while talking.' He wanted an excuse to go to the new bride's house.

'I shall go for a short stroll with Raju.'

'No no, my son, you should not stir out of the house at night. The world is not good and the influence of wicked people lasts lifelong. Tomorrow morning before it gets hot you can go out.'

Akram knew the futility of persisting with his father, so he went straight to his room and to bed.

'Go to Akram's room and put out the light after ten. He sleeps leaving the light burning. I am going for a walk. I shall return soon,' said Kabeer to Raju.

'Master is gone out. Do you want to go to the missy?' said Raju to Akram. There was no sense in hiding his association with Rose from Raju.

'He will return soon.'

'He goes to a house near the market. Last night he came at three.'

Akram jumped out of his bed without a minute's delay and began to dress.

'Suppose father comes before I return. What will you say?'

'I shall put out the light and say you are fast asleep.'

'Very well. You will be a rich man in no time. Be careful and don't let him peep into my room through the key hole.'

'You don't worry, Sircar. I know what to do in that case.'

'But tell me what you will do then.'

'I shall put your pillows on the cot and cover them with your blanket.'

'Put something separately for the head.'

Akram went straight to a shop and bought sweets, chocolates and a bottle of wine. Then hiring a taxi he went straight to Rose.

George had not come that night, so mother and daughter were listening to the news on the wireless. When they heard a car parking near the gate both ran to see.

'Here I am again Granny, as you asked me to come. This parcel is for you,' said Akram to Mary.

'How sweet of you to think of an old woman. God bless you, my master. It is needless to say how I shall enjoy it,' said Mary taking the parcel.

'Mummy, unpack it. Let us all enjoy it,' said Rose. The things were served on a teapoy.

'What a lot you have brought. They will last for ages. Why, I can send some to Alexander,' said Mary tasting a bit of each one. All of them ate and drank with the sweet music on the radio. Rose suggested dancing.

'I don't know how to dance. I have never tried it in my life,' said Akram.

'I shall teach you in no time. My mother is a good dancer and she taught us all.'

Akram stood up at once. He needed no coaxing. Rose held him as she taught him, and both of them laughed at the funny steps Akram made.

Suddenly, without a sound, George stood on the threshold. He was so shocked that even if he had wanted to move he could not. It was past eleven and he did not expect to see Rose. He had been detained in his office for a long time so he just passed Rose's house as he usually did. Seeing the lights on he entered.

'George my dear, come and sit down,' said Mary, who knew the grave situation, and wanted to put him in a good humour. He entered slowly and thoughtfully, and sat down. Mary offered him the sweets but he refused. The music stopped and the dancers sat down. Rose got up from her seat, ran to her fiancé's chair, sat on the arm and put her arm round him lovingly.

'Darling, you are very serious today. Is anything the matter? How was your boss today? He is such a nasty man. I wouldn't work under him even for a day. You should not depend upon his job. Be on the lookout for another.'

'He is all right. There is nothing wrong with him. If he sacks me the army is a home for the disheartened,' said George.

Rose felt his remark was rather cold but she did not understand the cause of his seriousness. Mary knew it all right, and was talking with Akram.

The music began again. Rose pulled George's arm to dance with her.

'Come, don't be fussy. It is against your sweet nature. Don't spoil it by trifling.'

'I am tired and not in a mood to dance,' said George. Rose sat down seriously.

'If you don't mind I shall teach you dancing. You can learn quicker from an experienced teacher than from a beginner,' said Mary to Akram.

'I would love to dance with you, Granny.' They swung away to the other end of the room.

'You are very light on your feet. How quickly you have learnt the first steps. In a week's time you will be a good dancer. Come every day. I shall teach you,' said Mary.

'Don't flatter me, Granny. I shall take months to learn it.'

The dance and the talk of Mary and Akram cooled George's temper. He thought after all it was as well to humour Akram and encourage Rose to teach him dancing. So much depended on his support. His income being insufficient he needed his wife's help to run a home. How could she get on with him if he tried to be nasty to her benefactor?

Rose pulled George a second time for a dance. He jumped up.

'You dance with Master Akram and I with mother,' said George.

They danced, ate and drank till one o'clock. Then Akram looking at his watch said, 'I must run like a Russian soldier. Otherwise I will be killed.'

All of them including George protested to no use.

'It will mean the end of my liberty,' said Akram and left, George accompanied him for some distance and suggested a taxi.

'No, I have to enter the house like a thief. Thanks for your kindness.'

They parted as good friends.

Chapter XX

Craftiness and craziness are qualities which are found side by side in human character. In general one leads the other and both act and react. It is rather difficult to put a mark on the extent of their success as human nature undergoes modification at all stages of life. This much is certain that in the young these are violent, daring and blind to consequences, whereas in the elderly their effect is more moderate.

Kabeer's sense of the justice of his behavior after his fourth marriage had reached the peak. It seemed to him as illuminating, as unfallacious as the morning star. He said to himself that he lived exclusively with his first wife for some year, and he did the same with the second and the third. If he did not do the same with the fourth he would be doing her an injustice. Doing justice to one's wife is compulsory as it is laid down in the holy book and was emphasized by the originator of Islam. It was his bounden duty to think of her and satisfy all her needs for some years by forgetting those who had already has such privileges for years and years.

How long were those old hags desirous of monopolizing the luxuries of life? They should be considerate and forgo their interest in favour of others. Have not the great religions of the world taught the precept love your neighbor as you would love yourself? What does it mean if not sacrifice one's happiness in preference to others'? If he persisted in his changed behavior towards them he would be teaching them a lesson which would prove advantageous all their lives. Selfishness had made them heartless, inconsiderate and vile creatures. He being the ruler of their bodies and minds it was his primary duty to train them to be agreeable to one another. They were in no way better than vultures who would devour their prey to the very bones. There was no need to inform them of the cause of his isolation from them. If they by chance came to know of it he would give them hell as revenge for all their ill-treatment of him. Kabeer's visits to the zenana had become merely nominal. He went there to see his mother who talked about nothing but Akram's wedding. No wife could be so bold as to come and talk to him in the presence of his mother. Zuhra herself sometime sent for Nazni to ask her about the things she needed in connection with the wedding preparations. Kabeer's and Nazni's eyes never met on these occasions.

Nazni thought that he was angry with her and she racked her brains to think of the cause. But she found that the other two also were afflicted by the same epidemic. Since all the three creatures had the same grievance they were united and disclosed the secret to one another. They often held a three-cornered table conference in either Nazni's or Maghbool's room. They were not jealous of each other, on the other hand the common ailment had made them friends against the formidable enemy. It was a disease that could not be cured so it had to be endured.

Akram kept his promise to bring Rose to Maghbool without caring for her advice not to accompany her. Rose's first visit created a great sensation in the family, and it became a topic of daily talk among the chief members excluding Maghbool. To make Rose's visits interesting she prepared tea for her out of her own money and had it with her and Akram. When Zuhra came to know of it she had the plates used for the purpose kept outside the kitchen and ashes thrown over them. When the next tea was to be taken things were brought from the kitchen and arranged for them in the quadrangle.

Maghbool thus created a fresh cause for Zuhra's anger. Nazni increased it by delivering additional information about the growing romance between Akram and Rose. Her motherly intuition made her exaggerate minor details about their talk and laughter in Maghbool's room.

'This will end in his ruination. We must hurry up with his marriage. Once he is married all these fancies will automatically be dropped. We shall send word to the bride's people to perform the marriage at once and postpone the preparations which can be finished and given afterwards,' said Zuhra.

Nazni agreed. A messenger was sent with the news but the other party flatly refused. Then it was decided that a betrothal ceremony should take place immediately to prevent Akram from going astray. This alternative did not vex the bride's people. A day was fixed. It had to be performed on two consecutive days, one in the bride's house and the other in the bridegroom's.

Akram had made it a point not to go empty-handed to Rose's house. The fuss made over the things he took there and the regard shown to him by both daughter and mother tickled his vanity. He brought sweets and drinks, presents for Rose and Mary on alternate days.

The lavishness of his gifts to a family where needs were always keenly felt produced the desired effect. Their attention was turned from George to Akram. The former being regarded as one of the family members needed no special attention. On the other hand it was his duty also to humour the whims and fancies of the generous benefactor. In eating, talking and dancing he was passed over for the newcomer. Even if Akram advanced the most absurd argument he was supported at the cost of George.

There is a limit to patience. When that is passed nothing can be tolerated. One's sense of one's own dignity varies according to one's valuations, but it is a thing of some importance to oneself. George's dignity was wounded at every snub he got and the obvious indifference shown to him. He felt ever more out of place. His objections to their behavior were condemned and he was called vain and selfish. Gradually he reduced his visits to Rose's house. He found that his absence was not felt. He thought that it was better not to be an unwelcome guest.

'Rose, you are not the same person whom I used to adore,' said George one morning when she was alone.

'You are changed more than myself. You are a cad. You encouraged me to get on his good side and you did it yourself. You used to enjoy his parties and you accepted his presents. Now all of a sudden without any ground you have begun to suspect me. You openly insult us in his presence,' said Rose.

'Yes, it was a mistake. I realise it now. I can't go on like this. Tell me frankly what you want me to do. Do you still love me? Am I not fallen in your estimation? You care more for him because he is wealthy.'

'If I care for him it is to help you. Do as you like. Since you impute false notions to me you can't expect me to respect you.'

'So shall we separate as good friends?'

'It is left to you,' said Rose and began crying. Her last sentence was enough to drive him out of the place and he disappeared.

'Where is George? What is the matter? Why are you crying?' asked Mary.

'He is gone for good,' sobbed Rose.

'If he has no confidence in your love it is useless to have any trust in him. If he behaves ill when he still has to flatter you one can imagine how he will treat you when he is married. Let him go and hang himself. We can't forgo our needs for his fancies.'

'He says I don't love him as I used to.'

'Yes, love that beggar and worship his person. Look at the difference between him and Akram. One spends money for your comfort like water and yet without any selfish motive. He is just an unselfish friend. Whereas the other thinks only of himself and nobody else. Whom will you trust?'

'I don't feel I can be happy without him. Shall I go to call him?'

'It is just like chasing a wild goose. Let him come himself or else he will make a hell for you. He must have that much sense, that Akram's visits are harmless and beneficial. If he is such a fool as not to understand it he must suffer for his lunacy.'

After the failure of George's attempt to effect a reconciliation with Rose he grew to dislike her and stopped going to her. This did not mean the death of his love for her. He had taken years to reach the stage of blind love. The loss of love in a strong lover is often followed by a spirit of revenge towards both the object that created it and the other that caused it to be jilted. No punishment for them was considered too cruel and no effort in the execution of his purpose was felt too difficult.

In his anxiety and disappointment he began to live a wild life. The money he had gathered with so much pain for his marriage he now spent recklessly. He gave up the friendship of his equals where he could not show his face. He felt relief in the company of human beings who talked and laughed but never thought. Such people have their own world: they have formed a sort of cosmopolitan nation.[1] There were among them youths of all communities—Hindus, Christians and bigoted Muslims. One can easily judge the economic condition of such a nation. It was poverty-stricken; by foul means it made some money to carry on its congregations and spent it all the very day it was gained. George's membership of this gang was a boon that could not be easily thrown off. He was taken for a hero and was revered by all. He spent money on them ungrudgingly. He gave them free entrance in the picture house where he was working. Thus he won over the hearts of the youths who would do anything for him at any cost.

'You praise the chastity and the strong religious sense of Muslims without knowing that all of them are not real Muslims. There are many young men in this very country that have joined other communities,' said George one day in the congregation.

'You talk through your hat without knowing the facts. People of other religions in hundreds are brought into our fold but never has a Muslim changed his religion even in adverse circumstances,' said one of the Muslim youths. The rest were anxiously waiting for the argument to develop.

'I shall give you hundreds of instances to prove it,' said George.

'Give us one, we shall be satisfied. Hundreds of instances we neither want nor is it possible for you to get them,' said all jealously.

'Do you know Kabeer Sahib?'

'Is it the Nawab Sahib you speak of?'

'Where does he live?' asked George indifferently.

'He lives in a big mansion in the Chandni Chouk.'

'Is he a Nawab?' enquired George.

'They call him so. His father was called Nawab. He is a very good man and is a friend of the poor. Lately he married a poor girl just to support her. Otherwise he has three wives,' said one of the Muslim youths who made no different between relevant and irrelevant information.

'Do you know his son?'

'I knew him when he was young but now he does not come near us.'

'Because he has changed his religion and wears English suits he does not like your society.'

'How do you know that?'

'I know him personally. I used to go with him wherever he went. He eats, drinks and lives in an English woman's house. He wastes all his father's wealth on her. Your community will be decreasing and ours will be increasing day by day.'

'Is he keeping a Kafirni?[2] Is he wasting a Muslim's money on her?' shouted the bigots.

'He is doing an unpardonable sin! If we let such a thing go on our nation will become extinct, and we being the pillars of it will be held responsible by both God and man,' said one of the enthusiasts.

'Yes, yes, it is our first duty to save our brethren from a crime,' said all.

'I am single and have no responsibility. I shall murder the woman and go to the gallows as one of the heroes of Islam. Where does she live?' said a daring young man.

'It is not only your duty but it is the duty of all of us. Unless we nip such sins in the bud we will be neglecting the interest and progress of our nation.'[3]

'It is no use to say what we have to do. We must do it immediately. Success will give us all eternal fame. How grand will it not be when my dead body will be followed by thousands applauding me? Tell me where she lives and then I shall show what I can do.'

George drew on a piece of paper a plan of Kabeer's house and the roads that led to Rose's house. He gave it to the enthusiast and explained it.

'Don't murder anybody, but bring the man to his senses by explaining the futility of his life and the waste of money on a useless purpose. Warn him to leave her at once lest he should be punished for it. Why should you give your life for the sake of a thing which can be done by gentle means?' said George who in spite of his distress could not bear the idea of harming Rose.

'Murdering a person is strictly prohibited in our religion. We should never take that step. It is a sin,' said all.

'I shall be called a shaheed.[4] That honour is rarely achieved by us.'

'A shaheed is one who gives his life in the battlefield in saving his country.'

'You try to do things gently. If that method fails you can take the drastic step. If you live longer in the world you can help more people. Your life is valuable and it shouldn't be wasted for one person,' said George.

'Then tell us what to do. We shall obey you implicitly,' said they.

'Don't take any weapons.'

'Not even our staffs and clubs?'

'None. Go as you are now. Wait at the east end of the road that leads to that Englishwoman's house. When he enters the road stop him and explain to him gently the harm he is doing and ask him to go back to his house. Do this for a few days, then he will give up the idea of her friendship,' said George.

'At what time does he go there?'

'Between ten and eleven at night,' said one of them.

'Then his motive is wicked. If he were innocent he would have gone there in the daytime,' said one of them.

'Our waiting for him in the night is to our advantage. We will not be discovered if something goes wrong,' said the hero.

'It is our duty to do our bit for the nation. We will spare no effort in fulfilling it. We shall let you know the result only after we succeed. Till that time have confidence in us. We are under an obligation to you and this will make us grateful to you for life because disinterestedly you have thought of the name, fame and prosperity of our community,' said all.

'Because your community was the ruling nation when the English came…'

'Even today we are a ruling nation,' said all, and departed.[5]

George was thoughtful in his loneliness. He looked back at the events and was satisfied. He had taken a promise from them not to do anything harmful. His plan and instruction would in no way interfere with Rose's interests. They being Muslims would do no harm to Akram. So the matter would be handled smoothly and his purpose be achieved.

What was taking place in Akram's house and in which direction was the feminine world working? The night before Akram's betrothal ceremony was the occasion of great rejoicing. Kabeer's part that night was not very great. He went to Akram's bride's house for an hour and then resumed his routine duty. The ladies had to play an important part among the members of their sex. They returned home at three in the morning.

Akram's presence was not needed that day. He was at liberty to go to Rose. He came to know there that George had a quarrel with Rose and had stopped coming. He now went with the scamps of the town and was wasting all his money on them.

'God saved my poor child from him. Even after his marriage he would have led the same life. A man of that taste can never make a good husband,' said Mary to Akram.

'He is behaving like a wild creature. I shall help you financially and Rose will get her pay. Don't worry, Granny,' said Akram.

'She lost a husband and she will have to live a spinster all her life,' said Mary.

'I am not free as my parents, especially my grandmother, will disinherit me if I do anything against her. If Rose waits for some time when I shall be able to help her. I shall not fail,' said Akram.

The next day was Akram's ceremony. Hundreds of relations gathered from the morning. Akram was asked not to leave home. He expressed his dislike of these foolish customs. When he was forced by all he said 'perform the ceremony with my cane.'

'It is done for those who are far away, especially those fighting on the battlefield who want to get themselves married soon after their return. In such cases the betrothal ceremony is performed to fix up the marriage and the sword of the bridegroom is placed on the stage. Your silly talk will upset everybody. Ammajan will drive you out of the house. As it is she is annoyed with you,' said Nazni.

'Why don't you leave me in peace? Doing all these things you drive me crazy. You will be happy perhaps when I die.'

'Akram, you break my heart. Don't say ill-omened things when the happiest day of your life is commencing. I have lived to see this day and surmounted insurmountable difficulties. Do this for me,' said Nazni with tears in her eyes.

'At what time does the ceremony take place?' said Akram who had changed his mind.

'It can't be earlier than eleven or twelve o'clock at night. They will have dinner first. It will be a long affair,' said Nazni.

'I shall be present,' said Akram.

Akram thought of paying a flying visit to Rose and returning early for the function. The grand dinner started and Kabeer was extremely busy in entertaining guests. Akram gave instructions to Raju to be near his room and if he was wanted to tell them that he had a headache and was sleeping. He had asked him to wake him up at eleven. Akram left for Rose's house at nine, but he was restless.

'You are unusually serious today,' said Rose.

'Yes, I don't know why. Something is heavy on my mind.'

'You ought to be happy. It is your lucky day. All of them are enjoying themselves in your honour. Your prospective wife in very beautiful and wealthy.'

'Who told you that?'

'Maghbool praised her.'

'Such tidings have different effects on different people. I think that is the cause of my distress.'

'I don't see any reason way you should be depressed. You have to yield to your parents' wishes,' said Rose.

'Will you keep up the same friendship with me even afterwards?'

'Why not? It won't make any difference.'

Akram left the place at half past ten and walked along the long dark road. When he reached the turning he saw two young men in typical Muslim costume approaching him. They had emerged from the corner of a big building. This looked rather suspicious to Akram, who recognized one of them as a thorough loafer and bad character. He had for a long time avoided the company of the young men of the town, so pretending not to recognize them he began to walk briskly.

'From where are you coming, Nawab Sahib?' said one of them, standing in Akram's way.

'Who is Nawab? Have you gone off your head? What business have you to question me?'

'It is our duty to check a Muslim and to put him on the right way.'

'I am not a Muslim,' said Akram.[6]

'You deny your religion! There is no greater sin than that. Do you know what has happened to such men in our country? We know who you are and what you are doing.'

'Get away from here, you rascal. Try to know yourself and your life first before you correct others. They are much better than you.'

'You call us rascals? You are living a worse life than ours,' said they and one seized hold of Akram's collar.

'Promise us that you will never step into that kafirni's house again,' said the daring main.

'Do you know what you will get? You badmash, badzal, harami![7] You have come to teach me and dictate to me? Do you know who I am?' said Akram giving a slap on the opponent's face. He returned it with double force. Akram felt giddy yet he kicked the fellow in the stomach. The scamp fell down, but this was the signal for the gang to jump out of its hiding place.

'He calls us names and has killed one of our brethren. He shall not be left alive!' they shouted, and began to rain blow after below on Akram.

'Do you taste the result of your impertinence? See how respectable you are! You are disgracing our religion and your family, yet you imagine you are dignified,' shouted the mob, at the same time kicking the fallen Akram and giving him blows with their fists. Someone brought sticks and with them struck the unconscious man who responded neither in words nor in action. Seeing him motionless they made a plan to quit the place but one of them suggested that they should not leave a Muslim to die without reciting Kalima.[8] 'If his body is sent to his house when he comes to consciousness his people will make him die a Muslim's death.'

'No no, we will be caught,' said the rest.

'We shall take a carriage and tell the driver to take him,' persisted the kind-hearted man.

'Let us all disappear. One is enough to do the job, and he can easily slip away,' said they, and vanished.

A bullock cart was engaged and the driver was given directions and great hopes of a big reward for his kind deed.

The grand dinner for the monstrous gathering was over. The servants were sent to have their food. Raju also left his post of guard. Akram was sent for by the ladies. A search began and he could not be found. Raju was questioned, who said he must have left the house after he had gone for his food. Servants and friends were sent all over the neighborhood to bring him, but no one expected that Akram would be brought home in a bullock cart.

The news of his absence reached the zenana. A general wailing began. Kabeer was upset and in his uneasiness he went to the gate to wait for the messengers. Some of them came back unsuccessful. A bullock cart was seen slowly approaching the house.

'Who does it bring?' said Kabeer.

I found this man near the big gutter. As I had seen him coming out of this house I brought him here,' said the cart man.

'What do you say? Whom have you brought? Where was he?' ejaculated Kabeer and ran to the cart to see.

'My son, my Akram, my first-born! What has happened to you?' cried Kabeer. But before he could do more everything went black, he fell and was deprived of sense and motion, and his breathing was labored.

Kabeer and Akram were carried into the house and were placed on beds. Akram's face was swollen blue, and at first sight hardly recognisable. His white silk shirt and grey suit were wet with blood. 'He has vomited blood! Oh God,' said someone.

'The shaking and jerking of the cart has overstrained his injured nerves,' said one of the relations.

A doctor was immediately sent for.

'Life is extinct. The case is beyond control. Unless great care is taken there is no hope' said the doctor.

Akram was still unconscious. The ladies were allowed to see him. They raised a cry that could have brought life even to a dead body. Nazni was near his head, stroking it with a gentle hand.

'Akram, speak one word! I am going to hear it. Take me with you!' she cried.

Akram opened his eyes and looked round. He saw Nazni and stared in her face.

'Bibi, don't cry,' he said faintly.

'I don't cry. I promise not to as you are well,' said Nazni in excitement.

He closed his eyes and opened his mouth.

'He is feeling thirsty. Give him some milk,' said Zuhra. He drank two spoons of milk and shook his head to stop. Two nurses were sent for to look after him and Kabeer. Medicines and injections were given to both. Their effect on Akram was progressive. He slept. Kabeer's condition seemed serious but the ladies were not informed of his health. The doctor diagnosed the disease as 'hemiplegia.'[9] He had fit after fit and there was no improvement. His mind remained impaired and he did not regain sensibility for days.

Chapter XXI

Doulath Khan, Nazni's father, was one of the invitees to the betrothal ceremony. He was very old and needed two men to help him to go from one place to another, yet his desire to see the function of his grandson brought him. His presence was a blessing in disguise as it saved Akram's life. He was both bodily and mentally inactive till he heard that his grandson had been brought home unconscious and his son-in-law had fainted.

As there was no elderly male member he took charge of the situation, sent for his family doctor, nurses and male ayahas, converted the bedrooms into wards, sent the ladies from the mardana with the help of nurses, and made his home there.

The morning brought office bearers, visitors and relations. Every one of them was anxious to see the patients but none was admitted. Akram regained consciousness in the morning but found himself utterly unable to move his limbs. Gradually the swelling came down and the fever dropped. His recovery was slow but satisfactory.

While Akram made progress Kabeer continued in the same stupor. He could neither be called dead nor alive and remained for days and weeks unconscious. The only motion to distinguish him from a dead body was seen when he had fits which occurred at intervals of three or four hours.

Akram knew nothing of his father's illness. He expected him in his room every day but not seeing him thought that he must have come to know the cause of the attack on his son which had made him hate him. He listened to hear him talking or ordering the servants but in that too he was disappointed. He asked the nurse about him. She said that no one was permitted to come to him. As Nazni also did not come to see him but only sent messages through the nurse he was contented.

Though his body was inactive his mind was alert. He reflected on his conduct and the event which came so near to ending his life on the spot. Shame and repentance took root in his heart. What brought him to that condition was a dilemma and he concluded that it was the hand of God that had saved him miraculously and had punished him to make him realize his sin and lead a better life. Was he not following his father's footsteps in his own way? Was it a well-trodden road to make an ideal for his life? The miseries of the ladies in the zenana, his mother's weeping and grievances, the sad picture of Maghbool's woe-begone eyes, her songs, her apparent indifference to her life, Munira's slavery, her sarcastic remarks, and last but not least Mahmood's treachery against him and his consequent sufferings and the unhappy days and nights he passed all flashed across his mind. How could his father be so heartless as not to guess what were his wives' feelings and what kind of life he had given them? He recollected an Urdu quotation which meant that there is no relationship in the world where one finds two bodies but one heart. He felt that if something terrible did not happen to his father for having killed so many hearts he would be surprised. He said to himself that when it was so difficult to please one's own heart how was it possible to please others'?

During the second week Akram's progress was rapid and he was allowed to sit up. His relations and close friends were permitted to see him. One day an associate of his called Murtaza brought a letter.

'A very close friend of mine gave this to you.'

'Your friend gave this to me?' repeated Akram. 'I know this man: where is he? I was under the impression that he had disappeared from the city. I see he wants to see me. Ask him to come tomorrow,' said Akram reading the letter.

'They don't allow visitors to see you or else he would have come with me.'

'I'll give you a permit to be given to him. Ask him to show it to the nurse. I shall also speak to her about it.'

Murtaza intended to take George with him to see Akram but George was bent upon going alone.

'It is very kind of you to take the trouble of coming to see me. Do you want any help from me?' said Akram.

In the presence of his supposed rival George felt his throat and tongue paralysed. His conscience from the day of that unhappy incident had kept him miserable. He had resolved to go to Akram to confess what he had done and part from him as a friend. 'How is Rose? It is ages since I saw her last,' said Akram. Again no reply came from the statue in front of him.

'While I was coming to your room she saw me but turned her head. This is the first time I had a glimpse of her for months,' said George, exerting himself.

'So she is here. Shall I call her and bring about a reconciliation between you two?'

'No, please, don't do that. My conscience is not clear.'

'Your conscience is not clear?' repeated Akram. 'Do you mean you still think her faithless?'

'Her faithfulness is unimpeachable. She was too good for me to get on with her.'

'Then what is it that pricks your conscience?'

'I have been very inconsiderate to both of you and unbelievably cruel to you,' stammered George.

'I don't remember any wrong done by you to me.'

'I am a criminal and acted ungratefully towards you. I did not mean any harm but I did not realize the extent of injury that would be done by those thoughtless and pitiless people. They acted on my injunction so I am responsible for the catastrophe.'

'I don't understand you.'

'You are too noble to understand the baseness of my nature. I instructed the bandits and gave them directions to meet you but only to threaten you. To my regret they over-did it. I have come to beg your pardon. After achieving it I shall leave the town. I was sure of the magnanimity of your heart. I am here ready for anything you like to do with me. Either you can exile me or hand me over to the police.'

The revelation agitated Akram but another thought made him calm.

'Tell me sincerely if you still love Rose.'

'I adore her. I shall do so all my life. It is my devotion to her that made me act so treacherously.'

'Your devotion to her is a virtue. You should not be punished for it. In fact you don't deserve any punishment. I was an intruder in your happy life. I am punished rightly by both God and my own conscience.'

George was silent and Akram rang the bell. George was on pins not knowing the decision of the man on whose mercy he had thrown himself. The nurse entered.

'Fetch Rose this minute.'

'Your Grandpa has strictly ordered everyone in the premises not to allow Rose to see you. The very first day after the incident she tried to come but was snubbed. When the permission for relations was given she tried again but Doulath Khan plainly told her that she was not your relative.'

'Oh heavens, all these complications have arisen and I am unaware of them. Tell Grandpa that Rose's fiancé has come to see me and I should feel pleased to see them together. Ask him not to deprive me of a little pleasure.'

'Oh, no, no, Akram. She would not come here. You are taking unnecessary trouble,' interrupted George impulsively. The nurse had already gone to obey the command.

Rose, come in. Why are you standing so far away? Are you afraid of infection? Sit down here. I am very sorry to hear that you were not allowed to see me. Well at least you came to see your fiancé.'

'I shall come after some time,' said Rose, turning to go back.

'Rose, Rose, I call you and you disobey me openly!'

'I am not in a mood to talk to you, Master Akram.'

'Yes, I know, woman are moody, but when they are commanded by their master their spirit is killed,' said Akram, which brought a big smile to her face. She came back and sat down.

'Please tell me why you sent for me. There is a lot to be attended to in the office.'

'Postpone your work for a later hour. You have the whole day. Take papers and attend to them at home.'

'Don't tease me. The work is increasing day by day. I find no time even to breathe.'

'Unless you are patient and show calmness I won't say what I want to as it needs a lot of patience, wisdom and justice. I shall waste your time in wrangling and keep you in suspense.'

Rose had no alternative. 'I shall sit here the whole day to make up for all those days of anguish.'

'Now you are a good girl.'

George was both dumb and deaf for the present. The familiarity between them vexed him, but he was a man who had been jilted in love and who was condemned and left to their mercy. 'I want you to be reconciled with George.'

'What, you want me to be the wife of a murderer? Ask me anything but that.'

'How dare you call him a murderer?'

'If you only knew what he had done you would send for a policeman and hand him over to him this minute.'

'Who told you that? Do you believe in any rot talked by street beggars? I find no difference between you and an ordinary gosha woman.'

'It is not rot told by street beggars,' said Rose. 'A case is going on against him in the court. His associates have betrayed him. When you were brought home unconscious master lost consciousness and did not regain it till today. Your Grandpapa handed over the cart man to the police. He was innocent and gave the name of the man who directed him to bring you home. They have arrested ten scamps. Enquiries are made daily and new arrests are expected. The cad before you is on the point of arrest. The police are after him. So very slyly he has come to effect an escape through your unbounded generosity.'

George stood up impulsively. 'Please permit me to go,' said he.

'No, no, you can't go so soon,' said Akram. 'We haven't finished yet.'

This naturally perplexed George and he was trying not to show his anxiety.

'Don't be so rude without knowing the facts, Rose. You are very hasty in your remarks.'

'I am not at all hasty. I am studying and judging every event and every report brought by reliable persons. I am just waiting to see justice done.'

'The reports from your reliable persons are the most unreliable. Forget and forgive all that. Don't you like to please me? Not because I am your master but because I am sick? A man who has so narrowly escaped death must be humoured by all. Everybody should think that it is his duty to undergo a bit of sacrifice for him. Can't you do that much service for a person who came out of the jaws of death?'

'Akram, you are doing a wrong thing. You are trying to lodge a snake in your house. Don't believe in his present meekness. Any moment he gets a chance he may turn and bite you. Destroy it when you can and prevent others from being bitten by it.'

'It has already bitten me so it won't do it again. God who is the Saviour has saved me from its poison. When God is my protector no one will harm me. You will see the very snake will turn out to be a very fine and harmless insect.'

'Don't let your imagination run away with you. You can never expect an apple from a hazel tree.'

'Rose, don't exhaust your philosophy here but listen to reason.'

'Yes, act against my own conscience. If you had not survived I would have shot him dead before the law of the country did it.'

'It would have been my lucky day,' interrupted George whose patience had reached its end. Akram gave him a sign not to open his mouth.

'Saving a person's life is nobler than destroying it. My life is saved, so give me a chance of making someone's life. He is not directly responsible for all that happened. On the other hand I am the chief cause of it. When a sinner like myself is protected why should a lesser criminal be punished?' said Akram.

'He is a notorious gangster,' ejaculated Rose. 'He tried to murder you. Association with him has given me a bad name. Everybody here looks at me suspiciously. Hundreds of people are allowed to see you but not I, though I am here from morning to night.'

'He did no wrong to you. Whatever has been done is my own concern. You should not bother about it. I have forgiven him for it.'

'The police are after him. Let him undergo the punishment he deserves and purify his soul before he dreams of reconciliation. He has to train himself to be a husband before he can think of marrying. He is too ill-trained to hold that responsible position.'

'Leave the question of his arrest to me. I shall see that no one touches him.'

'My acceptance of him is a matter of my heart. You cannot change it. I work here because I am paid for it. Expect nothing more than that from me.'

'So you have no human feelings, no regard for my sufferings, no inclination to oblige a person who is sincere to you?'

'My uncle said that after the enquiries are made I shall be sacked from my job. Hence there is no question of obliging you against my conscience.'

'I promise you a promotion and a permanent post. Nothing will please me more and make me get well quicker than your compliance with my request. You will be doing me a personal favour.'

'What do you want me to do? Do you want me to kneel down before him and ask forgiveness for my sins?'

'I am not so heartless as to make you do that,' said Akram, and turning to George said, 'Show your chivalry if you really adore her as you confessed before she came in.'

George got up and knelt down before Rose who stood up surprised. Her dignity was wounded. Tears were falling from her eyes which blinded her. She did not see clearly what George was doing. 'Forgive him, Rose, won't you have pity on him?'

Rose wiped her eyes, saw the pathetic sight before her and stretched her hand without a word.

'George, raise your head, take that noble hand, respect and revere it all your life. Prove by your untiring efforts a worthy possessor of it.'

'Rose, I have given you leave today. Both of you go home to celebrate your reunion,' said Akram shaking hands with both.

Akram sent for Alexander and asked him about the case against George. He found out that he was held directly responsible for the event and would be arrested soon.

'He can't be held responsible for it. There is no proof of his being one of them.'

'He gave them a plan of your house drawn by himself.'

'Did he sign it?'

'No.'

'Then he can deny it flatly. Those loafers are up to anything. Hurry up, go to the court and explain the matter clearly to the judge before the orders for his arrest are passed. Take our car or else you will be delayed.'

Alexander was worried more than words could describe. He did not know any way to solve the problem unless Akram took up the matter. There was no other possibility of saving George from disgrace. He thought the opportunity was God-sent and he should make the best use of it.

'Since you are well you will be questioned. Thanks to the doctors' wisdom in prohibiting visitors to see you, the police people were prevented from entering your room. But for that George would have been in jail today.'

'When they come to me I shall see it through. You have confidence in my support.'

'Nobility is personified in you, my dear young man. You are really a worthy successor of your father and grandfather,' said Alexander.

The doctor came to see Akram.

'You have been having too many visitors. The strain of talking with them is too great. I must limit their number.'

'I am healthy. I feel quite strong enough to talk and act. I want to see father. You kept me in the dark about him. What happened to him? How is he now?'

'Who told you about him? What did you hear?'

'Doctor, when his life is in danger you need not be anxious about mine. You took precautions and saved me but I can't be irresponsible any longer. I must see him this minute.'

'Your Grandpa's permission is to be taken. I am obeying him in everything but medicine.'

'It is almost a fortnight since I had the accident. I am dying to see him, yet you hesitate to take me there,' said Akram. He got off his bed and struggled to stand up. The doctor held him.

'Master Akram, you don't listen to me.'

'I obeyed you patiently all this time and now that stage is gone. Help me to go to him or give me a staff. Don't bother, I feel fit.'

'What is wrong with him? He seems like a person deep in sleep,' said Akram seeing Kabeer. He did not lose his head or cry out. His sense of responsibility gave him calmness and wisdom.

'Apoplexy.'

'How did he get it?'

'It often results from sudden emotion, a violent passion or overloading the stomach.'

'So I am the chief cause of his condition. Has he regained sensibility since then?'

'His stupor is increasing day by day and there is absolutely no improvement in his condition. It will end in death.'

'So his end is near?'

'That is certain. It is only a matter of a couple of days.'

'Yet you wanted to send him to his grave without my knowledge.'

'We knew his case was hopeless and all our attempts were concentrated in your complete recovery.'

Akram went back to his room. His mind was disturbed. His father was leaving a heavy responsibility on his shoulders. What a condition he was in. A terrible kind of sickness which keeps a man alive yet unable to say what he wants to. He wantonly created a heavy responsibility before he fulfilled his duty to those innocent and helpless creatures. He is going away leaving them in the lurch. His three wives—who knows how many he had? His nocturnal visits must have been on some purpose. Well, the care and protection of his three wives and children is my duty. Loans were taken, properties were mortgaged and the income was limited. He had to take the reins in his hand and clear all debts, to find out exactly how much he could spend to live a decent life.

Mahmood, Akram's step-brother, was sent by Zuhra every day to enquire about the health of the patients. The nurses were given strict order to say nothing alarming to any enquirer. They said that the patients were getting better. If she wanted to see Kabeer they said that he was sleeping. Zuhra's patience was exhausted and she could not be satisfied with mere reports.

'If they are better why don't they come here?' she said often.

'Break down the door. I shall go to see him. Do they want to separate my son from me in my lifetime? It is something serious, otherwise he would not have stayed in bed without seeing me. Don't ask those wretches, the nurses, ask Akram. Tell him that I want to see my son.'

'Granny asked me to go to you and ask you of your health and father's. She keeps on crying day and night as she has bad dreams about him. She is almost bedridden. She wants to see him.'

'I shall ask them to open the middle door tonight. Tell them all to be ready to come here. Take a promise from every one of them not to raise a cry. They will only make his condition worse.'

The wicket gate was opened in the night. The male servants, doctor and other relations were all sent to a room to observe purdah for a change. Zuhra was led by two of her daughters-in-law. The shock of Kabeer's illness had undermined her health and sapped her energy. Akram himself came near the steps to receive them all and to take them first to his room to prepare them in advance to see Kabeer. As soon as Nazni saw Akram she forgot all about her mother-in-law. Without thinking she left her arm and went straight to Akram. Maghbool who always kept herself aloof ran reluctantly to hold Zuhra's arm.

'I was dying to see you. God knows what anxious days I have passed. But for father's timely information of your progress I would not have stayed there so long,' said Nazni touching her son's chin gently. All of them went into Akram's room.

'Where is my Kabeer? Where is my son? I don't want to sit here. Take me to him first,' said Zuhra.

'Granny, please sit for five minutes here. Doctor is giving him an injection.'

'Enough of their injections as medicine! What good have they done to him with all that?'

'His disease is a serious one. Many people of his age don't recover from it.'

'Manhoos, don't utter such ill-omened notions. You are wishing ill of him. Is it for this he sacrificed his life for you and brought you up to wish ill for him? His heart will break if he hears you talking so heedlessly of his life.'

'He can neither hear nor talk nor even open his eyes. From the day he fainted he is in a deep sleeping condition. I am not wishing ill of him but explain the plain truth.'

'Whatever comes out of one's mouth, it takes place. I want to hear nothing. Take me to him first.'

Zuhra was ushered into the room. As soon as she saw Kabeer she screamed, ran to him and embraced him.

'Kabeer, Kabeer, Bava, get up and sit down. Open your eyes and look at me.'

'Don't shake him, Granny. That arm has been injected. It may hurt him.'

'Let your doctors and your injections go to hell. They have brought this condition on him. This is nothing except Shaitan ka saya.[1] The evil spirit possessed him because he went after eating rich food in the middle of the night. No medicine will cure him. He must be treated by those who bring down the evil spirits by force. Send for Pariyanwali, they do it in no time.[2] Until the spirit comes down, he will neither open his eyes nor eat anything. They treated me like a child and kept me in the dark, frightened me with the names of doctors and nurses to bring this condition on him. It is a wonder they did not practise their operation on him. I am not going to allow your nonsense to go on any more. I shall put my foot down and see that he recovers,' sobbed Zuhra.

She threw the ice bag from his forehead and the hot water bottles from his lower limbs and abdomen. She put him straight and asked the cook to go at once to bring a pir. Meanwhile she burnt incense and scented sticks and recited verses from the Quran.

'Granny is bent upon treating father herself. She wants no one to come into his room,' said Akram to Doulath Khan.

'Tell her that his disease is a serious one. If proper treatment is not given his death is certain and soon. Let her do whatever she likes but not stop the doctor's treatment.'

'She was vexed when I said that many people do not recover from it. She said that I was wishing ill of him.'

'Let us consult the doctor and see what he says.'

'With all our care he has a life of forty eight hours. Our treatment will lessen his suffering and his death will be easier.'

'Do you want to stop your treatment then?'

'It does not matter much. If they with their treatment see that his bowels are free and nourishment is injected it means the same.'

It was decided to keep a nurse for the purpose and leave the patient to Zuhra who could not bear the sight of the nourishing injection. It was a long process and the place was swollen. The nurse refused to work with Zuhra and left.

Early in the morning a goat was sacrificed and a fowl, eggs, rice, salt, wheat and money were arranged in a tray and placed near Kabeer's head. These had to do the work of pacifying the evil spirits the whole day and were given to beggars in the night. Thaviz[3] and palithas[4] were brought from the Peers and were tied and burnt. Cheenees[5] were got written and washed and he was made to drink.[6] A pooja[7] was performed to bring down the evil spirit. Zuhra sat beside him day and night calling his name and holding his hand. To her satisfaction her voice made him feel her hand and by his facial expression she found that he wanted to speak but could not. This was a promising sign and the treatment in its different aspects increased.

The next morning a cart with ladies was announced.

'Take them to the zenana, we are worried to death and can't entertain guests,' said Zuhra.

'They have come to see master,' said the servant.

'Ladies want to see him?' repeated Zuhra. 'What nonsense! Wretch, tell them he is not well to discuss business. They may have come to get rent excused. Ask them to pray for him. When he is well their request will be satisfied.'

'They say that they want nothing from him. They came to see him because they heard of his illness and they have been praying day and night for his speedy recovery.'

'Very surprising! Women who know him? They know his illness and pray for him? They seem to claim a relationship with him,' said Zuhra

'Let them come and see him. What difference does it make?' said Maghbool who was ever ready to offer a little help to the needy.

Noorjahan, Kabeer's fourth wife, followed by her grandmother entered the room and both began weeping.

'My dear son, what has come to you? Let your misfortune come to me and make me die near your feet. You are our benefactor. You supported us when we were helpless. You gave us a home and made us see comfort,' cried the old woman holding Kabeer's cold feet.

The pathetic cry of the visitors made all in the room shed sympathetic tears as they did at the entrance of every newcomer. After some time everybody stopped crying except Noorjahan. The girl's sorrow was great. She had led a miserable life. The happy days were short. Before she could begin to enjoy them she was informed by Mustafa that Kabeer was seriously ill and the doctors had given up hope.

'Who are you,' asked Zuhra.

'We are your old tenants.'

'Who is this girl? She seems badly affected.'

'She is my granddaughter and your daughter-in-law.'

Zuhra and Kabeer's other wives opened their mouths and eyes in surprise and focused them on Noorjahan. Her beauty and youth had already created a desirable effect on them. Zuhra as usual recovered from the shock first.

'I have come across hundreds of people with such made-up stories on such occasions. Your plot is not well-planned. Such schemes have succeeded in connection with people who die unclaimed by relations. You can't claim relationship with him as he kept nothing secret from me. There was no need to bring a new wife. He had enough of them at home. When he was in the throes of getting his son married would he go and get a young woman married himself? The absurdity of the design is clear as the day!' raved Zuhra.

'Don't condemn us. We have not come here with stories. We are poor and dare not go to the rich with schemes. Tears do not come from one's eyes unless one's heart is burnt. Her married life has been very short and she sees her husband on his deathbed.'

'You wretched woman, don't take the name of death in this house! Let his bed be a lucky one to make his life long and let him sleep on it for a hundred years. Let the evil that has come to him go to his enemies. He is getting better. Women's tears are not scanty, they can shed any amount of them if they want to. Before you entered the house you said you were praying for him and now you are cursing him. This wretched woman allowed you to get in. I would not have done it even for the world!' cried Zuhra.

'Let him be well. Who does not want him to be cured? His loss means our loss. We dare not wish ill of him,' said the old woman.

'You are a liar. He will never do a thing without my permission. I can't believe you without a proper witness.'

'Ascertain it from Mustafa.'

'We have something better to do. Worries have driven us mad. Our only care now is to save his life. Don't be a nuisance to us. Take your dirty faces from here.'

'Don't drive us out. We don't leave the place till he is well.'

'Even if they kill me I shall die here happily,' interrupted Noorjahan.

'When did you become so loving? Those who have been living with him for years don't express such regard for him,' said Munira.

'Wait and see how many more wives will claim his relationship. I think there are as many as there are hairs on his head. There is nothing surprising in it. He must have married her secretly as he did others,' said Maghbool.

'Just because you came slyly do you think others did the same?' said Nazni whose dignity as the first wife was wounded.

'You will die a pig's death if you suspect and talk lightly of him. He is your Neema khuda.[8] You tortured him and tormented him all your life. You don't leave him in peace even now. Noble wives hide the failings of their husbands and you talk ill of him even though there is nothing. What kind of death will you die, I wonder?' howled Zuhra.

Akram was announced and the newcomers had to leave the room to observe purdah in front of him.

'My grandson is coming. Leave the room,' said Zuhra turning to the old woman.

'I am an old woman, let him come. He is like my grandson,' said Noorjahan's grandmother.

'Let that shameless creature go. Ask her to go and sit in the cart,' said Zuhra.

'I am not going to stir from here. Let not one but hundreds of men come. I shall crave for justice from them. Women can never be just to women,' said Noorjahan boldly.

'So young and so audacious. See how she bosses everybody. Slap her and send her inside the room. She has enticed away one member of this family already. Now she wants to try her tricks on that unmarried boy,' said Zuhra.

'She is hurt to the point of boldness. If she does not care for her purdah let her sit here,' said

Maghbool and called Akram in. The others dispersed. Zuhra's spirit had cooled down from the time Kabeer feel ill. Maghbool felt free to speak out.

'Bava, this is your stepmother recently married but your grandmother refuses to acknowledge her,' said the old woman.

'When did he marry her?'

'Last Ramzan, that makes nine months.'

'All lies. He never did it. They have come with a made-up story to get a share from your property. Don't listen to them,' said Zuhra.

'Why don't you keep quiet, Granny?'

'Why should I when my son's honour is at stake? And specially when he can't speak for himself?'

'What proof have you of it?'

'The jewels and clothes on her body are the sure proof. We are poor people and could not afford to buy them.'

'This is not sufficient proof.'

'Ask Mustafa. He will give you the details. He is the man who arranged and performed the marriage.'

'You did not come here when he was well.'

'He kept it a secret. Even his visits were made at night. We knew nothing of his illness till yesterday when Mustafa himself came and asked us to come here,' said the old woman.

Akram remembered Kabeer's disappearance from home after dinner on the pretext of short walks and left the place without a word.

'Did you hear the history of your angel? You blamed me for suspecting him,' said Maghbool who had become unusually bold.

'Ungrateful wretches, do whatever you like to him since he is helpless. God will transfer all his misfortunes to you.'

Mustafa was sent for and enquiries were made. The newcomers were allowed to stay. Munira extracted every detail of Noorjahan's marriage from her and the old woman. Maghbool left the house with all her belongings. With all the care Kabeer's condition grew worse and he passed away. Zuhra lived only for two days separated from her son. Just before her end all her daughters-in-law were near her.

'I knew that my end was not very far when I saw Noorjahan with dimples in her cheeks.'

'People say that very beautiful wives cause their husband's death soon. Within a year of her marriage she sent him,' said Munira.

'Her dimples are sending me to my grave,' said Zuhra.

The icy hand of death was not gentle on Zuhra. She suffered terribly before she died. Nazni achieved the coveted position. Munira and Noorjahan, being helpless, continued in the same house under Nazni's regime.

Contexts and Criticism

Photograph of Iqbalunnisa Hussain, courtesy of Behram Ahmed

Iqbalunnisa Hussain (1897–1954)
A Biographical Sketch
Arif Zaman

In the 1940s, it was often said that there were two women who were the first to put women on the map in India: Sarojani Naidu (a Hindu) and Iqbalunnisa Hussain (a Muslim). These female activists and writers knew each other and worked together. They both inspired many women, among those who came to know of them and their writings.[1] However, while Naidu is very well known and appears prominently in most histories of the period, Iqbalunnisa Hussain, who remained unassuming and modest despite her achievements, remains little known. As her publisher, John Spiers of the Hosali Press, said in his 1940 foreword to *Changing India*, 'like the book itself, the author of these writings is unique. Considering the vast size of India, writers are all too few; and still less is the proportion of women writers. But as for Muhammadan women writers, where are they? In this respect, it is probable that Mrs Iqbalunnisa Hussain holds a lonely and courageous place. Here, for the first time, is the voice of a hitherto silent section of Indian women … [arguing for] the clearing away of religious dogmas and the reassertion of the true Islamic status of womanhood, or the hammering away at age-old social traditions which fetter Indian women, or her eloquent pleas for the means to achieve women's liberation, or education.'[2]

The time has come, finally, to bring Iqbalunnisa Hussain to the wider prominence that she deserves.

She was born in Bangalore on 5 February 1897. Her mother's family hailed from Central Asia and were descendants of Tipu Sultan. Her mother inherited a pension from her grandfather, who had died along with Tipu Sultan in the Mysore war against the British. Presenting a copper *sanad* to the General Post Office every few months, she would collect the pension given only to Sultan's family members, until her death. Hussain's father hailed from a family of bureaucrats and was part of the educated Muslim elite. He was a superintendent in the British police and had also served in Hyder Ali's army.

A 'simple village girl' who knew only 'a smattering of Arabic and Urdu'—as her daughter, Salima, puts it—Iqbalunnisa did not to go to school as a girl, though she was taught some languages at home. She was married by the time she was fifteen years old, to Syed Ahmed Hussain.

Syed Ahmed Hussain was a student of engineering in Bombay, and an official in the service of the Mysore government at the time. Together, they stayed in Bombay for a while at a student hostel but it was a difficult experience for Hussain. She observed purdah at the time and because there were no other female students, mostly kept to herself. Her husband, however, a far-sighted and in many ways, a revolutionary man,[3] was not bound by the confines of a conservative outlook on the role of women in the social sphere. He therefore encouraged his wife to learn how to read and write in English, even after she returned to Bangalore without him. According to Spiers, 'Mrs Hussain already knew Urdu and Persian, but her knowledge of English was limited to simple and not always reliable books of the self-taught variety. Now she had a husband who helped her to study and approved of every step she took to further her education.'

He undertook Iqbalunnisa's education from Bombay through a personal correspondence course of his own. Over the years, and continuing after her husband returned to Bangalore to work, she completed her secondary and higher education—while having seven children. As there was no women's college in Bangalore, she moved to Mysore for two years to study for her BA exam. She attended both college and university there, going on to earn a gold medal from Maharani's College for Women. She was accompanied by her two-year-old daughter, Nayeema, while the other five children remained under the care of her husband in Bangalore. During this time, she lived in a hostel and was pregnant (with Salima). As one can imagine, it is no simple feat to care for such a young child whilst expecting another, and carry on with one's studies.

Having become convinced of the importance of female education, in 1933, she made the courageous decision to travel to England to pursue her postgraduate studies in Education at the University of Leeds. It was a long and arduous journey by ship, via Colombo and Italy, and a round trip took three months. There was no coming back during holidays. Although it was becoming more and more common to travel to the UK, in those days, hardly any Muslim women from South India, not many from other parts of India, and few Muslim men went alone to study in England. Iqbalunnisa decided to take her eldest son, Bashir Zaman,[4] with her, once again leaving the rest of her children in her supportive husband's care.

Her decision to study abroad made her part of a small but increasing group of Indian women, who, since the late nineteenth century, had gone to study there. They included Pandita Ramabai who went in 1883 with the intention of pursuing medical study; Cornelia Sorabji, who went in 1889 and became the first Indian (male or female) to study at a British university as well as the first woman of any background to read for and pass the Bachelor of Civil Laws exam at Somerville College, Oxford. She became India's first woman lawyer. Ameena Tyabji and Zubeida Futehally, from the prominent Tyabji clan, went to London in 1894. Atiya Fyzee went to the UK in 1906 to study (which was also unusual since she belonged to a middle-class family) and kept a travelogue in Urdu about her journey which was later published.[5]

Iqbalunnisa also followed in the footsteps of those Elleke Boehmer calls 'remarkable Indian "arrivants"—scholars, poets, religious seekers, and political activists including Toru Dutt and Sarojini Naidu, Mohandas Gandhi and Rabindranath Tagore'—who arrived in London in increasing numbers in the late nineteenth and early twentieth centuries. Their presence and participation in the life of the metropolis brought with it attitudes and ideas forged in the colonies and informed by their transcontinental movement. As Boehmer argues, their ideas about the West, cultural decadence, urban modernity, and cosmopolitan exchange were more influential on British attitudes at the turn of the twentieth century than has previously been recognized.[6]

When she left for her studies in the UK in 1933, Iqbalunnisa was sent off like a queen. There were farewell parties. For months, she was garlanded every single day and gifts filled her home. At every station, dozens of Muslims with garlands and sweetmeat flooded the stations. There were, however, some people who were disturbed by the idea of a Muslim woman with seven children, studying English, going without her husband to England, the land of heathens and the sworn enemies of Muslims. According to Iqbalunnisa's daughter, Salima Ahmed (the last of Iqbalunnisa's children who passed away while this was going to press), it later became clear that many plots were hatched to do away with the entire family. As Spiers comments, 'like all pioneers, [Iqbalunnisa Hussain] has had to bear the bitter burden of a highly scandalized, critical, and bigoted orthodoxy. In this respect, not only did she have the joyous experience of flying far outside the bars of the purdah cage, but also the delight of sharing in the freedom of women in Europe, and [eventually of] the stirring example of the freed Muslim women of Turkey.'[7] Many delegations of Muslim religious men and others came to Syed Ahmed Hussain and advised him not to send Iqbalunnisa or his family would not be given a burial place in the Muslim graveyard. He told them that he would probably not need that heavenly place as he was thinking of not only sending his family to England but later, joining them himself! Three years passed and her husband made it almost his sole job to look after the children. His support of Iqbalunnisa's education meant that he refused promotions twice, because it would mean having to leave Bangalore. His support of his wife and his family is worthy of mention because of his incredible ability to challenge patriarchal conventions and stand up to societal pressures.

Group photo of 1933–34 Lyddon Hall residents with Iqbalunnisa Hussain, centre, standing, University of Leeds, 1934. (Reproduced with the permission of Leeds University Library)

At the same time, it should be noted that a commitment to university education for women was by no means universal, even in the UK, against which Iqbalunnisa's time at Leeds becomes even more significant. As Juliet Gardiner points out, 'by the 1930s, women [in the UK] were out in the world, visible in society, employment, politics, and the economy in numbers and ways that they had not been before the First World War. Since 1923, Oxford had caught up with London and provincial universities in awarding degrees to women (Cambridge held out until 1948), though the number of women undergraduates was tiny compared to men. In 1936, only around 500,000 girls were receiving secondary education in state or local-authority schools.[8] And as Jane Robinson has highlighted, at Leeds itself, there was 'a clear split in the 1935 cohort of leavers [Iqbalunnisa's batch] between those with little money, heavy family responsibilities, and an eagerness to take part in the cultural and corporate life of the university, and those spoilt by too much cash and with too little imagination', who were much less dedicated to their studies.[9] Iqbalunnisa's middle class and family background would have situated her firmly within the first category and among those to whom an education at Leeds was a serious undertaking.

While studying there, Hussain became involved with the growing community of Muslims and established herself, taking her passion for the education of Muslim girls to a wider audience. In February 1935, she was invited to speak on the subject of 'Muslim Women's Education' to a gathering of men at the Muslim Society of Great Britain (MSGB) in London at 59 Baker Street, in the heart of the establishment. At the opening of the speech, Iqbalunnisa worried that she would not be able to express her ideas 'as forcibly as I would do to an audience of women.'[10] Her lecture, however, was a clear and passionate argument for women's capacities and their need for education. As Asiya Alam points out in her introduction to *Changing India*, Iqbalunnisa's talk 'highlighted the importance of women's education with special emphasis on equivalence of temperaments between men and women. Insisting on fundamental similarity between men and women, she argues that "woman as an individual has the same power of feelings, sentiments, and emotions as a man."'[11] The speech makes it clear that she considers that women have the same 'faculties of mind' as men and that they possess the same modes of 'observation, reasoning criticism, and power of expression.'[12] They are also 'susceptible to the joys and sorrows of this world to the same extent as men. They, like men, continually fall prey to the ills of existence. They have to encounter in the battles of this world the same amount of evil as men. If philosophy is a solace of mind to a man, it is the same to a woman'.[13] A woman too can take as keen an interest in 'literary pursuits…if she is given the same opportunity and facility'.[14] Certainly, Iqbalunnisa's own life serves as an example of the points she makes in her lecture.

As Alam further points out, Iqbalunnisa thought that education was crucial for the potential of women to develop as fully-rounded human beings. 'Within Iqbalunnisa's ethical frame of human development, to be deprived of the moral sentiments of compassion and respect was a denial in certain possibilities of human life, a rejection of what life could be. Iqbalunnisa's specific conception of the "individual" as a "human being" enabled her to build a normative view of a good human life based on "development", involving the cultivation of intellectual, emotional, and social capabilities through education.'[15] The essay, 'Character and Education', discusses the ways in which human capacity and moral character develop through training, showing how abilities in 'reasoning and thinking; creative play; artistic pursuits like music, poetry, and painting; cultivation of virtues such as courtesy, obedience, kindness; and a passion for justice and fairness' must be nurtured in girls and women as well as boys and men.[16] She makes the case for a system of education for all that includes both creative and utilitarian tasks and works to bridge the 'gulf between home and school life'.[17]

Iqbalunnisa's interest in the development of well-rounded girls and young women drew her to the growing Girl Guides movement. Girl Guides, or 'guiding', began in 1910 to provide an option for girls who were attracted by the practice of 'scouting', which had begun for boys a few years before. The first Girl Guide Association in the UK was led by Agnes Baden-Powell, sister of Robert Baden-Powell, the founder of the Boy Scouts. By 1912, there were groups in several other countries and the movement grew internationally after World War I. It hosted its First World Conference in 1920.[18] Iqbalunnisa attended the eighth World Conference of the World Association of Girl Guides and Girl Scouts in Adelboden, Switzerland in October 1934. Throughout her life, she remained devoted to the movement as a way for girls to develop the 'full play of their spirit of adventure and service'[19] and helped to encourage and establish the movement in India.

Iqbalunnisa's concern with establishing a certain conception of learning, especially in teacher-student relationships, was one of the features of her interest in education, which she internalized at Leeds and advocated later in life. After returning from England in 1935, she decided to teach. Her husband founded a school for her, where she encouraged Muslim girls to come and acquire education. It was not easy. She went door to door to speak to the patriarchs of the family and convince them to allow their daughters to study. Bullock-carts were arranged to pick and drop off the girls. Iqbalunnisa paid eight annas (half a rupee) to every girl who learnt English. Her school trained girls in durri/carpet making, cane weaving, pottery making, embroidery, cutting, and sewing. Her students participated in Girl Guides, were good debaters, and were keen performers in dramas and plays. Iqbalunnisa established more schools in villages outside Bangalore—a move which did not please everyone. Family members recount that many in those villages became very hostile and declared that she was converting their girls to Christianity. However, there were a large number of Muslims, whose children had been acquiring education in Iqbalunnisa's schools, who became her staunch supporters and admirers.

In the years following her return from England, Hussain was also actively involved in efforts to promote women's education more broadly and wrote frequently for the English language press in South Asia. She published essays in such journals as *The Deccan Times* (Madras), *The Punjab Review* (Lahore), *Life* (Bangalore), *The Muslim Review* (Lucknow), *The Daily Post* (Bangalore), and *The Eastern Times* (Lahore). These essays culminated into *Changing India: A Muslim Women Speaks*, published in Bangalore in 1940 by Hosali Press; republished by Oxford University Press in 2015. Referenced in this sketch, they illustrate her strong convictions about the need for reform of Islamic practice(s), and the liberation of Muslim girls and women from the rigid requirements of strict purdah. Historian Barbara Metcalf remarks of *Changing India*, '[Iqbalunnisa's] Islamic modernism ... resonates strongly with the ideas of her "namesake" Muhammad Iqbal ... It is also fascinating to see the intensity of her political ideas in 1940'.[20] Iqbalunnisa's advocacy for women's education, emancipation, and reform of religious tradition underscore her importance as a feminist within the movement toward Islamic modernism.

As part of her reformist efforts, Iqbalunnisa was a member of the All India Women's Conference (AIWC) and attended, as the delegate from Mysore, the fifth, sixth, and seventh sessions of the AIWC held in Lahore (12–16 January 1931), Madras (28 December 1931 to 1 January 1932), and Lucknow (28 December 1932 to 1 January 1933). According to Alam, 'at the sixth session, she supported a resolution for the welfare of school children involving provision of adequate playgrounds and medical inspection in schools. She also emphasized the introduction of mobile libraries and film screenings in promoting adult education' only four years after the first sound film was made.[21]

In 1944, with World War II in its final stage, Iqbalunnisa Hussain's novel *Purdah and Polygamy: Life in an Indian Muslim Household*, republished here after 73 years, became one of the first full-length novels by a Muslim woman. Within a few months, following a visit to Lahore, Iqbalunnisa's play, *Harem House* was also published.[22]

Throughout her life and work, concern with the matters of purdah and polygamy (or more properly, polygyny) appear again and again. In 'Woman as an Individual', Iqbalunnisa describes the damage done to women as a result of strict seclusion. She argues that 'it is a serious error to think that a woman who is carefully guarded at all times and checked at every action and thought can lead a successful life and manage her own affairs.'[23] She lives 'constantly in an atmosphere of ignorance and restriction' which kills 'her power of striving.' [24] In another essay, 'The Causes that Led to the Degeneration of the Muslims', she makes clear that the environment of a home where the man has unlimited powers 'creates an atmosphere of repression which kills the individuality and initiative among his womenfolk.'[25] In these essays, Iqbalunnisa shows the problems caused by women's repression and forced ignorance and argues that 'no nation can be called strong and progressive unless its womenfolk are strong and progressive.'[26]

Iqbalunnisa also frequently addresses the issue of polygyny, which she argues is a product of the overly-rigid practice of Islam, terming it 'Muhammadanism'. Insisting that 'there is no polygamy in Islam', she emphasizes the value placed on marriage in the Qur'an. As Alam puts it, 'she believed that polygynous marriages in the past were considered to be solutions for the lack of independence of women. In the absence of an education and improbability of a life without the husband, polygyny was meant to guard women from the evils of society, and human catastrophe, to give them shelter, and a respectful livelihood.' With the rise in education and other opportunities for women in the modern period, she felt that polygyny had become "unnecessary".'[27]

Iqbalunnisa showed her strong commitment to the women's suffrage and women's rights movements of the early twentieth century. In April 1935, she led the Indian delegation at the twelfth conference of the International Alliance of Women for Suffrage and Equal Citizenship (IAWSEC) held in Istanbul, Turkey and delivered a speech entitled, 'Woman's Rights and Duties as a Citizen.'[28] The conference was striking in bringing together women from the Caribbean, Australia, Africa, India, and Europe.[29] The speech was not included in the original text of *Changing India*, but published in the 2015 edition for the first time after being discovered by Asiya Alam in the papers of the International Alliance of Women in the Smith College libraries in Massachusetts. Iqbalunnisa discusses the special role of motherhood and a woman's value to society as the 'best and first educator of her children.'[30] She develops what Alam calls a 'gendered notion of citizenship' and argues that 'the destiny of the nation lies to a greater extent in the hands of the women.'[31] It is a powerful statement on feminism and motherhood, rooted in her identity as an Asian woman, and provided a contrast to the Western feminists at the conference, who focussed more on justice and suffrage. At the International Woman's Twelfth World Congress in Istanbul in September 1935, she delivered another address on 'Women of East and West in Cooperation'. Here, she argued that 'no region can live long unto itself' and comments that, contrary to common impression, the East is not ancient and unchanging but is modern and connected to ideas from other parts of the world.[32] She goes on to acknowledge that the cultural understanding between the East and West was not easy. Acknowledging the growth of fascism, and the hold of imperialism and Eurocentrism, she remarks 'for a variety of reasons, false ideas of race or cultural superiority have gained ground, but on that score, perhaps no nation or people or country has a right to cast the first stone in the new world to be. We want to use every agency: political, economic, educational, and social to prevent false ideas from dominating the intercourse of the people'.[33] She remained hopeful that nations would come to associate with each other and unite to 'exchange their ideas and ideals'.[34]

A few months after Partition, Iqbalunnisa accompanied her daughter, Salima, by ship from Bombay to Karachi in the newly established Pakistan (where Salima subsequently lived until passing away in June 2017). When the ship docked at Karachi, no one was allowed to get off the boat until the morning, owing to checks by port officials. However, trouble ensued. A crowd of 300–400 refugees on board tried storming through the first-class cabins to get out. A family with a sick child, who needed immediate medical attention, was trying to make its way out. The Captain, scared, was unable to calm them down. Iqbalunnisa came through from the first-class cabins to inquire about the matter: she was told about the family and their child. She said, 'Give me the child and I will look after it.' She nursed him/her all night and the fever came down. The following morning, she returned the child to the family and they calmly disembarked. Travelling during such troubling times, accompanied only by her daughter, Hussain had no qualms in tackling a difficult situation such as this, displaying great bravery and strength of character.[35]

Iqbalunnisa returned to India after a few weeks, but she and her husband became keen to join their sons in London. In 1951, they were able to do so. Her final years were not easy. Her vibrant networks in the UK and Europe had been disrupted by the war and intervening years. In contrast to her wide circle of friends and renown in India, she lived in London in very different circumstances, without the support structures she had been used to. She found the winters harsh and carrying coal for the heating arduous. Her last few months, however, were marked with tremendous excitement at the engagement of her son, Bashir (whom she was concerned was still unmarried in his early forties). Her spirits unaffected by age or hardship, she welcomed her daughter-in-law with much enthusiasm; 'her face used to light up and her eyes would twinkle with excitement.'[36] Sadly, she died just a few weeks before the wedding in London, on 22 October 1954, at the age of fifty-seven from a very acute and sudden heart attack.

She is buried in Brookwood Cemetery, Surrey, England in the oldest Muslim cemetery in the UK, once part of the largest cemetery in the world.

Iqbalunnisa's tombstone describes her clearly and unequivocally as an author, educationalist, and social worker, a rare combination of words to find on an epitaph, let alone that of an Indian woman from the first half of the twentieth century. Recent years have seen a world more volatile, uncertain, complex, and ambiguous[37] which calls for a response in which there is greater vision, understanding, clarity and agility. In this context more than ever, we need Iqbalunnisa's prescient and powerful voice, its loud volume and—with this book and its predecessor, *Changing India*—her renewed visibility.

Tombstone of Iqbalunnisa Hussain, Brookwood Cemetery, Woking, Surrey, UK, courtesy of Arif Zaman

Notes

1. Interview with Dr Fatima Sughra Ahmed, 29 July 2015.
2. John Spiers, foreword in *Changing India: A Muslim Woman Speaks*, ix.
3. According to Dr Salima Ahmed, after having been cured of the Bubonic plague by Western doctors, Syed Husain developed a strong abhorrence towards orthodox methods and was determined to follow more progressive routes. The strictness of his upbringing, and the fact that half his family died without medical aid, had a significant effect on him. According Dr Ahmed, he was well read in English literature and his 'concept of a human being was of a well rounded person who acquires education, learns arts and physical development, and above all, develops an elevated character of honesty, integrity and hard work.' Interview with Dr Salima Ahmed, 14 August 2016.
4. Her son, Bashir Zaman, then a junior Indian Civil Service officer in London, was one of many attending language classes in the spring of 1940 to learn German with an impending expectation that Britain was on the verge of falling.
5. See Siobhan Lambert-Hurley and Sunil Sharma, *Atiya's Journeys: A Muslim Woman from Colonial Bombay to Edwardian Britain*, (Oxford: Oxford University Press, 2010).
6. Elleke Boehmer, 'Description', *Indian Arrivals, 1870–1915: Networks of British Empire*, (Oxford: Oxford University Press, 2015), <https://global.oup.com/academic/product/indian-arrivals-1870-1915-9780198744184?cc=us&lang=en&#>.
7. Spiers, Foreword, *Changing India*, xi.
8. Juliet Gardiner, *The Thirties: An Intimate History of Britain*, (London: HarperPress, 2011), 551.
9. Jane Robinson, *Bluestockings: The Remarkable Story of the First Women to Fight for an Education*, (London: Penguin, 2010), 155–6.
10. Iqbalunnisa Hussain, 'Muslim Women's Education,' in *Changing India*, 182.
11. Asiya Alam in introduction to *Changing India*, x. The quotation is from Hussain, 'Muslim Women's Education,' 183.
12. Iqbalunnisa Hussain, 'Muslim Women's Education,' in *Changing India*, 183.
13. Hussain, 'Muslim Women's Education,' in *Changing India*, 184.
14. Ibid.
15. Alam, Introduction, *Changing India*, xxii.
16. Ibid.
17. 'Character in Education', in *Changing India*, 200.
18. World Association of Girl Guides and Girl Scouts, 'About Our History', <https://www.wagggs.org/en/about-us/our-history/>. Last accessed 21 March 2017.
19. 'The Educative Value of the Girl Guides Movement,' in *Changing India*, 201.
20. E-mail message to Arif Zaman, 15 February 2016.
21. Alam, Introduction, *Changing India*, xv.
22. *Harem House*, (Lahore: n.p., 1944).
23. 'Woman as an Individual,' in *Changing India,* 223.
24. Ibid, 222.
25. 'The Causes that Led to the Degeneration of the Muslims,' in *Changing India*, 22.
26. Ibid, 23.
27. Alam, Introduction, *Changing India*, xxiv–v. The quotation is from Hussain, 'Polygamous Marriages,' 109.
28. Reprinted as an appendix to the 2015 edition of *Changing India*, 229–33. See Alam, xxviii, for more on the IWSA, which drew its leadership from Europe and the U.S. and drew participants from around the world to its conference.
29. The Australian Women's Weekly, Web National Library of Australia (22 June 1935), 3. <http://trove.n/a.gov.ou/newspaper/title/112#>.
30. 'Woman's Rights and Duties as a Citizen,' *Changing India*, 231.
31. Ibid, 233.
32. 'Women of East and West in Cooperation,' *Changing India,* 166–7.
33. Ibid, 171.
34. *Changing India, 225.*
35. Interview with Dr Salima Ahmed, 25 August 2013.
36. Dr Fatima Sughra Ahmed, e-mail message to Zaman, 14 January 2012.
37. Rob Elkington, Madeleine van der Steege, Judith Glick-Smith, Jennifer Moss Breen, ed. *Visionary Leadership in a Turbulent World: Thriving in the New VUCA Context* (Bradford: Emerald Publishing Limited, 2017).

Purdah and Polygamy in a Changing India

Suvir Kaul

Not long after Bankimchandra Chattopadhyay wrote *Rajmohan's Wife* (serialized in 1864, now understood to be the first Indian novel in English), two women published novels. In 1878, Toru Dutt's unfinished novel, *Bianca: The Young Spanish Maiden*, was published by her father after her death. In 1887 and 1888, the *Madras Christian College Magazine* serialized Krupabai Satthianadhan's *Saguna: A Story of Native Christian Life* (the novel was published in 1895, also posthumously). Dutt's novel is set in England and has nothing to do with Indian lives. Satthianadhan's semi-autobiographical *Saguna* describes the social constraints that mar the lives of Hindu girls and women, but also the possibilities that conversion to Christianity and missionary education made available to some young women, particularly those with supportive fathers, older brothers, or even husbands. Her other novel, *Kamala: A Story of Hindu Life* (1894), is directly concerned with the difficulties of women's lives, and is to that extent a precursor to Iqbalunnisa Hussain's *Purdah and Polygamy*. Elizabeth I. Grigg, who knew Satthianadhan and who wrote the memoir that prefaces the first edition of *Kamala*, describes the novel in these terms:

> We are admitted into the secrets of an Indian household—the difficulties and the sorrows of a Hindu wife and mother. Happy children we meet every day but from the time when an Indian girl enters her mother-in-law's house, her life seems rarely to be a very happy one. She is not imprisoned in a zenana and denied the blessings of air and exercise, but her life is seemingly too often one of hard work, of misconstruction, and of covert rebellion against injustice and domestic repression.[1]

These sentences could well describe *Purdah and Polygamy*, written some fifty years later, except that Hussain's novel is set in a Muslim household, where women are in fact 'imprisoned' by the twin burdens that comprise its title.

The reformist impulse that drove Satthianadhan's writing characterized other early novels too. Shevantibai Nikambe, who like Dutt and Satthianadhan, belonged to a family that had converted to Christianity, wrote *Ratanbai: A Sketch of a Bombay High Caste Hindu Young Wife* (1895), a novel that illuminates the debate about female education that was a crucial feature of the contested advent of colonial modernity.[2] Not surprisingly, these early novels that stage the miseries of Hindu upper-caste women, of child-brides and widows, are circumspect about the forms and velocity of social change. While they emphasize the difference education makes to women, that education is enabled by kindly men, and produces more benign and cultivated domestic lives rather than any form of visible public change (though it is, of course, historically the case that the former is fundamental to the latter). Many Indian and English men, or for that matter, women, were not sympathetic to the idea of reform generally or of education for women in particular; Saguna, for one, has to confront their prejudices as she grows. Her encounters with discrimination make pointed the novel's critique (however limited) of patriarchy and colonial attitudes, and it is these moments that link the novel to broader debates in the late-nineteenth and early twentieth-century public sphere about the 'woman question' in India.[3]

Indeed, debates about women's lives, and about the policies designed to intervene in them, were the centerpiece of struggles between (male) nationalists and their British colonial counterparts. It was not only public, legal, and institutional issues like the appropriate age of marriage, widow remarriage, the practice of *sati* or even legitimate forms of education, that were under examination, but the very forms of Indian (largely Hindu) domesticity, for as Antoinette Burton puts it, 'house and home had long been highly charged ideological categories in the context of the Raj':

> The 'oriental' zenana, or women's quarters, was pathologized as dark, unhygienic, and indicative of Indians' incapacity for self-rule throughout the nineteenth century, with Victorian feminists taking the lead in extrapolating from this domestic space a host of judgments about the character of Indian men, women, and children from the 1860s onward … Elite Indian male nationalists, for their part, refracted metropolitan anxieties about the status of home into concerns about the integrity of 'Indian' domestic space, in part because they shared many of the patriarchal convictions at the heart of the British colonial project … In any case, the struggle over house and home that shaped debates about Indian modernity undoubtedly staged domestic space as historical time, thus guaranteeing that it would be seized on as an opportunity for modernizing interventions.[4]

Educated women reformers like Pandita Ramabai, Cornelia Sorabji, and Nazar Sajjad Hyder also contributed to these public conversations and helped shape what we now recognize to be the modern forms of Indian cultural nationalism, even when the reformers were not themselves against British rule. Nationalists of very different political persuasions agreed on the need for reforms in a range of social sectors but particularly in the lives of women; what remained contentious was the precise machinery and nature of legal, social and cultural change, and indeed the question of whether reforms were hindered or furthered by colonial rule.

The status of women and of their roles within the family, particularly as circumscribed by the practices of purdah and polygyny, became the focus of debates among Muslim reformers too. As Asiya Alam shows, 'Polygyny was the site of much contestation and debate during the colonial period. Late colonial discussions on polygyny raised the question about the sanctity and uniqueness of the conjugal bond. But polygyny went beyond the husband-wife relationship and cast its vexing shadow on issues of child rearing, property inheritances, and relationships within the extended family.' This debate became important both because colonial missionaries had 'often identified [polygyny] as a specific feature of Muslim societies'[5] and one that marked them as deficient. Alam notes that, 'Even though polygyny was also practiced amongst the Hindus, the issue acquired a particular salience for the Muslim community. The perception that it is allowed in Islam and has a Qur'anic sanction made it a marker of Muslim identity and provided a distinctiveness that it otherwise would not have had' (635). Muslim religious leaders had long differed about the precise nature and prescriptive power of Qur'anic injunctions about polygyny, but this debate was furthered largely by *ashraf* Muslims, who saw in such reformist efforts a legitimation of their claims to the post-feudal, indeed, modern leadership of their community.

This is the social context within which Iqbalunnisa Hussain made her contributions to Muslim reformist and Indian nationalist thought. But first, a word on her remarkable life: as we know,[6] she was born in 1897 into a household which maintained purdah, was married at fifteen and then—aided by her husband, Syed Ghulam Hussain—educated herself to a point where, in 1930, she took a BA degree from Maharani's College in Mysore. Even more unusually, perhaps uniquely, for a woman in her circumstance, three years later she moved to England to study for an MA in Education at Leeds University.[7] Leeds brought her into contact with a wider world of women's emancipation and activism. In 1934, she went to Adelboden, Switzerland to speak at a conference of the World Association of Girl Guides and Girl Scouts; in 1935, she gave a talk at the Muslim Society of Great Britain as well as travelled to Istanbul to attend a conference of the International Alliance for Suffrage and Equal Citizenship. As Asiya Alam puts it, Hussain's political affiliations and her 'stance against isolationism points to a politics of "internationalism"', where her class-affiliations and English education encouraged membership in Europe-based international movements even though she was aware of the racial discrimination that was a component feature of colonial rule across the world.[8] Once she returned to India, she taught and spoke widely about the importance of education for women's advancement and social reform. She also attended several meetings of the All India Women's Conference as one of the delegates from the princely state of Mysore. Her talks and essays on a series of interconnected topics—women's rights in Islam, education, gender difference, on poverty and beggary, on inter-religious differences and co-operation, on language acquisition, and on the benefits offered by the Girl Guides movement—were collected and published in 1940 as *Changing India: A Muslim Woman Speaks*.

It is important to remember that Hussain's life and writing challenged social conventions that governed and restricted both Muslim lives and the lives of women, and that her actions and opinions met with opposition. Her coming out of purdah in 1931 led to threats that her family would suffer a social boycott, and her articles that advocated a more egalitarian reading of the doctrines of Islam attracted parallel condemnation. Even though, for the last four decades, Muslim men and women had developed community organizations devoted to the welfare of women—schools; magazines like *Tahzib un-Niswan* (Lahore), *Khatun* (Aligarh) and *Ismat* (Delhi);[9] the All India Muslim Ladies' Conference or the Women's Education Section of the All India Muhammadan Educational Conference—these initiatives were often resisted by religious authorities, who feared the loss of their power or by others who argued that such initiatives would lead to the end of purdah and the loss of women's modesty.[10] Hussain's religious, social, and political views drew upon these legacies of reform, which also provided her key templates for acceptable reformist opinions. For instance, corrupt practices amongst Muslims could be blamed on unthinking clergymen, but always while celebrating the original purity of Islam and calling for a return to the example set by the Prophet.[11] If women were to be educated and brought out of purdah, it was always with a view to making them better wives and mothers who could contribute to the modernization and development of the community and the nation. And while Hussain advocated change, she drew back from a too-rapid transformation or 'revolution': 'Personally, I am not for revolutions as revolutions destroy too much, even though they may be productive for the time being. In the end, they are very harmful. Any progress or growth, if it is to be real and sure, must be gradual and slow.'[12]

This model of progress was, of course, the norm amongst the upper-class men and women who mobilized against corrupt practices in their communities. To read the talks Hussain gave and the articles she published is to trace the energizing possibilities as well as the cultural and political limits of (Muslim) liberalism in India in the early decades of the twentieth century. Women (and men) who lobbied for reform always did so with an eye to the sensibilities of the community, which were now conditioned by the perception that, post the Mughals, Muslim power was in decline, limited first by the political and military victories of the British, and now by the educational advantages and greater numbers of the Hindu community. Even as Hussain does not specify such historical factors in her writing, this sense of decline is palpable in her many accounts of all that ails her community. Not long after she went to Leeds, Hussain spoke to the Muslim Society of Great Britain, and she was remarkably forthright in her diagnosis of social debasement: 'Our homes are disorganized centers of quarrels, our schools are good for nothing, our society simply does not exist, and our mosques are monopolized by our selfish men on the plea that they are polluted by the presence of women.'[13] For her, the first step out of this morass was the education of women. As she argued in 'The Causes that Led to the Degeneration of the Muslims':

> Regeneration of the Muslim nation is only possible when its women are educated and are efficient and independent. The goal of the young girl's life should not just be marriage, but also efficiency and culture. The contemptuous attitude of the superiority of man and the inferiority of woman should be replaced with equality … The regeneration of our nation is possible only when our women become efficient, intelligent, and brave.[14]

Hussain was not alone in recognizing that there were limits to the options available to Muslim women, even as some, primarily from well-educated and highly placed families, did make major changes in their own lives. Nazar Sajjad Hyder's commentary on purdah is a case in point. She had given up purdah herself in 1923, and was sharp in her condemnation of the male paranoia and power that kept women confined at home. She wrote mockingly of '[male] fear that, when she who has been a prisoner for ages leaves her prison, then the desire to see the world will certainly stir in her, and she will peep out of the carriage, look at the shops, and many faces will pass under her eyes. [Men] do not like such changes in any circumstances.' Hyder pointed out that such male insecurity depleted the entire community, since the 'severe confinement' caused by purdah was a huge 'social and national waste'. However, she did not argue that women *en masse* should attempt a radical breach of community norms. Rather, she attempted a pragmatic solution by designing a burqa that would allow women to step out of their homes to perform their chores without any putative loss of honor.[15]

While Hussain addressed a wide variety of social inequities in her writing and her advocacy, both the institutions of polygamy and purdah were of particular concern for her. In each case, even as she appealed to the better sense of the male leaders of the community, she understood the education of women to be of primary importance. Educate young women, she argued, and they will, as better companions to their men as well as more competent mothers and managers of the household, prove the best argument against both institutions. Both men and women, she wrote, needed to learn how to deal with each other much more fluidly than social conservatism allowed; for her, 'if a society is to be prosperous, progressive, and happy it must have a reasonable amount of free mixing of both the sexes as we have been seeing here in the society of the most advanced nations of the world.'[16] Hussain's comparison here is with England and Europe more generally. However, she also drew lessons from a largely Muslim country, Turkey, and pointed out that 'co-education in Turkey has been very successful. It begins from primary education and continues up to university … The idea of marriage is not the only means of support for ladies abroad. The goal of their lives is all round excellence and development of all their faculties.' To balance what must have seemed a radical observation, she emphasized that the 'success of co-education in Turkey is partly due to the strict observance of Islamic principles which forbid familiarity or illicit relations between men and women, and is also due to the highly developed character, the strong sense of self-respect, and the dignified personality which is found among Turkish women.'[17]

For Hussain, Kemal Attaturk's modernization of Turkey suggested possibilities for change in Muslim communities in India, and while she did not develop such parallels at length, she was very hopeful of transformation at home too:

Great modern thinkers of our country have been making a real contribution to the welfare and progress of their communities in particular, and of Indians in general. These have been the real incentives in developing a spirit of self-realization, self-responsibility, and self-respect in most of them. A demand for self-expression, political liberty, religious freedom, social equality, and economic justice is expressed everywhere … There is unanimous support for women's education and progress. Equal rights and suffrage have been granted to them by many of the governments all over India through the passing of the following resolution: 'That sex shall form no disqualification to women entering any position or profession for which she shows herself capable.'[18]

Looking forward, Hussain wrote further: 'The fight for equal rights, status, and a democratic form of social organization is not an uncommon thing nowadays. Indian women today want to be self-reliant, self-respecting, and responsible.'[19]

This is the hope and the energy Hussain brought to her public speaking and institutional work as a teacher, school administrator, and spokeswoman for reform. Given the faith in the future suggested by the essays in *Changing India*, the novel *Purdah and Polygamy*, published four years later, comes as a great surprise, for it is unremittingly grim and pessimistic, and able to see little sunlight at the end of the dark tunnel that is life for women in an orthodox home. It depicts, relentlessly and unforgivingly, the evils of purdah and the consequences of patriarchal power confirmed in the actions of a man who takes four wives. Perhaps the most startling feature of the novel is its minute accounting of the harm women in such a household do to each other, across the generations and amongst the multiple wives. The novel's tone is bitterly ironic and angry. There is no doubt about its attitude to the stultifying, destructive insularity of the everyday life of this household (both for the women immured within its walls and for male children brought up in these circumstances). Hussain intersperses her narrative with a variety of comments on the belief systems that bred such insularity—these comments are not marked off from the narrative but incorporated in free indirect style.[20] She had no qualms about stating in matter-of-fact terms, and thereby holding up to ridicule, traditional verities, as this passage shows: 'It is a well-known fact that man is superior to woman in every respect. He is a representative of God on earth and being born with His light in him, deserves the respect and obedience that he demands. He is not expected to show his gratitude or even a kind word of appreciation to a woman: it is his birthright to get everything from her. "Might is right" is the policy of [this] world'(35).[21] The seamless movement from the seemingly theologically sound and conventionally sent-ious first sentence to the stark brutality of the last is quite remarkable in its moment (or indeed, even now). Hussain's anger and reformist passion surface in such moments, which interrupt and intensify the much noted 'social realism' of the novel.[22]

The novel focuses on the dead weight of unchanging conventions, all sanctified in the name of religion, and all designed to subordinate women. But it also makes clear that these conventions also limit men and stunt their imaginations, as this instance suggests, if only by indirection. When we read that Zuhra had selected a bride for Kabeer, the narrative seems to emphasize the hypocritical gaps between piety and social practice, and direct its ire at the way in which girls are forced to perform their conformity to alienating expectations:

> Soon after the marriage is decided, a girl confines herself in a corner, preferably in a pantry or a store-room, where no male member of her own family can see her. She keeps aloof. Her immediate needs are supplied by her mother or sisters … She is not expected to laugh or to hear the talk going on in the house. She should assume an air of dejection, disappointment, and despair at leaving the parent's house or else she will not be doing justice to all their sacrifices for her. She should cry during the marriage and show her unwillingness to meet a man (21).

These prescriptions of the pieties governing brides-to-be seem like an editorial voice-over, but in a remarkable narrative twist, we are told that they run through Kabeer's mind as he tries to imagine his fiancée. This is how his sister was before she was married, and that is his only model for female behaviour. It is these moments of irony, of slight but startling shifts in point-of-view, that alert us to Hussain's acute sense of the destructive effects of sequestered lives, for women in particular but also for men.

The house that is the setting of the domestic drama belongs to Umar, an urban landlord. 'Dilkusha' (that which gives happiness to the heart), is a citadel of patriarchal power, as the opening of the novel makes clear: its 'high blind walls made a stranger take it for an unguarded jail, and literally so it was for its women folk' (6). The women within are in purdah, though they do not maintain its strictures equally. As the story evolves and different women enter the house, three of them as wives to Kabeer (a fourth wife is discovered elsewhere only after his death at the end of the novel), their conflicted relations with each other, with their mother-in-law Zuhra, and with Kabeer detail the miseries of purdah and polygyny. The opening chapters of the novel speed through Umar's life and death. He leaves behind a wife, Zuhra, a son, Kabeer, and a twelve-year-old daughter, Jamila (now lacking a father, she is promptly married off to a cousin). Zuhra, who goes on to become a tyrant at home, particularly vis-à-vis Kabeer's wives, suffers horribly when Umar dies. Convention and superstition demand that she be blamed for her husband's untimely death, and that she be ritually humiliated as punishment. Umar's sister crushes Zuhra's bangles (they are symbols of marriage), her clothes are replaced by a widow's white, she is veiled so that no married woman might look upon her face and be contaminated by her ill-luck, and she is sequestered from her husband's body lest she pollute it by touching him. All this while funeral feasts are held for hundreds of invited mourners, as this sort of conspicuous, wasteful expenditure in required in order to confirm the social status of the family.

Zuhra recovers from her own humiliation as she comes to control the household, and particularly when she arranges for a bride, Nazni, for Kabeer. Zuhra routinely rebukes and demeans Nazni (who complains to her husband, but does accept that a woman's lot includes such suffering). When her father takes an ailing Nazni to a male cardiac specialist, Zuhra is uncompromising in her insistence that Nazni has lost her purity. Once Nazni moves to her natal home to recover from childbirth, Zuhra arranges another wife, Munira, for Kabeer. Zuhra has a simple justification for this second marriage: Kabeer must marry again to lessen Nazni's domestic burdens, since 'an extra healthy woman at home is no more than an extra servant' (47). Nazni is horrified by this second marriage, but moves towards reconciliation with Kabeer as she believes that 'The woman who makes her husband sorry goes to the Seventh Hell where the fire burns eternally. She is burnt alive and is recreated and burnt again' (61). The lives of the women in this novel are governed by such quasi-scriptural beliefs, which cement their oppression. As Nazni's grandmother puts it to her, a man can do anything he likes, whereas Nazni must conform: 'Your only duty is to obey him. He can marry many wives or keep many outside' (81). It is not as if there is no resistance to such ideas: Nazni's brother argues that she should not return to her betraying husband. His father is pleased with his son's progressive ideas, as they suggest an educated man, but dismisses them in practice on the grounds that Muslim girls are 'weak both bodily and mentally' and hence 'should be kept under restrictions' (75). Reformist ideas are occasionally articulated in the novel, but there are precious few occasions where they carry the day.

Munira, who has neither wealth nor good looks, is maltreated by both Zuhra and, because he feels she is not up to his station, Kabeer. He decides to find himself a third wife, and here *Purdah and Polygamy* expands its canvas of the wrongs done to women to include those suffered by educated women immured in illiterate households.[23] Maghbool is an educated poet, a talented singer, a painter, and skilled in needlework, but being over twenty years old, considered too old for marriage and thus a disgrace to her family, which is why her father has no qualms in marrying her off to a man who has two wives already. Maghbool cannot refuse her father, and thus finds herself caught up in the ugliness that defines the lives of the women of Dilkusha. To take just one instance, Munira delivers a son (the novel pays him no further attention), and Maghbool is the only one in the household who helps her, both during childbirth and also when the baby falls ill. Munira has no understanding of illness except as the dictate of 'God and qismat' (124). No one else in the household aids Munira. Maghbool is so shocked by this indifference, that she confronts her own father and accuses him of having transferred her from 'a semi-prison to a real one' (121). Her father—more amused than disturbed by her anger—responds with truisms and counsels acceptance: 'A woman enters married life with the emblem of self-sacrifice of her husband and his family' (122).

Over time, and not surprisingly, Kabeer, challenged by Maghbool's 'frankness, respect for right, and hatred for wrong' (126), begins to dislike his third wife. Finally, one evening when his dinner is delayed, he beats her with his shoe. Zuhra's response typifies her attitude to the other women in the house: 'You served her right. When a woman forgets her duties, she should be reminded of them by gentle means. If she is so obstinate as not to heed, she should be dealt with more forcibly' (151). Zuhra is particularly angered that Maghbool spends her days writing, and her poetry soon becomes a bone of contention between her and Kabeer too. Since Maghbool has an income arranged for her by her father, she plans to publish her poems, which Kabeer finds wasteful and forbids. When she goes ahead, he sees this as 'a living example that to give money to a woman is to give a dagger to her' (153). He has no comprehension of her desire to publish, and becomes even more hostile as she does not hand over her money to him.

Purdah and Polygamy is so determined to emphasize Dilkusha as a house of horrors that it represents Akram, Nazni's son—the first-born male in this family—as constantly being beaten by his grandmother, and then, once he is older, by his father. Akram grows up to join his father's business, where he comes into contact with two employees, Alexander and his niece, Rose. He becomes a regular visitor of Rose's home, becomes friends with her fiancé George, and learns to wear suits and enjoy movies and alcohol. This Christian, perhaps Anglo-Indian, family suggest another model of male-female relations, more informal and full of fun, and the novel does suggest that Akram's discovery of a Western-inflected social life is therapeutic for him (though disaster does lie ahead).[24] The only reason why he can get away from his home is that his father too leaves surreptitiously each night to go and visit his fourth wife, who he has married secretly. While visiting a long-term tenant, a poor elderly woman, to collect what she owes him, Kabeer forgives her debt when he notices that she has a granddaughter, Noorjahan, 'who was young, beautiful, and fair as a lily' (161). The old woman is nearly destitute, asks for his help, and Kabeer convinces himself that he is doing his moral and religious duty by taking Noorjahan off her hands: 'God says if one supports a destitute person, he will be blessed a hundred times…This marriage is definitely not for my own sake but is meant to help an unfortunate creature' (162). He begins to spend more time with Noorjahan, but does not tell either his mother or his other wives about her.

Akram's attentions to Rose finally irk George enough for him to break off their engagement and hire a group of toughs to beat up Akram. They injure him badly enough for the sight of his broken body to send Kabeer into a coma. Akram recovers slowly, but his father declines. When Kabeer's mother and wives are finally allowed to see him, they have unexpected visitors: Kabeer's fourth wife and her grandmother. When she learns of Noorjahan, Maghbool finally walks out of the house in protest. Kabeer dies not long after, followed in short order by his mother. At the end of the novel, we learn that all this suffering results in little change within Dilkusha; the characters shift positions, but the structure remains unchanged: 'Nazni achieved the coveted position' as the senior woman in the house, and 'Munira and Noorjahan being helpless, continued in the same house under Nazni's regime' (194). It is the case that Maghbool escapes, and while we might imagine that she establishes an independent life as a writer and poet, *Purdah and Polygamy* does not chart her life beyond Dilkusha. That sort of life, lived beyond the strictures of rigid patriarchal conservatism, or even as patterned upon Hussain's own journey from purdah to public speaking and activism, is nowhere to be found in the novel. The insularity of Dilkusha, its refusal to open out into the world, is corrosive and punishing, and that is the lesson emphasized by Hussain's novel. India in the 1940s was roiled by powerful political forces, including those of different forms of anti-colonialism, that precipitated social change, but they find no place in *Purdah and Polygamy*. The necessity for reform, and perhaps its possibility, is suggested by the many moments of friction in the novel, but Hussain does not fan those sparks into flame—if anything, the novel suggests the impossible weight of conventions and the stultifying power of the social conventions that ratify them rather than the capacity of women, or the desire of men, to successfully challenge or overthrow them.

However, there is no question that *Purdah and Polygamy* is an important early Indian novel, one of several that make clear the dimensions of the social problems that constricted women's lives. Hussain's own life superseded these constraints, but her novel is a powerful, even shocking, representation of the world of sequestered women, particularly those who are thrust, for a variety of reasons, into polygyny. It leaves us a legacy of uncompromising critique unmatched by most novelists and commentators who write on similar issues today anywhere in the subcontinent. As Pakistan, India, and Bangladesh struggle to address and act against the oppression of women, particularly against those forms of subordination supposedly sanctioned by different religions, we need to recognize that we can draw upon the work of a long tradition of courageous women who fought similar problems in an idiom appropriate in their own time and place. It is thus important for us to remember a reformer-activist-novelist like Iqbalunnisa Hussain and to engage with her writing, for her essays and her novel bring into sharp relief the subordination of women within families that decorous conventionality today requires us to ignore or to explain away as practices that have receded into the past. Many of them have not, and our efforts to contest them and to build more egalitarian, democratic societies can only be honed and enhanced by our reading of novels like *Purdah and Polygamy*.

NOTES

1. Mrs H. B. Grigg, 'Introductory Memoir' to Mrs S. Satthianandhan, *Kamala: A Story of Hindu Life* (Madras: Srinivasa, Varadachari & Co., 1894), p. xxix. We should note the patriarchal formality with which the title page names both the novelist and her memoirist.

2. Indrani Sen, in her commentary on *Saguna* and *Ratanbai*, points out that in 'many cases female negotiations with "colonial modernity" were mediated through interactions with white women, especially with missionaries and schoolteachers.' These early novels in English feature such colonial interactions, which range from positive and enabling to racist and demeaning. Sen offers a valuable discussion of the coming of social reform in Western India: 'Writing English, Writing Reform: Two Indian Women's Novels of the 19th Century', *Indian Journal of Gender Studies*, 21:1 (2014), 1–26.

3. For an overview of such issues, Susie Tharu and K. Lalitha's introductory essay on 'Literature of the Reform and Nationalist Movements' remains indispensable reading, as do the writers that they collect in *Women Writing in India: 600 B.C. to the Present*, 2 vols. (Delhi: Oxford University Press, 1991). Volume I, *600 B.C. to the Early Twentieth Century*, 143–86. Ellen Brinks, in *Anglophone Indian Women Writers, 1870–1920* (Surrey: Ashgate Publishing, 2013), discusses five early women reformers (including Krupabai Satthianadhan) in India.

4. Antoinette Burton, *Dwelling in the Archive: Women Writing House, Home, and History in Late Colonial India* (Oxford: Oxford University Press, 2003), 7–8.

5. Asiya Alam, 'Polygyny, Family and Sharafat: Discourses amongst North Indian Muslims, circa 1870–1918,' *Modern Asian Studies* (2011), 45, 632–3 [631–68].

6. For more information on Hussain's life, see the biographical sketch by Arif Zaman in this volume.

7. Hussain's perseverance, and the extent of her husband's support, can be gauged from the fact that while her eldest son went to England with her to pursue his own post-baccalaureate studies, her other children remained at home. Hussain's daughter, Dr Salima R. Ahmed, speaks of missing her mother in the years that she was away at Leeds in the Karachi Literature Festival video of the 2015 book launch of Iqbalunnisa Hussain's *Changing India*: <https://vimeo.com/123294309>. Last accessed on April 30, 2016.

8. Asiya Alam, introduction to *Changing India: A Muslim Woman Speaks*, by Iqbalunnisa Hussain, (Karachi: Oxford University Press, 2015), xxxi. (*Changing India* was first published in 1940 by the Hosali Press in Bangalore.)

9. For a useful survey of the kinds of topics addressed in these reformist magazines, as well as an account of their contentious reception, see Gail Minault, 'Urdu Women's Magazines in the Early Twentieth Century,' in *Manushi*, 48 (September–October 1988), 2–9, <http://www.manushi.in/docs/912.%20Urdu%20 Women%5C's%20Magazines%20in%20the%20

Early%20Twentieth%20Century.pdf;>. Last accessed on April 30, 2016.

10. For a summary account of contemporary arguments for and against the setting up of the Muslim Ladies' Conference, see Tahera Aftab, *Inscribing South Asian Muslim Women: An Annotated Bibliography & Research Guide* (Leiden: Brill, 2008), 201–8.

11. Hussain distinguishes between Islam and what she terms 'Muhammadanism,' the former being 'the religion taught by the Quran' and the latter being 'a religion created by a priest-class.' 'Islam and Muhammadanism,' in *Changing India*, pp. 1–4.

12. Hussain, 'Muslim Womens' Education,' in *Changing India*, 191.

13. Hussain, 'Muslim Womens' Education,' in *Changing India*, 189. As is clear to a reader today, elements of Hussain's complaint are still matters of great contestation, and are rarely spoken about with her degree of candour.

14. Hussain, 'The Causes that Led to the Degeneration of the Muslims,' in *Changing India*, 23.

15. The quotations from Hyder are from the extract on 'Purdah' published in Tharu and Lalitha, *Women Writing in India: 600 B.C. to the Present*, I, 393. The editors also mention Hyder's design of the burqa in their headnote to the writer on p. 391.

16. Hussain, 'Muslim Women's Education,' in *Changing India*, 183.

17. Hussain, 'Progress of Women's Education Abroad,' in *Changing India*, 181.

18. Hussain, 'Potentialities of the Future,' in *Changing India*, 225–26. Here, Hussain echoes Margaret E. Cousins, who recounted a resolution passed by the Social Reform Conference in 1917 and pointed out that it was a veritable 'Woman's Charter of Freedom of Opportunity,' that spoke of an equality not yet available to women in western countries. See Cousins, *The Awakening of Asian Womanhood*, 1922. Reprint. (London: Forgotten Books, 2013), 102–3.

19. Hussain, 'Potentialities of the Future,' in *Changing India*, 227.

20. This stylistic feature, as well as her focus on domestic relations, has encouraged commentators on Hussain to represent her as an Indian Jane Austen. While Austen is justly celebrated for her quietly precise observations about social pretensions and the minutiae of class distinctions in early nineteenth century England, Hussain's ironies interrogate the religious and social corruptions of her time and place with a ferocity and courage not imaginable in Austen's genteel world. Hussain likely learned her 'free indirect style' from the sarcastic comments directed at the social hypocrisy and religion-sanctified discrimination that had long been the targets of iconoclastic satire in Indian languages including Urdu.

21. Iqbalunnisa Hussain, *Purdah and Polygamy: Life in an Indian Muslim Household* (Bangalore: Hosali Press, 1944), 24.

22. I have a longer discussion of *Purdah and Polygamy* in my essay, 'Women, Reform and Nationalism in Three Novels of Muslim Life', in A History of the Indian Novel in English, ed. Ulka Anjaria (Cambridge: Cambridge University Press, 2015), 133–46.

23. In an extraordinary essay collected in *Changing India*, 'Educated Girls in Uncivilized Families', Hussain paints a grim picture of the life of women in traditional sequestered families:

> The majority of the women members of the homes are illiterate, ignorant, superstitious, unscrupulous, and selfish-mischief mongers…They are elated at anyone's sufferings…Education has no value to them (115).
> 'One can imagine the sad plight of modern girls,' Hussain writes, 'in the family that observes artificial purdah strictly and indiscriminately, to the ruination of their health, education, and personality' (117). Lives within Dilkusha play out these miseries.

24. One marker of the insularity of the world Hussain represents is that it contains only three non-Muslim characters, all Christians.

Iqbalunnisa Hussain
and
Early English Fiction by South Asian Muslims

Muneeza Shamsie

Some years ago, while I was researching a literary history which has now become *Hybrid Tapestries: The Development of Pakistani Literature in English* (2017), I realized that a literature could not be divided so neatly into the parameters of nationality and nationhood defined by a specific date: 1947. It was important to look at the genesis of this literature in colonial times. My ideas were reinforced by a question raised by the American publisher of my anthology *And the World Changed: Contemporary Stories for Pakistani Women* (2008). She asked, 'Why are these women writing in English?' Once again, I found myself looking back to the pre-Partition era and the links between the development of English-language writing by South Asian women and issues such as zenana reform, education for girls, and public life.[1] At the same time, my exploration of the use of English as a creative medium by Indian Muslims led me to a surprising discovery: a novel called *Purdah and Polygamy: Life in an Indian Muslim Household* by Iqbalunissa Hussain. Published in 1944, it is probably the only full-length novel in English written before Partition by an Indian Muslim woman.

I was astonished that this extraordinarily powerful and incisive work, 'clever in its irony, at times humorous and always brave in its depiction of injustice'[2] and 'one of the most striking narratives of its period'[3] was mostly unknown in Pakistan, as was its author. In my quest for answers, I found a brief reference to *Purdah and Polygamy* alongside Ahmed Ali's *Twilight in Delhi* (1940) and *Ocean of the Night* (1964) in M.K. Naik's *A History of Indian English Literature* (2005). There was also an extract from the novel in Eunice de Souza's excellent anthology *Purdah* (2004), which provided me with brief biographical details.

In time, I discovered that Iqbalunnisa Hussain (1897–1954) belonged to a family which was divided between India, Pakistan, and Britain at Partition.[4] Her sons had settled in Britain prior to Partition and she joined them in 1951; her daughter, Dr Salima Ahmed, migrated to Pakistan. Her legacy is rightfully shared by India, Pakistan, and the South Asian diaspora. In 2015, Oxford University Press, Pakistan, reprinted Iqbalunissa Hussain's 1940 book, *Changing India: a Muslim Woman Speaks*. These writings reveal her active engagement in the Islamic modernism of the 1930s with its links to the international feminist movements. All this provided the impetus for her attack on male-dominated traditions and status quo in *Purdah and Polygamy*. Her activism and literary output remain an important precursor to the women's movement in post-independence Pakistan. Furthermore, in an era when the entire use of English as a creative medium by subcontinentals remained the subject of heated nationalistic debate, before and after Partition, Iqbalunnisa Hussain's use of English as a creative vehicle was very unusual, particularly for an Indian Muslim woman.

Interestingly, the first major English-language novel by a Muslim writer—*Twilight in Delhi* by Ahmed Ali—which preceded Hussain's *Purdah* by four years, portrays with great sympathy the strict rules and difficulties by Muslim women in a Muslim home, even though Hussain's has a stronger and richer feminist narrative. At the same time, Hussain's choice of English, her education in England and the fact that she had discarded purdah in 1931, was also an indication of changes that were taking place among the Muslim Indian elite. Several Indian Muslim women had travelled to Europe and recorded the experience in travelogues.[5] In 1921, women were given the right to be elected into the legislatures of the British Raj. Indian Muslim women, such as Jahan Ara Shahnawaz (1896–1979)[6] and Inam Fatima Habibullah (1893–1974)—the mother of Mumtaz Shah Nawaz and the mother-in-law of Attia Hosain respectively[7]—discarded purdah and entered into public life. Both were among the Indian Muslim women to be elected into the Provincial Assemblies. As such, English as the language of government and that of university education in British India opened out new possibilities of empowerment, including professions such as medicine and education. Early Indian Muslim women doctors included Fatima Jinnah (1893–1967)[8] a dentist, and Rashid Jahan (1905–1952), a gynaecologist.

Hussain is a direct literary ancestor, however, to two significant younger writers: the Pakistani novelist Mumtaz Shah Nawaz (1912–1948) and the Indian novelist Attia Hosain (1913–1998). Both were among the growing number of Indian Muslim women graduates and both contributed English creative work to various publications in colonial India but published their first full-length books of fiction after Partition. Shah Nawaz's novel, *The Heart Divided* (1957), was the first full length work in English in post-independence Pakistan. Hosain's story collection, *Phoenix Fled* (1953), was among the earliest works of fiction in post-independence India, but in Britain where she lived, it distinguishes her 'as a precursor of a host of celebrated [South Asian diaspora] talents'.[9] In both instances, Shah Nawaz and Hosain were important postcolonial pioneers, regardless of gender and genre, and their work places the narratives of women as a leading trope in the literary history of South Asian English writing. Aamer Hussein also points out, 'although she was not a Pakistani, Hosain's work has been, and remains, of relevance to a Pakistani readership, largely because of the impact of her epic novel, *Sunlight on a Broken Column* (1962), with its meticulous reconstruction of pre-Partition Indo-Muslim society'.[10] Iqbalunissa Hussain's pre-Partition novel, *Purdah and Polygamy*, thus heralds an entire body of post-independence Muslim women's writing in India, Pakistan, and the diaspora.

In order to place Iqbalunnissa Hussain within the literary and social context of her time, it is important to look at issues of English and English-language writing by South Asian women, together with links to zenana reform, education for girls, and public life. As Tariq Rahman points out, the English language was embraced by Hindu reformers in the early nineteenth century, such as Rammohun Roy, as the symbol of progress. English provided them with a 'secular, intellectual space' which was free from orthodoxy and was neither Hindu nor Muslim.[11] English and an education in it came to be regarded as symbols of progress, modernity, and reform. The Indian contact with English literature in institutions such as the Hindu College in Kolkata (1817) and the Delhi College (1825), set up by the British to impart English to Indians, had led to the development of the earliest Indian English poetry, fiction, and drama.[12]

The Muslim elite, however, identified more with Persian, the language of the Mughal court and 'shied away' (165) from English. The establishment of the British Raj, and the assertion of British ascendancy after the 1857 uprising, was followed by Sir Syed Ahmed Khan's urgings to Indian Muslims to adapt to changing times and acquire a contemporary education and modern knowledge through English. Most Muslims, however, including Sir Syed Ahmed Khan, thought it sufficient that women should be educated at home as had been his mother.[13] Inevitably, great distances developed between Anglicized well-travelled young Indian men and cloistered Indian women.

Traditionally, subcontinental society, Hindu and Muslim, was segregated and for a long time, the acquisition of English by Indians remained gender specific. South Asian women such as Toru Dutt, Krupabai Satthianadhan, and Sarojini Naidu, who used English as a creative vehicle, were the exception rather than the norm. Reformist debates around women's education, Hindu or Muslim, 'focused more on what and how much they should be, rather than whether they should be taught in English.'[14] The earliest schools for girls were set up by the reformist Hindus of the Brahmo Samaj in the 1870's but those for Muslim girls emerged gradually in the early twentieth century.[15] Even so, the introduction of English for girls continued to be regarded with much greater misgiving by Indian Muslims than by the Hindus. This was accompanied by an added terror: that English meant that the young, impressionable Muslim girls would be converted to Christianity, particularly in convent schools run by missionaries.[16]

This background is immensely important to Iqbalunnisa Hussain (1897–1952) and the two older Muslim women to have published the only major creative work in English before her: Atiya Begum Fyzee Rahamin (1877–1967) and Rokeya Sakhawat Hosain (1880–1932).[17] Atiya Begum, who migrated to Pakistan at Partition, belonged to a prominent family of Suleimani Bohras in Mumbai. In the late nineteenth century, its women were among the first in the Indian Muslim elite to discard purdah. Atiya Begum was educated at a convent school and travelled to England to join a teacher training college in London. Her travel diary, *Zamana-e-Tahseel* (A Time for Education) was written in Urdu for serialization in India's new reformist women's magazine, *Tehsib-i-Niswan*.[18] At the time, literature was considered to be an important instrument of reform and Atiya Begum was also involved in the network of women's conferences. 'At the meetings, resolutions were regularly passed in favour of women's education, and against polygamy and the veil.'[19]

In 1912, Atiya's marriage to the cosmopolitan British-trained artist, Samuel Fyzee Rahamin and their subsequent travels led to her first book in English, *The Music of India* (1914). Her narrative provides an interesting blurring of genres: she combines factual knowledge of music and musicology with storytelling skills to recreate India's timeless music lore. Her aim was to educate and inform a non-Indian, Anglophone audience.

In 1905, Rokeya Sakhawat Hossain published her very first story 'Sultana's Dream'. This remained the only work of English fiction by an Indian Muslim woman to precede *Purdah and Polygamy* four decades later. Hossain's remarkable and fiercely feminist work of science fiction, 'one of the earliest depictions of a feminist utopia', challenges patriarchal South Asian mores as well as Orientalist/British depictions of Indian womanhood.[20] She reverses gender roles in a fictitious country called Ladyland, which is run by women. Here the narrator, Sultana, discovers the men are kept locked indoors and that being 'mannish' means 'shy and timid like the men'.[21] Sultana is so astonished by this in Ladyland that she tells her guide, Sister Sara:

> '...In India, man is lord and master, he has taken to himself all powers and privileges and shut up the women in the zenana.'
> 'Why do you allow yourselves to be shut up?' [asks Sister Sara].
> 'Because it cannot be helped as they are stronger than women.'
> 'A lion is stronger than a man, but it does not enable him to dominate the human race. You have neglected the duty you owe to yourselves and you have lost your natural rights by shutting your eyes to your own interests.'[22]

These themes emerge with great clarity in Iqbalunnisa Hussain's later novel *Purdah and Polygamy* which portrays the power enjoyed by appalling, selfish patriarchs across two generations. Interestingly, both Iqbalunnisa Hussain and Rokeya Sakhawat Hossain had been similarly educated in Urdu, Arabic, and Persian. But after her marriage, Hossain, who belonged to Bengal's Urdu-speaking elite, learnt both English and Bengali. She wrote only one story 'Sultana's Dream' in English. Thereafter, she employed Bengali to write fiction which continued with her biting and fearless critique of patriarchy and purdah. Throughout, she worked for the education and empowerment of women and set up the Sakhawat Memorial Girls School in Dhaka (1911), though she continued to wear burqa in order to allay fears of other Muslim parents.

These binaries—English vs Urdu (mother tongue), Anglicization vs tradition—were integral to the ferment of ideas and ideologies in India, regardless of gender, as reformist agendas and nationalist sentiment grew. In 1905, the educationalists and reformers, Sheikh Abdullah and Waheed Jahan, set up a girls' school, Aligarh Madrassah Zenana (1905). Their daughters included the writer and gynaecologist, Rashid Jahan (1905–1952), who discarded purdah at university. In 1932, together with fellow Marxists, Ahmed Ali, Sajjad Zaheer, and Sahibzada Mahmuduzzafar Khan, Rashid Jahan co-authored *Angarey* (Embers), the groundbreaking story collection 'which attacked a whole range of sacred cows', spawned the influential Progressive Writers' Movement, and transformed subcontinental literature.[23] It is worth noting, however, that Mahmuduzzafar's sole contribution was written in English but translated by Zaheer, a fellow graduate from Oxford, into Urdu for *Angarey*—an interesting insight into language/mother tongue as an anti-imperial tool.

Iqbalunnisa Hussain's *Purdah and Polygamy* has a clear relationship to the work of Rashid Jahan and the new radical Indian Muslim women's writing, which emerged in the early twentieth century. Her use of English as a creative vehicle, however, places her as the direct heir to the feminist traditions of Rokeya Sakhawat Hossain. But *Purdah and Polygamy* is a full-length novel which marks a major milestone in Anglophone writing by South Asian Muslim women.

At the same time, *Purdah and Polygamy* with its clear, precise, uncluttered prose also belongs to the new modern, South Asian Indian English novel. This was forged in the 1930s by Mulk Raj Anand (1905–2004), Raja Rao (1908–2006) and R.K. Narayan (1906–2001). In 1940, Ahmed Ali (1910–1994), became 'the Muslim fourth' to these three major writers, with the publication of *Twilight in Delhi*.[24] These pioneers made a radical break from earlier Indian English writing which had emulated Orientalist and British writers to create images of 'India' and 'Indian-ness' familiar to their Anglophone readers. In marked contrast, the modern South Asian English fiction was strongly shaped by growing nationalism as the Independence struggle gathered momentum. They employed fiction as a tool to challenge the imperial narratives of English and convey the Indian point of view to an Anglophone readership. Ali's *Twilight in Delhi* juxtaposes British power and panoply during the Coronation Durbar of George V in 1911 with memories of Mughal Delhi and British atrocities during the 1857 Uprising.

Purdah and Polygamy is markedly different because it addresses neither colonialism nor nationalism, but is firmly rooted in the universal politics of the women's movement. Hussain uses English to challenge the narratives of patriarchy and she employs a clear reformist and feminist voice of protest. Hussain's novel shares aspects of Ahmed Ali's *Twilight in Delhi*, which also revolves around a segregated, aristocratic, urban Muslim family with an inherited income. Ali's multi-layered *Twilight*, unlike *Purdah and Polygamy*, is replete with references to literature, music, and song, and is interwoven with nostalgia for the elegance and certainties of a bygone age. Ali also captures a decaying insular society and the limited options available to women. In both *Purdah and Polygamy* and *Twilight*, the family patriarch has little interest in giving his sons more than a modicum of education. In *Twilight*, the main protagonist, the elderly, Mir Nihal, presides over an extended family and clings tenaciously to the culture and customs of Old Delhi into which he was born. He is enraged that his spineless son, Asghar, has added English shirts and boots to his attire and wishes to join the Muslim University of Aligarh, which Mir Nihal abhors as an instrument of the alien and godless colonials. Asghar, lacking guidance and direction develops into a confused hybrid, 'a hodge podge of Indian and Western ways'.[25]

In Hussain's *Purdah and Polygamy*, the household of the tight-fisted and tyrannical Umar, a jagirdar in a nameless place, remains oblivious to change. Umar's son, Kabeer, is taught the scriptures at home by a maulvi[26] and sent to a madrasa to learn how to read and write Urdu, but even this proves too taxing for him. He becomes expert at playing truant, aided and abetted by his over-indulgent, doting, and unlettered mother, Zuhra. She does not see much point in daily school lessons anyway. A generation later, Kabeer's son, Akram, in turn, shows such little aptitude at school that he often has to repeat a class, but having been 'intelligent, energetic, and mischievous' from an early age (155), he is frequently thrashed by his father or grandmother. He is then taken out of school and put to work in the family business. There his interest in Rosy, a Christian employee, encourages his muddled and superficial attempts at westernization and almost destroys her relationship with her fiancé, George.

In *Twilight*, Mir Nihal has but one wife, Begum Nihal. At the beginning of the novel, she waits dutifully for him to come home and summons Dilchain, the maidservant, to bring him his dinner. Much later, Ali slips in the fact that Mir Nihal had fathered a child by Dilchain, as a result of which Begum Nihal had had a nervous breakdown. Asghar attempts to discuss this with Begum Waheed, his married sister, only to be hushed into silence. None of this detracts from the novel's representation of Mir Nihal as a man of integrity, a character described by the Urdu critic Hasan Askari as 'the balanced and culturally harmonious whole which Delhi's culture has produced'.[27] Mir Nihal is the exclusive patron of a young courtesan, Babban Jan, and has set her up in a household of her own, as was customary for gentleman of means in his day.

In *Purdah*, Kabeer embarks on his polygamous career (sanctioned by religion, unlike dalliance with courtesans), encouraged by his widowed mother, Zuhra. She has been shattered by the cruel rites and taunts of becoming a widow. She is soon reminded that she must find the 19-year-old Kabeer a wife, which gives her a raison d'etre and new-found power, as a mother, mother-in-law, and matriarch. She manipulates and controls the self-indulgent Kabeer and his household to mitigate her own suffering as a virtual servant in the lifetime of Umar, her late and parsimonious husband. He had married only once, because more wives would have meant more expense. Umar did not entrust Zuhra with money, nor did he allow vendors in the house. He gave her new clothes as an act of charity once a year. Umar believed that 'no virtuous woman will step out of the house and will see no third person' (6). Zuhra was denied normal social interaction with other women. Hussain adds 'cinemas she had never seen' and later she is horrified that her daughter-in-law, Nazni, goes to a film with Kabeer and her family, though Kabeer explains that cinemas have separate arrangements for *purdah* women. These incidents are built in quietly to suggest a changing world outside Zuhra's cloistered household. The fact that a generation later, Kabeer's teenage son Akram takes a Christian girl, Rosy, to see *Gone with the Wind* is one of the few indications of a specific time frame for the novel which spans approximately the first four decades the twentieth century (whereas *Twilight* ends with World War I and the influenza epidemic of 1919).

Both novels portray the gradual induction of a Western-trained doctor into a rigidly conventional household as a symbol of a new, scientific world, which is applauded for its learning and related advantages. In *Purdah and Polygamy*, the conflict between traditional and modern medicine is a recurring theme: Umar dies of cancer because he prefers to be treated by a hakim, rather than see a doctor. Modern medicine finally infiltrates the widowed Zuhra's household, when her daughter, Jamila, almost dies giving birth at the hands of the traditional midwife. But Kabeer's first wife, Nazni, and her broad-minded parents overstep the bounds of propriety because her prolonged heart ailment is treated by a specialist who happens to be a man. The outraged Zuhra declares 'A man can't own a woman as his wife after she has been touched by a man' (45). This becomes yet another lever used to encourage Kabeer to find a second, more obedient wife.

Both *Twilight* and *Purdah and Polygamy* provide a biting critique of a segregated society, where marriages are often arranged on the basis of hearsay and the negotiations of a go-between. In *Twilight,* Mir Nihal's daughter, Mehro Zamani nurtures romantic dreams of a handsome young bridegroom and is engaged to Meraj, scion of a wealthy family in Bhopal. But when he arrives in Delhi for his wedding, Mehro's family is horrified to discover that he is disfigured, has a missing ear, and 'a black bushy beard and the ferocious eyes of a madman.'[28] Mir Nihal longs to break off the engagement but is counselled that if he does 'no one will blame him [Meraj]. They will all say there is some defect in the girl. We will then have no face to show anyone.'[29] Mehro must reconcile herself to her fate.

Purdah and Polygamy states 'Marriage among Muslims is a lottery' (82). Zuhra finds a bride for Kabeer with the help of the cook's sister—a professional matchmaker—and settles upon the rich and beautiful Nazni. Zuhra, a demanding and malicious mother-in-law, constantly finds fault with the naïve young Nazni; and soon creates differences between husband and wife. When the pregnant Nazni leaves for her parent's home to have her baby (as is the custom) and prolongs her stay due to ill-health, Zuhra urges Kabeer to remarry. She selects a girl from a humble family in the belief that she will be more compliant than Nazni—only to find that she is the victim of clever deception. The new bride, Munira, turns out to be 'dark, with deep pock marks' and '…her upper teeth projected prominently' (48). Repulsed, Kabeer spurns her and defies his mother, to marry for the third time. His new wife, the rich, beautiful, talented and well-read Maghbool, has little in common with Kabeer but her parents accept Kabeer's proposal for her—though they know that he is twice-married—because she has reached the ripe old age of twenty and Kabeer agrees to give her a generous marriage settlement. The tension of the novel is built up through the complex and intricate power plays, intrigues and shifting alliances, between Kabeer, his mother, and his wives. Before long, Kabeer marries for a fourth time, albeit secretly: he glimpses the beautiful young granddaughter of a very poor tenant and decides to marry the girl, instead of claiming the rent owed him.

Twilight has a clear historical trajectory interwoven into the lives and emotions of its Muslim protagonists. It juxtaposes memories of Mughal rule and Delhi suffering during the 1857 Uprising, with George V's Coronation Durbar in 1911 which embodies British ascendancy. The power of Hussain's *Purdah and Polygamy* lies in the very absence of politics, place, and history: the protagonists' unawareness of events in the outside world accentuates their self-involved lives as well as the continuing strength of their customs and attitudes despite the challenges of modernity. Interestingly, both *Twilight* and *Purdah and Polygamy* portray Muslim families as so insular that Hindus hardly impinge on their consciousness. *Purdah and Polygamy* follows a cycle that is repeated through Zuhra's life and later that of Nazni: the self-abnegating, suffering wife and devoted mother develops into domineering widow, mother, and mother-in-law. In marked contrast, *Twilight* describes (and laments) changing times, under British rule.

The earlier chapters of *Purdah and Polygamy* approximate the same era as *Twilight*, but most of *Purdah* covers the later period treated in two early post-independence novels about Partition: Mumtaz Shah Nawaz's *The Heart Divided* and Attia Hosain's *Sunlight on a Broken Column*. But *Purdah and Polygamy* makes no mention of the nationalist struggle and the debate between the Congress and the Muslim League, so central to both the novels of Shah Nawaz and Hosain. *Purdah*'s portrayal of an enclosed, patriarchal society, in which women become willing accomplices in the battle for power and control within the home, derives its significance from its sense of timelessness. *Heart*, which is written from a Pakistani point of view, ends with the 1940 Lahore Resolution. *Sunlight* presents the Indian Muslim perspective, with the first three sections leading up to the 1937 Provincial Assembly elections and the fourth, set in 1952, showing the aftermath of World War II, Partition, and independent India's sweeping land reforms.

Both *Heart* and *Sunlight* are important milestones in South Asian writing, and have a strong feminist trajectory.[30] Both are heirs to Iqbalunnisa Hussain's writing. In *Purdah and Polygamy*, Hussain portrays the *status quo* in a cloistered, rigid, patriarchal society and holds up a mirror to the gender-bias and ignorance that Hussain battled against as an activist and educationalist. The later *Heart* and *Sunlight* portray similar conservative social mores as *Purdah and Polygamy*, but show a trajectory leading to a new life and new possibilities for women: education, activism, freedom, the right to marry of one's own choice—although this shining path is paved with difficulties, challenges, and heartache. The binaries of modernity vs tradition are at the core of all three of these narratives. In both *Heart* and *Sunlight,* the main protagonist is an aristocratic and nationalistic young woman: her struggle for empowerment embodies her country's struggle for independence.

Mumtaz Shah Nawaz belonged to an Oxbridge-educated landowning family in the Punjab which was in the forefront of the movement for political and social reform and independence. She followed her mother, the future parliamentarian Jahan Ara Shahnawaz, to Queen Mary College, Lahore, and graduated from the Lady Irwin College in New Delhi. Shah Nawaz, an ardent feminist, nationalist, and political activist, first joined the Congress Party and later the Muslim League (to which her mother and grandfather belonged). Both mother and daughter were Muslim League activists and did not observe purdah, not even when they campaigned in the conservative areas of Khyber

Pakhtunkhwa. Shah Nawaz translated her political gestation into her novel, *The Heart Divided*. In 1948, Shah Nawaz died in an air-crash, leaving behind a first draft, which her family finally published, unedited.

Interestingly Shah Nawaz had started work on *Heart* in 1943 and finished it in 1948. As such, the two novels provide both interesting links and contrasts. Shah Nawaz's novel revolves around the household of Sheikh Jamaluddin, an eminent and Cambridge-educated lawyer in Lahore. He is drawn to western ways but his traditional wife and first cousin, Mehrunissa, has no wish to discard purdah—nor would his parents have approved of it. Over the years, he began to believe 'that perhaps the old ways were the best …[and] it was best for Muslim ladies to remain in purdah.'[31] In this respect, he is similar to Nazni's father Doulath Khan in *Purdah and Polygamy*. On the other hand, Nazni's brother is enlightened and well educated, but Nazni is not. When Kabeer remarries, Nazni's brother is outraged and wants her to leave Kabeer, but her father does not consider this an option: the uneducated Nazni has 'no power of decision, no judgement or practical knowledge of the world.' (74).

The difference between Doulath Khan in *Purdah and Polygamy* and Sheikh Jamaluddin in *The Heart Divided* is that the latter is persuaded by his educated sister-in-law to send Zohra and Sughra, his daughters, to a well-known school 'for girls of aristocratic families.'[32] Both girls go on to college too, although they remain in purdah. The sixteen-year-old Zohra hopes to become the first woman graduate in her family. Sughra cannot nurture such dreams: she has been engaged since childhood, to her cousin Mansoor. She is to be married soon, even though Mansoor has proved a disappointment to Sheikh Jamaluddin. Mansoor left school without a diploma and has no intention in furthering his education, let alone acquiring the foreign university degree that Sheikh Jamaluddin would have wished for his son-in-law. However, Sheikh Jamaluddin cannot break off the engagement without besmirching his honour or that of Sughra, which in turn would render her unmarriageable. Thus the educated, learned Sughra is married to a comparatively uneducated man, as is Kabeer's third wife, Maghbool in *Purdah and Polygamy*. Sughra's marriage is as much 'a lottery' as it is for the protagonists of *Purdah and Polygamy*. Sughra finds herself married to an easy going but thoughtless man in an old-fashioned household, in conservative Multan, with a mother-in-law as dictatorial, interfering, ignorant, and manipulative as Zuhra in *Purdah and Polygamy*. Sughra's son, Khalid, contracts typhoid and dies because her mother-in-law refuses to keep a nurse and disobeys the doctor's instructions. In Shah Nawaz's hands, this tragedy provides the catalyst for Sughra to move away from Multan. The novel opens out more worthy, modern commitments for women: social welfare and politics.

Both *Heart* and *Purdah and Polygamy* portray the vulnerability of young women to malicious rumours, gossip, and innuendoes. In *Heart,* Zohra finds herself falsely accused of secret assignations with 'boys', because she is sighted unveiled in the bazaar, in the company of her friend Surraya, who does not observe purdah. In *Purdah and Polygamy*, Maghbool's friendship with Azeem, a younger boy cousin and her mother's protégé, is used by Kabeer's suspicious mother to throw aspersions on Maghbool's fidelity. In *Heart*, Zohra has to ask her family for permission to participate in an inter-university debate (where she would not be in purdah). This causes such outrage that she is held responsible for her grandfather's subsequent heart attack. In *Purdah and Polygamy*, Maghbool is told that if she publishes her poetry it will be read by strangers and thus bring shame upon her.

The difference between the empowerment enjoyed by Hindu girls compared to *purdah nashin*, well-educated Muslim women who observe purdah, is also highlighted in *Heart*. The restrictions that Zuhra chafes under act as a foil to the autonomy enjoyed by her Hindu friend, Mohini, who is passionately involved in the independence struggle. Mohini sees herself 'as a girl volunteer marching among the others, a soldier of freedom.'[33] Mohini is arrested during a protest march, whereupon the spirited Zohra chooses to defy family and tradition by reading out Mohini's statement of protest on the radio. Eventually, Sughra and Zohra are allowed out of purdah and become political activists in the Muslim League and the Congress Party, respectively. Their England-returned brother and Mohini fall in love, thus breaking the laws of both his community and hers, but Mohini's untimely death embodies the parting of the ways between the Congress and the Muslim League. All their stories are linked to political events, although the detailed socio-political discussions, debates, and description detract greatly from plot and character.

Shah Nawaz's *Heart* is imbued with an idealism which is very different to the unflinching pragmatism and indeed, pessimism of Hussain's *Purdah and Polygamy*. Attia Hosain's novel, *Sunlight on a Broken Column*, strikes a rather different, more omniscient note. It looks back at the past from the distance of time and place, since Hosain was living in London by then. Hosain also extends her canvas to cover a much wider social spectrum, including friendships between learned, scholarly Englishmen and well-born Indians—Muslims, Hindus, Sikhs and Indian Christians—and the suffering of aging courtesans, spirited, defiant, servant girls, and exploited tenants, among others.

Hosain (1913–1998) was born into great privilege as was Shah Nawaz. Her Oxbridge-educated family of feudal lords (the Taluqdars of Oudh) was committed to education, reform, and nationalist causes. Hosain did not observe purdah, was educated in Lucknow at La Martiniere School for Girls, and graduated from the Isobella Thoburn College. She was closely associated with the left-wing Progressive Writers' Association and strongly influenced by Congress socialists, while her mother-in-law, Inam Fatima Habibullah, was a Muslim League activist and parliamentarian. Hosain defied family convention to marry of her own choice, her first cousin, the Cambridge-returned, Ali Bahadur 'Sonny' Habibullah, a civil servant. The couple was posted in London, at the Indian High Commission, when the Partition of India was announced. Hosain stayed on in London, though she continued to identify with India and is regarded today as one of the earliest writers of the South Asian diaspora. Her critically acclaimed fiction, a story collection, *Phoenix Fled* (1953) and a novel *Sunlight on a Broken Column*, reclaim the Lucknow in which she grew up and which vanished almost overnight in 1947.

Sunlight is often compared with Ahmed Ali's *Twilight* since it portrays an Indo-Muslim culture on the verge of extinction. Both capture an entire way of life, which encompasses literature and the performing arts, religious festivals, and religious rites. Hosain and Ali also comment on the role of courtesans and the tragic future which awaits most of them, once their beauty and talent fades. In Ali's narrative, the courtesan remains a part of the world of men—the *mardana*—but Hosain's portrayal of purdah life includes a visit to the zenana—the women's quarters—by an aging, once beautiful courtesan. She is renowned for her magical voice, which was destroyed by an illness, and has 'turned to God to expiate the sins of her life'[34] and become 'a wandering mendicant.'[35] Her plight evokes both sympathy and courtesy from the purdah women: they had once seen her in better days, through 'the thin slits of the bamboo curtains'[36] which divided their quarters from that of the men where she performed, danced, and sang at a grand wedding.

Sunlight portrays a more complex, multi-hued purdah life than *Twilight, Purdah,* and *Heart.* At the same time, it presents stark contrasts between zenana living patterns in sophisticated urban Lucknow and the ancestral family village at Hasanpur. The novel begins symbolically with intimations of imminent change. Baba Jan, a Taluqdar[37] and the paternal grandfather of the main protagonist, the orphaned heiress, Laila, is dying. She lives with him, in a segregated household, which includes his two daughters, the widowed Majida and the unmarried Abida. The novel contrasts Majida's pliable and conventional daughter Zahra, who has received a traditional education in Urdu and Qur'anic studies, with the intelligent and rebellious Laila, who has been brought up by Abida and educated at an English medium school (in purdah), according to the wishes of her late father.

In *Purdah and Polygamy,* Kabeer's household and its foetid atmosphere, suspicions, intrigues, and lack of generosity, belie the normal social responsibilities of the rich, benign family patriarch towards less fortunate relatives. Instead, this sense of social responsibility emerges through Maghbool's extended family, which includes her mother's poor, widowed sister and her son, Azeem, though her mother-in-law uses Maghbool's friendship with Azeem to throw aspersions on her character. In *Sunlight,* Baba Jan looks after Asad and Zahid, the orphaned sons of a poor relative. In both, Maghbool's home and Baba Jan's, purdah is not observed between boy protégés and the daughters of the house and they are friends. In *Sunlight,* the nationalistic Asad is Laila's window to the outside world, as the struggle for independence gathers strength, but Asad is almost killed in a Hindu-Muslim riot, which breaks out after an accident during a Moharrum procession and foreshadows Partition's horror. The wounded Asad falls into a delirium and reveals his love for Zahra. This is considered such a great slur on Zahra's chastity, that Zahra mother weeps and Zahra cries, 'How could he do such a terrible thing?' To avoid scandal, Zahra is to be 'married off to the first suitable person' and Asad is sent away.[38] *Sunlight* reaffirms that in traditional society, marrying of one's own choosing is not an option: in fact, it is considered positively immoral. In the same way, in *Purdah,* the talented, educated, well-read Maghbool, would have preferred to marry Ahmed, but her father chooses the rich polygamous, Kabeer.

Sunlight indicts the rampant hypocrisy of a society that is obsessed with the virtue of its women, but is rife with secrets revolving around illicit liaisons and misdemeanors. Nandi, a servant girl, tells Laila, 'We poor people get a bad name because we cannot stay locked up. But what of those uncles and cousins who wander in and out of the zenana. They're men, aren't they? Thieves steal the best guarded treasure.[39] Both *Purdah and Polygamy* and *Sunlight* refer to purdah women travelling in a car covered with curtains at the back. In *Sunlight*, Laila and Zahra peer discreetly through the curtains during their scenic journey to their ancestral home in Rajanpur, where the zenana is guarded by 'the centuries-old heavy, wooden, copper studded door.'[40] This is a world apart from the one Laila inhabits in Lucknow and more isolated, with a series of family houses interlinked by a courtyard. Laila and Zahra are only allowed to walk across if Nandi goes on ahead and cries out 'Purdah! Purdah!' to ensure no male servant sees them.

Both *Purdah and Polygamy* and *Sunlight* highlight the helplessness of the single women in an extended family, whether they are unmarried or widowed. They are left utterly dependent on the whims of others. In *Purdah,* the dying Umar's teenage daughter, Jamila, is married off as soon as possible; a generation later, Kabeer's widows are left with no recourse to a life of their own. They are at mercy of his successor Akram. The one exception is Nazni who can manipulate Akram, her son. She discovers a new power as Akram's mother and assumes the role of the household matriarch. In *Sunlight*, Baba Jan's death leaves the fate of his daughters and granddaughters to his undemonstrative son, Hamid, who admires westernized i.e. Victorian forms of behavior and is so aloof and distant 'that each time he came home, it was like meeting a stranger masquerading as family' (86).[41]

Hamid decrees that Laila should come out of purdah—as has his ambitious wife, Saira. In keeping with their 'progressive' ideas, Laila joins college in Lucknow, but her transition from Baba Jan's traditional and loving household, to Hamid's Anglicized and loveless home, is filled with heartache: everyone familiar leaves. Zahra is married and goes away with her husband, but a truly cruel fate awaits Hamid's sisters, Majida and Abida. Majida is sent to live in the zenana of the ancestral home in Hasanpur 'in one part of the large house, surrounded by closed empty rooms with blind-eyed windows.'[42] While Abida, the woman who managed her father's entire estate once—as Maghbool had in *Purdah and Polygamy*—is married off to an elderly widower and retired civil servant, Sheikh Ejaz Ali, who lives in a village near Hasanpur.

Sunlight follows a trajectory radically different to the enclosed world of *Purdah and Polygamy* and is permeated with Laila's awareness of, and engagement with, political events. At school, Laila's Hindu friend, Sita, is very much at the forefront of the nationalist struggle as Mohini in *Heart*. At college, Laila's close friends include Nita, a fiery nationalist, whose views she shares and who is killed during an anti-British protest; and Nadira, who has a strong sense of her Muslim identity. Soon Hamid's son, Kemal, and Saleem return from university in England. They befriend Laila and introduce her to new ideas. Ameer, the university lecturer she falls in love with, is one of their friends. Through all these characters, *Sunlight* continues to build in communal tensions, political division, and the conflict between the Congress and the Muslim League.

The cloistered existence that Laila's much-loved Aunt Abida is subjected to, has clear echoes with that of the women protagonists of *Purdah and Polygamy*. Laila thinks often of visiting her in the village and finally does so. Abida is overjoyed to see Laila but has 'a withdrawn, settled sadness' about her.[43] Abida's husband, Ejaz, spends most of his time in a different part of the house with male friends and relatives; his mother-in-law is 'wrinkled, near blind, and partially deaf' and the dependent single women in his family—sister-in-laws and stepdaughters—whether widowed or unmarried, consider Abida an outsider and resent her. The festering zenana tensions in *Purdah and Polygamy* and in Abida's home in *Sunlight* have clear resonance. Events in the outside world, let alone politics, neither penetrate the zenana nor have any place in it. 'The jealousies and frustrations of that household of women were intangible like invisible webs, spun by monstrous unseen spiders. Yet without each other they had no existence. Physically and mentally, their lives crushed each other.'[44]

Purdah and Polygamy, which was written before an independent India and Pakistan came into being, provides a biting critique of this very patriarchy. *Sunlight* carries the narrative forward to describe the cataclysm of Partition, which *Purdah*'s characters could not have imagined, yet the claustrophobic, patriarchal mores that *Purdah* captures so vividly finds echoes in post-independence South Asian English writing. The fact that independent India, Pakistan, and Bangladesh all have witnessed a strong women's movement and that today, a college education and career is the accepted norm for many Muslim women from privileged or professional families, does not alter the fact that glaring inequalities of gender still exist. The harsh reality of women's lives across South Asia, regardless of class, faith, and gender emerges strongly in post-independence South Asian English fiction.

For example, in Pakistan, Bapsi Sidhwa's five novels all tell of ancient customs and rules—whether Parsi, Hindu, or Muslim—which thwart and restrict women's lives. Her second novel, *The Bride* (1982), portrays a tribal society that expects a young woman to be completely subservient to her husband and mother-in-law and where her suffering is accentuated by dire poverty. Rukhsana Ahmad's *The Hope Chest* (1992) includes a rich, highly educated, but emotionally fragile young woman, struggling to cope in a marriage with a callous ambitious man, chosen by her mother. Kamila Shamsie's six novels all have strong feminist trajectories. Her *Salt and Saffron*, (2001) a tale of Partition, class, and gender in modern Pakistan, excavates a family's lost pre-Partition matriarchal narratives, and reveals links to *Sunlight on a Broken Column* by Attia Hosain—Shamsie's great-aunt.[45] Uzma Aslam Khan's four novels all focus on the struggle of women for empowerment but in *Trespassing*, a widow in modern Karachi, having been humiliated and demeaned by her husband throughout their marriage, hardly waits for him to be buried, before she exercises her new found power to arrange her son's marriage to a traditional girl of her choice. Rafia Zakaria's creative memoir, *The Upstairs Wife* (2015), a tale of Pakistan and the author's family, draws a poignant portrait of her childless aunt, coping within a polygamous marriage in which her husband takes a younger, second wife.

As this short survey shows, today a larger number of Pakistani English writers are women whose work addresses the varied challenges posed by gender across Southeast Asia. Their writing continues

Iqbalunissa Hussain's biting attack on patriarchy over seventy years ago. Iqbalunnisa Husain remains a bold pioneer and her novel, *Purdah and Polygamy*, deserves recognition as an important literary ancestor to an entire body of contemporary writing in English by women of South Asian origin.

NOTES

1. See Muneeza Shamsie, introduction to *And The World Changed: Contemporary Stories by Pakistani Women* (New York: The Feminist Press at CUNY, 2008), 1–52.

2. Teresa Hubel, 'Dutiful Daughters (or not) and the Sins of the Fathers in Iqbalunnisa Hussain's *Purdah and Polygamy*' in *Postcolonial Text* 10, 2 (2015), 2.

3. Jessica Berman quoted in Hubel, 'Dutiful Daughters,' 2.

4. See the biographical sketch in this volume by Arif Zaman for more information.

5. These travelogues included *Zamana-e-Tehseel* by Atiya Fyzee (1922—first serialized in *Tehsib-e-Niswan* 1904–1905); *A Trip to Europe* by Maimoona Sultan, Shahbano Begum of Bhopal, translated from the Urdu by G.B. Bakhsh (Calcutta: Thacker Spink 1913); *Tazkirat-e-Safar-e-Europe* by Inam Fatima Habibullah (Lucknow: self-published, nd).

6. Later Jahan Ara Shahanwaz was one of two women—the other being Shaista Suhrawardy Ikramullah—to be elected into Pakistan's first Constituent Assembly. See Jahanara Shahnawaz, *Father and Daughter: A Political Autobiography* (Karachi: Oxford University Press, 2002. First published, Lahore: Nigarishat, 1971).

7. Inam Fatima Habibullah was the great-grandmother of the Pakistani novelist, Kamila Shamsie. See Muneeza Shamsie, 'Discovering The Matrix', *Critical Muslim: 4: Pakistan?* (2012).

8. Fatima Jinnah is best known for her political activism, as a leading figure in the Muslim League, and as the sister of the Quaid-e-Azam, Mohammed Ali Jinnah. In 1964, she courageously stood for election against Pakistan's incumbent dictator, Field Marshal Ayub Khan, and became the first woman in Pakistan to head a political party and aspire to be the executive head of state.

9. Aamer Hussein, afterword to *Distant Traveller: New and Selected Fiction* by Attia Hosain, selected and edited by Aamer Husein and Shama Habibullah (New Delhi:

Women Unlimited, 2013), 227.

10. Aamer Hussein, introduction to *The Young Wife and Other Stories* by Zaib-un-Nissa Hamidullah, (Karachi: Oxford University Press, 2008), xv.

11. Tariq Rahman, *Language, Ideology, and Power* (Karachi: Oxford University Press, 2002), 163.

12. See Muneeza Shamsie, prologue to *Hybrid Tapestries: The Development of Pakistani Literature in English* (Karachi: Oxford University Press, 2017): 8–15.

13. Shamsie, *Hybrid Tapestries*.

14. Meenakshi Mukherjee, *The Perishable Empire: Essays on Indian English Writing* (New Delhi: Oxford University Press, 2002), 69.

15. See Muneeza Shamsie, introduction to *And the World Changed*.

16. This emerges with great clarity in the English memoirs of Shaista Suhrawardy Ikramullah, *From Purdah to Parliament* (Karachi: Oxford University Press, 1998); Jahanara Shahnawaz, *Father and Daughter* (Karachi: Oxford University Press, 2002); and Ismat Chughtai, *Kaghazi Hai Pairahan: The Paper Attire,* translated from the Urdu by Noor Zaheer (Karachi: Oxford University Press, 2016).

17. See the biographical sketch by Arif Zaman for more on these figures.

18. The English translation is now available in *Atiya's Journeys: A Muslim Woman from Colonial Bombay to Edwardian England* (eds.) Siobhan Lambert-Hurley and Sunil Sharma (New Delhi: Oxford University Press, 2010).

19. Uzma Aslam Khan, *Trespassing* (New Delhi: Penguin India, 2003), 11.

20. Tahmima Anam 'My Hero, Rokeya Sakhawat Hosain,' 28 May 2011, *The Guardian* <https://www.theguardian.com/books/2011/may/28/rokeya-sakhawat-hossain-hero-tahmima-anam>

21. Hossain (np).

22. Ibid.

23. Ali Hussein and Raza Mir, *Anthems of Resistance: A Celebration of Progressive Urdu Poetry* (New Delhi: India Ink, 2006), 3.

24. Bruce King, 'From Twilight to Midnight: Muslim Novels of India and Pakistan', *Worlds of the Muslim Imagination,* (ed.) Alamgir Hashmi (Islamabad: Gulmohar, 1986), 255.

25. Ahmed Ali, *Twilight in Delhi* (Karachi: Oxford University Press, 1984; first published London: Hogarth Press, 1940), 251.

26. A cleric.

27. Hasan Askari, 'A Novel by Ahmed Ali,' *Annual of Urdu Studies,* 9, 1994. (First published 'Ahmed Ali Ka Aik Navil'; *Makhzan*: Lahore, 1949), 79.

28. Ali, *Twilight,* 194.

29. Ibid., 194.

30. Khushwant Singh's novel *Train to Pakistan* was published in 1956 and is regarded as the first South Asian English novel about Partition; Shah Nawaz's *The Heart Divided* appeared a year later—nine years after she died.

31. Mumtaz Shah Nawaz, *The Heart Divided* (Lahore: ASR Publications, 1990. First published Lahore: Mumtaz Publications, 1957), 5.

32. Ibid.

33. Ibid., 20.

34. Attia Hosain, *Sunlight on a Broken Column,* (London: Virago, 1988), 66.

35. Ibid., 66.

36. Ibid., 65.

37. A land holder to whom taxes were due. For a detailed discussion on the role of the Taluqdars of Oudh as feudal lords and virtual rulers of their territories in British India, see Thomas R. Metcalf, *Land, Landlords and The British Raj: Northern India in the Nineteenth Century* (Berkeley: University of California Press, 1979).

38. Hosain, *Sunlight,* 81.

39. Ibid., 97.

40. Ibid., 93

41. Ibid., 86.

42. Ibid., 118.

43. Ibid., 250.

44. Ibid., 251.

45. See Muneeza Shamsie, 'Sunlight and Salt: The Literary Landscapes of a Divided Family', *Journal of Commonwealth Literature,* 44.1. (2009), 135–53. This essay combines memoir and criticism to trace the links and disparities between Hosain's *Sunlight* and Shamsie's *Salt.*

Appendix
Foreword

From Changing India: A Muslim Woman Speaks *(Karachi: Oxford University Press, 2015). It was written by Iqbalunnisa's daughter, Dr Salima Ahmed, and is published here to honour their memory.*

It is said that a prophet is seldom appreciated at home. This was the case with my mother. We failed to realize her sterling character and work. She was a simple village girl. When she was married, her only education was a smattering of Arabic and Urdu. It was my father who gave her learning through correspondence while he was studying in Bombay. It is amazing how she learnt English and was able to produce book after book in fine English.

She bore seven children while acquiring a degree in India and later in the UK. Her thoughts always lay with the unfortunate poor Muslim women: women in pain and trouble who would come to her for help and sympathy. She held them in her arms to comfort them and wept with them. She even went to their husbands, fathers, or brothers, whom she admonished to fight for the women's rights. She showed them the honourable and Muslim way. She threatened them and most often brought peace between them.

This simple, little-educated woman made friends with personalities like Lord and Lady Baden-Powell, Lady Astor [the first female MP], and Pearl Buck [Nobel Laureate in Literature]. She kept correspondence with Princess Durru Shehvar of Hyderabad Deccan and Lady Mirza Ismail [wife of Sir Mirza Ismail], until she passed away. She had a two-hour long interview with Kemal Atatürk. She also met poet Muhammad Iqbal and painter Abdur Rahman Chughtai, and they both gave her the same book of pictures by Abdul Rahman Chughtai and a book of Omar Khayyam's poetry. She was held in great esteem by all organizations and personalities in India. Yet she was the most unpretentious and humble person possible. I have known her to run and fetch chairs for her children at parties if she found them without a seat.

I am indeed honoured and grateful that I am able to write a few words about her. I could write volumes. We seven children treated her with the utmost honour and respect, which she so richly deserves. I hope this book is a befitting tribute and will make her happy.

All proceeds from this publication will go to charities decided by her family members.

Dr Salima R. Ahmed

(1926–2017)
President, Pakistan Federation of Business
& Professional Women's Organization
Karachi, 2015

Explanatory Notes

Foreword

1. Probably Bezwada Gopala Reddy, 1907–97, an Indian politician who studied with Tagore and translated his work into Telugu. In 1989, he was awarded the Raja-Lakshmi Award, given out by the Raja Lakshmi Foundation, Madras, annually to honor outstanding work in science, literature, humanities, and Indian culture.

2. One of the original members of the Department of English at Andhra University, who later became director of its press.

Chapter I

1. In this introduction to the house, where most of the action will take place, the novel makes clear that we are to understand the rigid practice of purdah—including both spatial separation and veiling—as a kind of imprisonment. Later chapters also use the term 'prison' to describe the house and its women's quarters, or zenana.

2. In Urdu, literally 'corner' or 'a secluded place'—another word for purdah. The practice was for men to announce their presence by repeating 'gosha' three times. The women would have to run inside and shut the doors and windows to the house before it was called out the third time.

3. It was customary in many households for men to handle all monetary transactions. The ironic tone of this passage, like others surrounding the practice of purdah in this novel, displays the novel's critique of the practice.

4. Ramadan: The spelling 'ramzan' is a closer approximation to the pronounciation of the word in the Indo-Pakistan region.

5. Alms for the poor; from 'zakat'—literally 'that which purifies'. Offerings for the poor are a religious obligation for Muslims who have sufficient means. These are considered obligatory and therefore are more like a tax than a charitable donation. The Qu'ran specifies seven groups who should be paid from the zakat funds, including the poor and needy, and others who may not be paid from these funds. One may not support one's wife or family with zakat money.

6. A Muslim nobleman or person of high status.

7. Arabic: one who is wise; the word eventually evolved to mean physician.

Chapter II

1. Periods of consideration after a death in the family are not specified by Islam and vary regionally. During the period, the family is rarely left alone and food is provided so that the mourning is not interrupted by cooking or other duties.

2. Islam prescribes strict rules for washing, shrouding, and caring of the body following death. Given the circumstances, male bodies must be cared for by men, and female bodies cared for by women. A husband and wife, however, in the event of either one's death, (can) take care of each other's bodies. As the narrative indicates, the rules of purdah remain in place even after the person has died.

3. It is common to recite litanies in remembrance of the dead forty days after the event. There are a variety of other customs surrounding death that vary among Muslim communities around the world. Often, on the third day, a feast is given in the morning and trays of flowers are passed to the guests who dip them in scented oil. They then proceed to the grave and pour the oil and flowers over it. On the morning of the tenth day, this offering of flowers and scented oil is repeated. Other feasts are given on the fortieth day and at four, six, and nine months, and one year from the date of death.

4. This refers to the cultural practice of bringing the widow to the deceased husband's side and removing the bangles and 'latcha' (see below), worn by wives. She is then clothed in white and her face is covered so that other married women do not see it. This is not a practice specified in Islam, and is more closely connected to Hinduism, though as the text indicates, it was common among both Hindus and Muslims in India.

5. In Indian cultural practice, widowhood was often seen as a result of something the woman must have done. This was a common belief among both Muslims and Hindus.

6. There is no stigma against widows in the Qu'ran. The Holy Prophet married a widow. However, in both Hindu and Muslim communities in India, widows were widely reviled. They were ostracized and often unable to remarry. In some places, in earlier periods, the practice of sati, or widow immolation, was practiced, though this was outlawed by the British colonial government in their territories in 1829 and in 1861 across all of India. The stigma against widows is due in part to the notion mentioned above: that the she must have committed a sin or done something that caused the death of her husband.

7. These are customs surrounding widowhood in India. The practice of breaking the glass bangles worn by wives inaugurates the transformation of the wife into a widow especially in terms of her dress. As remarked in the text, hereafter she will not wear colours or jewels. The beads described are the black beads that are tied around the neck of a bride in the form of a necklace (better known as a 'mangala sutra' in Hindu practice), which signifies the bond between husband and wife. The word 'latcha' literally means 'skein' in Urdu, indicating the importance of the thread holding them together.

8. A traditional belief.

9. Once the man is dead, he is no longer a husband, so the wife must observe purdah in front of him just as any other unrelated woman, and therefore should not touch him. Also, since the widow was seen as unpure and having caused her husband's death, her touch would be potentially polluting. This is purely a cultural practice and has no basis in Islamic scripture.

10. 1 PM is the usual time for the Friday prayer service and sermon (khutbah) to begin.

11. Dying on Friday, the most important day of the week in Islam, indicates a good end, and the protection of Allah from the punishment of the grave. This is a cultural practice that is not specified in the Qu'ran.

12. Muslims in India and contemporary Pakistan practice the tradition—called 'khatam' (meaning 'to finish')—of observing the seventh day after a death by gathering and reciting the entire Qu'ran in one day. Sections of the Qu'ran are given to each person to recite. Afterwards, those present pray for the deceased and share a meal. This is a cultural practice with no specific basis in Islamic scripture.

13. Islamic scripture calls for acts of charity in the name of the deceased. It is believed that good deeds and acts of charity reach the deceased and have an effect on his/her wellbeing in the afterlife, especially when practiced by the deceased's children. Giving clothes to beggars in particular will ensure that the deceased, when dreamed about, will be well-clothed. This is a cultural practice with no specific basis in Islamic scripture and is no longer practiced.

14. It is common to recite litanies in remembrance of the dead forty days after the event. This is a cultural practice with no specific basis in Islamic scripture.

15. Arabic: An ascetic, saint; also often a person devoted to God who lives off of alms.

16. The Qu'ran establishes the period of 'iddat' or 'iddah' (a widow's seclusion) as four months and ten days. The widow is precluded from remarriage during the period. This is so that any pregnancy with her previous husband will become visible before potential remarriage. Cultural practice is that during that time the widow is also not allowed to wear perfume or jewellery and does not customarily comb or oil her hair.

17. Widows do not customarily comb their hair or use scented oils during the period of seclusion while brides often have elaborate hair treatments.

18. 'Pir' is an honorific used in India and Pakistan for a religious scholar or master, often those from families associated with particular shrines.

Chapter III

1. A Pathan is a person of Pashtun ethnicity. Primarily Muslim, they speak Pashto.

2. Syed is an honorific title adopted by those Muslims who are supposed to be descended from the Holy Prophet

3. 'Jageerdar' (also spelled 'jagirdar') refers to the jagirdari system, which was a system of land tenancy developed during the period of Muslim rule of India. The 'Jagir' (or holding land) was bestowed on the 'Dar' (or official) for some period of time with the right to collect rents and taxes. The bestowal was often made in exchange for some kind of consideration, such as the raising of troops or funds.

4. Muslim widows are not deprived of social privileges and may negotiate marriages and participate in social festivals. However, Hindu widows were not allowed to participate in any ceremonies such as those connected to birth or marriage.

5. Ammajan: dear mother. 'Amma' comes from the Arabic word for mother, 'Umm'. 'Jan' is Farsi for 'life',

and is used to denote reverence and/or endearment. See also, 'Abbajan', with 'abba' coming from the Arabic word 'abb', meaning father.

6. It is customary that the engaged girl enter into seclusion. She can only be seen by her mother, her sister(s), and her closest friend(s). No other men [even her brother(s) and father] and women are allowed to see her.

Chapter IV

1. The ceremony where the bride is first shown to the bridegroom.

2. This is an ironic reference to the principles of non-cooperation and non-violence espoused by Gandhi as part of India's independence movement.

3. The word 'rasm' (spelled here as 'rasam') is Arabic for 'custom' and in this context specifically, is referring to the practice of presenting the bride/bridegroom with presents from either side, or any practice that is related to wedding celebrations.

4. Nikha (usually spelled nikkah): Arabic; in Islam, the marriage contract and the ceremony surrounding it.

5. It is common practice to wash the bride's feet and hands upon entrance into her husband's house. Here it appears she is being washed after her return in preparation for her departure to the husband's house the next day.

6. The bride's departure from her parents' home would traditionally take place on the day after the nikkah. But in India, the various ceremonies surrounding the nikkah can often continue for three days, with some taking place in the groom's home and others in the bride's home. The bride goes to the groom's house and then she is taken back to her parents' home the next day. The groom is not allowed to go to her home until invited. The bride finally enters the groom's home on the fourth day after the nikkah. A variety of ceremonies also surround the event where siblings of the bride tease the groom, and dinners are hosted in both homes.

7. 'Bhai' from Sanskrit means brother; also a friendly and respectful form of address to a man who is older than the individual addressing him.

8. 'Begum' is an honorific title for Muslim women of higher status. Domestic attendants also use this phrase to refer to their employers.

Chapter V

1. This is likely a reference to the opening lines of Jane Austen's *Pride and Prejudice*: 'It is a truth universally acknowledged that a single man in possession of a good fortune, must be in want of a wife.' Though we do not know what Iqbalunnisa Hussain might have read, the fact that Hussain references this canonical English novel places *Purdah and Polygamy* not only in a lineage of English fiction in India but also in contact to the British tradition. It invites readers to hear potential echoes of Austen or other British writers throughout the novel and raises the importance of themes common in Austen concerning marriage and money or social standing, the limitations of prejudicial judgments about people, the complexity of family relationships within rigid social structures, etc. The writer of *Purdah and Polygamy*'s original foreword, Sir

Ramalinga Reddy, also compares Hussain to Austen, calling her 'the Jane Austen of India' because of her attention to the 'ordinary and the familiar, not with the romantic and heroic' (2).

2. Farsi: of the fire, belonging to Hell.

3. The festival of Eid.

4. Physician.

5. Arabic: 'speech', 'discourse', and/or 'to address'. Purely in an Islamic context, it refers to the sermon given at mosques at midday on Friday, and on Eid-ul-Adha and Eid-ul-Fitr.

6. Eidgah (spelled here as 'Idgah') is a place used for the public prayers on the festivals of Eid ul-Fitr and Eid al-Adha.

Chapter VI

1. While interaction between male physicians and female patients is not completely restricted, those observing strict purdah strongly prefer to be attended to by members of the same sex. On some occasions, they might be examined through small openings in a screening cloth.

2. There is a long tradition of colorism in India that dates back to the ancient period. Colonial thinking contributed to divisions based upon color or perceived race among Indian people, some of which persist today. Among many in the Indian subcontinent, fair skin is still considered more beautiful than dark skin and skin lightening products are very popular. See the 'Introduction' to this volume for further discussion of this history.

3. Maidservant.

4. Kichdi (usually spelled 'khichdi'), is a simple, traditional South Asian dish, popular in India and Pakistan. It is made from rice and lentils. The word 'khichdi' also means 'chaos' or 'hotchpotch' in Urdu and Hindi.

5. Farsi: the standard spelling is 'dastarkhwan'; any object around which people gather around to eat, usually a rectangular piece of cloth laid on the floor.

Chapter VII

1. A forty-day retreat or period of spiritual practice; the word 'chila' or 'challis' means forty. It was common practice for ascetics to observe fasts or commit themselves to prayers for a forty-day period.

2. Farsi: throne or an elevated bed.

3. Doula Bhai: 'Doula' or 'dulha' is from Sanskrit, meaning 'groom'. The term is often used to address one's sister's husband.

4. 'Apa': term of respect for an elder sister/female.

5. 'Bavajan' or 'Babajaan': a term of endearment for father. 'Baba' is a respectful term for father.

6. Arabic: In Islam, the mahr refers to the money or goods paid to the bride by the groom upon their marriage.

There are two kinds: mahr-e-ma'ujal (to be given immediately) and mahr-e-maujjal (to be given at a later date). The mahr is a religious right of the wife, not a gift, and is mentioned explicitly in the Qu'ran. It is an essential part of marriage, without which it is null and void.

7. According to Aayesha Rafiq, under Islamic law 'mothers are given preference while deciding custody of children…during a child's initial years (till 7 years).' At seven years of age, some traditions will give the child the choice between his parents if they are separated. 'According to Abu Hanifa, custody transfers to the father when the boy reaches the age of seven years and the girl when she attains puberty,' ('Child Custody in Classical Islamic Law and Laws of Contemporary Muslim World', *International Journal of Humanities and Social Science*, Vol. 4 No. 5, (March 2014, 268. <www.ijhssnet.com> Last accessed 21 July 2016.)

8. The life of renunciation, as practiced by a Hindu ascetic, or sanyasi.

9. See the introduction to this volume for a discussion of colorism in the Indian subcontinent. It is important to note the use of the specific word 'negress' here since it indicates a connection to racial thinking both inside and outside India. While in 1944, at the time of the novel's publication, the term was not always as derogatory as it is today, it necessarily references the evolutionary thinking that denigrated African–descended people as less advanced than Europeans as well as the racial hierarchies that supported slavery and oppression.

10. In Islam, Hell has seven gates, each reserved for different kinds of sinners. All of them are associated with fire, and the intensity of the fire increases as the number ascends. Thus the fire of the seventh hell is considered the most intense and a common insult might be 'may you burn in the seventh fire of Hell'.

11. Babar (or Babur) was the founder of the Mughal empire in India. Humayun was his son. The story told about his death is the following: In 1530, Humayun 'went to Sambahl as its governor. After some six months' stay there, he fell ill, was reported to be in a dangerous condition, and was at last brought by water to Agra. All the skill of the royal physicians was used unsparingly to cure the royal patient, but no improvement was visible. At last, when his life was despaired of, it was suggested that something of great value should be given away in charity. Many suggestions were made to help Babar to choose the right things, but the Emperor was more generous than his courtiers, and he decided to offer up his life in exchange for Humayun's. He thrice went round the sick-bed and pronounced that he had taken upon himself Humayun's fell disease. From that time onward, as Humayun progressed towards recovery, Babar's illness—for he was in indifferent health at the time—increased, and Humayun's recovery led to Babar's death on December 26th, 1530.' [Ram Sharma, 'The Story of Babar's Death', *The Journal of the Royal Asiatic Society of Great Britain and Ireland*, No. 2 (April 1926), 295–6. Web accessed 07 July 2016].

Chapter VIII

1. This comment implies that Nazni's nurses are English though Indian women were being trained as Western medicine nurses from at least the late nineteenth century. Nursing along Western lines was introduced by the British into India in the earliest period of colonization, primarily for the military. Later, Florence Nightingale took an interest in nursing in India. After the Crimean War, she wrote a report titled, 'Suggestions on a System of Nursing for Hospitals in India'. Nightingale's suggestions helped create the modern profession of nursing in India. Graduates of the Nightingale Nursing School in England were

sent to India to start similar schools there and the first hospital in India began to train Indian women as nurses in 1867.

2. See above for discussion on the word 'negress'. Here, the addition of the reference to Munira as an ape makes clear the racialized evolutionary thinking implied by these comments. The connection between black people and apes was considered by racist thinkers to be evolutionarily closer than that between white people and apes.

3. Bhabi, or 'Bhabhi': from Sanskrit, the wife of an elder brother.

4. See above for discussion on mahar. Here, the usage indicates that Munira's mahar needs to be paid in order for potential divorce proceedings to take place.

5. Shaitan: a devil, or Satan.

6. Probably 'Bhabhijan' from Bhabi.

7. A suit of clothes, typically involving a kurta (shirt), shalwar (a kind of trouser), and a dupatta (a rectangular piece of cloth that usually is supposed to cover the chest and/or head).

8. Mumani: Sanskrit for aunt (wife of the mother's brother).

9. Dai or 'daya': Sanskrit for midwife; also wet nurse.

Chapter IX

1. This discussion between Nazni's father and brother about her options raises many of the issues surrounding Muslim women's education, health, well-being, and independence that Hussain addresses in *Changing India*. See in particular, 'The Present Condition of Girls in Islam' where she says that the cause of backwardness among Muslim girls is caused in part by malnutrition, poor domestic conditions, and lack of physical conditioning (39); and 'Muslim Women's Education' where she claims that 'the spread of education among women is indispensable both for the sake of family happiness and national progress' (187).

2. 'Douli', 'dooley', or 'doli': Sanskrit; a palanquin usually used when women wanted to travel. A douli is a decorated palanquin used to transport the bride to the husband's house after marriage. The reference here implies that she is married and should not act otherwise.

3. Probably another form for 'douli'.

4. Maid, especially one who cares for children.

Chapter X

1. The part of the house belonging to women and girls, where they are secluded.

2. Or 'Shab-e-B'raat': 'Shab' is Farsi for 'night' and 'b'raat' is Arabic, meaning to acquit, grant immunity to or exemption, to absolve someone; it effectively translates to 'night of acquital'. On the 15th of Sha'ban, it is believed by some sects in the Muslim community that fortunes for the year are determined and/or Allah will forgive sinners. Participants stay up late into the night to worship and pray. While widely practiced in India and Pakistan, this practice is not specified in the Qu'ran.

3. A mineral preparation used in the treatment of a variety of ailments in both Unani and ayurvedic practices.

4. A black powder used as a cosmetic, also referred to as kohl. Zuhra asks for a dot to be placed on the baby's check to make him less fair or beautiful in order that others would not be jealous and cast an evil eye on him.

5. Folk practice to protect from evil eyes and enemies. In this passage, it is clear that Zuhra adheres to traditional and often superstitious practices.

6. Arabic, for 'word', 'spoken word'. This refers to one of the declarations of faith recited by Muslims during services and often at other times. Here the implication is that Kabeer references Doulath Kahn and Nanzi as often as if they were a kalima and as though their words and deeds had the same importance.

7. A lakh equals one hundred thousand.

Chapter XI

1. This passage introduces the notion that Maghbool is not a conventional woman, and even more so, that she has abilities and characteristics that are associated with men. Although she is described as beautiful, her independence, extraordinary literacy, ability to handle figures and money, and willingness to participate in the public sphere all mark her as significantly 'masculine' in the context of this novel. As such, she is a figure who challenges gender expectations. See the introduction to this volume for more discussion.

Chapter XII

1. Communication of the faith of Islam. 'Tabligh' means 'communication of a message or revelation or fulfillment of a mission'. It is interchangeable with dawah (propagation of faith) in modern usage; 'e-Islam' means 'of Islam'.

2. Urdu: happy or blessed home.

3. Kharoon: usually 'Qaroon' or 'Qarun', a figure in the Qu'ran. The Qur'an informs us that Qaroon possessed a great fortune and high status in Egypt despite being of the people of Moses. His wealth made him arrogant and insolent towards his own people. He boasted about his wealth and believed himself to be superior to others. However, his arrogance brought devastation upon him when Allah caused the earth to swallow him and his dwelling place. The reference to Qaroon's treasury here refers to the fleetingness of riches and the folly of hoarding wealth.

4. Farsi: spectacle, entertainment, or celebration.

5. Arabic: maiden or angel of paradise; nymph.

Chapter XIII

1. Or 'tehsildar': a revenue or tax collector.

2. See above for discussion on the gender implications of Maghbool's independence and financial abilities.

Here, Hussain also seems to be raising the question of women's economic independence more generally. The father seems to understand the danger of placing his daughter in a position where she will be completely dependent. One can also hear further resonance with Jane Austen in this passage, since the matter of income and financial dependence or independence of women is a key theme in her novels.

3. Farsi: provision for a journey.

4. Arabic: inauspicious; can also mean someone who is bad luck.

5. Arabic: 'naqis' means error, 'aql' means wisdom. The term itself means faulty intellect, foolishness; often applied to women.

6. Zam Zam is a sacred well of water in Mecca. It is believed to have healing properties and is drunk by pilgrims.

Chapter XIV

1. See above for discussion on the gender non-conformity represented by Maghbool's intelligence and independence. The matter of who makes a 'good wife' is one of the main themes of the novel.

2. In this conversation, Maghbool and her father discuss the expectations for Muslim wives living in seclusion and some of the conflicts or contradictions that follow from both purdah and polygamy. While the conversation is dispassionate, Maghbool's comment about being transferred from the semi-prison of being a well-cared for daughter in her tolerant natal household to the complete prison of being a neglected and criticized third wife in her husband's household, resonates with Hussain's critiques of purdah and polygamy in *Changing India* and elsewhere in this novel.

3. The basis of this statement is unclear. Islamic doctrine emphasizes the nikha or nikkah as the most important part of the marriage since it is the making of the contract. Many of the rituals that might be practiced surrounding the celebration of the actual marriage are not prescribed in the Qu'ran and might vary from place to place. According to sources, Ibn Al-Hajj had this to say about women in connection to marriage ceremonies in Egypt in the fourteenth century: 'As for what they did in wedding ceremonies, do not ask about the innumerable violations that they invented, for what they invented in childbirth is a drop in a bucket compared to what they do in marriage ceremonies.' [Quoted in Huda Lufti, 'Manners and Customs of Fourteenth Century Cairene Women: Female Anarchy versus Male Shar'i Order in Muslim Prescriptive Treatises', in Nikki R. Keddie and Beth Baron, eds. *Women in Middle Eastern History: Shifting Boundaries in Sex and Gender* (New Haven: Yale University Press, 2008), 106].

4. Arabic: destiny, luck.

5. Sanskrit: insect.

6. Azan or 'Adhan'—call to prayer.

7. See above for discussion of the gender non-conformity of Maghbool's literacy and willingness to participate in the public sphere. Being known in public by one's name once it has been published on a book of poems would be considered a violation of purdah in conservative Muslim circles in which a woman's name would be considered private and reserved for use by her close family.

Chapter XV

1. Zuhra's choice of a bedroom arrangement that affords her a view of all that transpires in the zenana means that she has the power of surveillance over those who live and labor there. While limited to the interior, domestic spaces of the house, the power of her view might be understood by way of Foucault's discussion of the panopticon. As Foucault makes clear, such all-encompassing and constant surveillance makes power automatic and more 'perfect.' [*Discipline and Punish: the Birth of the Prison* (translated by Alan Sheridan, New York: Vintage, 1977, 1995)]. It also inculcates the desire to behave appropriately within those who are constantly watched, so that the exercise of power can continue seamlessly.

2. Farsi: wives.

3. Or 'nalayak': Arabic—unintelligent; unworthy, lacking in ability.

4. Women were expected to refrain from their regular duties after childbirth. On the twelfth day, before resuming duties, they would cleanse and purify themselves with a bath.

5. Women who have just given birth or are having their menstrual periods were expected to refrain from cooking so as not to pollute the food with their unclean status.

6. Or 'Qarurah', from Farsi: urine sample.

7. This comment likely refers to the lack of restraints on the public movements of the women in this family.

Chapter XVI

1. Maghbool's questions surrounding traditional Islamic practice and women's lives echo some of the concerns raised in *Changing India*.

2. Traditional medicine: A 'traditional healing system prevalent in the Middle East, India, Pakistan, and neighboring countries, according to which the body comprises four basic elements—earth, air, water, and fire—and four humors—blood, phlegm, yellow bile, and black bile. An equilibrium in the humors indicates good health while a disturbance in this equilibrium results in disease.' (*Jonas Mosby's Dictionary of Complementary and Alternative Medicine*. S. V. 'Unani.' Accessed 22 July 2016, <http://medicaldictionary.thefreedictionary.com/unani>).

3. This comment by Zuhra makes explicit the pressure on gender norms in the household that Maghbool produces. Not only is her identity often described in terms associated with men or male behavior, but her presence in the household pushes others out of their roles. In this sense, she represents what might be called a non-normative or trans-gender force. Here, Zuhra makes it clear that gender roles or performances exist in relationships; if Maghbool steps outside the norm for female behavior, then it is difficult for Kabeer to inhabit the expected male role. For Zuhra, the fact that he is caring for her and providing her with food means that he is becoming feminized.

4. A long-sleeved knee-length coat with a stand-up collar, worn by men of India and Pakistan on formal occasions.

5. Referring to prayer beads, usually called a 'tasbeeh'.

Chapter XVII

1. Used to paint designs on parts of the body by Indian and Pakistani women as well as others in the Middle East and Africa.

2. Or 'wudu': washing certain body parts in a particular way before saying prayers.

3. Mazar: 'shrine or tomb'; 'pir' is an honorific used for a religious master. In this usage, Peeranepeer or 'Peeran-e-Peer' is a double honorific for one who is a 'Peer of Peers' i.e. a teacher of teachers or master of masters.

4. Thuhfa: Or 'taufa', 'tohfa'; Farsi (from Arabic) for 'gift'.

5. Murad: Farsi (from Arabic), meaning desire, wished for thing. Zuhra and the cook are speaking about whether or not a gift is required at the mazar in order to have the wish fulfilled.

6. Offering.

7. The use of the term 'Moharram's jalali' can be understood as an expression of Zuhra's contempt towards Maghbool. To provide some context, the month of Muharram witnessed the martyrdom of the Holy Prophet's grandson, Al-Ḥusayn ibn 'Alī, along with his followers, in the Battle of Karbala. Muslims all over the world, especially those who follow Shi'ite tenets of faith, remember and mourn this loss. Members of the Shi'ite community perform matham, a practice which involves the physical expression of grief in varying forms. It is customary to wear old, dark coloured (mostly black), shabby clothing during this time. Maghbool's fancy clothes, used by Munira to stitch together something for her son, are being referred to in that capacity i.e. as something so worn out that they're only suitable for Muharram.

8. A woman in post–delivery confinement.

9. Sanskrit: Nandi the bull. He serves as Shiva's attendant and mount, and symbolizes fertility and well-being.

10. Literally, 'the opening'; used to refer to the short first verse of the Qu'ran, which many are able to recite. It is often recited on various occasions and especially at graves or at a shrine or mazar (as in this episode).

11. The 'Rubáiyát' is a Persian poetic form based on quatrains. The Rubáiy (pl. Rubáiyát, from the Arabic *Rubá*, meaning 'four') is the shortest form in Persian poetry. The most famous example of a Rubáiyát, and the one likely referenced here, is by the 12th century Persian poet, Omar Khayyám, translated by the British poet, Edward Fitzgerald as *The Rubaiyat of Omar Khayyam, the Astronomer-Poet of Persia*, in 1859. This translation was extremely popular among English-speaking audiences and is still widely referenced. Many other translations in English and other languages have been made since 1859. The Urdu version of the Rubaiyat by Harivansh Rai Bachchan came out in the late 1930s and helped revive interest in Omar Khayyam in India. The 'Ghazal' (pl. 'Ghazaliat') was originally an Arabic verse form dealing with loss and romantic love, which was taken up by medieval Persian poets in India. The form is built of couplets with an intricate rhyme scheme. Each couplet ends on the same word or phrase (the radif), and is preceded by the couplet's rhyming word (the qafia, which appears twice in the first couplet). The last couplet usually mentions the poet's name. The most famous example of a Ghazaliat and the one likely referenced here is the collected work of the 13th century Persian poet and Sufi mystic, Jalāl ad-Dīn Muhammad Rūmī, popularly known simply as Rumi. The first influential English translation, 'Selected Poems from the Dîvâni Shamsi Tabrîz,' containing 48 ghazals, was published in 1898 by the British scholar, R. A. Nicholson. Many other

translations in English and other languages have been made since this edition. That Magbhool is translating these celebrated Muslim poets and also writing her own poems places her in an august intellectual and literary tradition, one that also merges East and West.

Chapter XVIII

1. Or 'tawaf'; the ceremony of circumambulating the Ka'bah (the most holy shrine in Mecca) seven times— required of those who make the Haj or pilgrimage.

2. Kabeer here is invoking the Holy Prophet as a justification for taking a fourth wife.

3. Sanskrit: the sehra is a headdress worn by the groom at his wedding.

4. Or 'Qazi'; Arabic for 'judge'.

5. Namaz: itself a Farsi word which means 'worship' (i.e. of any kind); in Arabic, 'salaat' refers specifically to the ritual prayers observed five times a day by Muslims.

Chapter XIX

1. Farsi: the part of the house reserved for men.

2. Arabic: dress.

3. 'Agaya' is Urdu for 'has arrived'.

4. Term for unbeliever, often derogatory.

5. Arabic: 'one who believes in God', a believer.

6. Probably slang for the Hindi 'chatukar', meaning flunky, yes-man, overly slick person, here likely in reference to his wearing an English-style suit in imitation of Alexander.

7. Or 'Sarkar'; a man in a position of authority, esp. a landowner; used by servants to address male employers.

8. Muslims.

9. Or 'namakool'; Arabic, for absurd, unreasonable, irrational.

10. Farsi: Literally means 'forgiveness'; here tip, or gift, bribe.

11. Breeze or air.

Chapter XX

1. This comment refers ironically to the group of wayward men, unaffiliated with particular community or religion, and without distinct social connections or mores. Historically, the notion of cosmopolitanism has often been linked to disconnection, lack of values, and a dissolute lifestyle. While cosmopolitanism is usually taken to mean simply 'being a citizen of the world', it has also been connected to an 'openness of attitude', which refuses the authority of any particular state, nation, or religion, especially among thinkers

of the European enlightenment. A cosmopolitan under this definition would not harbour any particular cultural loyalties and might be less likely to be governed by cultural or religious norms, habits, or tenets. Cosmopolitanism has sometimes been used to describe those who love to travel or have no fixed abode and are strangers nowhere (see, for example, in Diderot, *Encyclopédie*). And for Marx, cosmopolitanism was tied to the worst excesses of capitalism and the illusion of 'free' trade (see *Early Political Writings*). Hussain's use of the phrase 'cosmopolitan nation' is unusual and interesting in that it raises the possibility that those who refuse the ties of belonging to any state, nation, or religion might nonetheless themselves constitute a group with many the problems associated with those entities but none of the habits, values, or responsibilities that make them meaningful.

2. Female counterpart of 'kafir', non-believer.

3. Here, George invokes Muslim unity in order to manipulate the gang of young men into action. Hussain may well be offering ironic commentary on the base ways political, social, and religious claims may be put to use. While a notion of Muslim unity had been developing throughout the twentieth century, in the 1930s and 1940s Muslim cultural unity and nationalism grew significantly in India. It became increasingly clear to Muslim leaders that plans for a post-independence state as put forward by the Congress leadership would not include guaranteed representation and certain significant safeguards for Muslims. Leaders began to advance serious arguments for considering Muslims in India as a separate nation and for forging a two-nation solution. In 1940, Muhammed Ali Jinnah, who served as the leader of the Indian Muslim League from 1913 until the creation of Pakistan in 1947 (when he became its first Governor-General), spoke to the League, proclaiming that Muslims 'are a nation according to any definition of a nation, and that they must have their homelands, their territory, and their state'—which was to be named Pakistan (Qtd. in Barbara D. and Thomas R. Metcalf, *A Concise History of Modern India*, third edition [Cambridge: Cambridge University Press, 2012], 208). In the years that followed, the idea of Muslim nationality became tied not only to the creation of Pakistan as a state but also to the broader ideal of Islamic unity.

4. Arabic: one who is slain in the cause of religion, on the battlefield; martyr. In Islam, it is considered a great honor to be a shaheed.

5. The Mughal Empire ruled large parts of India from 1526 until 1858 when British crown rule was established. During the period leading up to independence and partition in 1947, Muslim leaders had argued for Muslim national identity. Muhammad Ali Jinnah issued a call for a Muslim homeland in 1940.

6. Akram here denies his family's faith. Hussain makes ironic commentary on the way the family practices Islam.

7. Language used to demean an individual; 'harami' means 'illegitimate'. These are all curse words, with harami being the worst.

8. It is ideal to die right after saying the kalima.

9. Paralysis on one side of the body.

Chapter XXI

1. This translates to 'the shadow of Satan'. 'Saya' is Farsi for shadow and 'shaitan' is an Arabic word which

refers to the quality of being mischevious, disobedient; also evil spirit. Calling someone shaitan is usually an attempt to associate them with the djinn, Iblees (Satan). Here, this means being affected by the evil eye.

2. Informal; referring to a pir who acts as a medium between humans and supernatural entities.

3. Or 'tha'wiz'; an amulet or locket containing verses of the Qu'ran, considered to carry good luck, good health, or protection.

4. This appears to be another amulet-like object.

5. From the Sanskrit 'cheeni', meaning sugar. This refers to sachets of sugar on which verses are inscribed. The sugar is then taken with water to aid in a cure.

6. This refers to a customary practice of writing something healing on a piece of paper which is then immersed in water to be drunk.

7. Or 'puja'—a prayer ceremony, or the act of worship, usually Hindu.

8. 'Neema khuda': Farsi, translates to half-god. 'Khuda' means god and 'neem' means half. Here, Zuhra tells Nazni that she should treat Kabeer as her god and the source of her prosperity.

References

Introduction

Alam, Asiya. Introduction to *Changing India: A Muslim Woman Speaks* by Iqbalunnisa Hussain. Karachi: Oxford University Press, xiii-xvii.

Anand, Mulk Raj. 'Pigeon-Indian: Some Notes on Indian-English Writing.' *World Literature Written in English* 21.2 (1982 summer): 325–36.

Austen, Jane. *Pride and Prejudice*. Oxford: Oxford University Press, 1986.

Ballantyne, Tony. 'Race and the Webs of Empire: Aryanism from India to the Pacific.' *Journal of Colonialism and Colonial History*, no. 3 (2001): 725–50.

Basu, Chirosree. 'Inner Persons: From the Kitchen to the Air Balloon.' *The Telegraph*. Calcutta, 25 July, 2003, accessed December 27, 2016, https://www.telegraphindia.com.

Berman, Jessica. 'Is the Trans in Transnational the Trans in Transgender?' *Modernism/Modernity* 24.2 (April 2017): 217–44.

_____. 'Neither Mirror nor Mimic: Late Colonial Indian Narratives in English.' *The Oxford Handbook of Global Modernisms*. Mark Wollaeger, ed. Oxford University Press, 2012: 205–27.

Chughtai, Ismat. *Lifting the Veil: Selected Writings*. New York: Penguin, 2001.

_____. *Quilt and Other Stories*. New Delhi: Kali for Women, 1996.

Dutt, Toru. *Bianca: The Young Spanish Maiden*. New Delhi: Prachi Prakashan, 2001.

Hossain, Rokeya. *Sultana's Dream: A Feminist Utopia and Selections from the Secluded Ones*. New York: Feminist Press, 1988.

Hussain, Iqbalunnisa. *Changing India: A Muslim Woman Speaks*. Karachi: Oxford University Press, 2015.

Iyengar, Srinivasa. *Indian Writing in English*. Vantage Press, 1973.

Jussawalla, Feroza. *Family Quarrels: Towards a Criticism of Indian Writing in English*. New York: Peter Lang, 1985.

Kaul, Suvir. 'Women, Reform and Nationalism in Three Novels of Muslim Life.' Ulka Anjaria, ed. *A History of the Indian Novel in English*. Cambridge: Cambridge University Press, 2015: 133–46.

Khadeeja Majoka, Zara. 'Lahore Literary Festival: Women's Writings about Women.' *Dawn Books and Authors*. Published March 3, 2013. Accessed February 2, 2015.

Kheshti, Roshanak. 'Cross-Dressing and Gender (Tres)Passing: The Transgender Move as a Site of Agential Potential in the New Iranian Cinema.' *Hypatia* 24, no. 3 (2009): 158–77.

Lambert-Hurley, Siobhan and Sunil Sharma, eds. *Atiya's Journeys: A Muslim Woman from Colonial Bombay to Edwardian Britain*. Oxford: Oxford University Press, 2010.

Lambert-Hurley, Siobhan. 'Fostering Sisterhood: Muslim Women and the All-India Ladies' Association.' *Journal of Women's History* 16:2 (Summer 2004): 40–65.

Making Britain: South Asians in Britain from 1870 to 1950. <http://www8.open.ac.uk/researchprojects/makingbritain>.

Malak, Amin. *Muslim Narratives and the Discourse of English*. New York: State University of New York Press, 2004.

Metcalf, Barbara and Thomas Metcalf. *A Concise History of Modern India*, third edition. Cambridge: Cambridge University Press, 2012.

Minwalls, Shabnam. 'Rediscovery of Formidable Voices from the Past.' *Times of India*, Mumbai. Published November 17, 2002, 11.39, accessed before February 2, 2015. <http://timesofindia.indiatimes.com>.

Mishra, Neha. 'India and Colorism: The Finer Nuances,' *Washington University Global Studies Law Review*, 14.4 (2015): 725–50, accessed February 20, 2017, openscholarship.wustl.edu/law_globalstudies/vol14/iss4/14.

Mukherjee, Meenakshi. *The Twice Born Fiction*. London: Heinemann, 1974.

Panandiker, V.A. Pai and Navnita Chadha Behera. *Perspectives on South Asia*. New Delhi: Konark, 2000.

Rao, Rahul. 'Hijra.' *Key Concepts in Modern Indian Studies*. Rachel Dwyer, Gita Dharampal-Frick, Monika Kirloskar-Steinbach, Jahnavi Phalkey, eds. New York: New York University Press, 2015: 99–101.

Ranasinha, Ruvani. *South Asian Writers in Twentieth-Century Britain: Culture in Translation*. Oxford: Oxford University Press, 2007.

————. Ed. *South Asians and the Shaping of Britain, 1870–1950: A Sourcebook*. Manchester: Manchester University Press, 2012.

Reddy, Gayatri. *With Respect to Sex*. Chicago: University of Chicago Press, 2010.

Risley, H.H. *The Tribes and Castes of Bengal*. Calcutta: Firma Mukhopadhyay, 1981. Orig. pub. 1891.

Satthianadhan, Krupabai. *Kamala: A Story of Hindu Life*. Chandani Lokugé ed. New Delhi: Oxford University Press, 1998.

————. *Saguna: A Story of Native Christian,* Chandani Lokugé ed. New Delhi: Oxford University Press, 1998.

Sorabji, Cornelia. *Love and Life Behind the Purdah*. Chandani Lokugé ed. New Delhi: Oxford University Press, 2003.

de Souza, Eunice. *Purdah: An Anthology*. New Delhi: Oxford University Press, 2004.

Stryker, Susan. 'De/Colonizing Transgender Studies of China.' *Transgender China*. Howard Chiang ed. New York: Palgrave, 2012: 287–92.

————. '(De)Subjugated Knowledges: An Introduction to Transgender Studies.' *The Transgender Studies Reader*. Susan Stryker and Stephen Whittle eds. New York: Routledge, 2006: 1–18.

————. *Transgender History*. Berkeley: Seal Press, 2008.

Tharu, Susie and K. Lalitha. *Women Writing in India: 600 B.C. to the Present*, 2 vols. New Delhi: Oxford University Press, 1991.

Iqbalunnisa Hussain: A Biographical Sketch (1897–1954)

Ahmed, Fatima Sughra. E-mail message to author. 14 January 2012.

————. Interview with author. 29 July 2015.

Ahmed, Salima. Interview with author. 25 August 2013.

————. Interview with author. 14 August 2016.

Alam, Asiya. Introduction to *Changing India* by Iqbalunnisa Hussain.

The Australian Women's Weekly, 24 June 1935. Web: National Library of Australia. <http://trove.nla.gov.au/newspaper/title/112#>.

Boehmer, Elleke. 'Description'. *Indian Arrivals, 1870–1915: Networks of British Empire.* Oxford: Oxford University Press, 2015, web.

Elkington, Rob, Madeleine van der Steege, Judith Glick-Smith, Jennifer Moss Breen, eds. *Visionary Leadership in a Turbulent World: Thriving in the New VUCA Context.* Bradford: Emerald Publishing Limited, 2017.

Gardiner, Juliet. *The Thirties: An Intimate History of* Britain. London: HarperPress, 2011.

Hussain, Iqbalunnisa. *Changing India: A Muslim Woman Speaks.* Karachi: Oxford University Press, 2015.

_____. *Harem House.* Lahore: n.p., 1944.

Lambert-Hurley, Siobhan and Sunil Sharma, *Atiya's Journeys: A Muslim Woman from Colonial Bombay to Edwardian Britain.* Oxford: Oxford University Press, 2010.

Metcalf, Barbara. E-mail message to author. 15 February 2016.

Robinson, Jane. *Bluestockings: The Remarkable Story of the First Women to Fight for an Education.* London: Penguin, 2010.

Spiers, John. Foreword to *Changing India* by Iqbalunnisa Hussain.

World Association of Girl Guides and Girl Scouts. 'About Our History', web: <https://www.wagggs.org/en/about-us/our-history/>. Last accessed 21 March 2017.

Purdah and Polygamy in a Changing India

Aftab, Tahera. *Inscribing South Asian Muslim Women: An Annotated Bibliography & Research Guide.* Leiden: Brill, 2008.

Ahmed, Salima R. Talk at the 2015 book launch of Iqbalunnisa Hussain's *Changing India* at the Karachi Literature Festival: <https://vimeo.com/123294309>. Accessed on April 30, 2016.

Alam, Asiya. 'Polygyny, Family and Sharafat: Discourses amongst North Indian Muslims, circa 1870–1918.' *Modern Asian Studies* (2011): 45, 631–68.

_____ Introduction. *Changing India: A Muslim Woman Speaks* by Iqbalunnisa Hussain. Karachi: Oxford University Press, 2015.

Brinks, Ellen. *Anglophone Indian Women Writers, 1870–1920.* Surrey: Ashgate Publishing, 2013.

Burton, Antoinette. *Dwelling in the Archive: Women Writing House, Home, and History in Late Colonial India.* Oxford: Oxford University Press, 2003.

Cousins, Margaret E. *The Awakening of Asian Womanhood.* 1922. Reprint. London: Forgotten Books, 2013.

Gail, Minault. 'Urdu Women's Magazines in The Early Twentieth Century,' in *Manushi* 48 (September–October 1988), 2–9. <http://www.manushi.in/docs/912.%20Urdu%20Women%5C's%20Magazines%20in%20the%20Early%20Twentieth%20Century.pdf> Accessed on April 30, 2016.

Grigg, H. B. (Mrs). 'Introductory Memoir.' In S. Satthianandhan, *Kamala: A Story of Hindu Life.* Madras: Srinivasa, Varadachari & Co., 1894.

Hussain, Iqbalunnisa. *Changing India: A Muslim Woman Speaks* (1940). Karachi: Oxford University Press, 2015.

_____. *Purdah and Polygamy: Life in an Indian Muslim Household.* Bangalore: Hosali Press, 1944.

Nazar Sajjad Hyder. 'Purdah.' In Tharu and Lalitha, *Women Writing in India: 600 B.C. to the Present,* I. 392–93.

Sen, Indrani. 'Writing English, Writing Reform: Two Indian Women's Novels of the 19th Century.' *Indian Journal of Gender Studies,* 21:1 (2014), 1–26.

Suvir Kaul. 'Women, Reform and Nationalism in Three Novels of Muslim Life.' In *A History of the Indian Novel in English*, ed. Ulka Anjaria. Cambridge: Cambridge University Press, 2015. 133–46.

Tharu, Susie and K. Lalitha. 'Literature of the Reform and Nationalist Movements.' *Women Writing in India: 600 B.C. to the Present*, 2 vols. Delhi: Oxford University Press, 1991. Volume I, *600 B.C. to the Early Twentieth Century*. 143–86.

Iqbalunnisa Hussain and Early English Fiction by South Asian Muslims

Ahmad, Rukshana. *The Hope Chest*. London: Virago, 1996).

Ali, Ahmed. *Twilight in Delhi*. Karachi: Oxford University Press, 1984. First published in London: Hogarth Press, 1940.

———. *Ocean of the Night*. London: Peter Owen, 1964.

Anam, Tahmima. 'My hero, Rokeya Sakhawat Hosain.' *The Guardian*, 28 May 2011. <https://www.theguardian.com/books/2011/may/28/rokeya-sakhawat-hossain-hero-tahmima-anam>.

Askari, Hasan. 'A Novel by Ahmed Ali.' Annual of Urdu Studies, 9, 1994. First published 'Ahmed Ali ka Aik Navil' Makhzan Lahore, 1949). 73–84.

Bhopal, Maimoona Sultan, Shahbano Begum of. *A Trip to Europe*. Translated from the Urdu by G.B. Bakhsh. Calcutta: Thacker Spink, 1913.

Chughtai, Ismat. *Kaghazi Hai Pairahan: The Paper Attire*. Translated from the Urdu by Noor Zaheer. Karachi: Oxford University Press, 2016.

de Souza, Eunice. Ed. *Purdah: An Anthology*. New Delhi: Oxford University Press, 2004.

Fyzee, Atiya. *Zamana-e-Tehseel*. Agra: Mutb'a Mufid-i-Aam, 1922. English edition 'A Time for Education' translated by Siobhan Lambert-Hurley and Sunil Sharma in *Atiya's Journeys*, see Lambert-Hurley.

Habibullah, Inam. Fatima, *Tazkirat-e-Safar-e-Europe*. Lucknow: self-published, nd.

Hosain, Attia. *Phoenix Fled*. London: Virago, 1988. First published London: Chatto and Windus, 1953.

———. *Sunlight on a Broken Column*. London: Virago, 1988. First published London: Chatto and Windus, 1961.

———. *Distant Traveller: New and Selected Fiction*, selected and edited by Aamer Hussein and Shama Habibullah. New Delhi: Women Unlimited, 2013.

Hossain, Rokeya Sakhawat. 'Sultana's Dream' from 'A Celebration of Women Writers.' Ed. Mary Mark Ockerbloom, Digital Library, University of Pennsylvania, transcribed from *Sultana's Dream and Padmaraag: Two Feminist Utopias* by Rokeya Sakhawat Hossain, translated with an introduction by Barnita Baghchi. New Delhi: Penguin, 2005. <http://digital.library.upenn.edu/women/sultana/dream/dream.html>

Hussain, Iqbalunnisa. *Changing India: A Muslim Woman Speaks*. Karachi: Oxford University Press, 2015. First published Bangalore: Hosali Press, 1940.

———. *Purdah and Polygamy: Life in an Indian Muslim Household*. Bangalore: Hosali Press, 1944.

Hussein, Aamer, introduction to *The Young Wife and Other Stories* by Zaib-un-Nissa Hamidullah. Karachi: Oxford University Press, 2008. ix-xvii.

———, afterword to *Distant Traveller: New and Selected Fiction*, selected and edited by Aamer Hussein and Shama Habibullah. New Delhi: Women Unlimited, 2013. 220–34.

Ikramullah, Shaista Suhrawardy. *From Purdah to Parliament: Revised and Expanded Edition*. Karachi: Oxford University Press, 1998. First published London: Cresset Press, 1963.

Kazi, Seema. Muslim Women in India. London: Minority Rights International, 1999.

Khan, Uzma Aslam. *Trespassing.* New Delhi: Penguin India, 2003.

King, Bruce. 'From Twilight to Midnight: Muslim Novels of India and Pakistan.' *Worlds of the Muslim Imagination,* ed. Alamgir Hashmi. Islamabad: Gulmohar, 1986.

Lambert-Hurley, Siobhan and Sunil Sharma. *Atiya's Journeys: A Muslim Woman from Colonial Bombay to Edwardian England.* New Delhi: Oxford University Press, 2010.

Metcalf, Thomas R. *Land, Landlords and The British Raj: Northern India in the Nineteenth Century.* Berkeley: University of California Press, 1979.

Mir, Ali Hussein and Mir, Raza. *Anthems of Resistance: A Celebration of Progressive Urdu Poetry.* New Delhi: India Ink, 2006.

Mukherjee, Meenakshi. *The Perishable Empire: Essays on Indian English Writing.* New Delhi: Oxford University Press, 2002.

Naik, M.K. *A History of Indian English Literature.* New Delhi: Sahitya Akademi, 2005. First published 1982.

Rahman, Tariq. *Language, Ideology, and Power.* Karachi: Oxford University Press, 2002.

Shahnawaz, Jahan Ara. *Father and Daughter: A Political Autobiography.* Karachi: Oxford University Press, 2002. First published Lahore: Nigarishat, 1971.

Shah Nawaz, Mumtaz. *The Heart Divided.* Lahore: ASR Publications, 1990. First published Lahore: Mumtaz Publications, 1957.

Shamsie, Kamila. *Salt and Saffron.* London: Bloomsbury, 2000.

Shamsie, Muneeza. Ed. *And The World Changed: Contemporary Stories by Pakistani Women.* New York: Feminist Press at CUNY, 2008.

_____. 'Sunlight and Salt: The Literary Narratives of a Divided Family,' *Journal of Commonwealth Literature,* 44.1, 2009. 135–53.

_____. 'Discovering the Matrix,' *The Critical Muslim* (2012). <http://www.criticalmuslim.io/discovering-the-matrix/>.

_____. *Hybrid Tapestries: The Development of Pakistani Literature in English.* Karachi: Oxford University Press, 2017.

Sidhwa, Bapsi. *The Bride.* London: Jonathan Cape, 1982.

Zakaria, Rafia. *The Upstairs Wife: An Intimate History of Pakistan.* Boston, MA: Beacon Press, 2015.